808.85 Prochnow, Herbert
PR   V.

The complete
toastmaster

$8.95

By The Same Author

THE TOASTMASTER'S HANDBOOK

THE SUCCESSFUL SPEAKER'S HANDBOOK

THE SPEAKER'S TREASURY OF STORIES FOR ALL
   OCCASIONS

THE NEW GUIDE FOR TOASTMASTERS AND SPEAKERS

THE PUBLIC SPEAKER'S TREASURE CHEST

TERM LOANS

AMERICAN FINANCIAL INSTITUTIONS

THE NEXT CENTURY IS AMERICA'S
(With Carroll D. Murphy)

THE
COMPLETE
TOASTMASTER

a new treasury for speakers

by

Herbert V. Prochnow

PRENTICE HALL PRESS • NEW YORK

Published in 1986 by Prentice Hall Press
A Division of Simon & Schuster, Inc.
Gulf + Western Building
One Gulf + Western Plaza
New York, NY 10023

Originally published by Prentice-Hall, Inc.

PRENTICE HALL PRESS is a trademark of Simon & Schuster, Inc.

Library of Congress Catalog Card Number: 60-14291
ISBN 0-13-164608-7

Manufactured in the United States of America

10   9   8   7   6

First Prentice Hall Press Edition

To Speakers and Toastmasters

This book is planned to be helpful to the thousands of persons who have charge each month of luncheon and dinner programs, conferences, conventions, service club meetings and discussion groups. As chairman, president or toastmaster, these persons are responsible for conducting the meetings efficiently and effectively.

The time of millions of people is given to attendance at these meetings. Consequently, the persons who have charge of the programs have the responsibility of making these meetings worthwhile by providing the maximum reward for attendance.

The material in this book is meant to assist specifically the chairman or toastmaster. In these chapters, there are many hundreds of items which the chairman can use on various occasions. These items include introductions and responses to introductions, illustrations and stories from speeches, quotable quips, literary quotations, humorous stories, biographical and inspirational material, business quotations, quotations from modern sources, proverbs and material for special occasions. There are also humorous definitions and quotations which are related to various vocations and professions.

This variety of material is obviously not only suitable for use by the chairman or toastmaster, but should also be helpful to speakers, attorneys, ministers, teachers, salesmen and many other groups.

If the book is found of practical value for those for whom it is written, it is hoped it will also provide more interesting and profitable meetings.

Herbert V. Prochnow

TABLE OF CONTENTS

1 ✦✦✦

Requirements of a Good Toastmaster

Most men who serve as chairmen and toastmasters take these assignments in addition to regular responsibilities which occupy all their time. Although they wish to be competent chairmen and toastmasters, they frequently have little time to read long discussions on the subject. Consequently, to be helpful, the requirements of a good toastmaster are presented in this chapter in concise form. One may check quickly in the outlines which follow the major points to be considered in acting as chairman of a luncheon, dinner, discussion group, conference, or other type of meeting.

Following these outlines there are many hundreds of items which will be helpful in preparing one's remarks as a toastmaster and also as a speaker.

WHAT TO REMEMBER WHEN YOU PLAN A PROGRAM

1. Choose a worthwhile subject for the meeting and select a speaker who is unquestionably competent to discuss it interestingly. Every precaution must be taken to be certain that the speaker chosen will reward those present for their time and attention.
2. Appoint committees to select the menu for the meal and to look after all aspects of hospitality and fellowship at the meeting.
3. There should be a clear understanding with the speaker regarding his subject, the date and location of the meeting, and the nature of the audience he is to address.

1

4. Arrange to have someone meet the speaker and look after him.
5. Select guests for the speaker's table who will be a compliment to the speaker and who are related to the subject of the program.
6. If there are several speakers, put the best speaker last on the program.
7. Prepare a precise time schedule of the meeting and follow it! Start promptly and close on time.
8. Inform the speaker of the time to be given him. This should be done in advance when he is invited and accepts. Be certain that announcements and other activities do not take any of his time.
9. Be certain that the meeting room is completely satisfactory in every way including such matters as ventilation, acoustics, adequate space so tables and chairs are not crowded and the absence of unnecessary kitchen and street noises.
10. Ask the speaker for biographical material for publicity and for your introduction.
11. Arrange for publicity for the meeting and see that the speaker gets copies of the publicity.
12. If the program is broadcast, allow time for the opening and closing comments of the announcer.
13. As a rule, arrange for a speaker's podium or stand. The speaker then has a place for his notes if he wishes it.
14. Arrange for a public address system if there is any question about the speaker being heard.
15. Plan to have those at the speaker's table meet the guest speaker before the program begins.

POINTS TO REMEMBER IN RUNNING THE MEETING

1. Have place cards for the guests and see that each person knows where he is to sit.
2. Start the meeting on time and keep it on schedule. If it is a long meeting, allow time for a brief break in the session. Do not clutter up the program with lengthy announcements that bore the audience and rob the speaker of the time you promised him.
3. Be sure the audience knows who you are.
4. Often it is desirable to give each person at the speaker's table a list of the guests. This is especially worthwhile if there is a long list of guests.

5. Give the speaker any helpful information he may not already have about his audience.
6. If it is necessary to change the order of speakers, be certain each speaker knows it.
7. Have the necessary information about each guest so you can introduce him properly. The correct pronunciation of the guests' names is essential. You must also know where each guest is sitting so you do not hunt for the guests as you introduce them. Even introducing the guests affords an opportunity to add sparkle and showmanship to the program. Add a light touch and perhaps some humor to your introduction, but never injure a guest.
8. Commend the speaker strongly in your introduction so the audience understands it is a privilege to hear him. The audience must feel it is about to have a real treat. However, do not overdo it and make it impossible for the speaker to live up to your introduction.
9. Make the introduction and let the speaker make the speech.
10. Always express appreciation to the speaker on behalf of the audience and also thank him personally later. If the speaker is receiving no honorarium, it is suggested that at least a small gift be presented as a token of appreciation, if the treasury has any funds available. A conscientious speaker—and no other kind should ever be invited—will spend a great deal of time in his preparation of an address.

SOME SUGGESTIONS FOR SPEAKERS

1. Never accept an invitation to speak on a subject about which you are not well-informed.
2. Never agree to speak without the preparation necessary to give a speech that will reward the audience for its presence and attention. You have no right to plead unpreparedness, as this simply means wasting the time of an audience. The audience deserves the best address you can give—nothing less.
3. Your thoughts must be well organized and presented in logical order. This will enable you to talk straight to the point without rambling.
4. Illustrations, stories, examples, epigrams and other tools of speech will help you make an effective speech.
5. As a rule it is best to stick closely to the material one has pre-

pared.   Otherwise, there is a great danger that one will go off on tangents and take valuable time that was meant to be given to one's carefully prepared remarks.

6. Find out how much time you are to be given and stay within these time limits.

7. Do not underestimate the intelligence of an audience and do not talk down to them.   The audience may be wiser than you think, and they will resent any idea that you are downgrading them.

8. Never tell a questionable story.   You are almost certain to offend one or perhaps many persons in your audience.

9. Speak clearly and sufficiently loud to be heard easily in all parts of the room.

10. The only way you can bring genuine enthusiasm to a speech is to know your subject thoroughly.   No one can enthuse about something of which he is not sure.

THE USE OF HUMOR

1. Every humorous story or epigram you use should be closely related to your remarks.   The story or quip must be pertinent.

2. Do not try to be humorous just to be humorous, unless you are a paid comedian.   Even paid comedians find this difficult.

3. Never laugh at and applaud your own story.   It is either funny or it isn't.   Let the audience decide.

4. Unless you are exceptionally able, avoid dialects in stories.

5. Do not tell stories that injure persons or make fun of serious afflictions.   A person in your audience who has lost an eye does not think stories about persons with one eye are funny.   However, near-sightedness or far-sightedness are so common one can make light of them.

6. The length of a story is not too significant.   A long story with a minor point or very little laughter is probably not worth telling.   On the other hand, a short epigram must be perfectly clear and understandable if it is to make its point.

7. Stories are best if they are related to subjects with which the members of the audience are familiar.

8. Be sure you speak clearly.   If any words are lost to the audience, they may miss the whole point of the story.

9. If the story fails to bring the response you expected, do not

repeat it or try to explain it. This could be more humorous than the story!

10. An audience often likes the speaker to tell a story on himself.

11. If your story or epigram is well received, don't repeat the line that brought the laugh. Once is enough.

12. If you can tell stories in which you use the names of living perpersons who are known to the audience you will often have a better response.

13. The climax of a story should come right at the end. No other secondary points or words should follow the major point or climax.

14. Almost everyone likes a humorous story or illustration. People also like stories which touch the heart and inspire.

2 ✦ ✦ ✦

Introductions and Responses to Introductions

Clinton Youle, *president of the Executives' Club of Chicago, introduces* **Ilka Chase.**

You know I must confess to pulling a dirty low-down trick—some of you guests might call it a man's sort of trick.

What I did was to look back to see what Miss Chase said the last time she was here at the Executives' Club.

One of the most impressive things I found was her long description of the undying love of a wife for her husband, the ferocity of a woman hanging on to her man! Really, it had practically all the men in the place bursting their buttons with pride on what fabulously valuable creatures we men are.

Then she lowered the boom! "Reason women fight for men is simple," she said. "It's pure statistics. There just aren't enough men in the world to go around." It was a cold example of feminine calculations, and it was, I might say, depressing to us men in the audience. But before we recovered, she gave us the second barrel. "Men," she said bluntly, "obviously are the frail sex. Furthermore, we might as well pamper them a little to keep them alive so they can support us women a little longer."

You know, Miss Chase, now that I think about it some more, I wonder how you got invited back here again today.

Well, I suppose we all know why she was invited. It's impossible to find elsewhere, in one fascinating package, a woman who is an actress, a writer, a lecturer, a TV celebrity, a fashions commentator, a little mother and a great wit—all at one time.

6

It's not that we don't believe you're possible, Miss Chase, we just want to see if you're real.

Here she is, a real live doll, Miss Ilka Chase.

✦ ✦ ✦ ✦

Ilka Chase *responds to the introduction.*

Thank you very much, Mr. Youle, and believe me, I come to you with love in my heart.

It's truly a pleasure for me to be back here, ladies and gentlemen, after all these years. I feel very much as though I have come home again, and I thank you especially for your warm reception. It means more to me than you might realize because it re-establishes my somewhat shattered ego.

I had an experience that has kind of haunted me recently. It was in New York, and I was walking on 49th Street from Fifth Avenue. I was going into the NBC Building. As I was walking, I saw coming along from Sixth Avenue a woman, and in the crowd of pedestrians there was something very curious about her silhouette. As she came nearer to me, I could understand why because she had on her shoulder an enormous, live eagle.

Well, I thought to myself, live and let live, you know. We have a dog. She had an eagle. Still it was kind of odd on 49th Street, so I turned to watch her. As I did, I kept walking, and I bumped into somebody. I turned around and I saw it was a young kid, a kind of a bobbysoxer. She had apparently seen this, too, because she said to me, "What did that woman have on her shoulder?"

I said, "An eagle." She focused on me for a minute and said, "Aren't you Ilka Chase?" I said, "Yes, I am." She said, "Now I've seen everything."

There was no pleasure in it, you know. Just how much can you take in New York in a day, was the idea, but anyway, you can see why I am very grateful for your kind reception.

✦ ✦ ✦ ✦

Professor Paul W. McCracken *of the University of Michigan speaking on the Economic outlook, begins an address as follows:*

Speakers at outlook sessions often display considerable reluctance about being the sacrificial lamb at such a ritual, and I cannot myself claim any great feeling of eagerness upon approaching this occasion. All of us know the very limited extent to which we can really say anything very definite about the economic future. How many here, for example, were predicting early last year the vigorous upswing that got under way after April?

On the other hand, we also know that the policy-maker in government or in business must form some judgment about future events. Indeed, it is probably true that decisions are important largely to the extent that they do involve effects that carry well into the future. Moreover, it is good discipline for economists to forecast. Here we do not have available the easy out that we are only making projections (not predictions), or that we are only prescribing what ought to occur but not necessarily what will occur. In forecasting, the economist's job is to see if his use of economic analysis is skillful enough to produce answers that mesh with those the economic forces he is trying to analyze will themselves subsequently produce. In short, he is subject to the disciplinary test of simply being right.

✦　✦　✦　✦

Ben C. Corlett, *a past president of the California Bankers Association, presents a past president's pin to the retiring president,* **Anderson Borthwick.**

A first-grader was describing to her father how her school day began. She said, "First, you have to be in your seat when the bell rings; then we say our morning prayers; then give the pledge to the flag; then we sing America, and then our principal, Mr. York, gives the commercial."

I am here today to give the commercial for the Past President's Association.

I note that the California Bankers Association is confronted today with the same old personnel problem. They get a good man as President, train him in the job, and just when he learns the ropes they fire him. The Past President's Association is a welfare organization designed to take care of these displaced officers. We have no dues—no By-Laws—no officers—no assessments—and no meeting place. But, we do have an initiation fee—one of the most difficult that it is possible to satisfy, namely, a candidate for our organization must have served as President of the California Bankers Association which means that he has given at least eight years of devoted service to the work of the

Association as a member of the committees, a member of the Executive Council, as Chairman of the Executive Council, Vice President and finally President.

I stated that we had no By-Laws, but we do have one rule. In order to obtain admission to this venerable organization, the candidate must receive at least one affirmative vote. This is sometimes difficult to obtain as the candidate comes to us with a questionable record, having just been fired from a position of trust and responsibility. You all realize also that a banker will never say "Yes" if he can help it. Consequently, it is necessary for the candidate to do a bit of electioneering to obtain his one favorable vote.

Recently a candidate for public office accosted one of his constituents on the street and requested his support. The constituent replied, "I wouldn't vote for you if you were St. Peter, himself." The candidate replied, "If I were St. Peter, you wouldn't be in my district "

Andy, I know the only pin you're concerned with—stands in the middle of a golf green, but—there is a pin which I have been commissioned to give you which indicates that you are a candidate for our ancient organization.

✤   ✤   ✤   ✤

G. E. Leighty, *Chairman, Railway Labor Executives' Association, responds to an introduction.*

I want to express my appreciation to your distinguished organization for your kindness in inviting me to appear before you today. I am well aware of the prestige of The Economic Club of Detroit and its members, and I am therefore all the more gratified at this opportunity to bring before this group of enlightened industrialists and others interested in economic affairs the viewpoint of one million railroad workers in the United States and Canada.

✤   ✤   ✤   ✤

Donald Gordon, C.M.G., *Chairman and President, Canadian National Railways, responds to an introduction.*

The reason I am here to speak to you on "Facing Facts in Financial Reporting" is that some old friends, who are members of your Institute, refused to listen to me when I pointed out that I had neither the pro-

fessional competence to address you on such a subject, nor the orator-
ical skill to conceal my ignorance.   Therefore, if my audience this
evening suffers as much in listening to my address as I did in the
preparation of it, I shall regard it as a form of poetic justice, and shall
hope that you will place the responsibility upon the members of your
Speakers' Committee where it properly belongs.   Nevertheless, I confess that I am greatly honoured by being asked to deliver this year the
Anniversary Lecture to commemorate the incorporation in 1880 of the
Institute of Chartered Accountants of Quebec and also pleased to be
given thereby an opportunity to meet so many old friends and business
associates.

✦   ✦   ✦   ✦

Martin J. Caserio, *General Manager, Delco Radio Division,*
General Motors Corporation, responds to an introduction.

It is a pleasure for me to have the privilege of speaking to you on
this Business-Industry-Education Day.

This day has been well named.   It ties us together as a team in
working together for the welfare of all of our people.

You know we have a very great joint responsibility.   Yours is to
see that the students of today receive the best possible education.
Ours is to produce and sell the best possible products at the lowest
possible cost and to offer good jobs and good wages to our people.

We on our side of the fence can do a better job with the new employees we get from you if those new employees have been taught to
use their minds as creative tools, if they have been taught to think.

When I was chief engineer for the AC Spark Plug Division of General Motors, I used to talk to all of the engineers we hired.   Now, all
of these men had engineering degrees and had spent four, five, or six
years in college.

In talking with them, I tried to ascertain how they intended to use
their minds—whether they had been taught to use them as computers
or merely as sponges.   I urged all of them to utilize their minds as
creative tools and not just as sponges to soak up knowledge.

In making a point with each of them, I would point to the book
cases which lined my office and tell them that the books there contained
a tremendous amount of engineering information—but that information in storage didn't do anyone a particle of good, that the information
was valuable only when it was used to create something.   In other

words, we needed computers, not sponges. We needed people who could think for themselves.

✦   ✦   ✦   ✦

Rudolph G. Rydin, *vice president of the Atchison, Topeka and Santa Fe Railway Company, introduces* **Daniel P. Loomis,** *president of the Association of American Railroads.*

Good afternoon, gentlemen. Most of you are no doubt familiar with the Biblical story of Daniel and the great courage he displayed when cast into the lion's den. The account does not reveal whether Daniel had a last name, but if last names were handed out in that day it would not be surprising to learn that his was Loomis.

Our speaker, like Daniel, whatever his last name was, has great courage and is virtually in a lion's den as he moves right into the middle of the railroad's current fight to end featherbedding. He is extremely well-equipped to lead his industry's battle against the perpetuation of obsolete work rules, for he combines the precision of a lawyer with the patience and human touch of a labor negotiator. This comes naturally, since he has been both during his more than 30 years of railroading.

It is almost as if he had been groomed from the start to become the nation's top railroad man, for he is not only a lawyer and labor expert, but he also bridges the gap between eastern and western schools of railroad thought. We railroad men remember Dan Loomis well when he headed up the Association of Western Railways and his headquarters were here in Chicago.

When he left the Western Association to head up the Association of American Railroads in Washington, he took with him not only proven abilities and experiences but some other qualifications which moved one of his associates to comment: "His greatest attribute is his plain old rock-ribbed character. He sets his feet in one place and tells 'em the truth, the whole truth and nothing but the truth, whether they like it or not. Yet he gets along with people, and is a fine administrator. He delegates authority, but sees to it that a job is done."

Small wonder he has become the focal point in the railroads' fight to end featherbedding!

Our speaker's stature in his chosen field is further indicated by the fact that over the years he has been called on to lecture on railroad labor problems at half a dozen of the country's leading universities.

These were chores he turned to readily, for he has always retained an attachment to the academic life. He is, in fact, a trustee of his first alma mater, Union College at Schenectady, New York.

It is with a great deal of pleasure that I present to you this rock-ribbed character from Vermont, Daniel P. Loomis, President, Association of American Railroads.

✦ ✦ ✦ ✦

Daniel P. Loomis *responds to the introduction.*

I want to discuss with you today a subject that intimately concerns every business leader in America, as well as all the people. This involves a problem of over-riding importance to the future not only of the industry I represent but of everyone. It also involves a weird kind of cold war against management . . . practices that threaten to sabotage collective bargaining . . . some of the forgotten men of our economy . . . and a most challenging opportunity for union leaders to contribute mightily to America's welfare.

Basically, this problem that concerns us can be expressed in two questions:

One, can we restore a realistic relationship between employee wage gains and productivity increases?

And two, can we put an end to featherbedding and stop paying men for work not done or not needed?

✦ ✦ ✦ ✦

Clinton Youle, *president of the Executives' Club of Chicago,* introduces **Robert F. Wagner,** *Mayor of New York City.*

As I talked at lunch today with Mayor Wagner about his job—and earlier, as I read about the problems of our big cities, I just thought—"I'm glad it's you who's Mayor of New York and not me."

What problems—eight million proud, independent and touchy inhabitants—very rich and very poor people almost side by side—a budget second only to that of the United States Government.

Yet Robert Wagner asked for it—in 1953 the first time and again in 1957, when he was elected by an enormous majority, 900,000.

He's got the background for public life. His father was the famed New York Judge and Senator—Father of the Wagner Labor Act.

Robert Junior first watched politics first-hand at the age of six—

when he was a page boy in the New York Legislature. As he grew up, he went campaigning with his father and to Washington with him. When he finished his education, he went out for office, and that autumn, 1937, he went to Albany as a state representative.

Except for his time in the Air Force, he's been a public servant since.

Incidentally, Mayor Wagner started his Democratic victories and his headline making early. In 1928 he astounded the faculty and friends of his very conservative eastern Republican prep school by organizing a torchlight parade and campaign so successful that for the first and only time in its history the students' straw vote came up three to one Democrats—for Al Smith.

Also, in passing, we might note the Junior Wagner's description by his graduating classmates. They called him the "Smoothest, all around—the most likely to succeed—and the youngster with the biggest beard."

Gentlemen, may I present the Honorable Robert F. Wagner, Mayor of New York.

♣   ♣   ♣   ♣

Mayor Wagner *of New York City responds to the introduction.*

It is indeed an honor for me to be here today, to address the membership of The Chicago Executives' Club and their guests. I have long heard of this renowned forum here and it is a very signal honor for me, as Mayor, and as a visitor, to be here.

I certainly feel at home here because I have had the opportunity to visit this great city, the second largest in the country, on many occasions. I do not feel like the person in the story, some of you may have heard it, of the very famous British author who lived in London all his life and decided that he would like to seek the quiet of the countryside for the last few years of his life and so he bought himself a very lovely home in the middle part of England, outside of a small city, and the day after he arrived in his home, a delegation from the nearby small city called on him and said:

"Mr. Jones, you are a famous author. We are a committee organized to raise money for a new home for the homeless and we would be highly honored if you would make the first contribution."

So he said: "Fine, gentlemen—I will give you ten pounds."

Well, the next morning he saw in the local papers: "Mr. Jones,

famous author, gives 100 pounds to home for the homeless." He was
a little concerned with that and called them back and said: "Gentlemen, I think there is some misunderstanding, you misunderstood me—
I said ten pounds and not one hundred pounds."

They said, "We can clarify that very easily. Tomorrow morning
we will have a headline in the paper, 'Famous author refuses to give
one hundred pounds'."

Well, he thought for a moment and felt that this would not be so
good and he said: "I will tell you what I will do. I will make an
agreement with you—I will give you the one hundred pounds if you
will allow me to write the inscription for the home for the homeless."

They had a fast huddle and said: "This is wonderful, we are not only
going to get the one hundred pounds but this famous author is also
going to write the inscription." They were agreeable and so he said:
"Give me a piece of paper and a pencil and I will give you your motto."
The inscription that he handed to them was: "I was a stranger but they
took me in."

Of course I am sure that I do not feel that way here in Chicago.

✦   ✦   ✦   ✦

Clinton Youle, *president of the Executives' Club of Chicago,
introduces* **Maurice H. Stans,** *Director of the Bureau of the
Budget of the United States.*

I am sure that you will be interested to know that our speaker here
today is the only visitor we've ever had who has shot a bongo. And
I don't mean a bongo drum either. I suppose a dozen of you hot
tempered members have shot a few holes in a bongo drum when the
noise got too out of hand late at night.

Mr. Stans' bongo is a very rare antelope found only in the Belgian
Congo and he also has a fine photograph showing him with his trophy.
Among other things, as you gather, Mr. Stans is an ardent hunter of
big game.

Actually, I suppose our speaker today is well-known to many of you
as a fellow toiler in the Chicago vineyard. He came here in 1925,
studied with outstanding honor at Northwestern University's night
school. He built up and eventually controlled a great accounting
firm, Alexander Grant & Company. He lives in Kenilworth when he
is not off in the jungles of Washington or Africa. The last half dozen
years, he's spent a good bit of time in both of these jungles.

Mr. Stan's power and authority in his present position as Director of the Budget is immense.   To begin with, President Eisenhower likes Mr. Stans personally and in addition he respects very much this gentleman's views on balanced budgets.   In the second place, the Director of the Budget sits in on practically every White House conference of significance.   He's present at all meetings of the Cabinet, and the security council; he sits on all major executive committees.   Beyond that, only the President of the United States can override Mr. Stans' recommendations on budget matters.

His recommendations on spending are, as he himself says, "conservative."

There's a large framed motto in his office—one word—it reads "Why?"

And Mr. Stans expects every member of our Government to ask himself that question, before spending a nickel of our money.

Gentlemen, may I present Mr. Maurice H. Stans, Director of the Bureau of the Budget of the United States Government.

✦   ✦   ✦   ✦

Howard D. Murphy, *Partner, Price Waterhouse and Company, introduces* **Basil Rathbone,** *distinguished actor.*

Being President of the Executives' Club is a lot of fun.   One of the most pleasant aspects is meeting and getting acquainted with people such as those at this table.   Also the weekly reading of biographical material in the course of preparation of an introduction adds greatly to the pleasure.   Of course, there are some self-imposed rules.   I shouldn't try to make the speech for the speaker (he's the only one you really came to hear).   I mustn't exceed three minutes, I must get the audience warmed up for the speaker.   I mustn't use the prosaic routine of "he was born, he went to school and so forth" for a great many speakers; it's easy.   They have many hidden facts that most of you haven't heard about, so I can tell about them.   But then along comes someone like today's speaker.   So much of his life has been spent in a goldfish bowl, that there can't possibly be anything that you don't already know about him.

There is no point in mentioning that for over forty years our speaker has been active on stage and screen—both silent and talkie. It would be a waste of time to remind you that he played Sherlock Holmes in sixteen movies as well as in a radio series.   You all know that some of the toughest critics have referred to him as "extraordinarily well-trained" and as "neat" and "accomplished." It's completely unnecessary to mention his work on "Peter and the Wolf" and "Manfred." What can you say about someone this famous?

I looked at back issues of the Executives' Club News to see what some of my predecessors did in similar circumstances. Chuck Hanson would have probably worked in something about Walla Walla being a good place for a carpet factory; John McDonough would have insisted that his lovely wife Ann do something; Stu Weyforth would have written some blank verse, which would have been surprisingly good; Rube Borsch told about his German grandfather and Jim Day, of course, talked about his grandmother.

My friends know that I can't write verse and my puns are really horrible. As to my family, who are well represented here today, I bow to no one in my willingness or ability to talk about them, but I'm darned if I will do it in a minute and-a-half. However, I just happen to have some pictures.

Consequently, it leaves me only one avenue of escape. Ladies and gentlemen, may I present the extremely talented well-known star of stage, screen and television, Mr. Basil Rathbone.

✤   ✤   ✤   ✤

B. Stuart Weyforth, Jr., *introduces* **Rear Admiral George J. Dufek.**

In preparation for my introduction today, I read a multitude of material on the Antarctic. I now consider myself an armchair specialist on weather, cosmic rays, geomagnetism, seismology and glaciology. Clint Youle, please note.

While the rumbling, restless continent of Antarctica is a fascinating study, even more fascinating are the lives of those intrepid souls, the men who invaded her mysterious and icy privacy. One of the most outstanding of these men is our guest today, Admiral George J. Dufek.

A living counterpart of the fictional figure Flash Gordon, our guest was born and reared in Rockford, Illinois.

After he was graduated from the United States Naval Academy in 1925, he served in the Submarine Service becoming one of the few officers earning qualification without attending submarine school. A few years later he earned his wings as a naval aviator, thereby attain- .

ing the distinction of a fully qualified air, surface and subsurface naval officer.

After thirty years of active service, involving almost all major areas of armed conflict—two arctic and three antarctic expeditions—Admiral Dufek was scheduled for retirement in 1955. By a special Act of Congress in July of that year, he was continued in his command and is the only senior retired naval officer in that status.

Gentlemen, I have the honor and privilege to present a great naval officer and a great American—Rear Admiral George J. Dufek.

❖   ❖   ❖   ❖

Wilfrid Smith, *Sports Editor of the Chicago Tribune, introduces* **Ford Frick,** *Commissioner of Baseball.*

It is always an honor to be asked to introduce a speaker as well known as the man who is to talk to you today, but this is a particular pleasure and one, I suspect, that even the men who arranged the program did not realize.

There is no point in concealing the name of your speaker, Ford Frick, but I want to tell you that we are cousins, because we were both born in Indiana. More important, he graduated from Depauw, at Greencastle, in 1915. I'm very happy he graduated in 1915, because he played first base on the varsity. I entered Depauw University in the fall of 1915, and the following spring took over his position.

I might add that he went just about as far in Colorado as I did in Florida!

Mr. Frick played semi-professional baseball, was a high school teacher, taught English, taught in college, and did War Department rehabilitation work. He became a sports reporter, a columnist and radio commentator, and was then made manager of the National League Service Bureau. He continued from there to become President of the National League, and is now Commissioner of Baseball.

After playing first base with the Walsenburg, Colorado, semi-professional team, he remained to teach English in the high school. From that position he became assistant professor of English at Colorado College, Colorado Springs.

He entered the newspaper field for a second time when he started writing for the Colorado Springs *Telegraph*. Even before he had entered school, he had been a part-time reporter for the Fort Wayne, Indiana, *Gazette*.

Then he went to work for the *Rocky Mountain News* in Denver, and because of his excellent work and very likeable column, he became an employee of the New York *American,* and there he was assigned to cover the New York Yankees. You might say then that Ford had arrived; actually, he had just got a good start.

In 1934 he took over the management of the National League Service Bureau, and very shortly after that became the President of the National League.

The rest is familiar to you, I'm sure. During his career as President of the National League, night baseball was legalized. He was the moving spirit behind baseball's centennial celebration in 1939. He was one of the founders of the National Baseball Museum in Cooperstown, New York, and also prepared and supervised baseball's history on film, "That National Game." In 1951 Mr. Frick took baseball's highest position as Commissioner.

Certainly, the recital of these biographical facts proves that by education and experience, Ford Frick is eminently qualified to talk to you today on the subject, "Baseball, An American Institution."

✦   ✦   ✦   ✦

Mr. Frick *responds to the introduction.*

I didn't realize what a guy I was until I heard that introduction. Apparently, I'm quite a man.

It's really a great pleasure for me to be here. I hope you can say the same thing after I'm through, though I wouldn't bet on it, particularly.

Strangely enough, I propose to talk to you gentlemen today for a little bit about baseball. I could talk about other things, but I don't think you'd expect me to and I do seriously want to talk just a little bit about this game of ours that has become so much a part of our lives, so much a part of our American way.

Before we go into the subject very deeply, we should define what baseball is. Baseball is something more than the major leagues, though they are part of it, of course.

Baseball is Babe Ruth, eternally pigeon-toeing his way around the bases after hitting a home run. Baseball is Don Larsen, pitching a perfect ball game. Baseball is made up of the great stars we have known, all part of the Hall of Fame.

Baseball is more than that.   Baseball is a kid on the sandlot, holding fast to a dream, hoping, dreaming of the days when he will be in major league baseball, too.   It is the old-timer, holding fast to his memories.

Baseball is a youngster from the Little League, going home heartbroken over a lost game.   It's the father who backs the Little Leaguer, rolling up his sleeves and helping to build a diamond.   Baseball is radio, and television, and newspapers.   Baseball is a headline of the box scores that commuters read as they crowd into the trains going to work in the morning and going home in the evening.   Baseball is a little old lady, rocking on her front porch and listening to the radio, and getting some satisfaction and some happiness out of the things that are going on within her sphere in baseball.

Too, it is a sick man in a hospital, watching on television, and perhaps finding some surcease from his pain as he watches a ball game develop.

Baseball is a newspaperman, chattering a telegraph instrument, talking over radio or television, writing about the game in order that you may know what is going on.

Baseball, is hot dogs, peanuts, fans sitting in the sun in the bleachers. As a matter of fact, baseball is a part of our way of life; something that is just as important to us, through the years, as those other great institutions we have.   Maybe that is the reason why a former President of the United States, in a speech in New York a few years ago, said, "Next to religion, baseball has had a greater impact on the American people than any other institution."   The man who said that was Herbert Hoover, former President of the United States, and I believe he was thinking of baseball in its broad scope.

✦   ✦   ✦   ✦

Dr. J. L. Morrill, *president of the University of Minnesota, begins a commencement address to a School of Banking class at the University of Wisconsin.*

Any college president will feel himself at home with the captive audience of a Commencement—but this one is a bit different, and disconcerting!

Most of us, at one time or another—college presidents included—are the captives of our bankers.   We need a loan, for ourselves or our

institutions, and our fate is in your hands.   Some of the respectful awe
of such moments overwhelms me now—even though, just at this
minute, I think there is enough in the bank to meet outstanding obligations and that I am not overdrawn.

But if there is anyone here from the First Nationa Bank in Minne-
apolis, I hope he won't check back to find out—and you never can tell.
My wife told me of a chap she'd seen recently on TV who went to his
doctor to have some obstruction removed from his ear.   The doctor
probed and pulled out a dime, a ten cent piece.   "How long," he inquired, "Has this been troubling you?" About a year, he was told.
"Then why wait all this time to have it out?"   the doctor asked.
"Well, I didn't need the money until now," the fellow said.

My congratulations to the members of this Graduating Class spring
from my respect for this School of Banking as a productive enterprise
in American adult or "continuing professional education," and for the
great University which welcomes and participates in its ongoing.

✣   ✣   ✣   ✣

H. A. Speckman, *Vice President of the McCandlish Litho-
graph Corporation of Philadelphia, responds to an introduction.*

I was a little disturbed when Ralph said that last year you had three
speakers on Saturday morning while this year you have but two.

It seemed to indicate that next year there will be but one speaker,
and I can assure you I am very much inclined to agree with this prog-
nostication.   Many times after I speak they close the meeting, and I
have known occasions on which they have fumigated the hall.   Therefore, if the only reaction to this forthcoming effort on my part is the
reducing of the number of speakers next year from two to one I shall
feel that I have been let off very easily.

✣   ✣   ✣   ✣

Howard D. Murphy, *president of the Executives' Club of
Chicago, introduces* **Willy Ley,** *distinguished rocket scientist.*

The line between success and mediocrity is a very thin one.   I think
I can illustrate that by one of the few times when I have crossed that
line and enjoyed the acclaim of my fellow men!

I sat in a hotel in New York in my official capacity as Program Chairman of the Executives' Club, and called a man whose writings I have always admired—our speaker. One hour later, Art Stewart called me and said our speaker for October 11 had just died so that date was open. When today's speaker arrived at the hotel a few minutes later, he agreed to appear on the 11th. We rushed off pictures and biographical material to Art, and we were in business. I came back to Chicago, happy in the knowledge that we had another outstanding speaker. Four days later, on October 4, to the surprise of most of the world, the Russians sent up the first Sputnik. Within hours, reservations were piling into the office—and a good attendance had already been assured. All of the news services were on hand together with the major networks to interview our guest.

Murphy was a hero for being so farsighted! Isn't it easy?

Our speaker's very substantial fame soared to new heights after the Sputnik. His voice which had been crying in the wilderness for a great many years suddenly grew in volume and cried from the mountain tops. Here was a prophet who suddenly had honor, in his adopted country and in his own house—St. Matthew to the contrary! It had taken twenty-two years for him to be proven right, but I'm sure it was worth it.

The romantics of rocketry have somewhat obscured our speaker's many other talents. Here is a man who has fluent knowledge of seven languages, education in paleontoloy, astronomy and physics, not to mention engineering. He has an insatiable curiosity and an inquisitive mind that seems to be always a hundred years ahead of its time. He also has a delightful accent that lets him use such expressions as "propaganda battle."

May I present one of the foremost rocket scientists of the world, Mr. Willy Ley.

❖   ❖   ❖   ❖

Clinton Youle, *president of the Executives' Club of Chicago,* *introduces* **Professor C. Northcote Parkinson.**

If you glanced more than casually at the caricature sketch on your invitation to today's luncheon you probably thought: "Oh yes, Colonel Blimp is coming to us—in civies;" or, maybe you thought, "That's the way this fellow Parkinson looks."

By now you've had a chance to peer at him over your neighbor's shoulder and see he doesn't look "blimpish." And I can assure you he doesn't talk "blimpish," although I did wonder uneasily a couple of times during our luncheon conversation if he were examining me— sort of "stewing me up" in his mental pot—to be a character in some future essay on financial folk—or toastmasters—or ex-weathermen.

Do you remember *THE SECRET LIFE OF WALTER MITTY?* James Thurber wrote that rather haunting piece on the dreams of men some years ago—and later it was made into a movie.

Professor Parkinson strikes me as a fit character for Walter Mitty's and our imagining one could look at this quietly shrewd face and say, "Ah, there sits Sir Sherlock H. Parkinson—the world's greatest living detective."

When he smiles he looks like a clergyman—when he talks he sounds like a British diplomat—when he writes, seriously, he is clearly an outstanding historian and philosopher. When he writes for fun, he's completely delightful—but with an edge.

One of the book reviews somewhere described him as "Bugs Bunny with a Ph.D."

Gentlemen, may I present C. Northcote Parkinson, Visiting Professor at the University of Illinois and California, retired Raffles Professor of History at the University of Malaya.

* * * *

Professor Parkinson *responds to the introduction.*

This is a very pleasant occasion for me—not merely in itself, but as one in a series of progression.

Some weeks ago I received from this Club a hectic, last-minute invitation, "Would I come to Chicago?" A short notice because this Club was due, the next day, to be addressed by Mayor Wagner, of New York, but the weather was uncertain, and it was by no means clear whether His Honor was going to make it. Would I stand by in case Mayor Wagner failed to arrive? Well, that is an honor, of a kind. And it gave me some of the sensations of the understudy standing in the wings, hoping that the prima donna will break her leg.

The next step in my progress to fame was when I was invited to address a Conference on Agricultural Industries at Urbana; and this time, because the Secretary of Agriculture had fallen ill.

You notice the progression—one; he really had fallen ill and stayed ill; and the other; presumably a Secretary of Agriculture ranks, perhaps by a fraction, a Mayor of New York—not a Mayor of Chicago, but a Mayor of New York. So I felt I was getting on in the world and was flattered by the invitation; and I told the meeting as much, though I pointed out that I was running some danger of assassination.

Anyway, I represented the Department of Agriculture to the best of my ability on that occasion, and I am glad to be able to tell you, Mr. Chairman, that I reduced an audience more or less to hysterics merely by reading a list of publications produced by the government, by the Department which I had undertaken to represent.

The third stage in my progress to fame happens today, and on this occasion I was told that if Mr. President Truman failed to be present today I should have the honor of substituting for him.

You notice, step by step, rising higher. If we can continue the graph upwards, in about a year's time you will hear of President Eisenhower being asked, at rather short notice, to take my place.

✦   ✦   ✦   ✦

Howard D. Murphy, *Partner, Price Waterhouse and Company, introduces* **George Romney,** *President American Motors Corporation.*

They said it couldn't be done! Couldn't be done! Couldn't be done! Tucker said it! Muntz said it! Kaiser said it! "You can't beat city hall—or the Big Three in the automobile industry." The only thing they didn't know was how many times our speaker had been told that before!

Five years after our speaker's birth in Mexico, Pancho Villa kicked out all Americans. After that, our speaker's father had numerous ups and downs in business. One experience was that of going broke in potatoes in Idaho. That gave our speaker the claim to knowing more ways to cook and eat potatoes than anyone else in the country.

As a missionary in England for the Latter-Day Saints, he learned about hecklers. After that he worked in Washington, in and around the government, and became a business executive by the unusual route of trade associations. Even his bride-to-be said "No" for a couple of years.

In 1948 he became a special assistant to George Mason, the head of Nash Kelvinator. The two of them staked their reputations and careers on a belief that the major car manufacturers were leaving a gap unfilled in the small car field. Mason died shortly after the merger with Hudson, and our speaker became President. Since then, the story is well known. He did it!

Now, for a moment I would like to get on my own soapbox. I fervently and sincerely hope that our speaker is the Moses who can lead his fellow car manufacturers out of the wilderness.

Will someone tell me why I shouldn't be able to sit in a car with my hat on? And just why can't I buy a car that will fit in my garage without alterations? And why must I have a car seat so low that my orthopedist assures me it is bound to cause back trouble? And why is repair service getting less reliable, more expensive and harder to get? Mister, that is real wilderness!

May I present the man who has already surprised Detroit with a lot of new answers and may still have some up his sleeve. The President of American Motors Corporation, Mr. George Romney.

✦   ✦   ✦   ✦

George Romney *responds.*

Thank you very much, Mr. Murphy, for that very pleasant introduction, pleasant in a number of ways.

No. 1, I won't have to sing my own commercial here this afternoon. It is quite true that at five I was driven out of Mexico, and as I started kindergarten in Los Angeles, I was greatly annoyed by the fact that the kids all called me a Mexican because I was quite proud of my American citizenship, having been born an American in Mexico.

It perplexed me until I finally lit on the right argument. I guess that is when I found out that ideas are really the things that count in this world, because I finally said to the kids, "Now, look. If a kitten was born in a garage it wouldn't make it an automobile, would it?" And that seemed to take care of that.

Throughout life there is a constant fight against the human tendency to inertia. Again by way of preface, let me say that I am glad the Chairman took care of my commercial, because I would like to talk about ideas and things that I think are far more fundamental than hat room and entrance room and sitting room and the other things that could be improved in other people's cars. America is the result of stimulating and unleashing the innate capacities of its citizens. The effectiveness of our total effort has been greatly multiplied and im-

proved by those who have voiced new ideas and criticized old ones
While critics and the non-conformists have played a vital role, it is
becoming more difficult as our country's accomplishments produce
undreamed of contentment and comfort.

If you don't think so, just try it. Just voice some viewpoint that
isn't the viewpoint of your industry, and see how many doghouses you
get into!

Emerson voiced a great thought when he said: "To be a man you
must be a non-conformist," and further, "It is easy in the world to live
after the world's opinion. It is easy in solitude to live after your own,
but the great man is he who in the midst of a crowd keeps with perfect
sweetness the independence of solitude."

❖   ❖   ❖   ❖

Clinton Youle, *president of the Executives' Club of Chicago,*
introduces **William Veeck,** *president of the Chicago White*
Sox.

Practically every Chicagoan able to read, see, or hear knows all
about Bill Veeck. You know he's the most colorful guy in the game
since the Mighty Casey of Mudville, and he has been a whole lot more
successful than Casey ever was.

You've heard him described as the greatest promoter in the game
More important, you know he is the fellow who brought the Indians
their first pennant in 26 years, and that was just a warmup for the
White Sox, of course.

A couple of things you might not know. It's almost a tossup which
Bill loves most—kids or baseball. The tip-off maybe is that he's got
seven of his own youngsters, but so far has only had four ball clubs.

He likes practical jokes, too. He started early, and once got invited out of junior-school for seizing the two minutes his arithmetic
teacher's back was turned, to whip out a barber apron, shears, clippers
and hair tonic and starting to cut the long hair of a classmate—with
the help, I should add, of Phil Clarke, Jr., the son of the gentleman
down here.

Bill's big hearted, too.

Maybe you haven't heard about the time he presented his manager,
Charlie Grimm, with a big birthday present right on the baseball field
at Milwaukee just before the game.

It seems the Brewers were short of pitchers, the team was in a stretch race, and Charley was worrying day and night. ᴊo on Charley's birthday, Bill Veeck had a trailer towed out onto the field and on the trailer was the biggest, fanciest birthday cake you ever saw —the blooming thing was seven feet tall.

Charley was overwhelmed, but finally trotted out to take a bow and try the cake. Just as he got there, the top of the thing shot up in the air, and out popped a brand-new, left-handed relief pitcher. That was Charley's birthday present from the boss.

And to make it perfect, the pitcher won the game, and the Brewers won the pennant—just like in the story books. Remember that, Bill? O.K. It's yours.

✦   ✦   ✦   ✦

William Veeck *responds.*

I am a little—not a little, I am greatly ill at ease today. You see, I haven't been in Chicago long enough to get used to crowds.

I operated the St. Louis Browns for several years. We played secret games.

As a matter of fact, when I would see those people in the upper deck, I kind of figured we are going to play a double-header. And I know that all of you gentlemen came as a tribute to the White Sox, and the secondary reason to get World Series tickets.

I am just delighted to be here. I find that one is entitled to speak on anything they want, and I figured that the proper thing for my address today would be the "Impact of Mr. Khrushchev on the United States."

I had originally planned to talk about baseball, but you see, coming in I heard so many more expert people than I, there is no sense of my talking about it.

✦   ✦   ✦   ✦

C. W. D. Hanson, *Western Manager, Life Magazine, introduces* **His Excellency Dr. Konrad Adenauer,** *Chancellor, Federal Republic of Germany.*

Chancellor Adenauer told Secretary of Defense Wilson that "A good diplomat is one who accomplishes the possible." At the ripe—and in his case, zestful—age of 80, Chancellor Adenauer has accomplished very much indeed.   So much, in fact, that Churchill has called him "One of the greatest men Germany has produced since Bismarck."

He makes it quite clear that the Federal Republic of Germany is now free and independent.   At the same time, he scrupulously carries out his agreements with NATO and the Western Powers even though he reportedly thinks some of the agreements foolish or wrong.

The Chancellor's skill in government is no accident.

He has long and assiduously been applying his talents at some government post.   He started in 1906 as a Town Counsellor in his native Cologne, and he was Mayor there from 1917 to 1933.

He confounded the Christian Democratic Union—a political combination of Protestants and Catholics—and has been his party's Chairman since 1946.   He was President of the Parliamentary Council, which drafted the constitution in Bonn in 1948–49, and very soon after was elected Federal Chancellor.

He has done much to develop democratic rights and responsibilities among the people in Western Germany—and it's particularly apparent to their unfortunate countrymen just across the Iron Curtain.

Speaking of the Iron Curtain, I believe no leader has gone to Moscow, gained some basic objectives and stuck to his guns like this indomitable diplomat.

Gentlemen—it's one of our finest moments that we can be host and audience to such a great man and that he would select ours from the myriad platforms offered him to make an address.

I am very happy indeed to welcome to the Executives' Club of Chicago—and present to you—the man who accomplishes the possible—the Chancellor of the Federal Republic of Germany, His Excellency Konrad Adenauer.

❖   ❖   ❖   ❖

Dr. Adenauer *responds.*

First let me thank you for permitting me to make my remarks in my mother tongue.   My knowledge of the English language is too inadequate to enable me to present my views to you on so difficult a subject in your own language.   Do not expect me to say anything very new because, gentlemen, there simply is nothing new.   My whole aim is to bring some clarity into the thinking of the present situation and in our future.

Let me make another preliminary remark.   I want to speak to you ,
realistically; I do not want to paint too rosy a picture nor do I want to
suppress anything, nor do I want to be unduly pessimistic, but I do
believe that in the very difficult foreign political situation in which we
find ourselves, the citizens of the United States in particular should
contemplate the situation very realistically.   For it lies in their hands,
in the hands of the people of the United States of America, whether
the world is to be led toward good or toward evil.   I do not say that
to tell you something pleasant, but I give expression in that way to a
conviction which I have had since 1945.

✦   ✦   ✦   ✦

B. Stuart Weyforth, Jr., *introduces* **Fred C. Foy,** *Chairman of
the Board and President of the Koppers Company, Inc.*

American industry has achieved an enviable place in world history
by its ability to create and mass produce.   One of the notable con-
tributors to this reputation is the ever-expanding chemical business.

To the ordinary layman modern industrial chemistry is a miracle—
a lump of coal in one end of the machine and out comes a pharmaceu-
tical—a slight change in formula and out comes a pair of stockings—
oversimplified, but true as well as bewildering.

The Koppers Company, a great force in the chemical industry, not
only achieves similar miracles with materials but apparently also with
men.

Our guest, Mr. Fred C. Foy, after eighteen years as an advertising
executive, joined Koppers in 1948 as Vice President and General Manager of its central staff sales department.   Seven short years later he
was elected to the Presidency and in March of this year was elected to
the dual post of President and Chairman of the Board.

Although a young man himself, Mr. Foy is particularly interested in
developing the potentialities of younger executives with which Koppers
is plentifully supplied.   He is a tireless organizer of community enterprises and is an important factor in the progressive rehabilitation of
Greater Pittsburgh.

Gentlemen, I have the pleasure to present the relaxed, affable and
fluent Chairman and President of the Koppers Company—Mr. Fred
C. Foy.

✦   ✦   ✦   ✦

Mr. Foy *responds to the introduction.*

I hope I have a lot of stockholders in the room, and that they listened carefully to everything you had to say. I wish I could believe it myself. I am amazed that there are so many people in Chicago that don't have anything to do at noon.

I am a little perturbed by this apparatus in front of me because these things always bother me just a little bit, but I am positive with this large a group I couldn't make myself heard for as long as I want to speak without losing my voice if it weren't here. Nevertheless, every time I see one of these boxes, I am made nervous because of the situation which arose when a particularly boring speaker had rambled on and on for some twenty-five or thirty minutes. In the middle of the discourse apparently it went dead, and you know, those of you—and I imagine most of you in this room have occasion to make talks from time to time—you know that when one of these goes dead, you can tell right away because your voice doesn't sound the same. It just doesn't feed back to you any more, and he became aware it had propably gone dead. It sort of threw him a little bit, and he stopped. He hit it a couple times like people do, and looked out at the audience. He said, "Can you hear me out there?" He said, "I don't think this thing is working. Can you hear me?"

He said, "I can't hear myself," and some guy in the audience spoke up, and said, "Don't worry, brother, you ain't missed a thing."

❖   ❖   ❖   ❖

C. W. D. Hanson, *Western Manager, Life Magazine, introduces* **Dr. Paul Dudley White,** *distinguished physician and cardiac specialist.*

A heart is something without the ace of, you can't make a grand slam in.

A heart is something you have if you're charitable and don't have if vou won't let Junior go to the movies.

A heart, indeed, is many things, and it takes half a page in Noah Webster's stout lexicon to list them.

To Paul Dudley White, M. D., the heart is the chief and central mechanism of the body, whose mysteries, until recent years, were pretty unfathomable. He has fathomed them more, perhaps, than any other man, and he has obviously had a very interesting time of it.

For example, he ran down a one-ton whale near Alaska to check
its heart beat.   After practicing on this minnow, he caught up with a
fifty-ton gray whale near La Jolla, whose heart action he also charted.
Obviously, mere man has no choice but to cooperate with this intent
medico who is doing so much to solve one of our chief health problems.

Although Dr. White's experiments have been largely with people,
he has also clocked the vital organs of even higher animals like hum-
mingbirds, mice, primates, shrews and that unforgetting but Republican
species, the elephant.   In the latter case, Dr. White tells me he found
the heart all right after he found out which direction the elephant was
going.   Incidentally, Mayor Daley tells me it's easier to find out which
way elephants are going than Republicans.

About all I could say after reading up on Dr. White was—WOW!
His is one of the busiest and most remarkable careers I've heard of.
He has quite literally seen everything and done everything that the
field of medicine—and, indeed, the world—has to offer.

He has been in most of the countries of Europe and the Near East,
and he was a specialist on the Point 4 Program in India, Pakistan and
other Asian nations.

He has donated much in both time and money so that heart disease
would be brought under control.   He is a thoroughly dedicated man
on the subject.

His list of decorations and honors is as long as my arm, and, believe
me, all of the top ones are there from both here and abroad.   You
know, of course, that Dr. White attends President Eisenhower, and he
is given no little credit for putting a winning candidate back into the
lists.

I'm delighted to present one of the founders of the American Heart
Association, a bicycle rider of note, author, teacher, thinker, foremost
physician—Dr. Paul Dudley White.

✤   ✤   ✤   ✤

Dr. Paul Dudley White *responds to the introduction.*

I'm a bit embarrassed after that introduction.   I'm really just a
plain doctor, a practitioner of medicine.   My chief interest is the care
of the patient, but many things have happened, and I have had a busy
few years.   I may have the opportunity to tell you a little of that, but
I want now to present to you the problem of your own health, and the
challenges posed thereby.

✤   ✤   ✤   ✤

Howard D. Murphy, *Partner, Price Waterhouse and Company, introduces* **Ezra Taft Benson,** *Secretary of Agriculture.*

You will agree that freedom is the foundation of our country, and therefore our business and agricultural economy must also remain free. Our speaker is one of the greatest exponents of this philosophy.

His personal background and farming experience are a matter of public record. Did you know that he has spent over thirty years of active participation in the Boy Scout Movement and is presently a member of their Executive Council? Those of us here in the Midwest will appreciate the fact that he is a distant relative of the late Senator Robert Taft.

That you may know him better, here are a few things he has said: "The virus of subsidies permeates the economic body and eats it up, once it gets its proboscis under the skin." That was way back in 1943. In 1957 came this statement: "Since we apparently cannot legislate scarcity, we must learn to live with abundance." Then, this year, these words: "I think we have also learned that you cannot, over the long pull, fix prices by government mandate, so we must move in the direction of greater freedom for the farmer to produce, and less government regulation and control."

I am personally very thankful for a man who has the depth and strength of conviction to stand, sometimes almost alone, against a Brannan Plan, a Proxmire Plan and all such socializing schemes. I am equally thankful that we have a President who has the courage to support him against his many critics in both parties.

It is a great pleasure to present the Secretary of Agriculture, the Honorable Ezra Taft Benson.

❖   ❖   ❖   ❖

Ezra Taft Benson *responds to the introduction.*

This is a signal honor and a challenging responsibility. I was just reminiscing. In my travels, which have averaged almost 100,000 miles per year for the last five and a half years, I have probably made more trips to Chicago than any other city in America, and possibly have spoken more times in this city than possibly any other city.

I love to discuss the agricultural problem. I don't know that I enjoy talking about agriculture any more than a three-term Governor we once had in Idaho, C. Ben Ross. He loved to talk. He loved to campaign, and he loved to talk about agriculture.   In fact, it was his favorite subject.   It wasn't the one he understood the best, but that didn't make any difference.   He went right ahead and talked about it.

In those days I was doing county agent work in southeastern Idaho in Pocatello.   Just west of Pocatello there was a great, dry Michaud flat, we called it unproductive, and this night Governor Ross was orating at a rally in Pocatello.

I was sitting way in the back of the room, and true to form, when he got to the height of his oratory, he went right to the subject of agricultural expansion and agricultural opportunities in the great Democratic state.

He said, "Ladies and gentlemen, all we need to make this Michaud flat to the west of us, one of the most productive areas in this whole inter-mountain country, is good people and water," and a heckler in the back of the room—it wasn't me—yelled out and said, "Hey, Governor, that's all hell needs."

✢   ✢   ✢   ✢

Arthur O. Dietz, *president of the C.I.T. Financial Corporation, begins an address.*

Whether you are an optimist or a pessimist, you will agree that these are uncertain times.   Therefore, as we look into a changing future, it is good for the banks and finance companies in the installment credit business to re-examine our responsibilities, to check our directions and operations and to determine exactly how we propose to meet today's and tomorrow's problems.   I would like to direct such a re-examination this morning to the field of the general public interest—to the question of "What We Owe Our Customers."

3 ✦ ✦ ✦

Stories from Speeches and Other

Helpful Illustrations

GETTING SOMEWHERE

"You never stub your toe standing still," said Charles F. Kettering. "The faster you go, the more chance there is of stubbing your toe, but the more chance you have of getting somewhere."

NO ORDINARY VICE PRESIDENTS

Judging from the business news pages, the title of Vice President has got so common that nobody pays attention to it any more. To get a tumble you have to be some special kind of V.P. So Madison Avenue is showing us the way; already, along that splendid thoroughfare there is at least one firm with no fewer than three Executive Vice-Presidents; several have a whole platoon of Senior Vice-Presidents; and it is rumored that a concern faced with a temperament problem is considering the appointment of a second First Vice-President. *Management Briefs. Published by Rogers, Slade & Hill*

EDUCATED

Whom, then, do I call educated?

First, those who manage well the circumstances which they encounter day by day; and those who possess a judgment which is accurate in meeting occasions as they arise and rarely misses the expedient course of action.

Next, those who are honorable in their dealings with all men, bear-

33

ing easily what is unpleasant or offensive in others, and being as reasonable to their associates as it is humanly possible.

Furthermore, those who hold their pleasures always under control, and are not unduly overcome by their misfortunes, bearing up under them bravely and in a manner worthy of our common nature.

Most important of all, those who are not spoiled by their successes, who do not desert their true selves, but hold their ground steadfastly as wise and sober-minded men, rejoicing no more in the good things that have come to them through chance than in those which through their own nature and intelligence are theirs since birth.

Those who have a character which is in accord, not with one of these things, but with all of them, these are educated—possessed of all the virtues. *Socrates (470–399 B.C.)*

MY GET UP AND GO

How do I know that my youth is all spent?   Well, my get up and go has got up and went.   But in spite of it all I am able to grin when I recall where my get up has been.

Old age is golden—so I've heard it said—but sometimes I wonder when I get into bed, with my ears in a drawer and my teeth in a cup, my eyes on the table until I wake up.

Ere sleep dims my eyes I say to myself, "Is there anything else I should lay on the shelf?"   And I'm happy to say as I close my door, my friends are the same, perhaps even more.

When I was young, my slippers were red, I could kick up my heels right over my head.   When I grew older, my slippers were blue, but still I could dance the whole night through.

But now I am old, my slippers are black, I walk to the store and puff my way back.   The reason I know my youth is all spent, my get up and go has got up and went.

But I really don't mind when I think, with a grin, of all the grand places my get up has been.   Since I have retired from life's competition, I accommodate myself with complete repetition.

I get up each morning, and dust off my wits, pick up my paper and read the "obits."   If my name is missing, I know I'm not dead, so I eat a good breakfast and go back to bed!

A COMMON EXPERIENCE

Dr. James R. Killian Jr., who recently resigned as special assistant to the President in the field of science and technology, told a luncheon group about the trials and tribulations of his space age job.

"During my trip thru the outer space of Washington, I experienced many novel sensations," he said. "I experienced very high accelerations and decelerations . . . test failures . . . the exhilaration of orbital flight and successful landings. And as does everyone who ventures on this kind of man-in-space flight, I have, on occasion, known the sensation of weightlessness."

CUT IT SHORT!

A certain South African tribe has one custom that might well be introduced in this country. Considering long speeches injurious to the orator and to the audience as well, they have an unwritten law that a public speaker must stand on one foot while addressing his listeners. As soon as the other foot touches the ground, the speech is brought to a close—by force if necessary!

JUST WAIT!

You can't pick a lock with a pickle, you can't cure the sick with a sickle, pluck figs with a figment, drive pigs with a pigment, nor make your watch tick with a tickle.

You can't slacken your gait with a gaiter, you can't get a crate from a crater, catch moles with a molar, bake rolls with a roller.

But you can get a wait from a waiter! *Sunshine Magazine*

THE SORE FINGER

Many years ago Dwight W. Morrow, the father of Anne Lindbergh, told a group of friends that Calvin Coolidge had real presidential possibilities. They disagreed, saying that Coolidge was too quiet, and lacked color and political personality. "No one would like him," objected one of the group.

But up piped little Anne, then aged six: "I like Mr. Coolidge." Then she displayed a finger with a bit of adhesive tape on it. "He was the only one who asked me about my sore finger."

Mr. Morrow nodded. "There's your answer," he said.

STILL CONFUSED

Comdr. William B. Van Dusen, a navy ordnance officer who can explain what makes guided missiles tick, tells of a lady who heard a lecture on missiles and reported that "She was still somewhat confused —but on a much higher plane than before."

GOOD QUESTION

Allen W. Dulles, head of the Central Intelligence Agency, reports that at a communist meeting in Russia, one of the quietest party members, Sergei Popsky, arose.

"Comrade leader," he said, "I have only three questions. You say we have the greatest industrial system in the world. If so, where are our automobiles? You say we have the finest agriculture in the world. If so, where is our bread? And you say we raise more cattle than any country in the world. If so, where is our meat?"

"The hour is growing late," said the presiding officer. "I will answer your questions in full next week."

A week later at the opening of the meeting, a party member arose.

"Comrade leader," he said, "I have only one question: Where is Comrade Popsky today?"

PUBLIC ECONOMY

Almost 200 years ago Thomas Jefferson wrote the following sage counsel to the American people:

I place economy among the first and most important virtues and public debt as the greatest of dangers to pursue our independence. We must not let ourselves load up with perpetual debt. We must make our choice between economy and liberty, or profusion and servitude. If we can prevent the government from wasting the labors of the people under the pretense of caring for them, they will be happy. The same prudence which in private life would forbid our paying our money for unexplained projects, forbids it in the use of public money.

NOT EASY TO SAVE

B. K. Nehru, secretary for economic affairs in India's ministry of finance, in thanking the United States for a loan for his country's economic development, made his point clear that it is not easy for a society living on the bare margin of subsistence to provide funds for its own development. He said, "There is not much room for the tightening of belts worn by skeletons."

IMPOSSIBLE

It's hard to feel that life on Mars is possible, when so often it seems almost impossible here on earth. *Presbyterian Life*

HE KNEW THEM

Representative Sid Simpson recalled recently that when he was a boy in Carrollton, Illinois, Memorial day was observed with services at which a local minister read the names of those who had crossed the Great Divide.

One year, Simpson said, the solemnity of the reading was interrupted by a member of the local G. A. R., a gentleman who took a dim view of most of his old colleagues in arms and who aired his views when he had dallied with the bottle.   This day he had dallied.   His irritation mounted as he noticed that as the minister intoned the name of each departed brother he paused to gaze heavenward.   Finally he blurted:

"If you are looking for any of them stinkers, Reverend, you are searching in the wrong direction."

JUST A WORM

Senator Carl Hayden of Arizona, the oldest senator in continuous service 'n the Senate chamber, illustrated with a story his point that danger ust be known before fear can be felt.   He told of a dude rancher .om Brooklyn who returned to his lodge after a day in the mountain. waving a formidable set of rattlers.

"Where did you get those rattlers," asked an astounded dude wrangler.

"Off'n the biggest woim I ever saw," was the calm reply.   .

BIG TREES FROM LITTLE ACORNS

A shirt waving on a clothesline was the beginning of a great balloon, forerunner of the Zeppelin.

A spider web strung across a garden path was the inspiration for the suspension bridge.

A teakettle singing on the stove suggested the steam engine.

A lantern swinging in a tower gate gave rise to the pendulum.

An apple falling from a tree was the cause of discovering the law of gravity. *The War Cry*

THE UNDEMANDED THINGS

A nurse I used to know was unusually capable and helpful in her care of the sick, relates Harold Blake Walker, a writer in the Chicago *Tribune*.   On one occasion she remarked, "It is the extra, the unde-

manded things I do that give me the greatest satisfaction." In those
words she put her finger on one of the greatest sources of joy in human
life.

Whether we are laying brick, carpentering, serving the suffering, or
whatever may be our occupation, it is doing the undemanded things
that offer the greatest satisfaction. Doing more than is expected of
us, inspires the inner glow that is the token of a rewarding life. The
clock watchers, the indifferent who merely do enough to collect their
pay, find no joy in the hours from 8 to 5, and not much satisfaction in
life thereafter. *Sunshine Magazine*

UNKINDEST CUT

Chief Justice Peter A. Quinn of the City court of New York City
told the Friendly Sons of St. Patrick in Washington that he probably
received the unkindest introduction from a toastmaster ever visited on
a speaker. Shortly after his decisive defeat for re-election to Congress, Quinn said, a Washington toastmaster introduced him as follows:

"The next speaker bears a slight resemblance to the earth. You
know the earth is not a perfect spheroid, because it is flattened at the
poles. So was your next speaker."

GEORGE GOBEL TAKES A MOTH POLL

George Gobel describes Adolphe Menjou as the man whose clothes
closet was voted by the moths of America "As the one we'd most like to
spend the summer in."

OLD MOTHER GOOSE

"Old Mother Goose" was a real person whose maiden name was
Foster. Born near Charlestown, Massachusetts, in 1665, she married
Isaac Goose, who died years later, leaving her a widow with ten children. For the entertainment of her large brood, she wrote a great
number of nursery rhymes, which were collected and published by her
son-in-law, Thomas Fleet. When Old Mother Goose died at the age
of 92, she was buried in Old Granary Cemetery, Boston, where her
grave may still be seen.

CHINESE PHILOSOPHY

A Chinese philosopher once said that parents who are afraid to "put
their foot down" usually have children who step on toes.

IT WASN'T FAIR

Secretary of State John Foster Dulles continued to brood about a scholastic mark he received at Princeton 50 years ago. Talking about American education at a Senate foreign relation committee hearing, Dulles said:

"When I went to college, I had spent much time with French speaking families in Europe and could speak better French than my professor. But because I couldn't conjugate a verb, I got a C. All the rest of my marks were A's and B's. I never quite got over the injustice of it." *Walter Trohan in The Chicago Tribune*

HE GOT HIS WISH

Speaker Sam Rayburn of Texas was once asked if his childhood ambition was to serve as speaker of the House of Representatives.

"No," he replied thoughtfully, "but I did realize another childhood ambition. Once when my teacher in Roane county, Tennessee, pulled my hair, I fervently wished I hadn't any."

NO TIME LEFT

Senator William E. Jenner of Indiana reported a constituent from his home town came to the capital and registered in a hotel.

"Breakfast is served from 7 to 11," the clerk explained. "Lunch is from 12 to 3 and dinner from 6 to 8."

"My goodness!" exclaimed the guest. "When am I gonna get time to see the town?"

WILLING

Secretary of the Treasury Robert B. Anderson told a story about a New Englander who wanted to buy a yoke of oxen and called upon a neighbor who had a pair for sale. The neighbor showed him the two, Ed and Tom.

"Are they a willing pair?" the prospective buyer asked.

"Very willing," the owner replied. "Ed, here, is willing to do all the pulling, and Tom is willing to let him."

ARE YOU SURE, HENRY?

Henry Morgan says marriage is a give and take affair. The husband gives his wife everything he makes and she takes it.

IN ANOTHER'S FOOTSTEPS

Great God, let me walk three weeks in the footsteps of my enemy, carry the same burden, have the same trials and temptations as he, before I say one word to criticise him. *An Indian Chief's prayer*

OLD TREES

Old age comes to trees, as to all living organisms. Each tree has its life span. Gray birch is old at 40. The sugar maple lives long, occasionally to 500 years. Some oaks may live 1500 years, junipers 2000 years. A few of the giant Sequoias are believed to be around 4000 years old.

Old trees are like old people—the infirmities of age are upon them. They have difficulty with respiration (its rate in old plants is much lower than in young plants). The annual shoots are not so vigorous as they once were. Fewer wood cells are formed, annual rings become narrower, and as the rate of growth decreases, dead branches appear in increasing numbers.

In old trees the recuperative capacity is impaired. Wounds do not heal so easily as before. The leaves become smaller; their moisture content decreases; the tree finds it more and more difficult to provide water for its life functions; the inflow of food lags, and life activities in general are slowed down or impaired.

But no tree has yet died of old age. Death usually is readily traceable to such things as drought, insects, fungi, malnutrition, destructive winds, or perhaps, a crushing burden of sleet.

Some of these causes are beyond human control. But the lives of trees can usually be indefinitely prolonged by providing intelligent care. *The Davey Bulletin*

THE RAMPAGEOUS CORYLUS

A farmer who was much troubled by trespassers during the nutting season consulted with a botanical friend. The botanist furnished him with the technical name of the hazelnut, and the farmer placed the following notice at conspicuous points:

"Trespassers, take warning! All persons entering this wood do so at their own risk, for, although common snakes are not often found, the Corylus Avellana abounds everywhere, and never gives warning of its presence."

The place was unmolested that year, and the farmer gathered his crop of hazelnuts in peace.

HE WANTED TO BE SURE

Representative Sidney R. Yates in a recent letter to his constituents said partisanship is not always to be condemned because, frequently it can be beneficial. Unfortunately, he wrote, it too often takes the form demonstrated by Thaddeus Stevens when he rushed in to the House of Representatives to vote on an election contest and asked a colleague which of the two men he should vote for.

"You can take your pick—they are both miserable scoundrels," the colleague replied.

"I know they are both miserable scoundrels, but which is our miserable scoundrel," cried Stevens, according to Yates. "I want to vote for him."

TOO FAST FOR HIM

Sports announcer Clem McCarthy talked so rapidly that many listeners complained about being unable to understand his blow-by-blow accounts of prize fights. The climax came the night Maxie Baer leaned over the ropes in the third round and shouted down into the press row, "Hey Clem, slow down. I can't keep up with you."

SOUNDS FAMILIAR

Here is a description of "modern" youth:

"Our youths love luxury. They have bad manners, contempt for authority; they show disrespect for their elders, and love to chatter in place of exercise. Children are now tyrants, not the servants of their households. They no longer rise when their elders enter the room. They contradict their parents, chatter before company, gobble up their food, and tyrannize their teachers."

Just right for the twentieth century, isn't it? Well, it was written by Socrates, the great Greek philosopher, in 400 B.C.!

HE COULDN'T EITHER

They told him it couldn't be done. With a smile he went right to it. He tackled the thing that couldn't be done, and found that *he* couldn't do it.

WHAT JEFFERSON OMITTED

Thomas Jefferson (1743–1826). Born April 13 in Virginia. Lawyer, architect, inventor, statesman; best known as author of the Declaration of Independence, written in 1776. Served as governor of

Virginia, minister to France, and Secretary of State in Washington's first administration. Vice-President during John Adams' administration. Wrote his own epitaph, but neglected to mention that he had been President of the U. S.

STILL HAS SAME JOB

An American in London, at a party, saw a pretty girl whom he recognized—but couldn't place. He walked over to her and said, "How nice it is to see you again," to which she replied, "Why thank you, sir."

This didn't help much so he said, "How is your mother?" to which the pretty girl replied, "She's fine, thank you." This didn't help either, so the embarrassed American said, "How's your brother?" to which the pretty girl replied, "Why, I'm sorry, but I have no brother."

In a panic, the American said, "Well, then, how is your sister?" to which the pretty girl replied:

"She's still Queen."

BELIEVE IT OR NOT

Did you know that Panama hats originally came from Ecuador? That the Irish potato came from Peru? That bananas grow pointing up? That there are more people of Irish descent in the United States than in Ireland? That it would take 9,000 years to count up to one billion?

IN THE OLD DAYS

We came across an old letter from one friend of the late 1920's telling us news of another. "Dan says he gets 5000 miles from a set of tires. But you know what a blow-hard Dan is."

COFFEE BREAKS

Do you know that a ten-minute coffee break five days a week amounts to forty-three and one-third hours during a year—over a week's vacation in time?

LOSING A MILLION DOLLARS

Representative Joseph W. Martin Jr., Republican House leader, is often twitted by his colleagues about being a bachelor. Representative Clarence Brown likes to say that in his youth Martin narrowly missed being married and being a millionaire to boot. According to Brown's fanciful tale, Martin paid court to a young lady who confided

she had a million dollars.   Brown said the following passage ensued:
"Will you marry me?"   Martin asked the girl.
"No," she said.
"I thought so."
"Then why did you ask?"
"Just to see what it feels like to lose a million dollars."   *Walter Trohan in The Chicago Tribune*

PRETTY AWFUL

Business trends note from Dave Garroway: "When the price of duck feathers increases, down will be up!"

NOT IMPRESSED

Senator Andrew F. Schoeppel recalls that when he was first elected to the Senate he found that new honors impressed him a bit, but he was soon brought to earth.   One morning shortly after his election, as he walked into a hotel dining room for breakfast, a man arose.
"Sit down, sit down," Schoeppel said condescendingly.
The startled man sat down and then asked plaintively, "Why can't I get the salt from the next table?"

NOT SUFFERIN'

A taxpayer from the midwest sent in his report of his 1959 income on form 1040, his check, and the following comment to the internal revenue service:

No longer does 1040 scare me;
   I fill it without any sufferin'.
I read the instructions,
   Grab hold of my pen,
And my aspirin, my anacin
   And my Bufferin.

THE GOOD OLD DAYS

Our forefathers did without sugar until the 13th century; without coal fires until the 14th century; without buttered bread until the 15th century; without potatoes until the 16th century; without coffee, tea, and soup until the 17th century; without pudding until the 18th century; without gas, matches, and electricity until the 19th century; without canned goods until the 20th century.   Now, what was it we were complaining about?   *Sunshine Magazine*

SERENITY

Submarine navigators tell us that no storms ever reach very deep into the ocean. The water is perfectly calm a hundred feet down, no matter how high the breakers may rise on the surface. There is a quietude in the depths that no surface storms can disturb. This is possible, too, in human lives—there can be serenity and peace within, undisturbed by the storms of the world.

LANGUAGE

Professor Ernest Brennecke of Columbia University is credited with inventing a sentence that can be made to have eight different meanings by placing the word "only" in all possible positions in it:
"I hit him in the eye yesterday."

NOT A TOTAL LOSS

Wife: "I've been asked for a reference for our last maid. I've said she's lazy, late for work, and impertinent. Can I add anything in her favor?"

Husband: "You might say that she has a very good appetite and sleeps well."

MODERN FARMING

A western farmer, who had the reputation of being close, had two hired men and a maid. Rumors got around that he was paying too low wages, so a federal inspector called on him.

"I understand that you are violating the law by paying wages below the minimum," stated the inspector in a tone of authority.

"I am, huh?" the farmer retorted indignantly. "Well, there's Jake, who milks the cows an' does the chores around the barn. Go ask 'im."

"Forty dollars a week, sir," Jake informed the inspector.

"An' there's Clem," the farmer said, calling over the other hired man. "Clem, tell this inspector yer wages."

"Forty dollars a week, sir," Clem said.

"How about the maid?" demanded the inspector.

"Hannah? Ask 'er," offered the farmer.

"Thirty dollars a week and room and board, sir," replied Hannah.

"All right, any more?" the disgruntled inspector asked.

"Well, no—only the half-wit," the farmer replied. "He gets $10 a week fei his terbacco an' his board and room."

"Let me speak to him," demanded the inspector.

"Well, you're speakin' to 'im now," the farmer said with a smile.
Capper's Weekly

DIFFERENT VIEW

A man was driving in the country one day and he saw an old man sitting on a fence rail watching the automobiles go by. Stopping to pass the time of day, the traveler said, "I never could stand living out here. You don't see anything, and I'm sure you don't travel like I do. I'm on the go all the time."

The old man on the fence looked down at the stranger and drawled, "I can't see much difference in what I'm doing and what you're doing. I set on the fence and watch the autos go by, and you set in your auto and watch the fences go by. It's just the way you look at things."

SMART MORON

Then there's the one about the little moron who cut a hole in the rug so he could see the floor show. He later sewed it up, of course, because he didn't want to see the hole show.

A GERM OF TRUTH

Sam Levenson observes: "The modern mother is so busy going to parent-teacher meetings her children become juvenile delinquents in the meantime."

CONFUSED

A centipede was happy quite until a frog, in fun, said, "Pray, which leg comes after which?" This raised her mind to such a pitch she lay distracted in a ditch, considering how to run.

IT WORKED

One day as I sat musing, sad and lonely, and without a friend, a voice came to me from out of the dark saying, "Cheer up, things could be worse." So I cheered up, and sure enough, things got worse.
Doings in Denton

COULDN'T LEARN

A six-year-old lad came home from school one day with a note from his teacher in which it was suggested that he be taken out of school, as he was "too stupid to learn." His name was Thomas Alva Edison.

DOUBTFUL

Benjamin Franklin's prospective mother-in-law hesitated about permitting her daughter to marry a printer. There were already two printing shops in the United States, and she was dubious about the country's being able to support a third. *Sunshine Magazine*

ALONE

"Mother's in the hospital," explained the six-year-old Sonny James when a neighbor lady called, "and me and Daddy and Georgie and Margaret and the twins are here all alone." *Oren Arnold*

TROUBLE

One friend to another: "You sure look worried."
The other: "Boy! I've got so many troubles that if anything should happen to me today, it would be at least two weeks before I could start worrying about it."

PAYOLA

A baseball club was organized by a boys' organization. The team was challenged by another boys' club. One man gave a special contribution of five dollars to the captain, stating that the money should be used to buy bats, balls, gloves, or anything that might win the game.
On the day of the game the man was surprised to observe nothing new in the club's equipment. He called the captain to him. "I don't see any new balls or gloves," he said.
"We haven't anything new," the captain admitted.
"But I gave the five dollars for that purpose," the man exclaimed.
"Well, you see, it's this way," came the hesitant answer. "You said we could spend it for bats or balls or gloves, or anything else that we thought might help win the game—so we gave it to the umpire!"

BLAMES GRANDMA

Sympathetic person: "What's the matter, little boy? Are you lost?"

Little boy, sobbing: "Yes, I am.   I shoulda know better'n to come out with Grandma.   She's always losin' somethin'!"

PERSISTENCE

When you feel that being persistent is a difficult task, think of the bee.   A red clover blossom contains less than one eighth of a grain of sugar; 7,000 grains are required to make a pound of honey.   A bee, flitting here and there for sweetness, must visit 56,000 clover heads for a pound of honey; and there are about sixty flower tubes to each clover head.   When a bee performs that operation 60 times 56,-000, or 3,360,000 times, it secures enough sweetness for only one pound of honey!   *Sunshine Magazine*

AS YOUNGSTERS SEE THE WORLD

Helen G. Meyers, supervisor of elementary education in Long Beach, California, was captivated by the talk and writings of first graders—uninhibited, cliché-free, straight to the point.

Over a two-year period she collected the youngsters' descriptions of everyday things.   Among them:

"Cats are for dogs to chase."

"Dogs are made to like people."

"A door is to answer."

"A dream is something you think when you're asleep."

"Ears are something that big people put hearing things on . . . Ears are to wiggle."

"A face is a thing that holds your head and hair in place."

"Mashed potatoes are things to have steak and gravy with."

"Mountains are a place that's hard to go up but easy to come down."

"A package is something to say, 'Yoo hoo!   Look what I got'."

"The world is something to come down to after you've been up in space."   *Associated Press*

UNUSUAL FELLOW

A celebrated vocalist was in an accident.   A paper, after recording the accident, added: "We are happy to state that he was able to appear the following evening in three pieces."

A BIG JOB

Here is a copy of a bill rendered by a painter employed to make extensive repairs to fresco work in a church.   When his charges were disputed, this modern Michelangelo submitted this itemized bill:

1. Corrected the Ten Commandments .... $ 3.02
2. Put new ribbons in Pontius Pilate's hat 5.12
3. Replumed and gilded left wing of guardian angel 4.18
4. Renewed Heaven, adjusted the stars and cleaned the moon ... 7.10
5. Revived the flames of hell, put an extra joint in the devil's tail, mended his left hoof, and did several jobs for the damned ... 7.13
6. Shoeing Balaam's ass 3.02
7. Mended shirt of the prodigal son and cleaned his ears 4.00
8. Put new stone in David's sling, enlarged head of Goliath and extended his legs 3.00
9. Decorated Noah's ark 3.00

Total $39.57

SUCCESSFUL SPEAKER

We gave him twenty minutes, he finished up in ten.   Oh, there's a prince of speakers and a servant unto men.   His diction wasn't very much, he hemmed and hawed a bit, and still he spoke a lot of sense, and after that—he quit.   At first we sat plum paralyzed, then cheered and cheered again; we gave him twenty minutes, but he finished up in ten!

THANKSGIVING PROCLAMATION

Proclamation by Governor Wilbur L. Cross, of Connecticut (1938), considered one of the most beautiful of all Thanksgiving documents.

As the colors of autumn stream down the wind, scarlet in sumach and maple, spun gold in the birches, a splendor of smoldering fire in the oaks along the hill, and the last leaves flutter away, and dusk falls briefly about the worker bringing in from the field a late load of its fruit, and Arcturus is lost to sight and Orion swings upward that great sun upon his shoulders, we are stirred once more to ponder the Infinite Goodness that has set apart for us, in all this moving mystery of creation, a time of living and a home.   In such a spirit I appoint Thursday, the twenty-fourth of November,

A Day of Public Thanksgiving

In such a spirit I call upon the people to acknowledge heartily, in friendly gathering and house of prayer, the increase of the season nearing now its close: the harvest of earth, the yield of patient mind and faithful hand, that have kept us fed and clothed and have made for us a shelter even against the storm. It is right that we whose arc of sky has been darkened by no war hawk, who have been forced by no man to stand and speak when to speak was to choose between death and life, should give thanks also for the further mercies we have enjoyed, beyond desert or any estimation, of justice, freedom, loving kindness, peace—resolving, as we prize them, to let no occasion go without some prompting or some effort worthy in a way however humble of those proudest among men's ideals, which burn, though it may be like candles fitfully in our gusty world, with a light so clear we name its source divine.

PROGRESS IS SLOW

America's first bathtub was built in Cincinnati in 1842. Constructed of mahogany, lined with sheet lead, it was exhibited at a Christmas party. The next day the local newspapers denounced it as a "luxurious and democratic vanity." Doctors warned that the bathtub would be "a menace to health." The next year, in 1843, Philadelphia undertook by public ordinance to prohibit bathing between November 1 and March 15. Two years later Boston made bathing unlawful except when prescribed by a physician.

DOCTORING

Father: "Yes, you may ask a question, but make it short."

Small son: "Well, when a doctor gets sick and another doctor doctors him, does the doctor doing the doctoring have to doctor the doctor the way the doctor being doctored wants to be doctored, or does the doctor doing the doctoring of the doctor doctor in his own way?"

VACATION

Help Wanted: Millions of people for 2 weeks of hard outdoor labor, 12 to 16 hours per day, 600 miles a day of driving. Experience helpful, but not necessary. Crowded working conditions, intense sunshine, sweltering temperatures, rain, gales, etc. Many hazards involved. Little time for meals. No coffee breaks, chats. No wages or salary. Applicants must agree to pay all expenses. No others need apply.

What is this—Drudgery? Maybe, but it's commonly called "vacation."

ADVICE

Learn this and you'll get along, no matter what your station: An ounce of keep-your-mouth-shut beats a ton of explanation.

MARY AND THE LAMB

Mary had a little lamb—you've heard this oft before—and then she passed her plate again, and had a little more!

HE HAD TO DO IT AGAIN

Johnny was taking part in a local concert.   He was only seven, but performed so well that he was encored.

"Well, Johnny, and how did you get on with your part?" asked the proud father when he returned home.

"Why, I thought I had done it all right," replied Johnny, "but they made me go and do it again."

THE BARD UP-TO-DATE

If Shakespeare were alive today, writing for radio or television, we might have commercials reading something like this:

"Let me have about me men that are fat, sleek-headed men, and such as sleep o' nights with 'Sanka.' "

"Yon Cassius has a lean and hungry look.   Me thinks he has not had his 'Wheaties' this morn."

"The quality of mercy is not strained; it falleth like the gentle rain from heaven upon the place beneath it.   Like gifts from Ye Olde Giftie Shoppe, 2032 West Hamilton Drive, it blesseth him who gives and him who takes." *Upward*

UNIVERSITY EDUCATION

I never had the advantage of a university education.   But it is a great privilege and the more widely extended, the better for any country.   It should not be looked upon as something to end with youth but as a key to open many doors of thought and knowledge.   A university education ought to be a guide to the reading of a lifetime. . . One who has profited from university education has a wide choice. He need never be idle or bored.   He is free from that vice of the modern age which requires something new not only every day but every two or three hours of the day. . . The first duty of a university is to teach wisdom, not a trade; character, not technicalities.   We want a lot of engineers in the modern world, but we do not want a world of modern engineers. *Winston Churchill*

DEBT

There are two ways in which a gigantic debt may be spread over new decades and future generations. There is the right and healthy way; and there is the wrong and morbid way. The wrong way is to fail to make the utmost provision for amortisation which prudence allows, to aggravate the burden of the debt by fresh borrowing, to live from hand to mouth and from year to year, and to exclaim with Louis XVI: "After me, the deluge!" *Winston Churchill*

A FORECAST IN 1835

There are at the present time two great nations in the world . . . The Russians and the Americans. . . The American relies upon personal interest to accomplish his ends and gives free scope to the unguided exertions and common sense of the people. The Russian centers all the authority of society in a single arm. The principal instrument of the former is freedom; of the latter servitude. Their starting point is different, and their courses are not the same; yet each of them seems marked out by the will of Heaven to sway the destinies of half the globe. *Alexis de Tocqueville, Democracy in America, 1835*

THE HIGHEST REWARD

The highest reward for a man's toil is not what he gets for it, but what he becomes by it. *O jay Bulletin*

PICNICS

Humans are a simple breed, yet kindly in their way; they'll travel miles at breakneck speed on a hot and dusty day, and scrabble through the biggest bunch of poison ivy plants, to bring a lovely picnic lunch to all us hungry ants. *Sunshine Magazine*

A PERSON WHO CONSTANTLY ASPIRES

Did you ever hear of a man who had striven all his life faithfully and singly toward an object, and in no measure obtained it? If a man constantly aspires, is he not elevated? Did ever a man try heroism, magnanimity, truth, sincerity, and find that there was no advantage in them—that it was a vain endeavor? *Henry David Thoreau*

CAN YOU?

To be able to carry money without spending it; to be able to bear an injustice without retaliating; to be able to keep on the job until it is finished; to be able to do one's duty even when one is not watched; to be able to accept criticism without letting it whip you.

SPOKE TOO QUICKLY

Whatever I said in anger, whatever I shouted in spite, I'm sorry I spoke so quickly—I thought up some worse ones tonight. *Sunshine Magazine*

FOREVER

His fuel was rich, his speed was high; he parked in a ditch to let the curve go by. *Straight*

DOUBLE MEANINGS

Some interesting items inadvertently creep into print, as, for example, the following, gleaned from a number of sources:

Fifty guests assembled at the Domestic Forum, and thirty have been married to the same man for more than twenty years.

The fatal accident occurred at the corner of Broadway and Henry Streets just as the dead man was making an attempt to cross the street.

Leo Drau is at the Memorial Hospital. He is suffering from head injuries and shock caused by coming into contact with a live wife.

It is with real regret that we learn of Mr. Shaigh's recovery from an automobile accident.

At the Ladies Aid Meeting many interesting articles were raffled off. Every member brought something they no longer needed. Many members brought their husbands.

TRAVEL—THE TIE THAT BINDS

I found in the course of various extended trips with one's own dear mate that there may come certain days when you begin to grate just a little on one another's nerves, you know. Now this doesn't mean that the marriage isn't radiantly happy. It doesn't mean that either partner would look at another member of the opposite sex, so much as a glance at them. It does mean you are getting a more concentrated dose of your husband or wife than is normally the case.

After all, here at home in the United States of America the fellow usually goes off to his office in the morning. He comes back in the evening, and there are the children for distraction or friends are coming for dinner or you are dining out or going to a play or something, and you know you are not so completely dependent on each other for social intercourse, but when you are traveling, unless by a fluke you meet another very congenial couple, you are pretty much thrown together.

Also, when you are traveling, there is no doubt, no matter how divine it is, it is exhausting and you are together when you are tired, when you are kind of upset by all that oil the Spaniards use in cooking or by the dubious water or vegetables of the Orient, or by the rich sauces of the French.   And the husband is doubtless concerned about his office or wishes he could get a game of golf or do a little flycasting instead of traipsing through another museum, or get a gander at those bills you've run up in Paris or Hong Kong and Tokyo.

There are, in short, an infinite number of reasons why one's nearest and dearest can seem not quite the creatures of dream that we one time imagined them to be.   But be of good cheer.   Remember that the irritation is transitory.   The underlying love is real, and few things bind two people together more happily than travel experiences and memories shared, and especially if you take pictures as we did.   We are great picture fans.   You can relive the ventures with amusement and excitement and nostalgia, bore your friends a little, too, through many a long winter evening.   *From an address by Ilka Chase before the Executives' Club of Chicago*

THE FIRST TIME I MET JOHN FOSTER DULLES

The first time I met John Foster Dulles was an experience I shall never forget.

The Secretary and I had discussed travel over the world.   I commented that my major interest in visits abroad was in the economic and financial problems of foreign nations.   As the discussion turned to other nations, the Secretary became deeply reflective.   When he spoke, his words came with great feeling.   "When I travel in various parts of the world," he said, "I seem to see different things than many other persons.   For example," he explained, "many persons who visit Egypt marvel at the pyramids as great monuments of earlier civilizations.   But the pyramids do not appeal to me primarily as great monuments of earlier civilizations.   When I see the pyramids, I see tens of thousands of poor, under-nourished Egyptians carrying heavy

physical burdens as they painfully struggle to build the pyramids.   I
see these poverty-stricken people carrying for years the oppressive
burden of the great costs of the pyramids.   Thousands toiled, suffered
and died to build them.   This is what I see when I look at the pyramids."

After a moment the Secretary continued, "and when I look at the
world today, I see hundreds of millions of men and women carrying
on their backs the crushing burden of the costs of government and the
costs of war.   We must remove from the backs of the common people some of the great burdens of the mounting costs of government
and armament so that men and women over the world may enjoy the
fruits of their labor.   We must find the way to lasting peace for all
mankind.   This is what I see when I look at the world."

The Secretary was speaking with a profound conviction.   He was
pouring out thoughts that were deep in his heart.   This was his great
challenge and his great goal.

Later, as we walked to the door, the Secretary said, "Every man
needs to make the decision to dedicate at least a part of his life to his
country and to the attainment of these objectives."

We also say that today our people need to make great decisions.
We are heirs to a priceless and costly legacy.   In our hearts you and
I know that there are no easy devices by which men or nations attain
distinction and greatness.   We know that sound economic and fiscal
policies require principles to which men hold fast.   We know that
hard work and thrift require character and self-denial.   We know
that balanced budgets rest on financial integrity.

If we have the courage to make the right decisions in these times,
and if we have an abiding faith that only the right will ultimately survive, we shall meet the difficult problems of our time with a deep inner
serenity and a calm confidence.   We shall know that we are helping
to build a nation and a world in which the finer values of man's spirit
may flower.   *Herbert V. Prochnow*

THE CONSUMER'S WISHES

Fifty years ago we were still in the horse and buggy era.   Today
we can hurtle through space at 600 miles an hour to attend a business
meeting in a distant city.

Fifty years ago many manufacturers produced products without
making any attempt to find out what the public really wanted.   Today the manufacturer who makes no attempt to find out what the

public wants does so at his peril.   Not only must he know what the public wants, he must make a constant effort to find out what it will want next week, next year, in five years, in ten years.

I might say that in most large companies today the future plans department is considered a major staff function. *Thomas B. Mc-Cabe, President, Scott Paper Company*

A NATURAL BORN SALESMAN

The other day a fond and doting mother said to me, "My boy is a natural born salesman.   What would you suggest I do with him," and I answered in my usual bright and cheery manner, "Madam, I'd shoot him."   A natural born salesman—merciful Heaven, save our profession from the natural born salesman.   What have we ever done—the eight million of us—to deserve this fate.   You know the picture—if he has the gift of gab, if he can talk on any subject whether he knows anything about it or not, if he would rather talk than listen, he is a natural born salesman.   Well, I'll tell you what you can do with your natural born salesman, no I won't either because you wouldn't do it, but if I were offered all the natural born salesmen in the world I'd trade them for six—yes just six—good, hard-hitting, run-of-the-mill salesmen who can think.   Give me a man who can think.   Give me a man who can think and plan, and I have the basic.   Then throw in a dash of good old horse-trading ability, and I believe we have the makings, and then to top it off if he has the willingness to work and is resourceful —look out customers, here we come! *Harold Speckman*

THE WAY YOU LOOK AT LIFE

Because of the housing shortage near the military base where he was stationed, a young doctor and his wife and three children had to live in cramped quarters in a hotel.   A friend said to the doctor's six-year-old daughter, "Isn't it too bad that you don't have a home?"   To which the philosophic young one replied, "Oh, we have a home; we just don't have a house to put it in."

THE GOOD SPORT

The fellow who is a good sport has to lose to prove it.

BLOWING YOUR TOP

Speak when you are angry and you'll make the best speech you'll ever regret.

THE EFFECT OF MODERN BEAUTY PRODUCTS

To judge from the grandmothers we know, Stonewall Jackson (or Whittier speaking for him in "Barbara Frietchie") would today have to revise his famous command and begin, "Who touches a hair of yon blue head . . ."

TWO EXPERIENCES

The first experience was in Greece. On top of a great hill, the Acropolis, in the center of Athens, there stand the proud columns of the ruins of the Parthenon, one of the most magnificent and inspiring architectural works man has ever created. Late one afternoon, Mrs. Prochnow and I were climbing those long, steep stone and gravel steps that lead to the Parthenon, in order to see the golden rays of the setting sun fall on those majestic ruins.

A large unit of the American fleet was in Greek and Turkish waters. Two American marines on shore leave were walking with us, and as we climbed the stairs one marine said to the other, "I suppose the day will come when others will walk up stone and gravel steps to the ruins of the White House, and they will say as they look at the ruins, 'This was a great civilization before it fell.' "

The second experience was in Lebanon. It is only a short drive by automobile from Beirut to the little city of Byblos. This city is one of the oldest in the world. There the ruins of many early civilizations are now exposed by the excavations of archeologists. Here one can stand and look down through seven thousand years of history. Each civilization was built on top of the ruins of the last. The floor of a home of one civilization may be seen only a foot above the floor of a home in a preceding civilization. There one sees the Stone Age, the civilizations of the Egyptians, Phoenicians, Babylonians, Assyrians, Greeks, Arabs, Romans, Crusaders and Turks. One after another, through seven thousand years, great empires and great nations rose and then fell from power. It is a sobering thought.

Through the centuries great empires have risen and declined—Spain and Portugal in the Western Hemisphere; the Netherlands in the Far East; France in Indochina and the Middle East, and now struggling to retain her position in Northern Africa. In this generation we have witnessed the decline in power of a great empire upon which it was said, with understandable pride, that the sun had never set.

Now another power—the United States—is striding majestically across the horizon of world affairs. Its armies, its planes, its ships, its money, its merchandise, and its industrial genius are moving to the remote parts of the world. We are far richer than any nation in history has ever been. The call of economic comfort is loud. Leisure becomes more attractive than labor. Spending becomes more alluring than saving. Lest we forget: every great nation which has risen to power has declined. Confronted with the challenge of Communism over the world we must remain strong and we must hold fast in our minds and hearts to those great ideals upon which our freedom and our very survival ultimately rest. *Herbert V. Prochnow*

LASTING WORDS

Should you wonder how many of the books published last year will still be on the library shelves in 2059, you might get a clue from the century-old items still extant.

Of all the new books published in 1859, the five still to be found in 1959 were Darwin's "Origin of Species," Dickens' "Tale of Two Cities," Eliot's "Adam Bede," Mills' "Essay on Liberty," and Tennyson's "Idylls of the King." *The Postage Stamp*

DO-IT-YOURSELF STATUS SYMBOLS

There may be significance for the historian—as there certainly is for the manufacturer—in the vast increase of things that have gained sales oomph by acquiring what used to be called "snob appeal." (The modern, more charitable, and probably more accurate description is to say that these items have become "symbols of status".)

Our fathers, of course, had their status symbols and many of these are still with us: membership in much-desired clubs, residence in the "right" part of town, Social Register listing; driving a certain make of car . . .

Now, the list of "status symbol" products has vastly expanded: imported sports cars, summer homes, swimming pools, foreign travel, the winter vacation (in addition, of course, to the regular summer vacation, and for true distinction in the Caribbean,) stereophonic hi-fi . . . and many more.

So far, it appears, most status sfmbols have become smart as spontaneously and mysteriously as this or that woman's style becomes fashionable. But there is increasing ground for the belief that a few of the more recent arrivals have been judiciously helped along by purposeful design, by careful distribution, and by subtle suggestion in

advertising. *Management Briefs, published by Rogers, Slade &
Hill*

HUMBLE CHALLENGE

There is a challenge in the words of a humble Hindu woman who
heard the Word of God and became a Christian.

Her husband was very angry and lost no opportunities to vent his
feelings.

"What do you do when your husband is cruel?" she was asked.

She replied quietly: "I cook his food better.   When he complains,
I sweep the floor cleaner.   When he speaks unkindly, I answer him
mildly.   I try to show him that when I became a Christian, I also
became a better wife and mother."

COMMATOLOGY

The afternoon's activities require rather greater study; and I claim
to be the founder of the latest of the biological sciences, the science of
Commatology.   "Commatology" is the study of the life cycle of the
committee.

Now I'm sure we all realize, by now, that a committee is not a structure but an organic growth.   It is something that is planted and it
grows up.   It throws out branches, sub-committees, like this (illustrating), in all directions, and it flourishes; decays; and dies.   And in
dying scatters the seed from which other committees spring up.   How
does this happen?

Let me try to put this in rather more concrete form.   The committee, when first seen under the microscope, consists of five members;
you actually only want three, but you have two to allow for wastage.
With five nominal members you feel tolerably certain of having a
quorum of three on any occasion, as it first appears—and that is
probably the ideal number.

But it's very difficult to keep a committee down to five.   Some
people feel they have been unjustly excluded, and having this feeling
of unjust exclusion, they criticize.   They "bellyache" if I may use the
expression, about what the committee does or does not do.

Now, in Soviet Russia the answer to that will be simple.   The
critics would be liquidated.

In what we call the Anglo-Saxon world, we have another method.
We bring them on to the committee.   Which method is the more
humane I don't know.   But the result of this process is that you shut

up the critics, but in doing so you enlarge the committee; and from its original number of five, it gradually rises, to seven; to nine; to eleven; to thirteen—until it finally reaches what is known, technically, as the coefficient of inefficiency, which lies, as you will all know, between 19 and 23.

Now, this inefficiency is reached because for some historical reason the table at which the committee meets is practically always a long table—not a round table. Round tables are only used for round table conferences. That is something entirely different.

A committee meets at a long table, and, of course, as the committee is enlarged, the table has to get longer. So, it gradually draws out. This table (indicating speakers table) would do very well but you'd have to be straight; and you'd see it extending in either direction, and when the coefficient of inefficiency had been reached, different conversations would have developed at either end. No agreement is even remotely possible because people aren't even discussing the same subject.

And at that point the original five members—just this little group in the middle here-say to each other, "Well, next time we'll have lunch the day before and settle everything then."

And so you have the inner committee of the committee, back to the number five, but of course the pressure begins and that, too, is enlarged until you have the inner committee of the inner inner committee, and so on, in a majestic cycle of nature, from spring to winter, from dawn to dusk. *Professor C. Northcote Parkinson*

THE LESSON IS CLEAR

A squad car policeman was covering a quiet beat out in the suburbs when he was amazed to find a former lieutenant on the police force covering the beat. He stopped the car and said, "Why, Mike, this wouldn't be your new beat way out here, would it?"

"That it is," Mike grimly," "ever since I arrested the judge on his way to the Masquerade Ball."

"You mean, you pinched his honor?" asked Pat.

"How was I to know that his convict suit was only a costume!" demanded Mike.

"Well," mused Pat, " 'Tis life and there's a lesson in this somewhere."

"That there is," replied Mike. " 'Tis wise never to book a judge by his cover."

FREEDOM

When the Athenians finally wanted not to give to the state, but the state to give to them, when the freedom they wished most for was freedom from responsibility, then Athens ceased to be free and was never free again.   *Edith Hamilton*

4 •••

Three Hundred Quotable Quips

The most welcome person is the one who knows when to go.

Iceland is so cold that most of the inhabitants have to live somewhere else.

The person who brags lacks confidence in himself.

A smart cat would eat cheese and breathe down the rat hole with baited breath.

Few persons have good enough sight to see their own faults.

No dime ever looks so big as the one you didn't get back from the telephone box.

No one has his ups and downs like the person in the end seat at the theatre.

Life begins at forty, but so do lumbago, bad eyesight, arthritis and the habit of telling the same story three times to the same listeners.

Government is an institution through which sound travels faster than light.

To be a leader you need a lot of people dumb enough to follow.

Modern education has changed the commandment to read, "Parents, obey your children."

Love makes the world go round, but so does too much red pepper in the chili.

No one ever gets paid for being disagreeable, except a traffic cop, a head waiter and theater ticket agent.

If you can look interested when you are bored, your social success is certain.

Winter comes but once a year, and that's enough.

An efficient business man who found a machine that would do half his work at the office bought two.

One reason you can't take it with you is that you don't have any left when you go.

If a person wants to get ahead, he has to start without all the advantages others have.   *Herbert V. Prochnow*

Money won't make you happy, but it may make you feel a little less miserable.

The fellow who says the church is losing ground is probably the same one who says the sun is losing heat.

Figures don't lie, and that's exactly what makes tailoring so difficult.

Too often when conscience tries to speak the line seems to be busy.

A highly commendable government expenditure is any spending that helps my community.

Money is the root of all evil and also of a good many family trees. *Herbert V. Prochnow*

A statesman is a person who takes his ears from the ground and listens to the still small voice.

With a small boy cleanliness is not next to Godliness, but next to impossible.

If you're going to make a pal of your boy, don't do it until after he has had quadratic algebraic equations.

There are 100,000 useless words in the English language but they come in handy in college football yells.

Nothing in the world is fool-proof as long as there is a fool.

The green light is the signal for the man behind you to blow his horn.

You never know how many friends you have until you rent a cottage at the beach.

God made the country, but the cars on all sides of you keep you from seeing it.   *Herbert V. Prochnow*

Once upon a time, a young man took the garage keys and came out with the lawn mower.

A picture window will bring the outdoors into your living room, but a ten year-old boy can bring in a lot of it with only two feet.

Horse sense in banking is the ability to say "Neigh."

Getting out of a rut is the highest mountain most of us have to climb.

Hardening of the heart ages people more quickly than hardening of the arteries.

In the old days a husband lost his shirt in the stock market. Now it's the super-market.

It's strange how few of the world's great problems are solved by people who remember their algebra. *Herbert V. Prochnow*

When it comes to helping you, some people stop at nothing.

Every time you give someone a piece of your mind you make your head a little emptier.

It's remarkable how easy it is to read the traffic signs if a motorcycle cop is just back of you.

Only one or two persons in 25 or 50 are illiterate, and yet they insist on writing those letters to the newspapers. *Herbert V. Prochnow*

Nothing helps adult education like children.

No collision injures an automobile like a trade-in.

It's surprising how many persons believe they can break up a traffic jam by blowing an auto horn.

Some persons pick one hobby to go crazy about instead of letting the world generally drive them nuts.

One thing about mischievous youngsters is that they get their parents home from the party early.

Life is pretty rugged if you have to keep on driving a car with a standard shift.

Keeping up with the Joneses is bad enough but passing them on a hill is worse.

If you are ignorant, you can get into some very interesting arguments.

A person who may be too polite to talk when his mouth is full will talk when his head is empty.

Just because a person grows older, it doesn't mean he necessarily grows up.

The main thing you learn from radio and television is that the country is full of people who can't sing.

A friend is someone who will listen while you gossip about someone else. *Herbert V. Prochnow*

To be a gentleman is an asset, but it is a great handicap in a traffic jam.

Enough is just a little more than the neighbors have.

If you think you can't take it with you, it's because you never packed a car for a vacation.

Some fishermen catch their best fish by the tale.

Gentleman Farmer—A farmer who has more hay in the bank than in the barn.

One advantage of being married: You can't make a fool out of yourself without hearing about it.

The dollar doesn't go as far as it did, but its acceleration is much better developed.

A girl baby triples her weight in her first year and tries to halve it in her fortieth.

Many a young girl is as old as her mother tries to look.

It takes more than a shoeshine and a manicure to give a person polish. *Herbert V. Prochnow*

Clothes may make the man but his wife's break him.

The modern woman seldom cries, but what has she to cry about?

We suppose it would be worse to be born old and have to look forward to growing young and silly.

If a person says he won't argue, it means he won't listen after having his say.

The way for nations to do away with war may be to pray more and prey less.

A self-made man is generally a combination of dollars and sense.

If you could sell your experience for what it cost you, you would have a fortune. *Herbert V. Prochnow*

If an automobile doesn't get a pedestrian, an automobile salesman will.

Most self-made men are smart enough to employ college professors to train their sons.

If children now can spell better than their fathers, why don't they?

Another thing that seems to improve the longer you keep it is your temper.

Double jeopardy is when a man with a two pants suit discovers both pairs need to be replaced.

After listening to many parents we are convinced brilliant children spring from parents who are not so bright.

Don't criticise anyone for wishing for what he doesn't have. What else could he wish for? *Herbert V. Prochnow*

Clothes may make the man, but we've seen some where the job still wasn't finished.

A committee meeting is a long and tortuous route to an obvious conclusion.

It never pays to plant a bigger garden that your wife can weed.

A teen-ager is grown up when he thinks it is more important to pass an examination than to pass the car ahead.

They lived cheaper in the horse and buggy days with the mud roads, but was that living?

Many a family that seems to be on Easy Street is only on Easy Payment Street.

It's a fine thing to be a gentleman, but it's a handicap when you drive a car on some highways. *Herbert V. Prochnow*

The advisability of passing a car at a curve depends upon whether your widow thinks the loss will be covered by insurance.

No wonder children are confused when we tell them they're too little to stay up at night and too big to stay in bed in the morning.

Every man likes a woman with brains enough to tell him how wonderful he is.

Every girl should remember in seeking a model husband that there are two models: sport and working.

Who gets the last word when one woman talks to another?

It is a strange fact that there is no connection between what a man knows and the time it takes him to tell it. *Herbert V. Prochnow*

A banker says marriage promotes thrift. Demands it, he means.

The way to pass a twenty-ton truck on a two lane highway is on a parallel road in the next county.

A man may be on the right road and get run over if he just sits still.

It is said we spend more on wild life than we do on child life in this country, but parents will find this a puzzling distinction.

What obstructs the vision and is called smog in our big cities is called "defining the issues" in politics.

He who hesitates loses the place to park his car. *Herbert V. Prochnow*

Travel is broadening, especially if you stop at all those restaurants recommended along the road.

The husband who brags that he never made a mistake has a wife who did.

If you have a high batting average, don't worry. The big leagues will find you.

It isn't easy to keep your mouth and your mind open at the same time. *Herbert V. Prochnow*

The trouble with a household budget is that there is generally too much month left at the end of the budget.

Etiquette is the noise you must swallow your soup with.

A lot of time could be saved if salary checks were sent directly by the employer to the installment people.

No one has the independence of a farmer who can get to work anytime in the morning just so it isn't after 5 A.M.

When parental control is remote control, you have juvenile delinquency.

Every married woman gets a man's wages, sooner or later.

The fellow who drives this year's car on next year's salary probably wears last year's suit and shoes. *Herbert V. Prochnow*

Prosperous times are those in which all of us have more installment payments than we can afford.

The person who says you can't mix liquor and driving must not read the traffic accident lists.

There are now enough automobiles in this country so every man, woman and child can ride at the same time, and on Sunday afternoons they do.

Every once in a while we see a television program that makes us yearn for the good old days of static radio.

A decathlon is any combination of ten athletic events such as painting the garage and falling off the ladder.

The person who tells you his troubles keeps you from thinking of your own. *Herbert V. Prochnow*

Another thing the installment buyer pays is the salary of the installment collector.

To have national prosperity we must spend, but to have individual prosperity we must save—which clears up everything.

With most of us money talks, and it usually talks about more money.

Some women not only meet their husbands half way, but on pay days they go right to the office.

America has more transportation facilities than any other nation, but they're so crowded you can't use them.

When you try to reduce, the problem isn't keeping up with the Joneses, but keeping down with them.

We know one family that has no washing machine, no television, no mink coat—just money in the bank.

You don't get much help out of a spade merely by calling it one. *Herbert P. Prochnow*

No one leads the orchestra without turning his back on the crowd.

When youth calls to youth, the telephone company makes money.

Among other things we're paying for on the installment plan are two World Wars.

Nothing keeps the American people moving like the "no parking" signs.

Some people know how to live everyone's life but their own.

An antique is a piece of furniture that is paid for.

What you hear never seems as exciting as what you overhear.

Flattery is when people say nice things about you that you always knew were true.

The person who is too busy to be courteous is too busy.

There is no such thing as a secret.   Either it is too good to keep or not worth keeping. *Herbert V. Prochnow*

The dollar doesn't do as much for us as it did, because we don't do as much for a dollar as we did.

Women can keep secrets as well as men, but it takes more of them to do it.

It's surprising how people will agree with you if you keep your mouth shut.

If you think of the things you don't have and don't want, you'll find you're pretty rich.

A rich man is only a poor man with money.

If you can get in the last thought, you don't have to worry about getting in the last word. *Herbert V. Prochnow*

Sooner or later a person who carries tales makes a monkey of himself.

The boss may not be able to make you do anything, but he can make you wish you had.

Man starts life young and broke and winds up old and bent.

No one gets too old to learn a new way of being stupid.

It's difficult to climb a ladder with your hands in your pocket.

No boy expects to grow up and be as dumb as his father.

When a person is always right, there is something wrong.

A Dutch treat is when two businessmen have dinner and each uses his own expense account.

The first thing a pickpocket learns is not to fritter away his time on a man with three children in college. *Herbert V. Prochnow*

A person ought to be thankful when he has the means to live beyond.

Conscience is what makes a small boy tell his Dad before his sister does.

If at first you don't succeed, you're about like everyone else.

A good listener usually dozes or has his mind on something else.

After you hear two witnesses in an automobile accident, you have some doubts about historians.

A reckless driver is a person who passes you when you are exceeding the speed limit.

A traffic policeman is a man who stays mad all the time.

A diplomat is a person who can make his country's greed seem like altruism.   *Herbert V. Prochnow*

Why are the ignorant always so certain and the intelligent so uncertain.

A person has good manners if he is able to put up with bad ones in others.

He was the kind of cautious person who thought things over carefully before going off half-cocked.

Don't worry about what people think of you because they seldom do.

If all the officers in a business agree, some of them aren't thinking.

No woman wants a perfect husband, because it leaves nothing for her to do.

No other labor-saving device beats a wastebasket.

Happiness is the result of being too busy to be miserable.

A married couple lives happily if only one is spoiled and selfish. *Herbert V. Prochnow*

Nothing is easier in life than getting up early in the morning the night before.

It is strange why other people do not profit when we point out their mistakes.

Some persons speak when they think and some oftener.

Profits may be bad but they meet the payroll better than losses.

Early to bed and late to rise and you won't see any soap operas or old movies on television.

With television, radio, and phonographs the American family is more sound than ever.

We sort of like the moron who said when his feet get hot he turns the hose on them.

Sometimes a go-getter is sorry he gotter.

It's easy to pick out the best people because they'll help you do it.

What every married man would like to buy is a three-pants and two-coats suit.   *Herbert V. Prochnow*

Americans sink millions of dollars in unsound financial schemes, one of which is keeping up with the neighbors.

We've often wondered why a car always makes a chicken think it lives on the other side of the road.

There are more than 200,000 useless words in the English language and at some committee meetings you hear all of them.

In these days when you see silver threads among the gold it's time for another color hair rinse.

Be it ever so humble, there's nobody stays home.

Women today expect their husbands to bring home the bacon, but only after the delicatessen has fried it.

The automobile may ruin some youngsters, but there are also some youngsters who ruin the automobile.

A road hog and reckless driver is any other motorist.

No driver needs manners who has a horn and a ten-ton truck.

A politician is a fellow who shakes your hand before the election and shakes you after the election.

It always pays to smile in the morning, because later in the day you may not feel like it.

You never have to know all the answers because you won't be asked all the questions. *Herbert V. Prochnow*

We like the fellow who is reasonable and does things our way.

In the grammatically correct home the wife says, "you shall" and the husband says, "I will."

It's pretty hard to believe in improvement through evolution if you have been listening to television programs for two or three years.

The blessing in being poor is that a woman can pay $1.98 instead of $25 for a $1.98 hat.

It's strange in a progressive country how some persons are so backward they don't buy anything until they have the cash to pay for it.

The husband has to make money first and his wife has to make it last.

A business is too big when it takes a week for some gossip to go from one end of the office to the other.

It's terrible the way those careless drivers keep so close ahead of you.

You can win $5,000 at the race track if you're the horse.

If all the cars at a busy cross road were laid end to end some dumbbell would pull out and try to pass.

Most of us would prefer to be miserably rich than happily poor.

A chrysanthemum by any other name would look the same—and be easier to spell.

Out in Los Angeles we understand the children learn subdivision in school. *Herbert V. Prochnow*

Occasionally you can make someone else happy by just leaving him alone.

You can really mess up the traffic if you signal left and turn left.

Sometimes a business is so busy that the officers don't have time for long committee meetings.

Some men are born meek, get married and have to stay that way.

This would be a pretty discouraging world if you couldn't get ahead of the Joneses occasionally.

Most persons not only keep their youthful figures as they grow older; they double them.

You seldom hear of a mob rushing across town to support the Golden Rule.

A middle-of-the-road policy may succeed in politics, but it gets you into lots of trouble on a highway.

Some of the stuff that comes to TV and the radio through the ether makes any other anaesthetic look weak.

Modern Boy: You're the best father in the world, including outer space.

Many couples are unhappily married but fortunately don't know it.

A good many homes are still without bathtubs, but after all, a good many people seldom stay home.

A parking space is the thing that disappears when you make a u-turn.

An army private may be the captain of his soul and still have to salute a second lieutenant. *Herbert V. Prochnow*

We like the man who says yes better than the one who says no, but the trouble is the former seldom has any money to lend.

Ten years from now we'll laugh at the clothes women wear today, but can we hold in that long?

A boy is grown up when he walks around a puddle.

With a high standard of living people are often better off than they are better.

Nature abhors a vacuum and she sometimes fills an empty head with conceit.

A person can win a lot of arguments by avoiding them.

We've noticed that nothing seems to need reforming so much as other people's faults.

We still think there is something to be said for the old days when some child welfare work was done in the woodshed.

In a life time most persons decide whether they are going to be wise or otherwise.

Progress means taking risks, for you can't steal home and keep your foot on third base.

Sometimes a person gets so busy hunting for advantages that he forgets there is work to do.

You don't judge a person's generosity by the amount of advice he gives away.

It takes a man a lifetime to work himself up from the country to the country club and back again.   *Herbert V. Prochnow*

No two persons are alike and they're both glad of it.

When a person really knows himself, he probably wonders why he has so many friends.

Most of us find that it's hard to take advice from people who need it worse than we do.

If you have had some hard bumps, you are probably traveling out of the rut.

The person who spends what his friends think he makes is probably in debt.

"What you don't know doesn't hurt you" doesn't apply to the hidden taxes in the things you buy.

Wise words are sometimes spoken in jest, but many more foolish ones are spoken in earnest.

It doesn't do any harm to dream if you get up and hustle when the alarm goes off.

You can tell a person's real age by the pain he feels when he gets a new idea.

One of our troubles is that too many persons recognize their duty in time to avoid it.

If Aladdin lived today, they could use him as minister of finance in a number of countries.   *Herbert V. Prochnow*

An American is a person who yells about the government spending too much and then asks for a handout for his community.

The world would be better off if people paid as much attention to their consciences as they do to their neighbors' opinions.

Money doesn't make fools of persons, but it does tend to show them up.

Most of us are so busy trying to get what we don't have that we can't enjoy what we do have.

It's all right to be optimistic, but no smart cook breaks an egg directly into the pan.

A punctual person is patient, because he gets that way waiting for those who are not punctual.

We only need one safety slogan—"Drive as if a police car were ahead of you."

Sign outside a small town: "Speed limit 50 miles per hour. You can't get through here too fast for us."

Opportunity doesn't knock now, but it rings the telephone and a quiz show asks you a silly question.

On television they don't always seem to know the difference between a beautiful singer and one who can sing beautifully.

A pessimist forgets to laugh, but an optimist laughs to forget.

Some people who laugh out loud at the family album look in the mirror and never crack a smile.

Little things count, and three of them give you a nice tax exemption.

If you want to learn to tell fortunes, you need to read Dun and Bradstreet.

A successful man generally has a wife who saves his time by making the decisions.

Conceit makes some persons think they are on the way to greatness when they are only on the way.   *Herbert V. Prochnow*

A person gets into trouble if he thinks success depends on how many he can do instead of how much.

Before criticising your wife's faults, remember that they may have prevented her from getting a better husband.

If you aren't too conceited, people will give you credit for knowing more than you do.

What you don't know won't hurt you, but it will amuse a lot of people.

The trick of making women beautiful is done with the help of mirrors.

Today's children don't think much of anyone who can't spell a word two or three different ways.

Famous last words—no woman is going to tell me what to do.

As the man said, "If you will lend me $10, I'll be everlastingly indebted to you."

A woman doesn't make a fool of a man, but she often directs the performance.

No one is unemployed who minds his own business.

If you're not sure what it is, it may be your wife's hat.

As the student said, "Persia gave us the dismal system of mathematics."

A tourist is a person who changes the car oil every four days and his shirt once a week.

Some people keep you so busy listening to their troubles that you haven't time to worry about your own.

The nice thing about life is that one extravagance always suggests another.

We are not prejudiced against a two-dollar bill as it will buy a dollar's worth of groceries any time.   *Herbert V. Prochnow*

The person who goes on a vacation and wants to forget everything discovers that he has when he opens his suitcase.

A smart wife has the steaks on when her husband returns from his fishing trip.

All things come to him who crosses the street without looking.

Conscience is the voice that says you shouldn't have done something after you did it.

An optimist is a person who drops a quarter in the collection plate and expects a five-dollar sermon.

An optimist is a person who thinks that when his shoes wear out he will be back on his feet.

Conscience helps, but the fear of getting caught doesn't do any harm either.

Can you remember way back when governments got along without something if it cost too much?

The hardest job for a rugged individualist is to keep the government from looking after him.

No woman is a good housekeeper until she can slight her work and not have the neighbors notice it.

It's difficult to be content if you don't have enough, and it's impossible if you have too much.

What most of us need is more horsepower and less exhaust.

The average golfer just putters around.

No honest man is a successful fisherman.

The fellow who explodes doesn't necessarily have a dynamic personality.

The seven ages of woman—the right age and six guesses.

When all is said and nothing done, it's time for the conference to break up.

Every small boy wonders why his father didn't go into the ice cream business.

Homes never before were so comfortable and young people so seldom in them. *Herbert V. Prochnow*

"I think" is not only an over-worked expression, but is usually an exaggeration.

At home you can say what you please because no one pays any attention to you.

Those rainy days for which you save often come during your vacation.

A shallow thinker never leaves a deep impression.

The recipe for a good speech includes some shortening.

Man has never discovered perpetual motion, but he is close to perpetual commotion.

In Russia a person can talk his head off very easily.

A yawn at a committee meeting may be bad manners, but it's an honest opinion.

When the going seems easy, you may be going downhill.

It's hard for a youngster to learn good manners without seeing any.

It's a good thing we don't pay taxes on what we think we are worth.

Two heads are not better than one with the present price of haircuts.

When a husband sees the kind of men most women marry, he is sure his wife did pretty well.

A man's mind may be so broad that it is shallow.

Marriage is a mutual partnership if both parties know when to be mute.

Too often television is merely an advertisement with knobs on it.

A person who never makes a mistake gets pretty boring.

No one is so disappointed as the person who gets what's coming to him.

The person who keeps pulling on the oars doesn't have much time to rock the boat.

Tact means looking around to be sure no one is related to the person about whom you are going to gossip.

The person who loses his head usually is the last one to miss it.

A deficit is what the government has when it hasn't as much as if it had nothing.

All things come to him who waits, but not soon enough.

Happiness is often punctured by a sharp tongue.

The only fool bigger than the person who knows it all is the person who argues with him.

The man who says money can do everything hasn't any.

The man who says he is boss in his house has a wife who never stays home.

Fools rush around on tires no good garage man would tread.

The person who claims the old-fashioned winters were harder probably has a son who shovels the sidewalk for him.   *Herbert V. Prochnow*

The government issues thousands of checks a day, which explains how the other half lives.

If you never make a mistake, you may live and die without anyone ever noticing you.

You can lift your head up if you keep your nose at a lower level.

The first of the month bills fall like due drops.

George Washington may have slept many places, but the modern politician also moves from bunk to bunk.

A catty remark often has nine lives.

You must speak up to be heard, but you have to shut up to be appreciated.

If you spill ink on the rug, all you have to do is listen.

As the sweet young thing said when she took a golf lesson, "Now which club do I use for a hole-in-one."

It isn't easy for an idea to squeeze into a head filled with prejudices.

No one has a finer command of language than the person who keeps his mouth shut.

To make money last you have to make it first.

Some persons jump at conclusions, but others dig for facts.

No married man can understand what a bachelor does with his money.

Remember, your relatives had no choice in the matter either.

A person's reputation is a mixture of what his friends, enemies and relatives say behind his back.

No perfume holds a husband like the aroma of a pot of hot coffee.

When a fat man laughs, a great deal of him has a good time.

If the boss were any smarter, a good many people would be out of a job.

If you can make your guests feel at home when you wish they were, you are a good host.

5 •••

Interesting Excerpts from Speeches

THE AMERICAN CITIZEN

I have unlimited faith in the American citizen. He is not following, he is way ahead of the politician. He runs his own affairs well. He knows that this country is nothing more nor less than millions like himself, and he wants the affairs of the nation run the way he runs his own affairs. That is the sound way. He is increasingly aware that the tax dollar is his dollar, and he wants his money's worth! He wants his job, and he's willing to compete with the world and win to keep it. He only wants the opportunity to lift himself and his family by his own efforts and ingenuity to a constantly better life and give his children a little better break in life than he had himself. He wants his individual freedom preserved to worship, to come and to go, and to run his own affairs as he thinks best.

His voice will be heard! It will rise in a great crescendo to run this country soundly and well! *George M. Humphrey, Chairman, National Steel Corporation*

HOW NATIONS GROW

In a free society, free men choose to save and invest for economic growth. In a regimented society, the state dictates the rate of saving and the character of the investment. In any society, investment must be for productive purposes if the standards of living of the people are to be improved. Building pyramids did not make a thriving, vigorous Egyptian economy. There is no easy route to economic growth.

76

Saving means self-denial. It means not consuming now in order to produce more later. To achieve economic progress, every nation must save and invest. There are no short cuts through easy money and artificial low interest rates. There are no exceptions. These are economic imperatives. The nation that neglects them does so at the risk of its economic survival. *Herbert V. Prochnow*

THE WORLD BALANCE OF POWER

Since the end of World War II, we have witnessed a number of revolutionary developments—events of great historical significance.

We have seen the production of goods and services in the United States doubled and resulting benefits in the form of higher incomes and greater leisure.

We have seen the triumph of the Marshall Plan, and the beginning of the Common Market . . . a dramatic demonstration that at long last, major countries in Western Europe are beginning to adopt the American philosophy of broad consumer markets and an economy of the working man.

We have witnessed a technological renaissance in science . . . in the atom, in missile development, in satellites and space exploration, in electronics, and in chemistry.

We have seen emerge a new world balance of power, with a Soviet Union that has made formidable strides on every front: economic, social, and scientific.

Finally, and perhaps most important of all, we have seen the emergence . . . the political birth or achievement of independence . . . of 22 new nations. These new nations are concentrated in the non-western world. They are found in Africa and the Middle and Far East. Largely, their names are unfamiliar . . . their locations obscure.

IN AFRICA: Ghana, Guinea, Libya, Morocco, Sudan and Tunisia.

IN THE MIDDLE EAST: Israel, Jordan and the United Arab Republic.

AND IN THE FAR EAST: Burma, Cambodia, Ceylon, India, Indonesia, North and South Korea, Laos, Malaya, Pakistan, The Philippines, and North and South Vietnam.

I mention them all for in the years to come, many of them will become tremendously important to the western world.

These nations have a total population of about 800 millions . . . One-third of the world total. They have a great deal in common . . .

despite their different cultures, backgrounds, histories, political institutions, and varying stages of economic development.

They have all undergone—or are undergoing—radical changes . . . political, economic and social. These changes are inspired by a nationalistic fervor; an almost fanatic desire to thrust off the yoke of colonialism; to free themselves from imperialism; to establish self-rule, and to achieve in their own right the dignity of being free. These nations are most anxious to eliminate poverty and to secure a standard of living and a degree of security commensurate with what mid-20th century technology can provide.

It's appalling to realize while we sit in our warm comfortable America that almost a billion people have an average per capita income of about $150 per year. It seems obvious that these people are susceptible to a new governmental philosophy in the future. What that philosophy will be will depend largely on how interested we Americans become in the problem and how well we sell our ways to these people.

Therefore, I believe that one of the major keys to a peaceful and prosperous world is to be found in these under-developed and largely uncommitted areas of the world.

In the great ideological contest of our times—that of Western democracy and Euro-Asian Communism—these uncommitted nations will play a strategic part; indeed, as they grow in power and strength, their weight may be great enough to shift again the entire world balance of power. *Thomas J. Watson, Jr., President of International Business Machines Corporation*

OUR CHOICE

The choice of how America goes in the years ahead is squarely up to us. We can't lay the responsibility on our Government, our President, or our military leaders . . . for in the end, we are the policy makers.

The decision that we will make the sacrifices necessary for victory is a difficult one to reach. Our Government can reach it only if it is backed and led by a majority of people who clearly support its decision.

This country is a shining goal for nearly all the people on earth whether they admit it or not. The fact that nearly all Americans have a chance for success and that many or most do in fact succeed, is well known abroad. Most of the uncommitted nations want to follow us. Let's make it possible, even easy, for them to do it.

Thomas J. Watson, Jr., President of International Business Machines Corporation

WINNING POLITICAL RECOGNITION

Millions of voices down the ages tell us that every group that has wanted political recognition has had to fight for it, organize for it, work for it, pay for it—whether these groups be farmers, labor unionists, military men, businessmen or any other kind. *G. James Fleming, Professor of Political Science and Director of the Institute for Political Education, Morgan State College, Baltimore*

LOSING THE BENEFITS

We must not forget, to paraphrase the words of Harold Laski, the late noted British political economist, that "Those who are excluded from politics, or who exclude themselves from politics, are also excluded from the benefits of government." *G. James Fleming, Professor of Political Science and Director of the Institute for Political Education, Morgan State College, Baltimore*

THE VIEWS OF YOUNG PEOPLE

Liberty rides high in the hearts of the young people, and justice and tenderness and love for humanity. "Feed the children," they cry. "Make their bodies healthy so that you can educate their minds." "Let's open our doors to the displaced persons." "Do not destroy what America has stood for through the years."

The young people speak their minds with the deep shining hope that they will be listened to and taken seriously. They resent the emphasis on juvenile delinquency and the wholesale indictment of all youth. "If you take an actual count," they say, "how many of us are delinquents? And if there are so many, why isn't something done about it? All right, people get together in a neighborhood and start a recreation center. As if that's the answer!"

To the question, "What is the answer?" they come back quickly, "Lots of things."

"The home, the school, the church, the way people live." One young girl declared, "Most of it comes when children are not loved. Everybody wants love and affection. I come from a very crowded neighborhood—slums, I guess you would call it. But all the children aren't bad. Lots of them help their mothers after school and work hard and study. But some of them are terribly neglected. Their

fathers drink and their mothers work and they are left alone and that's
how they get into bad company. I guess for those children a place
for recreation and play is a good thing, but every boy and girl wants
love and affection."

A young girl from a very select private school looked across the
table at the last speaker with brooding eyes. She spoke slowly,
distinctly, clearly, "You are right, of course. Delinquents don't
come from the slums. There are Park Avenue and Fifth Avenue
delinquents too. Broken up homes, divorce, parents separating,
children living with one parent, then another. It isn't only the parents who work that neglect their children. The place of worship can
play a great part. Children must be taught moral values, faith in God,
the difference between right and wrong."

These opinions are not localized. They reflect general thinking
on the part of youth all over the country. There seems to be a
clarity of thinking among young people that defies the nostrums and
palliatives often suggested by older minds. And there is courage too.
Racial and religious prejudices are tackled courageously and attacked
at their roots. The young people state firmly that "people are not
born with prejudices. These are imposed upon them by their elders."

A quick statement came from another member of a panel. "For
that matter, any kind of hate is bad—hate of the rich, hate of the
poor, hate of one class of society by another class. People must learn
how to live together. It goes back to education. If all the children
of the world could be educated at one time to understand each other
and respect each other you could wipe out prejudice in one generation." *Dorothy Gordon, Moderator, The New York Times Youth
Forums*

A WORLD IN GRAVE CONFUSION

These are times when thoughtful men are sobered by the grave
confusion in world affairs and when there is a need for critical decisions.

In the distance one hears the ominous rumble of a ruinous struggle
for world power. In many countries, reckless revolution is pleading
its cause at every street corner. People upon whom the ragged mantle
of proverty has hung for centuries are no longer docile. The mind, as
well as the mood, of the illiterate and undernourished masses of the
backward nations is one of social and economic unrest. Despite
small savings and a great deficiency of capital equipment, hundreds of

millions of people in the underdeveloped countries are demanding that governments give them immediate industrialization and higher standards of living. In the meantime, the treasury of every major nation in the world is facing the relentless pressure of increasing expenditures for government and for instruments of mass destruction.

Freedom, the right to private property, and the ideal of exalting and enriching the individual in contrast to the state are cherished principles of this Republic, but today they are being boldly challenged across the world by Communism. In the midst of the perilous struggle in which we are now engaged, the United States has come to world leadership as the greatest economic power in history. We may pray that vision has come with power and wisdom with wealth. As we survey the tremendous forces now in conflict over the world, we may well be tempted to cry aloud with Shakespeare's Hamlet, "The time is out of joint; O cursed spite, that ever I was born to set it right!" *Herbert V. Prochnow*

PROFITS

Only a profitable business can generate or raise the capital that will enable it to grow, produce more goods, hire more people, and pay improving wages.

Only a profitable business can pay for research and development work to improve its products and services, create new ones, and reduce their cost and price.

Not only is profit a measure of efficiency—good profits actually promote efficiency by enabling a business to plan and invest soundly for the future. Where heavy plant investment is required, the financial ability to engineer and build in the most efficient increments makes possible important economies. Short-range, piece-meal construction, in contrast—when a business is pinched for money—results in higher unit costs and requires more capital in the long run. This of course makes for higher costs of operation and higher prices.

Again, the profit incentive stimulates imagination and the desire to provide better goods or services. If the telephone company, for instance, develops an optional service with special features, people may be willing to pay a premium for it. The test of the market will decide this. If the project is successful, the company may increase its over-all profit. Thus several gains are accomplished. Customers who elect to buy this optional service get something they want. The company improves its financial situation. Moreover—and most important—the company is encouraged to try another new venture. *Frederick R. Kappel, President, American Telephone and Telegraph Company*

THE BLIGHT IN URBAN CENTERS

The battle of the second half of this 20th century is that against blight in our urban centers, where two-thirds of our population lives. But unfortunately a dangerous proportion of our political and civic leadership is living in the first half of the century, and a few rest durably in the 19th century.

Last summer at Saloniki in Greece there met representatives of churches from all over the world to receive and discuss the report of a three year study on Areas of Rapid Social Change. They thought there only of Asia, Africa, and the Near East and Latin America.

But I assure you that the areas of greatest social change at this moment are in the 200 cities of these United States with 50,000 population or more. The blight that had grown, long unnoticed, at the cores of these cities (matched of course by much blight in smaller places) has now erupted, and shown itself as cancerous and threatening to our very life in the urban centers.

Surgery is what we are trying with every hope of success, but while the physically deteriorated buildings can be cut away, the people who occupied them are not only expendable, but they are human beings from whom may well come essential future leadership, and who in our Judeo-Christian civilization must be treated as of infinite worth. We must make our suburb-dwellers, our rural neighbors, and our unknowing fellow citizens in each of our states realize that this relocation and rebuilding is the task of the century, and a task in which every one of them must cooperate, in his own and the greater community's interest. *Charles P. Taft, Councilman and former Mayor of Cincinnati*

A CHALLENGE TO STUDENTS

One way you might challenge students is to tell them the story of the college professor talking to incoming freshmen. Here is what he said to them, "Suppose that by paying a modest sum you would be given a permit to go into the largest most luxurious store in the world and help yourself to everything—diamonds, watches, expensive clothing, the best of everything, with the only limit being what you could carry away in a four-year period . . . Only a fool would say, 'Guess I'll just take some cigarettes and liquor and some clothing for dates.' Only an imbecile would say that—and yet that is the position of the youth who pays for a college education entitling him, to the limit of his capacity, to absorb the accumulated wisdom of the ages, to offer him intimate acquaintance with the geniuses of all time, to provide him with a knowledge of the universe—but who says 'Guess I'll just take the snap courses and try not to flunk out.' "

To me that is a dramatic way of illustrating the opportunities open to students and in challenging them to get the utmost from their education.

Of course, it would not be enough to come away from school with a prefabricated storehouse of information. We must have graduates who can use their minds creatively, who can use that storehouse of information, who can apply the knowledge they learn. *Martin J. Caserio, General Manager, Delco Radio Division, General Motors Corporation*

FREEDOM AND HUMAN PROGRESS

To an overwhelming number of our friends abroad, America is still the nation that has written the most humane and productive chapter in the history of the world. And these friends are aware, also—sometimes more than we are—that the essence of America is not so much our physical wealth as the jealous way we have built freedom and inspired human progress.

Nevertheless, no one should know better than the American people that our leadership in any area can't be taken for granted. No nation has a monopoly on new ideas or creative talent. And no nation can count itself immune from competition. If the Russian space shots underscored anything, it is that other people do have brains and know how to use them. *G. Keith Funston, President, New York Stock Exchange, speaking before the Executives' Club of Chicago*

THE GOAL OF THE UNITED STATES

We seek a common goal—brighter opportunity for our own citizens and a world peace with justice for all.

Before us and our friends is the challenge of an ideology which, for more than four decades, has trumpeted abroad its purpose of gaining ultimate victory over all forms of government at variance with its own.

We realize that however much we repudiate the tenets of imperialistic communism, it represents a gigantic enterprise. Its leaders compel its subjects to subordinate their freedom of action and spirit and personal desires for some hoped for advantage in the future.

The Communists can present an array of material accomplishments over the past 15 years that lends a false persuasiveness to many of their glittering promises to the uncommitted peoples.

The competition they provide is formidable. We so recognize it.

But in our scale of values we place freedom first. Our whole national existence and development have been geared to that basic concept and is responsible for the position of free world leadership to which we have succeeded.

It is the highest prize that any nation can possess; it is one that communism can never offer. And America's record of material accomplishment in freedom is written not only in the unparalleled prosperity of our own Nation, but in the many billions we have devoted to the reconstruction of free world economics wrecked by World War II and in the effective help of many more billions we have given in saving the independence of many others threatened by outside domination.

Assuredly we have the capacity for handling the problems in the new era of the world's history we are now entering.

But we must use that capacity intelligently and tirelessly, regardless of personal sacrifice.

The fissure that divides our political planet is deep and wide.

We live, moreover, in a storm of semantic disorder in which old labels no longer faithfully describe.

Police states are called "people's democracies."

Armed conquest of free people is called "liberation."

Such slippery slogans make difficult the problem of communicating true faith, facts, and beliefs.

We must make clear our peaceful intentions, our aspirations for a better world. To do so, we must use language to enlighten the mind, not as the instrument of the studied inuendo and distorter of truth.

And we must live by what we say.

On my recent visit to distant lands I found one statesman after another eager to tell me of the elements of their government that had been borrowed from our American Constitution, and from the indestructible ideals set forth in our Declaration of Independence.

As a Nation we take pride that our own constitutional system, and the ideals which sustain it, have been long viewed as a fountainhead of freedom.

By our every word and action we must strive to make ourselves worthy of this trust, ever mindful that an accumulation of seemingly minor encroachments upon freedom gradually could break down the entire fabric of a free society.

So persuaded, we shall get on with the task before us.

So dedicated, and with faith in the Almighty, humanity shall one day achieve the unity in freedom to which all men have aspired from the dawn of time.   *Dwight D. Eisenhower*

SOVIET RUSSIA AND THE UNITED STATES

In 1835, Alexis de Tocqueville, a French author wrote as follows:

"There are at the present time two great nations in the world which seem to tend toward the same end, although they started from different points; I allude to the Russians and the Americans . . . All other nations seem to have nearly reached their natural limits . . . but these are still in the act of growth; all others are stopped, or continue to advance with extreme difficulty; these are proceeding with ease and celerity along a path to which the human eye can assign no term.   The American struggles against the natural obstacles which oppose him; the adversaries of the Russian are men; the former combats the wilderness and savage life; the latter, civilization with all its weapons and its arts; the conquests of the one are therefore gained by the plowshare; those of the other by the sword.   The Anglo-American relies upon personal interest to accomplish his ends, and gives free scope to the unguided exertions and common sense of the citizens; the Russian centers all the authority of society in a single arm; the principal instrument of the former is freedom; of the latter, servitude.   Their starting point is different, and their courses are not the same; yet each of them seems to be marked out by the will of Heaven to sway the destinies of half the globe."

This was striking foresight.   One hundred and twenty-five years later each of these nations is swaying the destinies of half the globe. Alexis de Tocqueville knew Russia only under the czars, and he could not have foreseen communism.   He could see only the fundamentals which were to shape the destiny of these nations.   As one looks now at the entire world in perspective, perhaps it was historically inevitable that these two nations, each with great natural resources, a vast land area and a large population, should one day confront each other in a titanic economic and political conflict in the arena of the world.   In this struggle perhaps it was also inevitable that each nation should seek—as it is now doing—to attract to its support the other nations of the world.

There are fundamental differences in the historical backgrounds of Russia and the United States which have persisted through the years. Russia has had a long record of oppression of its people over decades, together with violent changes in government and tyrannical rulers. Her economy has always been directed by the government. When the Communists came to power in 1917, they did not change the historical pattern under which the Russian people had lived. However, the revolution in 1917 made one extremely significant and far-reaching change. The ruling party imposed upon the Russian economy a rigid framework of state planning. This was the great change from the past in Russia.

Since 1917, the entire Russian economy, including family life, education, agriculture, industry, and even letters, science and the arts, has been placed in a planned pattern of economic development. The Kremlin authorities are determined to make tremendous gains rapidly, even if it means the loss of freedom and compelling people, especially in the satellite nations, to follow a course which they would not themselves choose.

The American process of growth may be slower and almost casual in some respects. It may sometimes even seem to be operating at cross purposes. However, the economy is vigorous and strong because the people themselves are making the decisions which determine the direction and pattern of economic growth.

If the ultimate survival of the United States and Soviet Russia is to be determined by military power, it may be cooperative suicide. If economic competition is to determine survival, the United States has certain significant advantages. In the Soviet Union, succession to power may be accompanied by internal violence and a serious interruption to the growth of the economy. The Soviet Union is also weak because there is no assurance that the satellite nations can be held in bondage forever. In the United States, under constitutional government one administration succeeds another in accordance with the will of the people. Our economic growth rests on the firm foundation of freedom in which we recognize the dignity of man and his aspirations, and with which we have combined an enlightened sense of broad social responsibility.

In order fully to understand the Communist challenge, we must recognize certain facts. Russia has the world's largest unbroken land mass under one flag, with an area approximately two and one-half times that of the United States.   The Soviet population of 210 million compares with 180 million for this country.   We cannot excel her in the size of her land area, population or labor force.   She is one of the wealthiest nations in the world in minerals.   She has a large part of the entire world's timber reserves.   We cannot assume that if her people work hard for long hours, restrict their consumption of consumer goods, save and invest heavily in the expansion of Soviet basic industry—as they are now doing—that she will not have remarkable economic progress in the years immediately ahead.   It is not wise either to assume that Russia will eventually have trouble with Communist China or with her own people, and that her challenge to our institutions and to the Free World can be lightly dismissed.   These are dangerous assumptions.   *Herbert V. Prochnow*

CHANGING POPULATION

We have estimated, at the Department of Labor, that the population of the United States will increase to 226 million by 1975.   The labor force in that period will grow to 95 million, an increase of 23 million. Eight million of that increase will be men and women over 45 years of age.

At present, because of senseless prejudices, because of changes in business technology, the older worker is often excluded from employment.   He finds that his age has erected invisible barriers around him, cutting him off from participation in the active economic life of his society.

Well, whose problem is this?

Is it the problem only of the mature worker himself, and one that he can meet only by recourse to his political power?

In New York and in other States there are now laws on the books that prohibit discrimination in employment because of age.   Is it possible, unless the managers and the leaders of our centers of private economic power realize that this is their problem too, that a national law might someday be on the books—and it will be there not because the Government is seeking to control but because millions of people, frustrated in their desire to join into society in an active way, have demanded such control.   *James P. Mitchell*

THE CHURCH IN RUSSIA

I had an unforgettable experience in one of several churches I visited behind the Iron Curtain.   Three services are held in this church in Moscow each Sunday as well as a number during the week.   On my visit I was seated at the railing in the balcony. The church was filled from top to bottom with the aisles crowded by those standing. For example, a mother entered with children and had to stand with the children at the end of a pew. Occasionally, someone who was seated arose to permit a person who was standing to be seated. Some in the aisles were on their knees. They may have found it difficult to stand through the entire service which lasted two hours with two sermons. The text for the first sermon was "Trust in the Living God," and it was from Timothy I, Chapter IV, Verse 10. Here and there throughout the congregation there was weeping. I saw very poorly dressed people generously contribute to the collection, and I was told that finances are not a problem of the church. As I looked into the many hundreds of earnest, deeply sincere faces in that congregation and saw the care-lined, gentle features of the older women with their babushkas, I felt certain that no government, no matter how determined and powerful, could completely destroy the living faith, the cherished ideals, and the eternal values of the common people of Russia. *Herbert V. Prochnow, Executive Vice President, The First National Bank of Chicago*

CHANGES IN OUR ECONOMIC LIFE

It seems that the evolution of our economic life is leading toward larger concentrations of economic power within institutions—power based not on the ownership of wealth but on the control of wealth.

These institutions are various: corporations, of which 500 now account for two-thirds of our total industry; pension and trust funds, already totaling some $40 billion and growing at the rate of $4 billion annually; labor unions, supported by 16 million members; mutual funds, trusts, insurance and banking firms and so on.

It has been estimated that 50 million citizens are now sharing in the profits of the 500 largest corporations, directly and indirectly. Since 1952, the number of direct stockholders in public corporations has risen from 6.5 million to 12.5 million.

In the United States more and more people are enjoying greater and greater degrees of wealth.

At the same time, the control of economic wealth is concentrated in greater degree in our economic institutions, and in the hands of the managers, administrators and leaders of those institutions.

Outside a free society, this might be a dangerous condition, but inside a free society it has an opposite effect; it places in the hands of private citizens both the power and the resources to attain the social and economic goals they set for themselves.

A free society has within itself the weapon to curb injustice that might result from a selfish or blind use of economic power; that weapon is the political power that the people have reserved for themselves.

We are all familiar with the use of political intervention, from antitrust laws through the regulation of transportation and broadcasting the regulation of labor-management affairs.

Intervention usually results when economic institutions have not lived up to the responsibilities that society has expected of them, either through incompetence or willful mismanagement and abuse of control.

We have, in America, a rapidly growing society, one with impressive needs, and even more impressive wants. *James P. Mitchell, January 1960*

WHAT GOOD BUDGETS PRODUCE

A Director of the Bureau of the Budget may hope to be respected, but if he is wise he does not look for honors. There is a reason for this. Just as in science and technology there is a law to explain practically every phenomenon, so in the field of finance we try to be fashionable and postulate laws. I have discovered the fiscal law that "Good budgeting produces a uniform distribution of dissatisfaction." I'm not sure I want this to be called "Stans' Law," but it goes far to explain why Budget Directors normally do not win popularity contests. *Maurice H. Stans, Director of the Bureau of the Budget*

HAVE WE A HAPPY SOCIETY?

Schopenhauer said that there are only two possible outcomes to our wishes: either we fail to get our wish, or we succeed—only to find out that we do not, after all, want what we got. Consider our own American society. Those whose memories go back to the depression days of the thirties realize how astonishingly we have fulfilled the fond dreams of those hard times, when it seemed that if only we could achieve full employment, raise wages and salaries, put a car in every garage and a chicken in every pot, then we should have a heaven on earth. Someone recently estimated that we have now reached the point where our entire population could ride all at once in our cars—and not occupy the back seats. Our homes are crowded with television sets, radios, automatic washers and dryers, vacuum sweepers, dishwashers, and a dozen other work savers—as they are sometimes called. Our yards are noisy with motor-driven lawnmowers. The cheaper cuts of meat are passed over for filet mignon and Rock Corn-

ish hens.   We feel deprived if we have not yet managed to get a boat
and a trailer, or to take a Mediterranean cruise.   And if as students
or teachers or other underprivileged types we may have been scrimp-
ing a bit—not very much, perhaps, but a bit—we do it cheerfully in
the full expectation that in short order we too will adorn our lives with
the gadgets that magazine advertisements prove to be the ingredients
of happiness.

Yes, truly, we are prosperous, affluent—no, let's say it right out:
rich.   And yet, heaven remains a destination and not an achievement.
Would any one dare to say that ours is a happy society?   America
leads the world in rate of homicide.   We lead the world in rate of
alcoholism.   We are internationally famous for the extent of our
juvenile vandalism, our racial disturbances, the instability of our marriages.   In the rate of suicide we lag behind Denmark, Switzerland,
Finland, and Sweden—notice that they are countries we think of as on
the whole prosperous, enlightened, highly literate, democratic—though
we have more than double the number, in proportion to population,
that Spain or Italy has.   Such are the more sensational indices, but the
testimony of our most sensitive social observers is, if anything, still
more disheartening.   They describe us as uneasy, insecure, restless,
worried.   With more leisure and more work-savers than any other
people, we gobble tranquilizers and sedatives in monstrous amounts.
We cannot provide enough treatment for our armies of psychotics and
severe neurotics.   We din into our dulled ears the trashiest music.
We are almost completely literate, but publish fewer books, counted
by title, than Great Britain, Germany, and Japan—not relative to our
numbers but absolutely.   In a survey intended to indicate how many
persons spent the preceding evening reading, Americans rank behind
the Danes, Swedes, Norwegians, Frenchmen, Dutchmen and Cana-
dians. *James L. Jarrett, President, Western Washington College of
Education, Bellingham, Washington*

A MEANINGFUL LIFE

One of the seven capital or deadly sins is acedia.   Translated
"sloth" it sounds to some ears more ridiculous than sinful, but acedia
has in it something worse than idleness or laziness.   It signifies the
"state of not caring," a state whose lineaments have been most horrify-
ingly drawn by Dostoyevsky.   For instance, in the superb story, "The
Dream of the Ridiculous Man," wherein the man speaks of "the terrible misery that was growing in my soul through . . . the conviction

that had come upon me that *nothing in the world mattered* . . . I suddenly felt that it was all the same to me whether the world existed or whether there had never been anything at all: I began to feel with all my being that there was nothing existing . . . I gave up caring about anything, and all the problems disappeared."

Such is the state of meaninglessness. The attitude is expressed with chilling precision by the enormously popular vulgarism: "I couldn't care less." Is the peace of the world in danger? Are our cities blighted by physical ugliness? Is there an election coming up? Is there a fine new novel just out? Does someone love me? *I couldn't care less.*

Now, I think that even those of us who are the most avid professional advocates of education—I count myself in this number—will have to admit, and indeed have a duty to declare, that our schools and colleges are not forestalling this utterance of disgusted boredom. Bachelor, Master, and Doctor,—all are quite capable of echoing it. No mastery of facts, no acquisition of skills is immunization against the disease of meaninglessness. I lay it down as a formula that the life without a sense of meaningfulness and purposefulness is an empty, unhappy life whatever its attainments in degrees, prestige, and money. Being busy is no evidence for the presence of meaningfulness. We may protect ourselves against an explicit avowal or even recognition of our inner emptiness by a day-to-day life of jangling telephones, crowded calendars, of speeding from place to place, and a resulting end-of-the-day, end-of-the-week, and end-of-the-vacation exhaustion, but victory is only apparent. *James L. Jarrett, President, Western Washington College of Education, Bellingham, Washington*

WHAT WE LIKE

Said the lady as she looked with supercilious eye at the artist's canvas, "Well, I don't claim to know much about art, but I do know what I like." Whereupon Mr. Whistler replied, "So does a cow, madam, so does a cow." True, in a sort of bovine way, we know what we like, but in a more complex way, most of us are frequently mistaken about our own likes and preferences. The man who said that he didn't know whether he could play the piano, never having tried, was scrupulously honest; which is more than can be said for the man who knows without trying that he doesn't like raw oysters. *James L. Jarrett, President, Western Washington College of Education, Bellingham, Washington*

WHAT A COLLEGE CAN FURNISH

A college, even the very best, cannot furnish ideals, but it can drive persons back on themselves, confront them with themselves and do much to make the not finding of ideals hard. College cannot make persons capable of genuine love, but it can promote an intellectual understanding of the conditions of love and an aesthetic grasp of its vibrant reality. College cannot grant people the gift of energy and drive, but it can shine a five watt bulb on the craggy, pathless way to knowledge beyond gossip and understanding beyond the conventional wisdom of cliché. College cannot give out life interests along with diplomas, but it can spread an intellectual smorgasbord that will ever afterward spoil one's appetite for hog jowl and hominy. *James L. Jarrett, President, Western Washington College of Education, Bellingham, Washington*

FREEDOM OF THE PRESS

Members of the public and many newspapermen are inclined to accept the idea that the American people are so steeped in the traditions of a free press and its part in a democracy that no public official would dare to attack our idealistic concept of an uncensored and independent press. There is the view that Americans, born and reared in this tradition, would rise in fury to strike down the government officials who would seek to control or suppress the nation's newspapers. We often hear it said that Americans, reared in an atmosphere of freedom, would not put up with the encroachments on liberty that have been forced on people behind the Iron Curtain. We are told that they would not put up with the kind of conditions that have stifled many freedoms in our own hemisphere.

It seems to me that this philosophy of the indomitable American presupposes that Americans are somehow braver, stronger, wiser and more valiant than people living in other parts of the world. I would think that the present stage in the space race would teach us that Americans have no monopoly on wisdom, enterprise, strength, or know-how. For years we kidded ourselves into thinking that simply because we are Americans, with many advantages over the Russians, that we were guaranteed a long lead in the fields of nuclear weapons, aircraft, and space exploration. In recent years we have seen our lead dwindle and vanish while many of our leading scientists have complained that nonsensical security on many matters interfered with our scientific progress.

Now, many realists are willing to admit that we Americans have no guaranteed superiority in scientific areas. We have been forced to learn the hard way that the rate of accomplishment in scientific areas is tied pretty closely to our willingness to work, to study and make sacrifices.

There is little in our lazy, well-fed, luxury-loving attitudes of the present to make me believe that any great number of Americans have awakened to the recognition that we are not a super race. There is little to indicate that any large segment of the American people recognize that we must work and study to recognize when there are encroachments on our freedoms, or risk seeing these freedoms go down the drain as has our lead in the scientific field.

My concern today is over the apathy where there are serious encroachments on the right of access to information. It is an apathy that covers not only the general public but a good many representatives of the press. This lack of concern is either the result of a lack of knowledge of what a free press means to a democracy, lack of enough interest to dig in and learn where some abritrary governmental secrecy policies can take us, or lack of guts to speak out.

It is time that more Americans recognize that we are no brighter, stronger, or more courageous than many people who have been crushed by totalitarian governments. We are only luckier—luckier because we are fortunate enough to be living in a free nation. *Clark Mollenhoff, Washington Bureau, Cowles Publications*

COMMUNISM AND COUNTRIES THAT LAG BEHIND

For many centuries, almost up to the beginning of the 1700's, living standards, social ideals and political concepts for the masses of people were essentially similar over the world. In many respects, life in the early 1700's was not wholly unlike life two thousand years ago. Candles and oil lamps were used for light, fireplaces for heat, horses and sailing ships for travel. No message could be sent faster than a man could travel.

As late as 1812, it took three months for the people as far away as Kentucky to know who had been elected President of the United States in November. When Benjamin Franklin first took the stagecoach from Philadelphia to New York, he spent four days upon the journey.

His driver spent his time knitting stockings as the coach jogged along. All the trade by land between Boston and New York was carried on with two stagecoaches and eight horses, and in winter the trip took a week.

When this nation shortly after its birth sent its first representative to the British government, the captain of the sailing vessel in New York harbor told him to come aboard at once. He hurriedly bought a sack of flour, three hams and a bag of potatoes and arranged on ship for a sailor to cook his meals. He expected the ship to sail any hour, but it was five weeks before the ship left the harbor, and six weeks more before the representative of the government of the United States saw the coast of Great Britain.

However, in the middle of the 1700's economic forces began to come into existence that were destined to change vitally the entire course of history. Unfortunately, these forces left great areas of the world untouched so that they now lag centuries behind the economic progress of other parts of the world. The sad fact is that while we all dwell on the same globe and use the same calendar, hundreds of millions of people are living centuries back in terms of economic, social and political progress. For them, the world has stood still. In some countries, oxen slowly thresh grain by treading it under foot just as they did two thousand years ago. The women of Jericho go to the well for water and carry it in earthen jugs on their heads just as they did in the days of Abraham, Isaac and Jacob. The nations that were left behind now provide Communism, with its promises of rapid industrial progress, a vast field of perhaps one billion five hundred million people in which to work. *Herbert V. Prochnow*

THE INFLUENCE OF TELEVISION

The impact of television on our nation is so considerable that it can influence our morals, our thinking and our culture for good or for bad. It is up to us to make certain that this greatest medium of communication is made to serve the public interest.

It is being asserted that we get our television broadcasts free. Is this true? I doubt that we obtain anything in this world without paying a price for it. Who is paying the billions of dollars of advertising to the TV stations if not the American public? The degrading of our taste, the corruption of our morals, the juvenile delinquency to which many of the TV programs make such an outstanding contribution are too high a price to pay for the so-called free television. In a recent remarkable speech on the subject "What More Is Left To Accomplish?", General David Sarnoff, Chairman of RCA, stressed the point that the only valid achievement of science and education is its effect on the individual human being.   He warned us that we run the danger of confusing democracy with mediocrity, and that we may grow softer, more pleasure-loving, content to squander our increasing leisure on the trivial if not on the harmful.   General Sarnoff admonishes us to embrace heroic goals and dedications and to accept the hard disciplines of the good life.   We had better heed his advice if we wish to respond successfully to the material and ideological challenges surging from the East and the Far East.   Because of its terrific impact, TV will have a considerable influence, for good or bad, on the kind of men we are bringing up to defend our moral values, our heritage and our way of life.   *Philip Cortney, President, Coty, Inc.*

TAXES AND GOVERNMENT SPENDING

Taxes and government spending are inseparable.   Spending must be followed in equal amount by taxes, sooner or later, inevitably, if our country is to remain solvent and if our precious freedoms are to survive.   The great preponderance of our taxes come from earnings of business, earnings from jobs in business, and earnings from those who serve in one way or another business and the people in business's jobs.   Good profits and good personal earnings and wages are the foundation for the support of our government and everything it does.   Where would we be in America without good earnings in business and jobs?   *George M. Humphrey, Chairman, National Steel Corporation, speaking before the American Iron and Steel Institute*

WHAT RUSSIAN CHILDREN LEARN

The Russian worker is not the only one who is constantly reminded of his responsibility to the state.   This indoctrination begins at a very early age.   From nursery school through kindergarten, the grades, secondary school and college the indoctrination of the child never ends.   Sacrifice for the state, devotion to his country, self-discipline, and good grades are all part of the program.   In the nursery school or the kindergarten, the child first becomes a "Little Octobrist."   Between the ages of nine to fourteen years, the child becomes a member of the "Young Pioneers."   There are 20 million "Young Pioneers."   Each one takes a solemn oath to be true to Lenin's cause and to live and study to become a worthy citizen of the country.   He meets with other Pioneers a number of hours each week in the "House of Pioneers" buildings.   Each Young Pioneer receives a red scarf or tie to wear. The child learns that he must live for the state, and that the state comes before everything else, even one's family.   He also learns that religion has no place in life and that there is no God.   When I asked a young Russian girl whether there were churches in her city, she replied, "Oh yes, we have churches.   They are for the people who believe in God— mostly the older folks."   As someone once said, "a nation may attempt to abolish God, but fortunately God is more tolerant."

After the Young Pioneers, the young people from 14 to 26 years of age who prove their merit become members of the Young Communist League, or Komsomol.   There are now over 18 million members of this League.   The final step for a select few is membership in the Communist Party.   This is not easy.   As one of my guides said when I asked if she had become a member of the Party, "No, I am not good enough to deserve membership in the party."   The Communist Party is the church for the dedicated believers in Communism, and it is not for those who may be weak in their faith in the communist system. An applicant for membership in the Communist Party must have several sponsors, and sponsorship is not a minor matter.   If a member later strays from, or repudiates, the party line, the sponsor may be in for trouble.   The Communist Party has about 7,200,000 members, or four per cent of the population.   *Herbert V. Prochnow, Executive Vice President, The First National Bank of Chicago*

THE VOICE OF THE FARMER

The strengths in agriculture are largely due to the freedom of our farmers.   If the voices of 20 million farm people in the United States could be united in one voice, that voice would, I feel certain, demand even more freedom for farmers.

The voice would say:

Give us more freedom to plant—so that we can run our farms efficiently.

Give us more freedom to market—so that we can increase our incomes.

Give us more freedom to meet our competition—so that we can expand our markets.

Give us more freedom from government interference—so that we may again be independent and self-reliant.

This Nation will never reach its full strength until our farmers have more freedom to plant, to market, to compete, and to make their own decisions.

Farmers want to produce for markets and not for government bounty.

Farmers want government at their sides, not on their backs.

Again I say, farmers know that the farms of America cannot be run from a desk in Washington.

Farmers know more than anyone else that socialized regimentation strikes at the very heart of the free enterprise principles which are basic to the high American standard of living and progress, which we enjoy.

Let's not sell America short. Let's not cave in to a doctrine which has been proven false in the courts of history.

My point is this:

There is a great reservoir of faith in our free institutions. There is excellent leadership, both active and latent, for this cause. If we bestir ourselves and shrug off our lethargy, the drift toward socialism at home and abroad can be slowed down, halted and reversed. This has been shown to be a fact in agriculture.

I would not for a moment imply that our agricultural problems have been fully solved or that our difficulties have been overcome. New problems will arise and new difficulties will beset us. The battle for freedom is a continuing one; freedom must be won anew by each generation. That is the thing we have come so disastrously near forgetting! *Ezra Taft Benson, Secretary of Agriculture*

HOW JOE CITIZEN FUNCTIONS

Joe Citizen is a two-fold fellow. He is a political citizen, and he is an economic citizen. That makes him an inconsistent citizen. As one citizen, he wants to take the economy road. As another, as a producer, consumer, laborer citizen, he may favor economic legislation which is both socialistic in nature and costly.

As a laborer citizen, he wants to ride the high wage bandwagon, but as a consumer citizen, he wants low prices. As a getting citizen, he wants a lot of free help of one kind or another from the government, but at the same time, as a paying citizen he wants low taxes. So, actually, when this Joe Citizen we are talking about makes up his mind to support something, he does it because he has formed an opinion on it. Whether he was right, or whether he was wrong, he has formed this opinion on the basis of what he knows, or what he thinks he knows.

There are honest differences of opinion, but one of the real tragedies in a democracy such as ours is that it is quite possible for too many opinions to be formed without proper knowledge of the facts, so education then becomes a prime factor in molding opinion.   When there are two sides to any question, as there usually are, the proponents of those two sides line up in a battle for the minds of people, the minds of Joe Citizen and his wife.

I submit to you, as in any other contest of this type, that the side which is most vocal and is persuasive has the best chance of winning, and certainly the side that doesn't speak at all has a very slim chance of winning. *Fred C. Foy, Chairman and President of the Koppers Company, Inc.*

THE THIN MAN

When I was a young actor in London, I was fortunate—more than fortunate—to make a rather early success.   To those of you who may look back over the theatre for quite a few years, that is putting it tactfully, isn't it, you may remember a very famous actress by the name of Mrs. Patrick Campbell.   I had just made a very big success in a play called "Peter Ibbetson" which has been played by John Barrymore and Constance Collier here in America—at the Blackstone Theatre in Chicago, incidentally, amongst other towns, naturally.

Mrs. Campbell had sent someone to scout for a young leading actor to play Alfred de Muss opposite her, Madame George Sand, in a play by Philip Muller then at the Theatre Guild.   I had been reported to be the actor.   She then went to see my performance, liked it, came home and decided to give me the role.   I was eventually assigned to it.

Seated shortly afterwards, either at a dinner or a tea or on some occasion, the famous Mrs. Campbell was asked by a friend of hers who this young man was that she had engaged to play this important role opposite her in her new play.

She said, "Darling, I have no idea what his name is, but he has got a face like two profiles stuck together." (Laughter)

All I can tell you is that it gets worse year by year.

So many, many years later one charming evening out on the Coast, when Mrs. Campbell was quite an old woman, I reminded her of this remark she had made.   I explained to her that at the time I was embarrassed by it.   I was inexperienced and very sensitive about how I looked.   I knew I was thin, and she apologized and said, "Darling, you must forget all about it because now you look like a folded umbrella taking elocution lessons." *Basil Rathbone, Distinguished Actor*

IT TAKES CHARACTER

Have we what it takes to face a call for discipline, to bring compulsive spending to heel, to stop dripping gravy on pressure groups, to discontinue living on Government credit cards, to distinguish between growth and inflation, to protect our money from debasement, to put priorities first and selfish pressures last? *Maurice H. Stans*

THE CHALLENGE CONFRONTING US

Modern capitalism in this country has given us the highest standards of living in the world. It has made this nation the greatest economic power in the history of the human race.

If Russia with its bleak and barren materialism becomes in history a blind Samson who pushes down the economic temple of the capitalist world, it will be because weaknesses had developed in the temple before the shoulders of communism were brought against its pillars. It will not be because of the spiritual and secular strength of communism. It will not be because communism has subordinated man and made him the serf of the state. It will be because you and I have failed. It will be because our ideals, our vision, our character and our minds were not equal to the challenge of democracy, freedom, and modern capitalism with its sense of social responsibility. *Herbert V. Prochnow*

BREVITY

It is my understanding that this Conference does not break up until tomorrow noon. What a lovely prospect this is for me! For once in my life I believe I shall be able to talk as long as I desire. From now until tomorrow noon stretches on as a beautiful infrequently encountered opportunity, so just get yourselves as comfortable as possible and settle down to the hours that lie before us as I drone on and on far, far into and through the night.

You may have gathered from the immediately foregoing that I am somewhat enraptured by the sound of my own voice, but why shouldn't I like to hear myself talk? On my father's side I come from a long line of pedagogs and theologs, and on my mother's side—well, mother was a woman. But I shall try not to be too long drawn out. Perhaps

I shall emulate that small lad who was told to write a brief biography of Benjamin Franklin. He wrote "Benjamin Franklin was born in Boston. At an early age he moved to Philadelphia. As he walked down a street in Philadelphia munching a loaf of bread, a lady standing in the doorway saw him and laughed at him. He married the lady and discovered electricity." *Harold A. Speckman*

GOOD GOVERNMENT

Our form of government is the best, the most effective, and the most equitable form of government ever devised. But our kind of government can only be the best kind of government if it is intelligently used by informed people determined to have the best government on earth. We must always remember, we must never forget, that a good form of government does not guarantee good government. You only get good government by using a good system vigorously and intelligently. *George M. Humphrey, Chairman, National Steel Corporation, speaking before the American Iron and Steel Institute.*

THE INDUSTRIAL REVOLUTION

One of the great forces which enabled some parts of the world to take gigantic strides ahead was the Industrial Revolution that began in Great Britian and spread to other countries, especially the United States. The Industrial Revolution was ushered in by a number of unusual inventions by which machines replaced men in industry after industry.

The old-fashioned spinning wheel gave way to the cotton textile factory, and as early as 1840 we had 1,240 factories with over two and one-quarter million spindles in the cotton industry. Horses gave way to the new steam engine and to water power. In 1807, Robert Fulton's Clermont made the historic one hundred sixty mile trip up the Hudson River from New York to Albany in thirty-two hours. In 1838, the Atlantic Ocean was crossed for the first time by steam.

In 1830, Peter Cooper's little steam locomotive, the Tom Thumb, proudly traveled thirteen miles at an average speed of six miles an hour. At that time, there were only twenty-three miles of railroad. By 1860, there were 30,000 miles and by 1890 over 160,000 miles. No other nation ever matched that expansion.

By 1860, the American factory system was firmly established. We had 140,000 manufacturing plants, and we were producing more goods by machine than by hand. This was a major turning point. The foundations of a machine economy had been firmly laid.

The country was making colossal strides in every field. The iron plow and the reaper were taking their toll from the prairies. New processes were revolutionizing the iron and steel industry. Typewriters, cash registers, arc lamps, electric lights, sewing machines, the telegraph, rotary presses, pneumatic tires, tank and refrigerator cars, air brakes, power shovels, electric locomotives in place of mules in mines, mechanical loaders, tractors and tractor-drawn farm equipment, automobiles, trucks, heavy industrial equipment and airplanes are only a few illustrations of the striking mechanization and the new products that were remaking the American economy and thrusting it dramatically forward in the world.

Great natural resources, a vast continent, insulation from major foreign wars for over a century, a rapidly expanding, hard working population and confidence that our economic system would reward men well gave our people enormous driving energy. *Herbert V. Prochnow*

A FREE SOCIETY

What I have wanted to say is that the prospects of our free society are almost boundless if we can perceive and protect the genius of freedom: freedom for discovery and diversity, for change and advance. I have tried to communicate my conviction that schools and colleges and universities are the most significant trustees of freedom among all the institutions of our society—that their problems point up, as clearly as any you can identify, the problems of our free society.

I have spoken to you as influential and educated citizens at the very center of our American business enterprise system—a system which I regard as an indispensable resource of American strength and leadership in the world today. And I am not thinking merely of money and financial strength.

I am thinking of the ideals under which it has developed—the ideal of "elbowroom" for individual initiative and intelligence and industry, and the rewards of these in a national climate of self-reliance; the ideal, indeed of freedom as we in America know it.

It is these I beg you to foster in your special capacity to appraise and encourage investment in the largest and finest sense of that word. Deeply I believe that the dividends of freedom will determine the dimensions of our American destiny.   *J. L. Morrill, former president of the University of Minnesota*

INNER STRENGTH

One of the wisest observers of American life and of communism is Dr. Charles Malik, currently President of the United Nations General Assembly, a Christian Arab who was educated in the American University in Beirut and who taught at Harvard before becoming his nation's Prime Minister.   In a *U. S. News and World Report* interview, Dr. Malik said:

"You have in your own traditions certain invaluable beliefs about man and society and history and human destiny and the nature of God —beliefs that you should not be ashamed of, that you should feel free to export and to teach others.   But first you must rediscover them yourselves and believe in them profoundly yourselves.   Many of you have taken life too much for granted.   Therefore, the great deposit of belief and convictions and interpretation of life which has come down to you, you simply don't honor enough.

"The Communist is a man who has received a tradition and honors it profoundly and believes in it and therefore is willing to propagate it.

"You are a bit different.   Many of you don't know your own traditions.

"My deepest fear—if you want it put bluntly to you—is that you don't know the infinite values that you have at the basis of your own civilization, and you don't believe in them strongly enough to put them strongly to the rest of the world.   You take life too easily.   You take things too much for granted.   You are not fighting for values as much as your forebears were."

In answer to the question, "Do you think the Communists will win in the end?", Dr. Malik said: "I myself am sure that they will never win in the end, although it may be after the ruination of the world. But it's impossible for a false doctrine to win—impossible."

Dr. Malik was voicing the experience of life and history; namely, that strength and weakness come from within, that nations and civilizations are destroyed by loss of conviction and purpose and decay from within.   Emerson recognized this in writing: "There is no weakness except from within.   There is no insurmountable barrier save our own inherent weakness of purpose."   *George Romney*

PROBLEMS THAT CONFRONT US

Less than one-fourth of the graduates of colleges and universities receive any education in the field of economics. How can we expect to preserve our private enterprise system when the rising generation is largely ignorant of its functioning and of its essential contribution to the well being and to the progress of the American people?

We should also ask ourselves how can we expect our democratic system of government to promote a sound economy when it is so largely controlled by pressure groups that effectively use their political power to promote their own interests without regard to the public interest. *A. L. M. Wiggins, Chairman of the Board, Atlantic Coast Line Railroad Company and Louisville and Nashville Railroad Company*

THE ROLE OF GOVERNMENT

Since the establishment of the United States, the role of government has grown steadily larger. Today there are scores of government agencies which regulate almost every important segment of the American economy. An objective analysis of the historical trend of the role of government indicates that it will grow larger, not smaller, in the years ahead. With great modern, power-driven, mass production industries, with great organizations of labor and with the Soviet Union challenging us as an economic and military power, it is highly improbable that government will return to its simple role in the days of Washington and Jefferson. However, if capitalism is to function at its best, it needs the utmost freedom consistent with the complex interdependence of modern life.

Millions of Americans condemn the expanding role of government. They protest increasing government expenditures, unbalanced budgets and high taxes. At the same time through their representatives in the Congress they demand of government vast new services, Federal aid, price supports, stockpiling of products on a gigantic scale, bonuses and subsidies. Approximately 100 Federal programs provide aid for states. We persist in indulging in the pleasant illusion that Federal aid does not come from local taxpayers. The increasing role of government over the years offers little encouragement to those who believe that government should perform essentially only those functions which individuals, businesses and communities cannot perform, or cannot perform as well as government. If this trend is to be halted, we shall need a major change in our thinking. This is not now evident. We shall need far greater self-reliance, or we shall inevitably lose more and more of the private economy of the United States and find ourselves finally embracing the economic socialization which now characterizes the communist world. *Herbert V. Prochnow*

FREE COMPETITIVE ENTERPRISE

One of the most important things for us to preserve, defend and improve through the exercise of our kind of government is our system of free economic choice—our free competitive enterprise system—and this, in practical form is our business system. It is our free business system that produce the jobs that make the goods and the wages and income by which we have gained the most satisfactory standard of living in man's history. It is from these jobs and goods and incomes— and only from these—that we draw the taxes to support our government, to defend our nation, to educate ourselves, and to provide us with our roads, harbors, social security and employment benefits, and to achieve the military and economic objectives of our foreign policy. It is from the jobs and goods and incomes of our free business system that we siphon off the wealth that supports our churches, our art and literature and music, our great private universities, our health and recreational facilities, and the entire material fabric of our cultural and spiritual life.

Business has been in the political dog house in this country long enough. It is shot at from every quarter. I'm proud to be a businessman. Almost every material benefit we have is created by business, and it's time every American businessman takes his proper place in leadership toward sound governmental objectives and fulfills his political duties and obligations. *George M. Humphrey, Chairman, National Steel Corporation, speaking before the American Iron and Steel Institute*

OBSERVATIONS ON RUSSIA

To understand and place in perspective what one sees in Russia some background of general knowledge regarding the country is helpful. Here is a nation extending 2,000 miles from North to South and 6,000 miles from West to East. It covers about one-sixth of the world's land surface, having approximately two and one-half times the area of the United States, including Alaska and Hawaii. This is the world's largest unbroken land mass under one flag. There are over

30,000 miles of coastline, but only one major unrestricted port—
Murmansk—with access to the open sea throughout the year.

The Soviet population of 210 million compares to 180 million for
the United States. Forty-three per cent of the people live in the cities
in contrast to 64 per cent in the United States. Moscow with five
million population, Leningrad with over three million and Kiev, Baku
and a number of other cities each with around a million population are
the largest cities. The people of this nation speak one hundred and
forty-nine languages. In the last thirty years the Soviet Union has
founded 503 new cities and over 1,350 smaller communities.

Forests still cover an area about equal to the area of the United
States and constitute a large portion of the entire world's timber reserves. The Soviet Union is also rich in oil, iron ore and manganese,
and is perhaps the richest country in the world in minerals. If you
combine important natural resources with hard work by the entire
population, austerity in the consumption of consumer goods, and substantial saving with heavy investment in plant and equipment, you
have the basic reasons why the authorities in the Kremlin believe they
will attain economic and political leadership of the world. Some of
the best informed observers of the Russian economy are convinced that
the Kremlin authorities believe it is only a matter of time until they
surpass us. *Herbert V. Prochnow, Executive Vice President, The
First National Bank of Chicago*

PARKINSON'S LAW

Well, my subject is PARKINSON'S LAW. And I will approach it
historically, as an historian should, by telling you how this discovery
was first made—a discovery, by the way, I emphasize—not an inven-
tion. It is a law of nature; and the discoverer of a law of nature, people like Archimedes, Pythagoras, or myself—well, we have a certain
status, definitely higher than that of mere legislators or people who
pass laws—these people who discover them.

Well, my law—the law to which I am modestly giving my own name
was first discovered during the second World War; and I, for one,
would not maintain for a moment that that war was worth-while
merely for this reason. Quite possibly that discovery might have been
made more economically. In fact, it was made during the second
World War, in the course of which I discovered that success in the
British armed forces depended on knowing as many people as possible
by their first name. Well, I have a very poor memory for names, and

so I ended the war in relatively humble rank, and such success as I had
—had to be achieved by a different method, and that method was to
place myself midway between the Army and the Air Force, each
imagining that I was assisting the other.

Now, this was done, as you would imagine, at a headquarters.
There is an Official Secrets Act which forbids me from telling you
what headquarters, but I will give you this inkling. It was not the
headquarters responsible for winning the war. I have already perhaps said too much.

Incidentally I could not tell you what the headquarters was for, because that I never discovered—but it was awfully busy. There were
about eighty people, and there was an Air Vice-Marshal, and a Colonel
from the Army, and he was assisted or impeded, or whatever it was, by
a Wing Commander from the Air Force; and he was definitely assisted
by myself, a Major from the Army. And we were all as busy as could
be.

Paper flowed onto our desks, and we worked on from day to day
until the day when the Air Vice-Marshal was called away to what I
think one might describe as a convention of air vice-marshals. Just
such a meeting as I see before me.

The work to be done dropped abruptly by 25 per cent; and shortly
afterwards, the Colonel went on leave. The work dropped to 50 per
cent.

After that the Wing Commander fell sick. I was in command—
not the disaster you might suppose; but I noticed, then, that the work
had dwindled to a point where I could deal with it in about an hour
after breakfast.

Now, of course I was very tempted to go away in my turn. I had a
precedent for it by then. And I am convinced that had I gone away
and handed the whole headquarters to the sergeant, he would have had
really nothing to do.

There never had been anything to do. All we had been doing was
write memoranda for circulation among ourselves; write minutes to
each other; and criticize each other's grammar and punctuation. This
was the beginning of my insight into administration.

Nothing, perhaps, might have come of it had I not, in the years
following the war, had the good fortune to marry a girl who had previ-
ously taught mathematics at a girls' high school. I'm sure all the
intelligent members of an audience like this will realize that in any serious scientific, economic, or social studies sort of book you must have

some mathematics from time to time. It doesn't matter what it is about; but you must have a graph, or something, just to show that it is scientific.

It is rather like in business—you must have IBM equipment somewhere in the building. This is what is known as a "status symbol." And ever since my marriage I have had an unfailing supply of mathematics for this decorative purpose, to break up the page. I turn to my wife and say, "Darling, I want an equation."

And my loyal wife, whatever she may be doing—she might be changing the baby's nappie—puts it down, writes the equation—possibly on the nappie—pushes it over to me, and I put it into the book—the equation, I mean.

Well, years afterwards, assisted by my loyal wife, I wrote an article called PARKINSON'S LAW. Now, the question arose as to what I was going to do with this; where should I send it?

I might have sent it to a humorist paper, because it could be fairly described—I wouldn't say as a funny article, but an unserious one, perhaps. And it could have gone to a humorist paper. And there are humorist papers in England, by the way—something called PUNCH, you can see in any dentist's waiting room.

But we didn't do that. Advised by my loyal wife, I sent it to the LONDON ECONOMIST; and the editors of the LONDON ECONOMIST, rather to their own surprise, published it.

Now I need hardly tell people here—but I will tell them, nevertheless, that the LONDON ECONOMIST does not rank among the humorist papers of the world. It is something rather like the WALL STREET JOURNAL. You don't expect to see people convulsed with laughter over it.

And so, the effect of my article in THE ECONOMIST was, I think, out of all proportion perhaps to its merits. Some readers had probably read it three times before they could quite believe their eyes; and the general effect might be compared, perhaps, with that of a short, sharp anchovy in a strawberry ice. Well, that article had a certain amount of success, which encouraged me to go further into my studies in administration. *Professor C. Northcote Parkinson, in an address before the Executives' Club of Chicago*

RUSSIA—A LAND OF CONTRASTS

Russia is a land of strange contrasts. Its Moscow and Leningrad subways are splendid, but tens of millions of its people are unable to own even the lowest priced automobile. It boasts of progress in education, but it denies the people the right to read newspapers and magazines from abroad or to hear foreign radio broadcasts. It produces a Sputnik, but it sharply restricts the production of refrigerators, washing machines, vacuum cleaners and other durable goods which would raise the standard of living of its masses. Its leaders encourage infiltration and subversion by Communists for the purpose of ruthlessly overthrowing foreign governments, and at the same time the common people of Russia desperately hope they may live at peace with the world. Russia denounces the Western World for materialism and simultaneously destroys religious institutions and concentrates the entire energy of its people on a dictated program of sheer, naked materialism. *Herbert V. Prochnow, Executive Vice President, The First National Bank of Chicago*

OUR NEVER-ENDING REVOLUTION

The American revolution was not a distant explosion, from which the dust has long since settled. It is a continuing process. We haven't begun to establish economic freedom in this country, and we haven't fully established political freedom.

We must be clear ourselves, that we are part of a living revolution, set in motion in our colonial times but not ended there, that we agree upon certain basic principles as essential to our way of living, and have a political method that will permit those principles to work for the benefit of society. Our responsibility and destiny is to keep them working.

The American Revolution is a continuing process of applying our basic principles to new problems that arise out of new experiences. *George Romney*

THE TIME WILL COME

Once the great Lord Melbourne, then Prime Minister of England, asked a young man named Disraeli, what he would like to be. Disraeli boldly replied, "Prime Minister of England." Few men in world history present a more remarkable illustration of the ability to overcome hardship than Disraeli. Without opportunity he struggled through the middle classes and the upper groups of his country. Three times he was defeated in parliamentary elections. When he made his first speech in the House of Commons he was ridiculed, hissed and jeered. He cried out, "The time will come when you will hear me." And the time did come. He was determined. With courage and confidence he fought his way from the back benches of the House of Commons to leadership as Prime Minister of the British Empire. *Herbert V. Prochnow*

THE BUSINESSMAN AND POLITICS

The American businessman must personally take a far greater, more active part in politics. The largest items in your cost sheet are fixed for you by political decree. Politically determined costs can price you out of your better markets. Politically determined regulations can restrict your exports and increase competitive imports against you.

Wages are an important item of costs, which are more and more in competition with wages abroad. We no longer operate or sell in a vacuum. If any of our costs become non-competitive, it will simply mean moving jobs from Pittsburgh, Cleveland, Detroit and Chicago and other areas here at home, to Britain, Germany, other European centers, and even Russia. They will work and produce the goods, and we will have less business and fewer jobs.

Both wages and prices are subject to competitive limitations that will eventually control them, no matter how powerful a union may seem to be or what the price levels in an industry may be for a limited time.

Both labor and business can price themselves out of the market with distressing results—labor with a high rate and no job, and business with a high price and no sale, but equally destructive to both. However, in all cases, the responsibility of the government should only be to prevent monopolistic, restrictive or compulsory practices by either, or the government itself, to the detriment of the public, or eventually the whole free system will be destroyed. Short of interference, the system is self-correcting and self-policing for the benefit of all concerned. *George M. Humphrey, Chairman, National Steel Corporation, speaking before the American Iron and Steel Institute*

THE PROGRESS OF AGRICULTURE

Agriculture provides a remarkable example of mechanization in a single industry. George Washington was the president of a rural nation with at least ninety per cent of the people engaged in agricultural pursuits.

By 1840, the iron plow had displaced the inefficient wooden plow. Then came the steel plow along with the reaper, mower, hay rake, thresher, seed drill, corn planter and cultivator to bring amazing changes. By 1860, an American farmer could produce his crops with one-third less labor than he required just twenty years earlier.

By 1880, only forty-four per cent of our people were engaged in farming, which compares with about forty-eight per cent in Soviet Russia today. By 1900 in the United States about thirty-six per cent of our labor force was engaged in agriculture in contrast to less than ten per cent today.

Moreover, between 1850 and 1950 the work week on the farm declined from seventy to forty-five hours. The increased use of science and equipment, including tractors, trucks, milking machines and great combines, as well as fewer but larger farms, has vastly increased farm production. The increase in tractors alone is one indication of the progress of mechanization on American farms. In 1910, there were 1,000 tractors; in 1915, 25,000, and by 1958 more than 4,700,-000.

In 1820, one farm worker in the United States produced sufficient food for four persons. Today he produces enough for twenty-four persons. In contrast, in Soviet Russia, one farm worker produces enough food for about two persons. Since 1932 the production of American farms has increased by fifty per cent at the same time the farm population has declined by more than twenty-five per cent. For at least twenty years the productivity of farm labor has risen at an average annual rate of more than twice the 2.2 per cent annual increase for the rest of our economy. The average acreage planted in 1958 was the smallest in forty years, but the crop output was eleven per cent greater than in any preceding year. These are some of the striking achievements in agriculture that resulted from mechanization and heavy capital investment, and they illustrate the remarkable progress that has been going on in industry after industry to give the United States the economic leadership of the world.

However, more than thirty per cent of the people of Europe, forty per cent or more of South America and as high as seventy to eighty per cent for large areas in Asia, Africa and the Middle East are engaged in agriculture. Today over one-half the people of the world still live in pre-industrial societies engaged in agriculture. Any nation in which a large percentage of the people must work solely to subsist will be greatly retarded in its industrial development. *Herbert V. Prochnow, Executive Vice President, The First National Bank of Chicago*

THE FINANCE COMMITTEE

The finance committee of, shall we say, the University of Chicago —assuming it has a finance committee (and this is mere supposition)—works somewhat like this:

The committee meets, and before it is an agenda; and the first item on the agenda comes, invariably, from the Department of Physics; and the Department of Physics always wants a reactor; a betatron, cyclotron—whatever you like—something of the kind; and the cost is approximately 20 million dollars. You never hear about a cyclotron going at nineteen and a half million dollars, or anything like that. It's always a good round figure.

And there it is—item one.

And the chairman looks around his finance committee and says, "You have the plans, specifications, the estimates, the blueprints. Any member anything to say?" He glances around like that (illustrating). No one has anything to say. Most of them don't know what a reactor is. But they all realize that it is something you've got to have. And so, after approximately two and a half minutes the chairman has got no views, and so he goes like that (rapping gavel), and says, "Item number one carried."

So he moves on to item number two. Now, item number two on the agenda comes from a professor of English literature, and he—rash man—wants a new blackboard for his classroom.

Now, the estimate for the blackboard is $34.80. But the members of the committee have a guilt complex about item one. They feel that item one went through rather fast, and that now the moment has come for them to justify their existence as a finance committee.

So, one member says, "Mr. Chairman, are we convinced that there is no other blackboard around the campus which is insufficiently used?" The dean of arts gets up and says, "Mr. Chairman, I can assure you every blackboard on the campus is in constant use, day and night." Another member says, "Yes, that may be so. And, of course, I realize this amount is not very large, but it's a question of principle."

As you all realize, there is always a time when it's a question of principle. And he goes on and says, "Yes, Mr. Chairman. Wasn't this the very same department that last year was wanting a duster? And apart from that, where is it all going to end? If we allow this to go through, by next year won't they be wanting some chalk?"

Now I don't want to emphasize how this acrimonious discussion ends, and whether the blackboard is obtained, or not—what I want to emphasize is the time taken, because whatever the result on this item of $34.80, the time spent will be approximately three-quarters of an hour.

Item three is the cost of refreshments for the committee itself. This comes to $9.20, for the semester. Now if item two took three-quarters of an hour, item three will take an hour and a half, and you will readily recognize the rule which is emerging, that the time spent on any item on the agenda is in inverse proportion to the amount involved. *Professor C. Northcote Parkinson, in an address before the Executives' Club of Chicago*

MAKING UP YOUR MIND

The ability to decide—to make up your mind—to quit straddling— to choose wisely and courageously under any circumstances—is unquestionably one of the earmarks of greatness in men and women. It means the ability to choose between the wise and the foolish, between wasting time and using it wisely, between the safe and unsafe, the sound and the unsound, the good and the bad, the beautiful and the ugly, the virtues and the vulgarities of life. It is in a large measure the only true test of whether a man is educated, regardless of how many years he may have spent in college. What choice does he make of books, of friends, of ways of recreation? It is the only assurance that parents have relative to the conduct of their children when they cannot watch over them personally. Let them be certain that a son or daughter will choose wisely—will make the best decisions—and serenity comes to them in mind and heart.

Every minute and every hour of the day we are confronted by choices. What are you doing now to improve and use your talents? How will you use your time today—tonight—tomorrow and tomorrow night and so through the weeks, months and years? Of course you will make intelligent decisions when it is easy, but, honestly, have you the courage to do the intelligent thing when it is not popular, or when it is inconvenient or possibly embarrassing? Will you decide to read some great literary work every week? Will you decide to take a constructive part in building up the community where you live? It is easier, you and I know, to let some one else do it and then criticize.

Many times decisions are not easy. For some men they have meant life itself. David Livingstone dying in a Negro hut in Central Africa for his ideals; Mark Twain at sixty years of age bankrupt, shouldering his debts and starting out on a heart-breaking lecture tour to earn enough money to be out of debt in four years so he could start life all over again at the age of sixty-four; Abraham Lincoln carrying on his shoulders the terrible burden of a nation engaged in civil war, his methods criticized by his own party and his generals denouncing him —these men could testify to the price men pay for courageous decisions.   Small minds, lazy minds, weak minds always take the easiest way—always make the easiest decision.   In life, the line of least resistance is always the busiest boulevard.

In the last analysis, life is going to be the sum total of the decisions we have made.   Nothing more—nothing less.   We can make it a blind experience or a great adventure.

A university president says that one spring time he was in the north of Canada when the frost was breaking up and the roads were almost impassable.   He comments that at one crossroad he saw this sign: "Take care which rut you choose; you will be in it for the next fifty miles."   One would like to say that to every young man and woman. Take care the kind of life you choose.   You will be in it for the next fifty years.   Choose to live without vision, without courage, without depth and breadth and height to your life and it will be simply a blind experience.   But make those decisions daily that give direction, meaning and character to life and it will be a great adventure.   *From an address by Herbert V. Prochnow, Executive Vice President, The First National Bank of Chicago*

LIFE OF A SALESMAN

I remember one time I was in Omaha.   I had hoofed the streets all day.   Orders—none.   When I got back to the Hotel Fontenelle that evening, they didn't even have to operate the revolving door—I walked under the rubber mat below it and didn't have to bend over.   Low—I was lower than that, but as in every salesman's life there came another day.   The next day orders fell into my basket so fast that I lost count of them and that evening when I went back to the Fontenelle they not only had to remove the revolving door, they also had to take out the door jam—in fact, they had to enlarge the entrance so that I could get into the lobby.   That, I suspect, is the life of a salesman boiled down to a typical two days.   Lights and shadows, down today and up tomorrow—but we love it.   *Harold A. Speckman*

JUST SIMMERING THROUGH LIFE

It was a great prophet, Paul, who said, "This *one* thing I do." In unmistakable terms he stated that his life was to have a singleness of purpose. *One* thing he would do.

"This day we sailed westward," were the simple words Columbus wrote in his book each day. How definite, how determined to do *one* thing. The crew might rebel, storms might come, but he had a single objective. Nothing was to interfere. And with that objective a new world was discovered and the history of mankind changed.

Many of us would be great in some field, but we are unwilling to sacrifice everything to that one ambition. We dilly dally with one thing or another, unwilling to pay the price demanded of giving up all for a single objective. Too many lives are like the man Voltaire described as an oven, always heating but never cooking anything. As Walt Whitman said, "I was simmering, simmering, simmering: Emerson brought me to a boil." Many of us in life may succeed to where we almost reach the boiling point. Nearly, you see, almost, but not quite.

The famous actor, Jefferson, spent a lifetime to become a great Rip Van Winkle; Webster spent thirty-six years on the single job of making a dictionary; Field crossed the ocean fifty times to lay a cable so men could talk across thousands of miles of water; Schumann-Heink's parents were so poor they could not buy her a good piano, but finally they got a dilapidated old instrument. For twenty years she fought off proverty to become one of the world's greatest singers. It is the slavery to a single idea or objective that has given to many a person of seemingly mediocre talent the ability of a genius.

Hand in hand with a determination to achieve greatness in a chosen field is the willingness to struggle through every kind of hardship. When we are confronted with the necessity of paying the price, we turn away.

Beethoven, the great musician, probably surpassed other musicians in his painstaking fidelity and persistent application. There is hardly a bar of his music that was not written and rewritten at least a dozen times. Gibbon wrote his autobiography nine times and was in his study every morning, summer and winter, at six o'clock; and yet young men and women wonder at the genius which could produce *The Decline and Fall of the Roman Empire,* upon which Gibbon worked twenty years. There are many of us who would envy the great master

Josef Haydn who produced over 800 musical compositions and at the age of 66 years gave to the world that matchless oratorio "The Creation." We envy his achievements, but we so often never look back to the days of his hardship. A Michael Angelo worked seven long years decorating the Sistine Chapel with his "Creation" and the "Last Judgment."

A leading magazine ridiculed Tennyson's first poems and consigned the young poet to temporary oblivion; Milton worked on *Paradise Lost* in a world he could not see; Balzac toiled in a lonely garret; *Pilgrim's Progress* was written in a Bedford Jail; Robert Louis Stevenson wrote his greatest works when he was blind and sick.

No struggles in life, no strength. No fight, no fortitude. No crises, no courage. No suffering, no sympathy. No pain, no patience. *From an address by Herbert V. Prochnow, Executive Vice President, The First National Bank of Chicago*

WHAT WOULD YOU HAVE IF YOU REACHED YOUR GOAL?

In a little country community a farmer had a dog who spent part of his time sitting by the side of a main-traveled highway waiting for big trucks. When the dog saw a large truck come around the corner, he would get ready and as it passed him would take out after it down the road, barking and doing his best to overtake it.

One day the farmer's neighbor said, "Sam, do you think that hound of yours is ever going to catch a truck?"

"Well, Bill," Sam replied, "That isn't what worries me. What worries me is what he would do if he caught one!"

Many of us in life are like that hound. We give our lives pursuing goals that have little value even if we reach them. Sometimes it pays to stop and ask whether we have objectives worth pursuing. *Herbert V. Prochnow*

6 •••

Useful Literary Quotations

ABILITY

Behind an able man there are always other able men. *Chinese Proverb*

We judge ourselves by what we feel capable of doing, while others judge us by what we have already done. *Longfellow*

ACHIEVEMENT

I wonder if we have really grown to the point where the size of a house in which a person lives will have little interest to his neighbors, but what he contributes in mind and character to the community will bring him respect and admiration. *Eleanor Roosevelt*

ACTION

Did nothing in particular
And did it very well. *W. S. Gilbert*

I took the canal zone and let Congress debate, and while the debate goes on the canal does also. *Theodore Roosevelt*

Theirs not to make reply,
Theirs not to reason why,
Theirs but to do and die. *Tennyson*

ADVERSITY

There is no education like adversity. *Disraeli*

Sweet are the uses of adversity;

Which, like the toad, ugly and venomous,
Wears yet a precious jewel in his head.   *Shakespeare*
Be still, sad heart, and cease repining,
Behind the clouds the sun is shining;
Thy fate is the common fate of all;
Into each life some rain must fall,—
Some days must be dark and dreary.   *Longfellow*

ADVERTISING

An advertising agency—85 percent confusion and 15 percent commission.   *Fred Allen*

So far as advertising is concerned, I repeat that it must survive as a thriving dynamic force.   Not only does it deserve to continue because of its contributions to our way of life but it has a job to do now.   *Leon Henderson*

You can tell the ideals of a nation by its advertisements.   *Norman Douglas*

ADVICE

Old men are fond of giving good advice, to console themselves for being no longer in a position to give bad examples.   *La Rochefoucauld*

Admonish your friends privately, but praise them openly.   *Syrus*

AGE

Youth is a blunder; Manhood a struggle; Old Age a regret.   *Disraeli*

If wrinkles must be written upon our brows, let them not be written upon the heart.   The spirit should not grow old.   *James A. Garfield*

Grow old along with me!
The best is yet to be,
The last of life for which the first was made.   *R. Browning*

As a white candle in a holy place,
So is the beauty of an aged face.   *Joseph Campbell*

Age acquires no value save through thought and discipline.   *James Truslow Adams*

To me—old age is always 15 years older than I am!   *Bernard Baruch*

AMBITION

When that the poor have cried, Caesar hath wept:
Ambition should be made of sterner stuff:
Yet Brutus says he was ambitious;
And Brutus is an honourable man. *Shakespeare*

Ambition has but one reward for all:
A little power, a little transient fame,
A grave to rest in, and a fading name! *William Winter*

> I had Ambition, by which sin
>   The angels fell;
> I climbed and, step by step, O Lord,
>   Ascended into Hell. *W. H. Davies*

AMERICA

Bring me men to match my mountains,
Bring me men to match my plains,
Men with empires in their purpose,
And new eras in their brains. *S. W. Foss*

ANGER

He that is slow to anger is better than the mighty; and he that ruleth his spirit than he that taketh a city. *Proverbs XVI, 32*

Anger is momentary madness, so control your passion or it will control you. *Horace*

APOLOGY

I asked Tom if countries always apologized when they had done wrong, and he says: "Yes; the little ones does." *Mark Twain*

APPEARANCE

Whited sepulchres, which indeed appear beautiful outward, but are within full of dead men's bones. *Matthew XXIII, 27*

Men in general judge more from appearances than from reality. All men have eyes, but few have the gift of penetration. *Machiavelli*

Things are seldom what they seem,
Skim milk masquerades as cream. *W. S. Gilbert*

ARGUMENT

Never argue at the dinner table, for the one who is not hungry always gets the best of the argument. *Whately*

When people agree with me, I always feel that I must be wrong.
Wilde

Strong and bitter words indicate a weak cause. *Victor Hugo*

It is impossible to defeat an ignorant man in argument. *William G. McAdoo*

ART

All passes.   Art alone
  Enduring stays to us.
The Bust outlasts the throne,—
  The Coin, Tiberius. *Austin Dobson*

ATHEISM

That the universe was formed by a fortuitous concourse of atoms, I will no more believe than that the accidental jumbling of the alphabet would fall into a most ingenious treatise of philosophy. *Swift*

The fool hath said in his heart, There is no God. *Psalms XIV, 1*

AUTHORS

The pen is the tongue of the mind. *Cervantes*

You don't write because you want to say something; you write because you've got something to say. *F. Scott Fitzgerald*

When audiences come to see us authors lecture, it is largely in the hope that we'll be funnier to look at than to read. *Sinclair Lewis*

BABY

Here we have a baby.   It is composed of a bald head and a pair of lungs. *Eugene Field*

Hush, my dear, lie still and slumber,
  Holy angels guard thy bed!
Heavenly blessings without number
  Gently falling on thy head. *Isaac Watts*

BEAUTY

A thing of beauty is a joy for ever:
Its loveliness increases; it will never
Pass into nothingness. *Keats*

. . . her beauty made
The bright world dim, and everything beside
Seemed like the fleeting image of a shade. *Shelley*

BELIEF

Blessed are they that have not seen, and yet have believed. *New Testament, John XX, 29*

Lord, I believe; help thou mine unbelief. *Mark IX, 24*

BIBLE

The English Bible—a book which, if everything else in our language should perish, would alone suffice to show the whole extent of its beauty and power. *Macaulay*

I call the Book of Job, apart from all theories about it, one of the grandest things ever written with pen. *Carlyle*

The Bible is a window in this prison-world, through which we may look into eternity. *Timothy Dwight*

A Bible and a newspaper in every house, a good school in every district—all studied and appreciated as they merit—are the principal support of virtue, morality and civil liberty. *Franklin*

BLESSING

God bless me and my son John,
Me and my wife, him and his wife,
Us four, and no more. *Anonymous*

We mistake the gratuitous blessings of heaven for the fruits of our industry. *L'Estrange*

"God bless us every one!" said Tiny Tim, the last of all. *Dickens, A Christmas Carol*

BOASTING

The fly sat upon the axle-tree of the chariot-wheel, and said, What a dust do I raise! *Francis Bacon*

BOOKS

All that Mankind has done, thought, gained or been: it is lying as in magic preservation in the pages of Books. They are the chosen possession of men. *Carlyle*

Except a living man there is nothing more wonderful than a book! a message to us from . . . human souls we never saw. . . . And yet these arouse us, terrify us, teach us, comfort us, open their hearts to us as brothers. *Kingsley*

Camerado, this is no book,
Who touches this, touches a man, . . . *Walt Whitman*
To produce a mighty book, you must choose a mighty theme.   No
great and enduring volume can ever be written on the flea; though
many there be that have tried it.   *Herman Melville, Moby Dick*

BORROWING

Neither a borrower nor a lender be:
For loan oft loses both itself and friend,
And borrowing dulls the edge of husbandry.   *Shakespeare*

BOY

A boy is, of all wild beasts, the most difficult to manage.   *Plato*
Across the fields of yesterday
He sometimes comes to me,
A little lad just back from play—
The lad I used to be.   *T. S. Jones, Jr., Sometimes*

When I was a beggarly boy,
And lived in a cellar damp,
I had not a friend nor a toy,
But I had Aladdin's lamp.   *J. R. Lowell*

BREVITY

Let thy speech be short, comprehending much in few words.   *Ecclesiastes XXXII, 8*
Since brevity is the soul of wit,
And tediousness the limbs and outward flourishes,
I will be brief.   *Shakespeare*

BROTHERHOOD

While there is a lower class I am in it.   While there is a criminal
class I am of it.   While there is a soul in prison I am not free.   *Eugene V. Debs*
A new commandment I give unto you, That ye love one another; as
I have loved you, that ye also love one another.   *John XIII, 34*

BUDGET

Let us have courage to stop borrowing to meet continuing deficits.
Stop the deficits.   *Franklin D. Roosevelt*

BUSINESS

Private capital and private management are entitled to adequate reward for efficiency, but business must recognize that its reward results from the employment of the resources of the nation. Business is a public trust and must adhere to national standards in the conduct of its affairs. *Harry S. Truman*

Tariff—a scale of taxes on imports, designed to protect the domestic producer against the greed of his consumer. *Ambrose Bierce*

CHAOS

And the earth was without form and void; and darkness was upon the face of the deep. *Old Testament, Genesis I, 2*

CHARACTER

When wealth is lost, nothing is lost;
When health is lost, something is lost;
When character is lost, all is lost! *Anonymous*

E'en as he trod that day to God, so
walked he from his birth,
In simpleness and gentleness and
honor and clean mirth. *Kipling*

The true greatness of nations is in those qualities which constitute the greatness of the individual. *Charles Sumner*

CHARITY

He who waits to do a great deal of good at once, will never do anything. *Samuel Johnson*

That charity which longs to publish itself, ceases to be charity. *Hutton*

My poor are my best patients. God pays for them. *Boerhaave*

Organized charity, scrimped and iced,
In the name of a cautious, statistical Christ. *John Boyle*

Though I speak with the tongues of men and of angels, and have not charity, I am become as sounding brass or a tinkling cymbal. *New Testament, I Corinthians XIII, 1*

And now abideth faith, hope, charity, these three; but the greatest of these is charity. *I Corinthians XIII, 13*

Verily I say unto you, Inasmuch as ye have done it unto one of the least of these my brethren, ye have done it unto me. *Matthew XXV, 40*

CHILDREN

When I was a child, I spake as a child, I understood as a child, I thought as a child; but when I became a man, I put away childish things. *I Corinthians XIII, 11*

Train up a child in the way he should go; and when he is old, he will not depart from it. *Proverbs XXII, 6*

A child should always say what's true
And speak when he is spoken to,
And behave mannerly at table;
At least as far as he is able. *R. L. Stevenson*

Suffer little children to come unto me, and forbid them not; for of such is the kingdom of God. *Mark X, 14*

CHRIST

Alexander, Caesar, Charlemagne and I myself have founded empires; but upon what do these creations of our genius depend? Upon force. Jesus alone founded His empire upon love; and to this very day millions would die for Him. *Napoleon*

CHRISTIANITY

Christianity taught men that love is worth more than intelligence. *Jacques Maritain*

. . . we may conclude from the close relationship of democracy and Christianity not that they will disappear together but that they will survive together. *Thomas Mann*

CHURCH

I never weary of great churches. It is my favourite kind of mountain scenery. Mankind was never so happily inspired as when it made a cathedral. *Stevenson*

CITY

The city is the place where men are constantly seeking to find their door and where they are doomed to wandering forever. *Thomas Wolfe*

One hears the hoarse notes of the great ships in the river, and one remembers suddenly the princely girdle of proud, potent tides that bind the city, and suddenly New York blazes like a magnificent jewel in its fit setting of sea, and earth, and stars. *Thomas Wolfe*

The reason American cities are prosperous is that there is no place to sit down. *A. J. Talley*

CIVILIZATION

Civilization means a society based upon the opinion of civilians. It means that violence, the rule of warriors and despotic chiefs, the conditions of camps and warfare, of riot and tyranny, give place to parliaments where laws are made, and independent courts of justice in which over long periods those laws are maintained. *Winston Churchill*

Civilization is, after all, but a coat of paint that washes away when the rain falls. *Auguste Rodin*

So I should say that civilizations begin with religion and stoicism; they end with skepticism and unbelief, and the undisciplined pursuit of individual pleasure. A civilization is born stoic and dies epicurean. *Will Durant*

COLLEGE

It is nonsense to talk of the college years as only a preparation for life. They are part of life, just as much as any other four-year period. *Paul Swain Havens*

COMMON SENSE

Horse-sense is a sterling quality, but let's skip what it did for the horse. *Louis Hirsch*

COMMUNISM

The theory of Communism may be summed up in one sentence: Abolish all private property. *Karl Marx and Friedrich Engels*

CONCEIT

He was like the cock who thought the sun had risen to hear him crow. *George Eliot*

A man who overindulges lives in a dream. He becomes conceited. He thinks the whole world revolves around him—and it usually does. *W. C. Fields*

CONSCIENCE

Conscience is a sacred sanctuary where God alone may enter as judge. *Lamennais*

Conscience is the guardian in the individual of the rules which the community has evolved for its own preservation. *William Somerset Maugham*

The soft whispers of the God in man.   *Young*

Conscience is God's presence in man.   *Swedenborg*

CONSERVATIVE

The most conservative persons I ever met are college undergraduates.   *Woodrow Wilson*

Conservative—a statesman who is enamored of existing evils, as distinguished from the Liberal, who wishes to replace them with others. . . .   *Ambrose Bierce*

CONSTITUTION

Constitutions should consist only of general provisions; the reason is that they must necessarily be permanent, and that they cannot calculate for the possible change of things.   *Alexander Hamilton*

In questions of power let no more be heard of confidence in man, but bind him down from mischief by the chains of the constitution.   *Jefferson*

The Constitution is what the judges say it is.   *Charles Evans Hughes*

CONTRACT

A verbal contract isn't worth the paper it's written on.   *Samuel Goldwyn*

COURAGE

Often the test of courage is not to die but to live.   *Alfieri*
A man of courage is also full of faith.   *Cicero*

COWARD

Cowards die many times before their deaths;
The valiant never taste of death but once.   *Shakespeare*

CRITICISM

The rule in carving holds good as to criticism; never cut with a knife what you can cut with a spoon.   *Charles Buxton*

Even the lion has to defend himself against flies.   *German Proverb*

What a blessed thing it is that nature, when she invented, manufactured and patented her authors, contrived to make critics out of the chips that were left!   *Holmes*

DAWN

Night's candles are burnt out, and jocund day
Stands tip-toe on the misty mountain-tops.   *Shakespeare*

DAY

Think that day lost whose low descending sun
Views from thy hand no worthy action done.   *Anonymous*

DEATH

Every moment of life is a step towards death.   *Corneille*

We begin to die as soon as we are born, and the end is linked to the
beginning.   *Manilius*

God's finger touched him, and he slept.   *Tennyson*

Death lies on her, like an untimely frost
Upon the sweetest flower of all the field.   *Shakespeare*

First our pleasures die—and then
Our hopes, and then our fears—and when
These are dead, the debt is due,
Dust claims dust—and we die too.   *Shelley*

Marley was dead: to begin with . . . Old Marley was as dead as a
door-nail.   *Dickens, A Christmas Carol*

Death be not proud, though some have called thee
Mighty and dreadful, for thou art not so,
For, those, whom thou think'st, thou dost overthrow,
Die not, poor death, nor yet canst thou kill me . . .
   . . . death, thou shalt die.   *John Donne*

> The little toy dog is covered with dust,
>   But sturdy and staunch he stands;
> And the little toy soldier is red with rust,
>   And his musket moulds in his hands;
> Time was when the little toy dog was new,
>   And the soldier was passing fair;
> And that was the time when our Little Boy Blue
>   Kissed them and put them there.   *Eugene Field*

Pale Death, with impartial step, knocks at the poor man's cottage
and the palaces of kings.   *Horace*

O death, where is thy sting?   O grave, where is thy victory?   *I Corinthians XV, 54*

There the wicked cease from troubling; and there the weary be at rest. *Job III, 17*

> Sunset and evening star,
>   And one clear call for me!
> And may there be no moaning of the bar
>   When I put out to sea.
>
>   . . . .
>
> I hope to see my Pilot face to face
>   When I have crost the bar. *Tennyson*

> The boast of heraldry, the pomp of pow'r,
>   And all that beauty, all that wealth e'er gave,
> Awaits alike th' inevitable hour.
>   The paths of glory lead but to the grave. *Gray*

Man goeth to his long home. *Ecclesiastes XII, 5*

Mausoleum—the final and funniest folly of the rich. *Ambrose Bierce*

You can't tell how good it is to be alive, till you're facing death, because you don't live till then. *John Galsworthy*

I never wanted to see anybody die, but there are a few obituary notices I have read with pleasure. *Clarence Darrow*

From birthday to death-day we continue to collect and weave together the materials of our minute private universe, as a bird builds its nest, and out of a myriad heterogeneous scraps we give it a certain shape and coherence, wherein to lay our treasured brittle eggs. *Walter de la Mare*

DECEIT

> O, what a tangled web we weave,
>   When first we practice to deceive! *Walter Scott, Marmion, VI*

DEEDS

> Great things are done when men and mountains meet;
> This is not done by jostling in the street. *William Blake*

> Something attempted, something done,
> Has earned a night's repose. *Longfellow*

How far that little candle throws its beams!
So shines a good deed in a naughty world.   *Shakespeare*

DEMOCRACY

It would be folly to argue that the people cannot make political mistakes. They can and do make grave mistakes. They know it, they pay the penalty, but compared with the mistakes which have been made by every kind of autocracy they are unimportant. *Calvin Coolidge*

Democracy needs more free speech, for even the speech of foolish people is valuable if it serves to guarantee the right of the wise to talk. *David Cushman Coyle*

When American democracy reaches its crisis and needs a "savior and a great one," out of its native earth, its native shrewdness and reality and common sense, it produces Abraham Lincoln, a backwoods politician and one of the greatest statesmen in all history. *Bernard De Voto*

In a democracy, the individual enjoys not only the ultimate power but carries the ultimate responsibility. *Norman Cousins*

As I see it, democracy encourages the nimble charlatan at the expense of the thinker, and prefers the plausible wizard with quack remedies to the true statesman. *Sir James Jeans*

We believe in democracy; we believe in freedom; we believe in peace. We offer to every nation of the world the handclasp of the good neighbor. Let those who wish our friendship look us in the eye and take our hand. *Franklin D. Roosevelt*

DESTINY

The significant questions of human destiny are not to be approached with a smile. God, misery, and salvation are no joke. *Irwin Edman*

DIGNITY

Perhaps the only true dignity of man is his capacity to despise himself. *George Santayana*

Too coy to flatter, and too proud to serve,
Thine be the joyless dignity to starve. *Tobias Smollett*

DISAPPOINTMENT

Oh! ever thus from childhood's hour,
I've seen my fondest hopes decay;

I never lov'd a tree or flower,
But 'twas the first to fade away.
I never nurs'd a dear gazelle,
To glad me with its soft black eye,
But when it came to know me well,
And love me, it was sure to die.   *Thomas Moore*

DISILLUSION

There's not a joy the world can give like that it takes away,
When the glow of early thought declines in feeling's dull decay;
'Tis not on youth's smooth cheek the blush alone, which fades
so fast,
But the tender bloom of heart is gone, ere youth itself is past.
Byron

EDUCATION

Education commences at the mother's knee, and every word spoken within the hearsay of little children tends towards the formation of character.   *Hosea Ballou*

Education makes a people easy to lead, but difficult to drive; easy to govern, but impossible to enslave.   *Attributed to Lord Brougham*

"Reeling and Writhing, of course, to begin with," the Mock Turtle replied, "and the different branches of Arithmetic—Ambition, Distraction, Uglification and Derision."   *Lewis Carroll*

Nothing in education is so astonishing as the amount of ignorance it accumulates in the form of inert facts.   *Henry Adams*

When we teach a child to read, our primary aim is not to enable it to decipher a way-bill or receipt, but to kindle its imagination, enlarge its vision, and open for it the avenues of knowledge.   *Charles W. Eliot*

Whether four years of strenuous attention to football and fraternities is the best preparation for professional work has never been seriously investigated.   *Robert Maynard Hutchins*

EQUALITY

All States, great or small, victor or vanquished must have access, on equal terms, to the trade and to the raw materials of the world which are needed for their economic prosperity.   *Franklin D. Roosevelt*

ERROR

Truth, crushed to earth, shall rise again;
    Th' eternal years of God are hers;
But Error, wounded, writhes in pain,
    And dies among his worshippers.   *William C. Bryant*
Errors, like straws, upon the surface flow;
He who would search for pearls must dive below.   *Dryden*

EXPERIENCE

Experience is the best of schoolmasters, only the school-fees are
heavy.   *Carlyle*
I have but one lamp by which my feet are guided, and that is the
lamp of experience.   *Patrick Henry*
Experience is the name men give to their follies or their sorrows.
Alfred de Musset
    A sadder and a wiser man
    He rose the morrow morn.   *S. T. Coleridge*
    Nor deem the irrevocable Past,
        As wholly wasted, wholly vain,
    If, rising on its wrecks, at last
        To something nobler we attain.   *Longfellow*

FAILURE

    And nothing to look backward to with pride,
    And nothing to look forward to with hope.   *Robert Frost*

I sing the hymn of the conquered, who fall in the battle of life,
The hymn of the wounded, the beaten who died overwhelmed in the
    strife.   *W. W. Story*

FAITH

An outward and visible sign of an inward and spiritual grace.
Book of Common Prayer
All I have seen teaches me to trust the Creator for all I have not
seen.   *Emerson*
I have fought a good fight, I have finished my course, I have kept
the faith.   *II Timothy, IV, 7*

Faith without works is dead.   *James II, 20*

    Strong Son of God, immortal Love,
        Whom we, that have not seen thy face,

By faith, and faith alone, embrace,
Believing where we cannot prove.   *Tennyson*

FAME

If you would not be forgotten as soon as you are dead, either write things worth reading or do things worth writing.   *Franklin*

The fame of great men ought always to be estimated by the means used to acquire it.   *La Rochefoucauld*

I met a traveller from an antique land
Who said: "Two vast and trunkless legs of stone
Stand in the desert. . . .
And on the pedestal these words appear:
'My name is Ozymandias, King of Kings:
Look on my works, ye Mighty, and despair!'
Nothing beside remains. . . .   *Shelley*

FAMILY

Woman knows what Man has too long forgotten, that the ultimate economic and spiritual unit of any civilization is still the family. . . .
Clare Booth Luce

FARM

Give fools their gold, and knaves their power;
    Let fortune's bubbles rise and fall;
Who sows a field, or trains a flower,
    Or plants a tree, is more than all.   *Whittier*

Farming looks nice—from a car window.   *Kin Hubbard*

FATE

We make our fortunes and we call them fate.   *Disraeli*

The Moving Finger writes; and having writ,
    Moves on; nor all your Piety nor Wit
Shall lure it back to cancel half a Line,
    Nor all your Tears wash out a Word of it.
Omar Khayyam, Rubaiyat

FATHER

When I was a boy of 14, my father was so ignorant I could hardly stand to have the old man around. But when I got to be 21, I was astonished at how much he had learned in 7 years.   *Mark Twain*

It is a wise child that knows its own father, and an unusual one that unreservedly approves of him. *Mark Twain*

FAULT

The greatest of faults, I should say, is to be conscious of none. *Carlyle*

The fault, dear Brutus, is not in our stars,
But in ourselves, that we are underlings. *Shakespeare*

FISH

Fish hold the honors for being brain producers, even though they haven't done as well as they might with their own organism. *C. C. & S. M. Furnas*

There is great pleasure in being on the sea, in the unknown wild suddenness of a great fish; in his life and death which he lives for you in an hour while your strength is harnessed to his; and there is satisfaction in conquering this thing which rules the sea it lives in. *Ernest Hemingway*

FLATTERY

'Tis an old maxim in the schools,
That flattery's the food of fools;
Yet now and then your men of wit
Will condescend to take a bit. *Swift*

FOOD

Vegetarianism is harmless enough, although it is apt to fill a man with wind and self-righteousness. *Robert Hutchinson*

Food is a trivial subject only to a man with a full belly. *Edgar Snow*

FOOL

Young men think old men are fools; but old men know young men are fools. *George Chapman*

Hain't we got all the fools in town on our side? And ain't that a big enough majority in any town? *Mark Twain*

A learned fool is more foolish than an ignorant fool. *Moliere*

There are two kinds of fools. One says, "This is old, therefore it is good." The other says, "This is new, therefore it is better." *Dean Inge*

FORGIVENESS

Forgive us our debts, as we forgive our debtors. *Matthew VI, 12*
> Good to forgive;
>   Best to forget!
>   Living, we fret;
> Dying, we live. *R. Browning*

The most difficult of all virtues is the forgiving spirit. Revenge seems to be natural with man; it is human to want to get even with an enemy. *William Jennings Bryan*

FREEDOM

Personal liberty is the paramount essential to human dignity and human happiness. *Bulwer-Lytton*

The only freedom which deserves the name is that of pursuing our own good in our own way, so long as we do not attempt to deprive others of theirs or impede their efforts to obtain it. *John Stuart Mill*

There is always one man to state the case for freedom. That's all we need, one. *Clarence Darrow*

FRIEND

I desire so to conduct the affairs of this administration that if at the end, when I come to lay down the reins of power, I have lost every other friend on earth, I shall at least have one friend left, and that friend shall be down inside of me. *Lincoln*

FUTURE

I never think of the future. It comes soon enough. *Albert Einstein*

For I dipt into the future, far as human eye could see,
Saw the Vision of the world and all the wonder that would be.
Tennyson

GENIUS

Doing easily what others find difficult is talent; doing what is impossible for talent is genius. *Amiel*

When a true genius appears in the world, you may know him by this sign, that the dunces are all in a confederacy against him.   *Swift*

GENTLEMAN

I like him.   He is every other inch a gentleman.   *Noel Coward*

GIFT

Whenever you see a man with handkerchief, socks, and tie to match, you may be sure he is wearing a present.   *Frank Case*

GIVING

You give but little when you give of your possessions.   It is when you give of yourself that you truly give.   *Kahlil Gibran*

It is more blessed to give than to receive.   *Acts XX, 35*

> Behold, I do not give lectures or a little charity,
> When I give I give myself.   *Walt Whitman*

> Not what we give, but what we share,
> For the gift without the giver is bare.   *J. R. Lowell*

GOD

> God moves in a mysterious way
>   His wonders to perform;
> He plants his footsteps in the sea
>   And rides upon the storm.   *Cowper*

"We trust, Sir, that God is on our side."   "It is more important to know that we are on God's side."   *Lincoln*

Everyone is in a small way the image of God.   *Manilius*

God is our refuge and strength, a very present help in trouble. *Psalms XLVI, 1*

If God be for us, who can be against us?   *Romans VIII, 31*

> A mighty fortress is our God,
>   A bulwark never failing.   *Martin Luther*

Let us hear the conclusion of the whole matter: Fear God, and keep his commandments: for this is the whole duty of man.   *Old Testament, Ecclesiastes XII, 13*

Suppose I had found a watch upon the ground. . . . The mechanism being observed, . . . the watch must have a maker; . . . *William Paley*

O God, our help in ages past,
Our hope for years to come,
Our shelter from the stormy blast,
And our eternal home. *Isaac Watts*

GOLF

Golf was, I should say offhand, the most useless outdoor game ever devised to waste the time and try the spirit of men. *Westbrook Pegler*

Golf is a funny game. If there is any larceny in a man, golf will bring it out. *Paul Gallico*

GOOD

Here's to you, as good as you are,
And here's to me, as bad as I am;
But as good as you are, and as bad as I am,
I am as good as you are, as bad as I am. *Old Scotch Toast*

Abhor that which is evil; cleave to that which is good. *Romans XII, 9*

GOVERNMENT

Though the people support the government the government should not support the people. *Grover Cleveland*

What government is the best? That which teaches us to govern ourselves. *Goethe*

I think we have more machinery of government than is necessary, too many parasites living on the labor of the industrious. *Jefferson*

Govern a great nation as you would cook a small fish. (Don't overdo it.) *Lao-Tze*

Themistocles said, "The Athenians govern the Greeks; I govern the Athenians; you, my wife, govern me; your son governs you." *Plutarch*

Government, even in its best state, is but a necessary evil; in its worst state, an intolerable one. *Thomas Paine*

Every country has the government it deserves. *Joseph de Maistre*

The whole of government consists in the art of being honest. *Thomas Jefferson*

In those days, the (Roman) government gave them bread and circuses. Today we give them bread and elections, but it is just a change in the style of periodical amusement. *Will Durant*

GRAFT

Public servant: Persons chosen by the people to distribute the graft. *Mark Twain*

GRATITUDE

He who receives a good turn should never forget it; he who does one should never remember it. *Charron*

Gratitude is the memory of the heart. *J. B. Massieu*

Gratitude is a duty which ought to be paid, but which none have a right to expect. *Rousseau*
> Two kinds of gratitude: the sudden kind
> We feel for what we take, the larger kind
> We feel for what we give. *E. A. Robinson*

GREATNESS

Everything great is not always good, but all good things are great. *Demosthenes*

It is the prerogative of great men only to have great defects. *La Rochefoucauld*
> That man is great, and he alone,
> Who serves a greatness not his own,
>> For neither praise nor pelf:
> Content to know and be unknown:
>> Whole in himself. *Owen Meredith*

But be not afraid of greatness: some are born great, some achieve greatness and some have greatness thrust upon 'em. *Shakespeare*
> Why, man, he doth bestride the narrow world
> Like a Colossus, and we petty men
> Walk under his huge legs and peep about
> To find ourselves dishonourable graves. *Shakespeare*
>> Ah vanity of vanities!
>>> How wayward the decrees of fate are,
>> How very weak the very wise,

> How very small the very great are! *Thackeray*

HABIT

Sow an act and you reap a habit. Sow a habit and you reap a character. Sow a character and you reap a destiny. *Charles Reade*

HAPPINESS

I have learned to seek my happiness by limiting my desires, rather than in attempting to satisfy them. *John Stuart Mill*

HATE

To harbor hatred and animosity in the soul makes one irritable, gloomy, and prematurely old. *Auerbach*

The hatred we bear our enemies injures their happiness less than our own. *J. Petit-Senn*

> For him who fain would teach the world
> The world holds hate in fee—
> For Socrates, the hemlock cup;
> For Christ, Gethsemane. *Don Marquis*

HEAD

And still they gaz'd, and still the wonder grew
That one small head could carry all he knew. *Goldsmith*

HEART

Where your treasure is there will your heart be also. *Luke XII, 34*
O hearts that break and give no sign
Save whitening lips and fading tresses. *O. W. Holmes*

HEAVEN

Lay up for yourselves treasures in heaven, where neither moth nor rust doth corrupt and where thieves do not break through nor steal. *Matthew VI, 20*

> It was a childish ignorance,
> But now 'tis little joy,
> To know I'm farther off from heaven
> Than when I was a boy. *Thomas Hood*

For a cap and bells our loves we pay,
Bubbles we buy with a whole soul's tasking:
'Tis heaven alone that is given away,
'Tis only God may be had for the asking. *J. R. Lowell*

HISTORY

There is properly no history, only biography. *Emerson*
History is indeed little more than the register of the crimes, follies, and misfortunes of mankind. *Gibbon*

What is history but a fable agreed upon?   *Napoleon*

The historian is a prophet looking backwards.   *Schlegel*

Rome's liberties were not auctioned off in a day, but were bought slowly, gradually, furtively, little by little; first with a little corn and oil for the exceedingly poor and wretched, later with corn and oil for voters who were not quite so poor, later still with corn and oil for pretty much every man that had a vote to sell—exactly our own history over again.   *Mark Twain*

HOME

Home is the place where, when you have to go there,
They have to take you in.   *Robert Frost*

> Name me no names for my disease
>   With uninforming breath;
> I tell you I am none of these,
>   But homesick unto death.   *Witter Bynner*

The foxes have their holes, and the birds of the air have their nests; but the Son of man hath not where to lay his head.   *Matthew VIII, 20*

HOPE

Hope is the poor man's bread.   *Thales*

Hope says to us constantly, "Go on, go on," and leads us thus to the grave.   *Mme. de Maintenon*

> Youth fades; love droops, the leaves of friendship fall;
> A mother's secret hope outlives them all.   *Holmes*

> The heart bowed down by weight of woe
> To weakest hope will cling.   *A. Bunn*

HUMILITY

Humility is the solid foundation of all the virtues.   *Confucius*

After crosses and losses, men grow humbler and wiser.   *Franklin*

In humility imitate Jesus and Socrates.   *Franklin*

I believe the first test of a truly great man is his humility.   *John Ruskin*

HUSBAND

All husbands are alike, but they have different faces so you can tell them apart.

IDEAS

No army can withstand the strength of an idea whose time has come. *Victor Hugo*

IGNORANCE

You may have noticed that the less I know about a subject the more confidence I have, and the more new light I throw on it. *Mark Twain*

I would rather have my ignorance than another man's knowledge because I have got so much more of it. *Mark Twain*

IMMORTALITY

No one could ever meet death for his country without the hope of immortality. *Cicero*

Oh, may I join the choir invisible
Of those immortal dead who live again. *George Eliot*

The nearer I approach the end, the plainer I hear around me the immortal symphonies of the worlds which invite me. It is marvelous, yet simple. *Victor Hugo*

Fool! All that is, at all,
Lasts ever past recall;
Earth changes, but thy soul and God stand sure;
What entered into thee,
That was, is, and shall be:
Time's wheel runs back or stops; Potter and clay endure.
R. Browning

Dust thou art, to dust returnest,
Was not spoken of the soul. *Longfellow*

Our Saviour, Jesus Christ, who hath abolished death, and hath brought life and immortality to light through the gospel. *II Timothy I, 10*

Happy he whose inward ear
Angel comfortings can hear,
O'er the rabble's laughter;
And while Hatred's fagots burn,
Glimpses through the smoke discern
Of the good hereafter. *Whittier*

The truest end of Life is to know that Life never ends . . . For tho' Death be a Dark Passage, it leads to Immortality, and that's Recompense enough for suffering of it. *William Penn*

JUDGMENT

There is so much good in the worst of us,
    And so much bad in the best of us,
    That it hardly becomes any of us
        To talk about the rest of us. *Anonymous*
Judge not, that ye be not judged. *Matthew VII, 1*
Why beholdest thou the mote that is in thy brother's eye, but considerest not the beam that is in thy own eye? *New Testament, Matthew VIII, 3*

KINDNESS

'Twas a thief said the last kind word to Christ:
Christ took the kindness, and forgave the theft. *R. Browning*

If I can stop one heart from breaking,
    I shall not live in vain;
If I can ease one life the aching,
    Or cool one pain,
Or help one fainting robin
    Unto his nest again,
I shall not live in vain. *Emily Dickinson*

KINGDOM

The ant finds kingdoms in a foot of ground. *Stephen Vincent Benet*

KNOWLEDGE

Our knowledge is the amassed thought and experience of innumerable minds. *Emerson*
As for me, all I know is that I know nothing. *Socrates*

There are four sorts of men:
He who knows not and knows not he knows not: he is a fool—shun him;
He who knows not and knows he knows not: he is simple—teach him.
He who knows and knows not he knows: he is asleep—wake him;
He who knows and knows he knows: he is wise—follow him.

Lady Burton (quoted as an Arabian proverb)
> Strange how much you've got to know
> Before you know how little you know.

Fullness of knowledge always and necessarily means some under-standing of the depths of our ignorance, and that is always conducive to both humility and reverence.   *Robert A. Millikan*

(About Kipling): He is a stranger to me, but he is a most remark-able man—I am the other one.   Between us, we cover all knowledge; he knows all that can be known, and I know the rest.   *Mark Twain*

LABOR

He who prays and labours lifts his heart to God with his hands.
St. Bernard

The labor union is an elemental response to the human instinct for group action in dealing with group problems.   *William Green*

> With fingers weary and worn,
>   With eyelids heavy and red,
> A woman sat in unwomanly rags,
>   Plying her needle and thread.   *Hood*

> Toil is the lot of all, and bitter woe
> The fate of many.   *Homer, Iliad*

Come unto me, all ye that labour and are heavy laden.   *Matthew XI, 28*

> Bowed by the weight of centuries he leans
>   Upon his hoe and gazes on the ground,
> The emptiness of ages in his face,
>   And on his back the burden of the world.   *Edwin Markham*

Share croppers, fruit pickers, cannery workers, and others drifting about in seasonal unskilled occupations, will never live the life of Riley.   *Raymond Clapper*

LAUGHTER

> And if I laugh at any mortal thing,
>   'Tis that I may not weep.   *Byron, Don Juan*

> Laugh and the world laughs with you,
>   Weep and you weep alone,

For the sad old earth must borrow its mirth,
  But has trouble enough of its own.   *Ella Wheeler Wilcox*

  On this hapless earth
There's small sincerity of mirth,
And laughter oft is but an art
To drown the outcry of the heart.   *Hartley Coleridge*

LAW

The law is a bum profession. It is utterly devoid of idealism and almost poverty stricken as to any real ideas.   *Clarence Darrow*

The law and the stage—both are a form of exhibitionism.   *Orson Welles*

A witness on the stand has some rights, or so the lawbooks say—freedom of speech is not one of them.   *Mitchell Dawson*

LAWYER

A lawyer's opinion is worth nothing unless paid for.   *English Proverb*

Most good lawyers live well, work hard, and die poor.   *Daniel Webster*

LIBERAL

A liberal is a man who is willing to spend somebody else's money. *Carter Glass*

LIBERTY

The God who gave us life, gave us liberty at the same time. *Thomas Jefferson*

LIFE

Life is a tragedy for those who feel, and a comedy for those who think.   *La Bruyere*

I wish to preach not the doctrine of ignoble ease, but the doctrine of the strenuous life.   *Theodore Roosevelt*

  Tell me not, in mournful numbers,
    Life is but an empty dream!   *Longfellow*
Why should there be such turmoil and such strife,
To spin in length this feeble line of life?   *Bacon*

When I consider Life, 'tis all a cheat.
Yet fool'd with hope, men favour the deceit;
Trust on, and think tomorrow will repay.

Tomorrow's falser than the former day. *Dryden, Aureng-Zebe*

A crust of bread and a corner to sleep in,
A minute to smile and an hour to weep in,
A pint of joy to a peck of trouble,
And never a laugh but the moans come double;
    And that is life! *Paul Laurence Dunbar*

Like leaves on trees the race of man is found,
Now green in youth, now with'ring on the ground:
Another race the following spring supplies,
They fall successive and successive rise. *Homer*

As for man his days are as grass: as a flower of the field, so he
flourisheth.
The wind passeth over it, and it is gone; and the place thereof
shall know it no more. *Psalms CIII, 15 16*

Tomorrow will I live, the fool does say;
Today itself's too late; the wise lived yesterday. *Martial*

A little pain, a little pleasure,
A little heaping up of treasure;
Then no more gazing upon the sun.
All things must end that have begun. *John Payne*

Life's but a walking shadow, a poor player
That struts and frets his hour upon the stage
And then is heard no more: it is a tale
Told by an idiot, full of sound and fury,
Signifying nothing. *Shakespeare*

    We are such stuff
As dreams are made on and our little life
Is rounded with a sleep. *Shakespeare*

And the wild regrets and the bloody sweats
    None knew so well as I:
For he who lives more lives than one
    More deaths than one must die. *Oscar Wilde*

It was not in the least likely that any life has ever been lived which was not a failure in the secret judgment of the person who lived it. *Mark Twain*

The crab, more than any of God's creatures, has formulated the perfect philosophy of life. Whenever he is confronted by a great moral crisis in life, he first makes up his mind what is right, and then goes sideways as fast as he can. *Oliver Herford*

I was sorry to have my name mentioned as one of the great authors, because they have a sad habit of dying off. Chaucer is dead, Spencer is dead, so is Milton, so is Shakespeare, and I am not feeling very well myself. *Mark Twain*

When a man stands on the verge of seventy-two you know perfectly well that he never reached that place without knowing what this life is—heartbreaking bereavement. *Mark Twain*

LONELINESS

The whole conviction of my life now rests upon the belief that loneliness, far from being a rare and curious phenomenon, peculiar to myself and to a few other solitary men, is the central and inevitable fact of human existence. *Thomas Wolfe*

LOVE

The fountains mingle with the river,
    And the rivers with the ocean;
The winds of heaven mix for ever
    With a sweet emotion;
Nothing in the world is single;
    All things, by a law divine,
In one another's being mingle—
    Why not I with thine? *Shelley*

LOYALTY

If you pick up a starving dog and make him prosperous, he will not bite you. This is the principal difference between a dog and a man. *Mark Twain*

There is no one on earth who is more patriotically devoted—verbally, at least—to the region from which he came than the American from the Southern portion of the United States. He is willing to do almost everything, in fact, for dear old Dixie, except to return permanently to her to live. *Thomas Wolfe*

LUCK

As for what you're calling hard luck—well, we made New England out of it.   That and codfish.   *Stephen Vincent Benet*

MAJORITY

Whenever you find that you are on the side of the majority, it is time to reform (or pause and reflect).   *Mark Twain*

MAN

There are times when one would like to hang the whole human race, and finish the farce.   *Mark Twain*

Man wants but little here below,
Nor wants that little long.   *Goldsmith*

Man passes away; his name perishes from record and recollection; his history is as a tale that is told, and his very monument becomes a ruin.   *Washington Irving*

God give us men.   A time like this
  demands
Strong minds, great hearts, true faith
  and ready hands!
Men whom the lust of office does not
  kill,
Men whom the spoils of office cannot
  buy,
Men who possess opinions and a will,
Men who love honor, men who cannot lie.   *J. G. Holland*

His life was gentle, and the elements
So mix'd in him that Nature might
  stand up,
And say to all the world, This was a
  man!   *Shakespeare*

Man is a reed, the weakest in nature, but he is a thinking reed.
Pascal

So God created man in his own image, in the image of God created he him.   *Genesis I, 27*

Thou hast made him a little lower than the angels.   *Psalms VIII, 5*

Man's inhumanity to man
Makes countless thousands mourn. *Burns*

Though every prospect pleases,
And only man is vile. *Reginald Heber*

Man, biologically considered, . . . is the most formidable of all the beasts of prey, and, indeed, the only one that preys systematically on its own species. *William James*

God puts something good and something lovable in every man His hands create. *Mark Twain*

It isn't the common man at all who is important; it's the uncommon man. *Lady Nancy Astor*

MARRIAGE

He that hath a wife and children hath given hostages to fortune; for they are impediments to great enterprises, either of virtue or mischief. *Bacon*

Matrimony—the high sea for which no compass has yet been invented. *Heine*

The whole world is strewn with snares, traps, gins and pitfalls for the capture of men by women. *George Bernard Shaw*

To have and to hold from this day forward, for better, for worse, for richer, for poorer, in sickness, and in health, to love and to cherish, till death do us part. *Book of Common Prayer*

What therefore God hath joined together, let not man put asunder. *Matthew XIX, 6*

It is not good that man should be alone. *Genesis II, 18*

Success in marriage is much more than finding the right person: it is a matter of being the right person. *B. R. Brickner*

The great secret of successful marriage is to treat all disasters as incidents and none of the incidents as disasters. *Harold Nicolson*

The conception of two people living together for 25 years without having a cross word suggests a lack of spirit only to be admired in sheep. *A. P. Herbert*

A man who can be a hero to his wife's relations may face the rest of the world fearlessly. *Meredith Nicholson*

MEMORY

Long, long be my heart with such memories fill'd!
Like the vase in which roses have once been distill'd:
You may break, you may shatter the vase if you will,
But the scent of the roses will hang round it still. *Thomas Moore*

Oft, in the stilly night,
Ere Slumber's chain has bound me,
Fond Memory brings the light
Of other days around me. *Thomas Moore*

MERCY

Blessed are the merciful: for they shall obtain mercy. *Matthew
V, 7*
Teach me to feel another's woe,
To hide the fault I see;
That mercy I to others show,
That mercy show to me. *Pope*

MISERY

Remembering mine affliction and my misery, the wormwood and
the gall. *Lamentations III, 9*
Preach to the storm, and reason with despair,
But tell not Misery's son that life is fair. *H. K. White*

MONEY

I cannot afford to waste my time making money. *Agassiz*

Money is honey, my little sonny,
And a rich man's joke is always funny. *T. E. Brown*
Get Place and Wealth, if possible with grace;
If not, by any means get Wealth and Place. *Pope*

Let all the learned say what they can,
'Tis ready money makes the man. *William Somerville*

MOTHER

God could not be everywhere and therefore he made mothers.
Jewish Proverb
Mother is the name for God in the lips and hearts of little children.
Thackeray

The angels . . . singing unto one another,
Can find among their burning terms of love,
None so devotional as that of "mother." *Poe*

MUSEUM

In a museum in Havana there are two skulls of Christopher Columbus, "one when he was a boy and one when he was a man." *Mark Twain*

MUSIC

Wagner's music is better than it sounds. *Bill Nye*

I can't sing. As a singist I am not a success . . . I am saddest when I sing. So are those who hear me. They are sadder even than I am. *Artemus Ward*

The man that hath no music in him-
    self,
Nor is not moved with concord of
    sweet sounds,
Is fit for treasons, stratagems and
    spoils. *Shakespeare*

Music hath charms to soothe a savage breast,
To soften rocks, or bend a knotted oak. *Congreve*

We are the music-makers,
    And we are the dreamers of dreams,
Wandering by lone sea-breakers,
    And sitting by desolate streams. *A. O'Shaughnessy*

It is not necessary to understand music; it is only necessary that one enjoy it. *Leopold Stokowski*

Classical music is the kind that we keep hopin' will turn into a tune. *Kin Hubbard*

NATION

There is no nation on earth so dangerous as a nation fully armed, and bankrupt at home. *Henry Cabot Lodge*

NATURE

There is a pleasure in the pathless woods,
There is rapture on the lonely shore,

> There is society where none intrudes,
> By the deep sea, and music in its roar;
> I love not Man the less, but Nature more,
> From these our interviews. *Byron*

> The meanest floweret of the vale,
>   The simplest note that swells the gale,
> The common sun, the air, the skies,
>   To him are opening Paradise. *Gray*

The heavens declare the glory of God, and the firmament sheweth his handywork. *Psalms XIX, 1*

. . . Nature is hitting back. Not with the old weapons—floods, plagues, holocausts. We can neutralize them. She's fighting back with strange instruments called neuroses. She's deliberately inflicting mankind with the jitters. . . . She's taking the world away from the intellectuals and giving it back to the apes. *Robert E. Sherwood*

NECESSITY

Necessity is the plea for every infringement of human freedom. It is the argument of tyrants; it is the creed of slaves. *William Pitt*

NEWSPAPER

A ration of one newspaper a day ought to be enough for anyone who still prefers to retain a little mental balance. *Clifton Fadiman*

The American country paper rests entirely upon the theory of the dignity of the human spirit. It is democracy embodied. It emphasizes the individual. *William Allen White*

OPINION

Good breeding consists in concealing how much we think of ourselves and how little we think of the other person. *Mark Twain*

OPPORTUNITY

> There is a tide in the affairs of men,
> Which, taken at the flood, leads on to fortune. *Shakespeare*

OPTIMISM

An optimist sees an opportunity in every calamity; a pessimist sees a calamity in every opportunity.

The optimist proclaims that we live in the best of all possible worlds; and the pessimist fears this is true. *Branch Cabell*

ORATORY

What the orators want in depth, they give you in length. *Montesquieu*

> I am not fond of uttering platitudes
> In stained-glass attitudes. *W. S. Gilbert*

PAIN

> Nothing begins, and nothing ends,
>   That is not paid with moan;
> For we are born in other's pain,
>   And perish in our own. *Francis Thompson*

PEACE

I am a man of peace.   God knows how I love peace; but I hope I shall never be such a coward as to mistake oppression for peace. *Kossuth*

It must be a peace without victory.   Only a peace between equals can last; only a peace, the very principle of which is equality, and a common participation in a common benefit. *Woodrow Wilson*

They shall beat their swords into ploughshares, and their spears into pruning-hooks: nation shall not lift sword against nation, neither shall they learn war any more. *Isaiah II, 4*

> Till the war-drum throbb'd no longer and
>   the battle-flags were furl'd
> In the Parliament of man, the Federation
>   of the world. *Tennyson*

POLITICIAN

The statesman shears the sheep, the politician skins them. *Austin O'Malley*

As long as I count the votes what are you going to do about it? Say. *William M. Tweed*

POVERTY

There are only two families in the world, the Haves and the Have Nots. *Cervantes*

The child was diseased at birth, stricken with a hereditary ill that only the most vital men are able to shake off.   I mean poverty—the most deadly and prevalent of all diseases. *Eugene O'Neill*

POWER

Power will intoxicate the best hearts, as wine the strongest heads. No man is wise enough, nor good enough to be trusted with unlimited power. *Colton*

Lust of power is the most flagrant of all the passions. *Tacitus*

Grim experience taught men that power is poisonous to its possessors; that no dynasty and no class can exclusively control the engines of power without ultimately confusing their private interest with the public well-being. *Harold J. Laski*

PRAYER

A prayer, in its simplest definition, is merely a wish turned heavenward. *Phillips Brooks*

Pray as if everything depended on God, and work as if everything dependent upon man. *Archbishop Francis J. Spellman*

He prayeth best who loveth best
    All things both great and small;
For the dear God, who loveth us,
    He made and loveth all. *S. T. Coleridge*

When the last sea is sailed and the last shallow charted,
    When the last field is reaped and the last harvest
        stored,
When the last fire is out and the last guest departed,
    Grant the last prayer that I shall pray, Be good to me,
        O Lord. *Masefield*

PRIDE

Oh, why should the spirit of mortal be proud?
Like a swift-fleeting meteor, a fast-flung cloud,
A flash of the lightning, a break of the wave,
He passeth from life to his rest in the grave. *William Knox*

Of all the causes which conspire to blind
Man's erring judgment, and misguide the mind,
What the weak head with strongest bias rules,
Is Pride, the never-failing vice of fools. *Pope*

PRODUCTION

A limitation on the production of the individual is pure waste.
Louis D. Brandeis

PROGRESS

My little grandson goes to (school). The other day he wrote a
letter to his aunt, up in Cincinnati. He has a uncle way up in New
York, but he can't write that far yet. *Mark Twain*

REFORM

At twenty a man is full of fight and hope. He wants to reform the
world. When he's seventy he still wants to reform the world, but
he knows he can't. *Clarence S. Darrow*

We are reformers in Spring and Summer; in Autumn and Winter
we stand by the old; reformers in the morning, conservers at night.
Emerson

Reform must come from within, not from without. You cannot
legislate for virtue. *James Cardinal Gibbons*

RELIGION

Men will wrangle for religion; write for it; fight for it; die for it;
anything but—live for it. *Colton*
If men are so wicked with religion, what would they be without it?
Franklin

REPUBLIC

Republics end through luxury; monarchies through poverty.
Montesquieu

REPUTATION

Who steals my purse steals trash; . . .
But he that filches from me my good name
Robs me of that which not enriches him,
And makes me poor indeed. *Shakespeare*

RICH

People who are hard, grasping . . . and always ready to take advantage of their neighbors, become very rich. . . . *G. B. Shaw*

SCANDAL

Assail'd by scandal and the tongue of strife,
His only answer was, a blameless life. *Cowper*

Have you heard of the terrible family They,
And the dreadful venomous things They say?
Why, half of the gossip under the sun,
If you trace it back, you will find begun
    In that wretched House of They. *Ella Wheeler Wilcox*

SILENCE

He had occasional flashes of silence, that made his conversation perfectly delightful. *Sydney Smith*

He knew the precise psychological moment when to say nothing. *Oscar Wilde*

SOLITUDE

Alone, alone, all, all alone,
Alone on a wide wide sea! *S. T. Coleridge*

I feel like one who treads alone
    Some banquet-hall deserted,
Whose lights are fled, whose garlands dead,
    And all but he departed! *Thomas Moore*

SPEECH

A sophistical rhetorician, inebriated with the exuberance of his own verbosity. *Disraeli*

Rhetoric is the art of ruling the minds of men. *Plato*

Blessed is the man who, having nothing to say, abstains from giving us wordy evidence of the fact. *George Eliot*

And 'tis remarkable that they
Talk most who have the least to say. *Prior*

While the right to talk may be the beginning of freedom, the necessity of listening is what makes the right important. *Walter Lippmann*

SUCCESS

All you need in this life is ignorance and confidence, and then Success is sure. *Mark Twain*

There are but two ways of rising in the world: either by one's own industry or profiting by the foolishness of others. *La Bruyere*

If you wish in this world to advance,
Your merits you're bound to enhance;
    You must stir it and stump it,
    And blow your own trumpet,
Or trust me, you haven't a chance. *W. S. Gilbert*

Success may go to one's head, but the stomach is where it gits in its worst work. *Kin Hubbard*

TALENT

If a man has a talent and cannot use it, he has failed. If he has a talent and uses only half of it, he has partly failed. If he has a talent and learns somehow to use the whole of it, he has gloriously succeeded, and won a satisfaction and a triumph few men ever know. *Thomas Wolfe*

TEACHER

The teacher is like the candle which lights others in consuming itself. *Ruffini*

TEARS

"I weep for you," the Walrus said:
    "I deeply sympathize."
With sobs and tears he sorted out
    Those of the largest size,
Holding his pocket-handkerchief
    Before his streaming eyes. *Lewis Carroll*

THEATRE

The American professional theatre is today at once the richest theatre in the world, and the poorest. Financially, it reaches to the stars; culturally, with exceptions so small as to be negligible, it reaches to the drains. *George Jean Nathan*

TIME

Backward, turn backward, O Time, in your flight,
Make me a child again just for to-night!   *Elizabeth A. Allen*

Gather ye Rose-buds while ye may,
  Old Time is still aflying:
And this same flower that smiles today,
  Tomorrow will be dying.   *Herrick*

To every thing there is a season, and a time to every purpose under
the heaven: A time to be born, and a time to die; a time to plant,
and a time to pluck up that which is planted. . . .   *Ecclesiastes
III, 1–8*

TOASTS

Here's a sigh to those who love me,
  And a smile to those who hate;
And whatever sky's above me,
  Here's a heart for every fate.   *Byron*

Here's to your good health, and your family's good health, and
may you all live long and prosper.   *Irving*

Here is a toast that I want to give
  To a fellow I'll never know;
To the fellow who's going to take my
    place
  When it's time for me to go.   *Louis E. Thayer*

TOWN

A hick town is one where there is no place to go where you
shouldn't be. . . .   *Alexander Woollcott*

TRAVEL

In America there are two classes of travel—first class and with
children.   *Robert Benchley*

TRUST

God's in his Heaven—
All's right with the world!   *R. Browning*

Who brought me hither
Will bring me hence; no other guide I seek.   *Milton*

TRUTH

Truth crushed to earth shall rise
  again:
Th' eternal years of God are hers;
But Error, wounded, writhes in pain,
  And dies among his worshippers. *Bryant*

Time is precious, but truth is more precious than time. *Disraeli*

To thine own self be true,
And it must follow, as the night the
  day,
Thou canst not then be false to any
  man. *Shakespeare*

God offers to every mind its choice between truth and repose.
Take which you please,—you can never have both. *Emerson*

I speak truth, not so much as I would, but as much as I dare; and
I dare a little more as I grow older. *Montaigne*

Truth forever on the scaffold,
Wrong forever on the throne. *J. R. Lowell*

When Mark Twain was introduced as the man who said, "When
in doubt, tell the truth," he replied that he had invented that maxim
for others, but that when in doubt himself, he used more sagacity.

VACATION

With me, a change of trouble is as good as a vacation. *David
Lloyd George*

VANITY

Lo, all our pomp of yesterday
Is one with Ninevah and Tyre! *Kipling*

WAR

What millions died—that Caesar might be great! *Campbell*

What distinguishes war is, not that man is slain, but that he is slain,
spoiled, crushed by the cruelty, the injustice, the treachery, the
murderous hand of man. *William Ellery Channing*

There is no such thing as an inevitable war.   If war comes it will be from failure of human wisdom.   *Bonar Law, Speech before World War I*

War is the greatest plague that can afflict humanity; it destroys religion, it destroys states, it destroys families.   Any scourge is preferable to it.   *Martin Luther*

They wrote in the old days that it is sweet and fitting to die for one's country.   But in modern war there is nothing sweet nor fitting in your dying.   You will die like a dog for no good reason.   *Ernest Hemingway*

There's many a boy here today who looks on war as all glory, but, boys, it is all hell.   *Gen. William T. Sherman*

> The tumult and the shouting dies,
> The captains and the kings depart.   *Kipling*

> Doughboys were paid a whole dollar a day
> and received free burial under the clay.
> And movie heroes are paid even more
> shooting one another in a Hollywood war.   *Kreymborg*

War hath no fury like a non-combatant.   *C. E. Montague*

The atomic bomb may help to decide a future war; like any other weapon it solves none of the problems which make for war.   *Hans Kohn*

As a rule a man does not remember his standards as a humanitarian when he stands behind a machine gun, or his standards as a Christian when he has to drop bombs from the air.   *Hans Speier*

WINTER

I met (an old man) out in Iowa who had come up from Arkansas. I asked him whether he had experienced much cold during the preceding winter, and he exclaimed, "Cold!   If the thermometer had been an inch longer we'd all have frozen to death!"   *Mark Twain*

WISDOM

The wisdom of this world is foolishness with God.   *I Corinthians III, 19*

> A sadder and wiser man,
> He rose the morrow morn.   *S. T. Coleridge*

WIVES

Us country women make good wives.   No matter what happens, we've seen worse.   *Keith Jennison*

WOMAN

Grace was in all her steps, heaven
  in her eye,
In every gesture dignity and love.   *Milton*

Woman's dearest delight is to wound Man's self-conceit, though Man's dearest delight is to gratify hers.   *George Bernard Shaw*

There is no such thing as romance in our day, women have become too brilliant; nothing spoils a romance so much as a sense of humor in the woman.   *Wilde*

I am very fond of the company of ladies; I like their beauty, I like their delicacy, I like their vivacity, and I like their silence.   *Samuel Johnson*

I expect that woman will be the last thing civilized by man. *George Meredith*

Women are wiser than men because they know less and understand more.   *James Stephens*

WORK

And only the Master shall praise us, and only the Master
  shall blame;
And no one shall work for money, and no one shall work
  for fame;
But each for the joy of the working, and each, in his
  separate star,
Shall draw the Things as he sees It, for the God of Things
  as They Are!   *Kipling*

Each morning sees some task begun,
  Each evening sees it close;
Something attempted, something done,
  Has earned a night's repose.   *Longfellow*

WORLD

This world is all a fleeting show,
  For man's illusion given;
The smiles of joy, the tears of woe,
Deceitful shine, deceitful flow,—
  There's nothing true but Heaven. *Moore*

Why, then the world's mine oyster,
  Which I with sword will open. *Shakespeare*

The world is so full of a number of things,
I'm sure we should all be as happy as kings. *R. L. Stevenson*

. . . this world is a comedy to those that think, a tragedy to those that feel . . . *Horace Walpole*

Twenty thousand years ago, the family was the social unit. Now the social unit has become the world, in which it may truthfully be said that each person's welfare affects that of every other. *Dr. A. H. Compton*

7 ❖❖❖

Humorous Stories

TACT

A meek little man in a restaurant timidly touched the arm of a man putting on an overcoat. "Excuse me," he said, "but do you happen to be Mr. Smith of Newport?"

"No, I'm not!" the man answered impatiently.

"Oh—er—well," stammered the first man, "you see, I am, and that's his overcoat you're putting on."

THEY'RE RELATED

An Alfred Hitchcock fan letter and reply: "Dear Mr. Hitchcock: My name is Hitchcock, and I wonder if we could possibly be related. I've been told that my maternal grandfather bragged that he was a horse thief. B.L.H."

"Mine would never admit it. Apparently we are not kin. A.H."

OLD NEWS

"Well, Father," the young man told the priest, "Susie and I are going to be married. How's that for news?"

"You just finding that out?"

THE OLD FOLKS ALSO ARE

Robert Q. Lewis says the kids in Texas are just like the kids any place in America: They love to get out in the back yard and play with piles of money.

A SAD FACT

Marriage vows might be a trifle more accurate if the phrase were changed to read, "Until DEBT do us part."

SAD STORY

Alec Templeton, the sightless pianist, collects music boxes. He has written a book about how he got them and their uses. Included in the volume is this bit of verse:

I'm an old music box from Chicago,
And I happen to play Handel's "Largo,"
    But now, Mercy me,
    I'm atop a TV,
So I listen each week to Wells Fargo.

CRITICS

A group of critics got together and started their own TV be-rating service.

WISER

Insurance salesman to prospect: "Yes, I know you told me yesterday that you weren't interested in buying a policy. But I thought that now, since you're older, you might be wiser."

X PENSIVE

After paying his doctor's bill, Walter Slezak says he knows what the x in X-ray stands for—expensive!

SERVICE

It was after midnight when the department store manager's phone rang. "This is Mrs. James Smith," said the voice, "one of your customers. I want to tell you about the hat I bought at your store the other day. It's lovely. I like it better than any hat I ever had."

The sleepy, tired manager was a little exasperated. "That's fine," he said, "but why did you call me up just now to tell me?"

"Because," said Mrs. Smith sweetly, "your truck just delivered it."

ARE THEY THAT SMALL?

Apartment house sign: "No baby carriages or foreign cars in the lobby."

THEY WANT IT BOTH WAYS

Jerome D. Fenton, general counsel of the National Labor Relations board, recently addressed a law student group and made a point with the following verse, the author of which he said he could not trace:

"Men never know exactly what is right;
So, caught between a promise and a doubt,
They first make windows to let in the light,
And then make curtains to shut it out."

A STRAIGHT FORWARD EVASION

Rep. Brooks Hays (D., Ark.) recalls the time he ran for governor 35 years ago, when the Scopes evolution trial in Tennessee was getting headlines. Hays was making a campaign speech in Flat Rock, Ark., about the proposed new state income tax.

A heckler stopped him and inquired: "Let's skip all that stuff, young fella. What we want to know is—how do you stand on evolution?"

Hays says he doesn't remember his answer, but a spectator commented: "If that boy is as good a two-stepper as he is a side-stepper, he shore will be popular at the ladies' social next Saturday night."

THEY'RE SO HANDY

Quin Ryan says another nice thing about one of those little cars is: If you flood its carburetor you can just toss the car over your shoulder and burp it.

THE LESSON HE LEARNED

Art Linkletter asked a member of his Kids panel what he had learned from reading nursery rimes.

"I liked Jack and Jill," one boy confessed, "and it taught me never to go up a hill with a girl with a pail."

SMART BOY

Woman to her 4-year-old grandson: "I can't kiss you with that dirty face."

"That," said the 4-year-old, "is what I figured."

NONSENSE

Hunter: "While wandering around the native village, I spotted a leopard."

Listener: "Nonsense! They come that way."

SMART GUY

"Why are you eating that banana with the skin on?"

"Why should I peel it? I know what's inside."

THEY CERTAINLY DO

Youngsters do brighten up a home. Whoever saw one of them turn off electric lights?

IT COULD BE

The doctor rushed out of his study. "I must go at once!" he shouted.

"Why, dad," asked his daughter, "what's the matter?"

"I've just had a message that this man can't live without me," gasped the doctor.

His daughter heaved a sigh of relief. "Just a moment," she said quietly. "I think that call was for me."

IS THAT THE WAY WE LOOK?

Bob Hope told what happened to him while he was busily practicing his swing during a golf lesson. The pro came over to him and asked: "What other imitations do you do besides the helicopter?"

JUST RESTING

George Gobel: "For some people life begins at 40, but most of us just spend that year resting up from being 39."

A SURE SUCCESS

An office boy noticed two women with the boss.

Office boy: "Who were those two girls?"

Boss: "Well, one was my wife and the other was Grace Kelly."

Office boy: "Which one was Grace Kelly?"

The Boss took a dollar out of his pocket and gave it to the boy.

Office boy: "What's this for?"

Boss: "Nothing. I just want you to remember, when you get to be president, that I once loaned you money."

WE THINK WE ATE THERE

Quin Ryan spotted this sign in a San Francisco restaurant: "Eat here once and you'll never live to regret it."

QUALITIES FOR SUCCESS

"Integrity and wisdom are essential to success in every business," said the boss to a new employe. "By integrity I mean that when you promise a customer something, you must keep that promise even if you lose money."

"And what is wisdom?" asked the new man.

"Don't make such fool promises."

THE FISH THINK SO

A little boy was fishing when a man came along.

"Is that bait any good?" he asked.

"I don't think so, but the fish do," answered the little boy.

THE WAY YOU FEEL SOME DAYS

Wife: "Don't you think it's about time we took Junior to the Zoo?"

Husband: "Why? If they want him bad enough, they'll come after him."

CHANGING TIMES

Lisa Kirk says times have indeed changed: "The man who used to bring home the bacon now brings home the TV dinners."

LINE'S BUSY

Boss to Secretary: "I've got to call home. Send my daughter a telegram to get off the phone."

HE WENT DOWN

Mother: "How did you do in your exams today, Billy?"

Billy: "I did what Washington did."

Mother: "What was that?"

Billy: "I went down in history."

HE UNDERSTANDS NOW

A soldier who lost his rifle was lectured by his captain and told he would have to pay for it. "Sir," gulped the soldier, "suppose I lost a tank? Surely I wouldn't have to pay for it."

"Yes, you would, if it took you the rest of your Army life."

"Oh well," said the soldier, "now I know why a captain goes down with his ship."

FOR HUSBANDS

Mrs. Walter Slezak told her husband: "I'm ready now. I thought you were dressed and waiting."

"I was," said Slezak, "but now you'll have to wait while I shave again."

A GOOD REASON

When little Jimmy returned from summer camp, his parents asked him if he had been homesick.

"Not me," replied the youngster. "Some of the kids were—the ones that had dogs."

HE HAD EXPERIENCE

First little boy (in hospital ward): "Are you medical or surgical?"

Second little boy: "I don't know—what does that mean?"

First little boy (disgusted): "Were you sick when you came or did they make you sick after you got here?"

FREEDOM

Allen Dulles, head of the Central Intelligence Agency, which dedicated its new 40 million dollar headquarters this week, tells of Jozef Rapacki, a minor official in the Polish ministry of trade who frequently was sent on missions to Russia and various satellite nations. On each trip he would send a postcard to a pal in his Warsaw office, Stephan. These were similar in pattern reading:

"Greetings from free Moscow."

"Having a wonderful time in free Prague."

"Best wishes from free Budapest."

One day Rapacki left unexpectedly. He did not tell Stephan of his departure. Days passed and Stephan began to worry. He feared arrest and a slave labor camp for his friend.

Finally, he got a card from New York which read:

"Greetings from free Jozef."

THE LETTER SAID A GREAT DEAL

A boy was sent by his doting parents to a big boarding school. He had been strictly ordered to write home regularly and tell them all about himself.

At the end of a week, his first letter arrived.

"There are 370 boys here," he wrote. "I wish there were 369."

HOW TO WIN FRIENDS

Psychiatrist: "Would you mind repeating what you just said."

Patient: "I said for some reason or other no one likes me. Why don't you listen, you fathead?"

THOUGHTFUL

A husband bought his wife a new summer outfit—a package of seeds and a rake!

DON'T WORRY

A hitch hiker was picked up by a big expensive car, driven by a wealthy Texan. Seeing a pair of horn-rimmed glasses on the seat between them, the hitch hiker remarked, "Shouldn't you be wearing your glasses while driving, sir?"

"Don't you give it no mind, son," said the Texan. "It's no trouble this way. The whole windshield is ground to my prescription."

COMPLETE EXAMINATION

Bob Hope reports that he had a complete physical checkup. "The doctor was real thoro," quipped Hope. "First thing he did was to examine my wallet."

FOOD

We have more food per person than any other country in the world. And more diets to keep us from eating it.

NO USE

The little first-grader came home from his first day of school.

"Ain't going to go to school tomorrow, Mom," he announced.

"Why not, dear?" his mother asked.

"Well, I can't read and I can't write, and the teacher won't let me talk, so what's the use?"

HE KNEW ONE

The minister asked for anyone who knew a perfect person to stand up. A meek looking fellow in the back stood. "Do you really know a perfect person?" the minister asked.

"Yes sir, I do," answered the little man.

"Won't you please tell the congregation who this rare perfect person is?" pursued the minister.

"Yes sir. It was my wife's first husband."

R U SATISFIED?

Bobby had a hard time pronouncing the letter "r," so his teacher gave him a sentence to learn: "Robert gave Richard a rap in the ribs for roasting the rabbit so rare."

A few days later she asked Bobby to repeat the sentence. He said: "Bob gave Dick a poke in the side for not cooking the bunny enough."

BUDGET HELP

A family budget is a good way to save money. By the time you figure it up every night, it's too late to go anywhere.

HE IS REALLY WORRIED

A businessman was extremely concerned over declining income. An acquaintance told him he looked worried.

"You're right," the man admitted. "I'm booked solid on worries on my mind that if anything occurs today it'll be 10 days before I can get around to worrying about it!"

WORKING FOR HIS COUNTRY

President Eisenhower recently received a letter from the heart of a 12 year old school boy. It read:

"Dear Mr. President: I would like to know if the law makes school teachers get drafted in the service. If they do, I know one who has not been. His name is James Smith. Thank You."

OSCAR WILDE'S IDEA

Oscar Wilde describes fox hunters as "the unspeakable chasing the inedible."

IT'S EASY

Discussing problems concerning teenagers, one woman asked her neighbor, "Is your son hard to get out of bed in the morning?" "No," replied the other, "I just open the door and throw the cat on his bed." The neighbor was puzzled. "How," she asked, "does that waken him?" Replied the other, "He sleeps with the dog."

FOREIGN AID

Walter Slezak's observation: "Not many Americans have been around the world but their money sure has."

OUR FISHER FRIENDS HAVE LONG ARMS

"The ability to sin differs among people," says one of our friends. "For example, a short-armed fisherman isn't as big a liar as a long-armed one."

THIS IS OUR EXPERIENCE

A man with a pair of glasses in need of minor adjustment dropped in at a store featuring the sign, "Glasses Repaired While You Wait." "You can call for these on Tuesday," he was told.

"But," protested the man, "how about your sign, 'Repairs While You Wait'?"

"Well," said the shopkeeper with unanswerable logic, "you'll be waiting, won't you?"

HE REALLY KNEW CATS

A grammar school boy handed in this composition on "Cats":

"Cats that's meant for little boys to maul and tease is called Maultease cats. Some cats is rekernized by how quiet their pur is and these is Pursian cats. Cats what has bad tempers is named Angora cats. And cats with deep feelings is called Felines. I don't like cats."

ANOTHER COMMANDMENT

When motorists ignored "No parking" signs put on the private lot of a minister of one church, he put up a placard reading "Thou Shalt Not Park." It worked. *Oren Arnold*

DIFFERENT THEN

The major looked up from his desk at the private first class and snapped:

"Now really, I ask you, in civilian life would you come to me with a puny complaint like this?"

"No, sir," was the reply, "I'd send for you."

REAL ABILITY NEEDED

Personnel manager to applicant: "What we're after is a man of vision; a man with drive, determination, fire; a man who never quits; a man who can inspire others; a man who can pull the company's bowling team out of last place!"

SHORT SPEECH

A banquet honoring Orville and Wilbur Wright, the late aviation pioneers, called to mind an occasion when the two famed brothers were guests at a testimonial dinner for them. Both were extremely shy. The toastmaster called on Wilbur to make a speech. Wilbur rose to his feet only long enough to stammer: "There must be a mistake. I think you want my brother." Wilbur quickly sat down and the toastmaster called upon Orville, who replied: "Wilbur just made the speech."

A HOT TIP

"Fortunes," said Baron Rothschild, "are made by buying low and selling too soon."

REST IN PEACE?

In the "hell hath no fury like a woman scorned" department, the latest example concerns a widow who learned when her late husband's will was read that he had left the bulk of his fortune to a pet charity. Enraged, she rushed to the stone-cutter from whom she had ordered a tombstone for her spouse's grave and ordered him to change the inscription.

"Sorry, lady," was the reply. "You ordered 'Rest in Peace' and that's what I inscribed. I can't change it now."

"Very well," the widow said grimly. "Just add the line 'Until We Meet Again.' "

CAME CLOSE

William E. Jenner, former member of the Senate from Indiana, is not averse to telling a joke on that august body now and then. He relates that a Washington business man instructed his switchboard operator, who was new on the job, to get him the local gas company. The operator dialed the wrong number and when a voice answered, asked if this were the gas company.

"I should say not," was the stuffy reply.   "This is senator whoozis speaking."

"Well," said the operator with a giggle, "I didn't miss it too far did I?"

ADVICE

Sage advice from George Gobel: "Never put off until tomorrow what you can do today—for tomorrow's gonna be bad enough as it is."

TOO BAD

Isn't it a shame that future generations can't be here to see all the wonderful things we're doing with their money?

SMILE WHEN YOU SAY THAT

The retirement of John L. Lewis as head of the United Mine Workers revived scores of stories about his salty exchanges with prominent figures.   When Lewis was suggested in 1950 to President Truman as ambassador to Russia, Truman said he wouldn't appoint Lewis dog catcher.

"The President could ill afford to have more brains in the dog department than in the state department," snapped Lewis.

ANY OTHER QUESTION?

An American tourist in London was caught in one of that city's famous fogs.   Hearing footsteps, he called out, "Could you please tell me where I'm going?"

"Into the canal," replied the unhappy voice from the mist.   "I'm just coming out."

THOUGHTFUL

Mother and Father (alarmed when their tot opened the door on their return after an evening out): "What are you doing opening the door?"

Tiny Tot: "Shhh!   I was watching for you.   The baby sitter's asleep and I didn't want you to ring the doorbell."

HE WILL

A clergyman received a phone call from the local income tax man inquiring about a $535 contribution listed as having been paid his church by a parishioner,

"Did he make this donation?" the tax man asked.

The clergyman hesitated, then replied:

"He will, he will."

CREDIT

Alex Dreier says: "This country is rapidly proving to be a place with two cars in every garage—neither of them paid for."

WRONG IDENTITY

"Say, Bill, I think I saw your wife downtown today. She was trying to park between two trucks."

"Did she make it?"

"Yes."

"Then it wasn't my wife."

THE SPACE AGE

Jack Herbert tells about the Martian who landed on earth and saw a guy carrying a portable TV set. The Martian stopped the man and asked indignantly: "How do you expect that kid to learn to walk if you keep carrying him all the time?"

GREAT CHANGE

You never realize how much the human voice can change till a woman stops arguing with her husband and answers the telephone.

VOCABULARY

Dr. You Chan Yang, Korean ambassador to the United States, addressed the girls nation of the American Legion for the third consecutive year. He began:

"I suspect that this year, as in previous years, I, too, shall learn from you. The last time I spoke at girls nation, I was struggling with the meanings of the teenage vocabulary of last year. Now will you help me 'dig' the new vocabulary? I don't want to be accused of having 'smog in the noggin' and I don't want to 'bug you.' Is this 'Kookie'?"

NO FRIENDS

Reporter: "Now that you are wealthy are you ever bothered by the friends you had when you were poor?"

Man of Wealth: "I never had any friends when I was poor."

NEXT QUESTION

Wife: "It says here that Minerva was the goddess of wisdom."
Husband: "To whom was she married?"
Wife: "She was the goddess of wisdom; she didn't get married."

PROGRESS

There, little deficit, don't you cry—
You'll be a bond issue bye and bye!

DIOGENES TODAY

Diogenes returned from his search for an honest man.
"Any luck?" a friend asked.
"Fair," replied Doig, "I still have my lantern."

IN MOST OFFICES

No one goes before his time, unless, of course, the boss leaves early.

CONVINCING

Representative Sidney R. Yates is aware that a member of Congress is sure to be criticized no matter which way he votes, but he consoles himself over the possibility that he will be at least as successful as the minister who returned wearily home to explain to his wife that he had attempted to persuade his congregation that it was the duty of the rich to help the poor.
"And," asked his wife, "did you convince them?"
"I was half successful," said the minister. "I convinced the poor."

GOOD ADVICE

Be kind to people until you make your first million. After that people will be nice to you.

NOT SO MANY

When Neil H. McElroy was appointed Secretary of Defense, he got the news in Cincinnati just as he and his wife were preparing to attend a formal dinner. McElroy stood before a mirror adjusting his black tie.
"Dear," he said to his wife, "how many really great men are there in the world today?"
"One less than you think," she answered brightly.

THAT WILL LEARN HIM

A little boy was pestering an air line stewardess. Finally, in desperation, she opened a door and said: "All right, go out and play."

PUNISHMENT

Sam Levenson tells the one about the prisoner who was only permitted to watch daytime TV and when asked what he thought of it replied: "I thought it was part of the punishment."

SIMPLE

A fellow was walking his long-haired dachshund and he met a friend who said, "What a funny animal! How do you tell his head from his tail?"

"It's very simple," the dog owner replied. "You pull its tail and if it bites you, you know it was his head."

THE REASON

The TV announcer, "And now a word from our sponsor who makes this program impossible."

WISH YOU WERE HERE

The inmate of a state prison penned a postcard to the district attorney who put him there. It read: "Having a dull time. Wish you were here."

STRANGE

A beatnik went to a psychiatrist.

"There's something wrong with me," he told the doctor, "I actually want to bathe and shave."

WE'VE WONDERED

Old politicians never die—they just run once too often.

IT HAPPENS OCCASIONALLY

The first mate of the ship, who was inclined to drink too much, happened to see in the ship's log one day this unfortunate item: "The mate was drunk today." No matter how he pleaded with the captain to change the sentence, the head man clung steadfastly to his resolve to let the record stand.

Sometime later it became the mate's duty to note the days' happenings in the log.   Remembering the permanent wrong done him a few pages back, the mate wrote: "The Captain was sober today."

IT'LL

You try to write—no ink will trickle.   Put pen in pocket, and instantly it'll.

EXPERIENCE

Don McNeill: "Experience may be the best teacher but the one I had in grammar school was prettier."

Again: "One small jack can lift a car, but it takes a lot of jack to keep it up."

TV REPAIR

TV is really educational: Just think of all the repair men's children it's putting thru college.

NO PLACE FOR NEUTRALS

"Are you a friend of the bride or the groom?" asked the usher of a guest at a formal church wedding.

"I'm a friend of both," the lady replied.

Said the usher: "I'm sorry, Madam, but you'll just have to choose a side.   You see, I haven't any instructions on where to seat neutrals."

HE WASN'T HELPED

Church was over, and the woman asked her husband if he had noticed the mink stole on the lady just in front of him.   The man said no, he feared he had dozed off.   "Well, my stars!" exclaimed his wife.   "A lot of good the service did you!"

NO REASON TO COMPLAIN

A man who had been married ten years consulted a marriage counsellor.   "When I was first married," he said, "I was happy.   I'd come home from a hard day at the store and my little dog would race around barking, while my wife would bring me my slippers.   Now, after all these years, everything's changed.   When I come home, my dog brings me my slippers and my wife barks at me."

"Well, I don't know what you're complaining about," said the counsellor.   "You're still getting the same service."

TOO MUCH TV

The cowboy movie star was lounging around on location in six-guns and belt when he was asked by a 5-year-old, "You a good man or a bad 'un?"

The cowboy answered, "Bad 'un."

The youngster said, "Boy, oh, boy!   I'd run you in, but I gotta go home for my nap."

SOUNDS REASONABLE

The motorist was filling in an accident report.   "I was backing out of a parking space, and by the time I backed out far enough to see what was coming it already had!"

JUST ONCE

The best way to remember your wife's birthday is to forget it once.

SMALL REPAIR

A Texan was visiting in Canada, and his host was showing him the sights.   But nothing was as big and fine as they have it in Texas. Finally the Canadian showed him Niagara Falls.   "You don't have anything like *that* in Texas, do you?"

"No, but we have a plumber down there who could fix that leak."

ALL OF US

A Hollywood actress was asked, "Are you living within your income?"

"No," she replied, "it's all I can do to live within my credit."

EXPERIENCE

A man learns from experience: That's how he recognizes a mistake when he makes it again.

DIET

Young mother (telling a visitor about her baby): "He is eating solids now—keys, bits of newspapers, pencils."

LET ME OUT OF HERE

The four-year-old and his father were in the rear of a crowded elevator.   A kindly elderly lady said to the father, "Aren't you afraid your little boy will be crushed?"

"Not at all," he answered, "he bites."

SON-UP TO SON-DOWN

A housewife, having finally tucked her small boy into bed after an unusually trying day, sighed, "Well, I've worked today from son-up to son-down."

GOOD JOB

A floorwalker tired of his job, gave it up and joined the police force. Several months later a friend asked him how he liked being a policeman.

"Well," he replied, "the pay and hours are only fair, but one thing I like—the customer is always wrong."

CLEAN EXPLANATION

A private and a sergeant were charged with striking an officer.

The sergeant told how the colonel, while inspecting the troops, had stepped on his sore foot.

"It was blind instinct," said the sergeant. "I threw up my guard, like anyone would do, and let him have it before I realized what was happening. It was an accident, and I'm sorry."

Then the private was requested to give his explanation. "Well, you see, sir," he replied, "when I saw the sergeant strike the colonel, I thought the war was over."

PECULIAR CIRCUMSTANCES

Heard about a coroner's jury that had trouble determining the cause of death. Finally it wrote this memorable verdict: "An act of God under very suspicious circumstances." *Oren Arnold*

WHAT WOULD YOU DO?

It was the usual muddy day in the country. Our first-grade teacher, Miss Brown, had just finished putting on the 18th pair of rubbers on the 18th pair of feet and quickly prepared to finish the last pair before lunch. The next pair of rubbers was for Johnny Smith, a quiet boy, who, as soon as the battle to get his rubbers on was won, looked blandly up into his teacher's face and said: "They aren't mine." Miss Brown groaned, but with grim gentleness removed the rubbers and straightened her aching back. Whereupon Johnny continued: "They're my brother's, but Mommy said I could wear them today."

SPACE PHOTOGRAPHY

Johnny Carson tells about the Air Force's sending up a camera 100 miles above the earth to take a picture. And then it didn't turn out well: Somebody moved!

TOGETHERNESS

Sam Levenson: "Family togetherness is beautiful. I was raised where there was nothing but togetherness. Eight kids in one room; man, that's togetherness."

COUNTRY AND CITY

Dave Garroway explains the difference between city and country living as seen by the farmer: "In the country you go to bed all in and get up feeling fine; in the city you go to bed feeling fine and wake up all in."

MORE THAN HE THOUGHT

Al Martino, the singer, tells about a guy who took out $20,000 insurance on his furniture and then asked what he could get if it was all destroyed by fire.

"Twenty years," the agent replied coldly.

SNAP ME OUT

Richard Helms, assistant director of the Central Intelligence Agency, tells the story of the communist hypnotist who put on a performance in East Germany. Selecting a meek looking worker from the audience, he convinced the subject that he was suffering, in turn, from thirst in the Sahara and shivering with cold in the Arctic. There was great applause.

Then the hypnotist told his subject:

"The worst thing of all has now happened to you. You have fled the protection of the communist people's republic and are in West Berlin. You are hungry, penniless, ground down under capitalism—"

"Snap me out of this one," interrupted the subject, his eyes still closed, "and I'll break your neck!"

NO BALL GAME

The new preacher looked coldly at Deacon Smith and said he had heard that the deacon went to a ball game instead of to church last

Sunday. "That's a lie!" the shocked deacon cried. "And I've got the fish to prove it."

OR WITH NO COFFEE

Doctor: "You should not give your husband strong coffee. It excites him."

Wife: "You should see how excited he gets when I give him weak coffee."

PROMOTED

A department store received the following letter from a couple to whom its billing department had written, requesting payment of a long overdue bill:

"Gentlemen: We have received your letter of the 23rd and would like you to know we have divided our creditors into three groups:

1. Those who will be paid promptly.
2. Those who will be paid sometime.
3. Those who will never be paid.

You will be happy to know that because of the friendly tone of your letter, we have promoted you from Group 3 to Group 2."

TRUE EVERYWHERE?

Young son: "Do you know, Dad, I read that in some parts of Africa a man doesn't know his wife until he marries her?"

Dad: "That happens in most countries, son."

TOO SMART

Two modern youngsters were discussing the subject of piggy banks.

"I think it's childish to save money that way," little Mary said.

"I do, too," Annie replied. "And I believe also that it encourages children to become misers."

"And that's not the worst of it," Mary exclaimed. "It turns parents into bank robbers."

WHAT DO YOU THINK?

Johnny's report cards had been far from satisfactory. One day one arrived a little worse even than those which had preceded it. Johnny's father announced that it would be a subject for discussion after dinner.

When the time came, the father appeared with the card in hand and, after reviewing it once more, said, "Well, Johnny, how do you account for such a miserable showing in your school-work?"

"I'm sure I don't know," answered Johnny. "What do you think it is? Heredity or environment?"

ADVICE

George Gobel: "Never look a gift horse in the mouth unless, of course, you happen to be a horse dentist."

THE GOVERNMENT DEFICIT

Accountant, to fellow employee: "For a minute this deficit had me worried. I forgot that I was working for the Government."

NOT IN WASHINGTON

Gen. Maxwell Taylor, retired as army chief of staff, tells of seeing a rating report on an officer which said:
"This officer is often confused when given conflicting orders."
Gen. Taylor wrote on the report: "Not suited for duty in Washington."

MORE THAN SATISFIED

Personnel director No. 1: "John Jones lists your firm as a reference."
Personnel director No. 2: "He worked for us one week, and we were satisfied."

NO PROBLEM

Rip Van Winkle slept for twenty years, but, of course, his neighbors didn't have a radio and television.

SKINNED AGAIN

Two Yankee traders met in front of the post office a few days after they had swapped horses. Each accused the other of having "skinned" him in the deal.
A stranger remarked to another bystander, "Why don't they just trade back?"
"Because," was the reply, "they're both afraid they'll get skinned again."

GOES TO SEE HIS LIBRARY

Stubby Kaye: "The neighbors have borrowed so many things from me that when I go for a visit next door it makes me homesick."

APPRECIATION

"Have I told you about my grandchildren?"
"No, and I appreciate it."

LOWER RATES

A little tot, in church for the first time, watched the ushers pass the collection plates. When they neared the pew, he piped up so everyone could hear: "Don't pay for me, Daddy; I'm under five."

ADVICE

It isn't a bad plan to keep still occasionally—even when you know what you're talking about.

HE IS A STORE CASHIER NOW

Jerry: "How are you getting along with your arithmetic?"
Joan: "Well, I've learned to add up the zeros, but the figures still bother me."

NEVER?

It is the proud, perpetual boast of the Englishman that he never brags.

YOU HAVE TO BE CAREFUL

A lawyer met a friend to whom he had recently given some simple advice, and to whom he had sent his usual sizable bill.
"Nice day, isn't it?" remarked the friend, and then added, hastily—"But I'm not asking you, I'm telling you."

MODERN YOUTH

A small child asked his father if he had any work he could do around the house to replenish his finances. The father assured him that he could think of nothing.
"Then," suggested the modern child, "how about putting me on relief?"

IT DOESN'T MATTER

A girl, wide-eyed and pretty, went into a library and asked for a good book.

"Do you want something heavy or do you prefer lighter books?" the librarian asked.

"It really doesn't matter," said the doll, "I have my car outside."

IS THAT CLEAR

Groucho Marx and Bergen Evans were talking about why English politicians stand for election and American candidates run.

"Have you ever seen an American politician?" asked Groucho, "He has to keep running."

CORRECT

Sen. Lyndon Johnson, a news commentator notes, has a sign on his office door reading: "You ain't learnin' nothin' when you're talkin.'"

TOURISTS

British steward working on a cruise ship full of American tourists:

"They manage not to dress for dinner . . . ice water, tea and coffee, beer and wine—anything and everything is served with meals. Even tossed salads."

WE'VE ALMOST FORGOTTEN HOW

Some city youngsters were visiting in the country. They saw a blacksmith putting a shoe on a horse.

"Hey," one of them called, "there's a man out there making a horse. He's just nailing the feet on."

HE LEARNED

Sam Levenson: "My folks were immigrants and they fell under the spell of the American legend that the streets were paved with gold. When papa got here he found out three things: (1) The streets were not paved with gold; (2) the streets were not even paved; (3) he was supposed to do the paving."

HOW SMART IS THE DOG

A service man stood looking doubtfully at the snarling, barking, dog. The lady of the house advised: "Don't be afraid of him. You know the old proverb 'A barking dog never bites.'"

"Yeah," said the service man. "You know the old proverb. I know the old proverb. But does this dog know the old proverb?"

INGENIOUS

A salesman was trying to sell a young wife an egg timer. "Your husband's eggs will be just right if you use this," said the salesman.

"But, I don't need it," replied the young wife brightly. "Jack likes his eggs the way I do them. I just look through the window at the traffic lights and give the eggs three reds and two greens."

SHELLING OUT

Sam Cowling: "A hen that lays three eggs a day is really shelling out."

ALMOST PASSED

"Did you miss any of these?" asked Johnny's father after reading over a list of five questions which his son had been called upon to answer in school that day.

"Only the first two and the last three," said Johnny.

IN FULL FLOWER

Little Mary was visiting her grandmother in the country. Walking in the garden, Mary saw a peacock, a bird she had never seen before.

After gazing in silent admiration, she ran into the house and cried out: "Oh, Granny, come and see! One of your chickens is in bloom!"

MOST OF US DO

Johnny Carson asked a friend how his wife was coming along with her driving lessons.

"She took a turn for the worse," he was informed.

ON TIME

The girl broke her engagement because her boy friend was always late.

"The only thing he ever did on time," she pouted, "was buy my ring."

SOUNDS LOGICAL

Sam Levenson: "The reason my father gives for not having come over on the Mayflower was that mama wasn't dressed in time."

EDUCATION

Dr. William E. Moran, President of Colorado State University, during a commencement address:

"Almost nobody listens to a commencement speech except, perhaps, a few parents engaged in one last effort to get something for their money.

GI LOAN

Sammy Shore was talking about trying to find a house at a reasonable price.

"But my wife and I were finally able to buy a house with a GI loan," he explained. "Generous in-laws."

WELL, IT'S A LONG WALK

A Texas millionaire bought a Volkswagen—to drive him from his house to the garage.

WESTERN

There are so many westerns on TV that every time you turn on the set all you get is a horse laugh.

INSOMNIA

Johnny Carson knows a fellow who finally was cured of insomnia.

"What a relief," the guy explained. "I still lie awake half the night thinking how I suffered from sleeplessness."

SLIGHT MISTAKE

Three professors were so absorbed in conversation that they didn't hear the train come in, nor did they hear the conductor's "All aboard" call. But they were attracted by the puffing of the engine as the train pulled away. Then they rushed for the train, and two of them managed to scramble on, leaving the third looking on sheepishly.

The agent, standing by, said, "Too bad, Mister, but don't worry. Two out of the three of you made it. That's a good percentage."

"Yes," sighed the professor. "The only trouble is that the other two came down to see me off!"

WE SAW HIM, TOO

The senator was campaigning for re-election in a rural section of the country. His long-winded address had been going on and on, punctuated only by occasional gulps of water. During one of these very brief pauses an old farmer turned to his neighbor and observed in a loud whisper, "First time I ever saw a windmill run by water!"

IT'S POSSIBLE

Hiker: "Can I catch the 6:45 if I cut through this field of yours?"
Farmer: "If my bull sees you, you might catch the 6:15."

NO USE

Mother: "When that naughty boy threw stones at you, why didn't you come and tell me instead of throwing stones back at him?"
Practical-minded youngster: "What good would that do? You couldn't hit the side of a barn!"

SURPRISED

A salesman was driving along a country road when he came to a ford. A native was standing by the little stream where some ducks were swimming. The salesman asked, "Friend, can I get through the creek with this car all right?"
"Yes, sir, just drive right on through."
The salesman drove into the stream, only to find that the water was so deep that it flooded his engine. He and his companion had to get out into the stream with the cold water up to their arm-pits and push the car to the bank.
The salesman turned and said, "What do you mean by telling me I could drive through that creek?"
"Well, sir," replied the native in surprise, "I never knew that the water was so deep. Why, it comes only halfway up on my ducks!"

EASY TO EXPLAIN

Said the hired man: "I've been with you 25 years, and I've never asked you for a raise before."
Retorted the farmer: "That is why you've been here 25 years!"

WE KNOW THE ANSWER

Two women were discussing a third who had just entered the room.
Said one of them, "Her husband is a judge, isn't he?"
Replied the other, "Everybody thought so till he married her. What do *you* think?"

DRAMATIC

A class in English was assigned the task of writing four lines of dramatic poetry. The results were variegated, and, selecting the verse of a bright boy, the teacher read: " 'A boy was walking down the track; the train was coming fast; the boy stepped off the railroad track to let the train go past.' This verse is very well done," commented the teacher, "but it lacks the dramatic. Try again, Johnny, and make it more dramatic."

Whereupon, in a short time, Johnny produced the following: "A boy was walking down the track; the train was coming fast; the train jumped off the railroad track to let the boy go past."

TOO SUDDEN

Charley had taken his girl friend to lunch, and she had spoken to a nice-looking man at the next table.

"Is that man a friend of yours?" asked Charley.

"Yes," she replied.

"Then I think I'll ask him to join us," said Charley.

"Oh, Charley, this is so sudden!" exclaimed the girl.

"What's so sudden?" asked Charley curiously.

"Why—why, he's our minister."

UNNECESSARY QUESTION

"Son," said a Texan to his offspring, "I just heard you asking that man what state he is from. Now, my boy, I want you always to remember this: If a man comes from Texas, he'll tell you; and if he isn't from Texas, there's no need to embarrass him."

CIVIL WAR

Two Ohio boys got lost driving through Tennessee. Along the deserted road trudged a native of whom they asked, "Which way to Chattanooga?"

The man stared at them, and then asked, "Where you boys from?"

"Ohio."

"I thought so," he exclaimed. "Wal, you found it in 1863. Let's see you find it now!"

AGREE TO DISAGREE

Two ministers, given to arguing about their respective faiths, were in a very heated discussion. "That's all right," said one calmly.

"We'll just agree to disagree. After all, we're both doing the Lord's work, you in your way and I in His."

WE CAN'T REMEMBER ONE

A woman with a newly developed interest in government wrote to the editor of a big newspaper—"I want to get into politics. Do the taxpayers have a party?"

The editor answered—"Very seldom, lady, very seldom."

NOT SO DUMB

Employer: "Have you any references?"
Applicant: "No, sir, I tore them up."
Employer: "That was a foolish thing to do."
Applicant: "You wouldn't think so if you had read them."

NO CHANGE

"They say brunettes have sweeter dispositions than blondes."
"Well my wife has been both and I can't see any difference."

TEXAS AND ALASKA

A Texan who sent an 8-lb. cucumber to the editor of an Alaska newspaper apologized, saying, "The big ones are too heavy, but I thought you would like to see a Texas gherkin." In a few days the editor replied with a 40-lb. cabbage, "The same is true of our cabbages," he wrote, "but I thought you'd like to see an Alaska Brussels sprout!"

EXPECTING TOO MUCH

Professor: "Why don't you answer when I call your name."
Student: "I nodded my head."
Professor: "You don't expect me to hear the rattle all the way up here, do you?"

CORRECT

Officer (very angry): "Not a man in this division will be given liberty this week-end."
Voice in Ranks: "Give me liberty or give me death."
Officer: "Who said that?"
Voice: "Patrick Henry."

BUDGET

Living on a budget is the same as living beyond your means except you have a record of it.

CAMERA FAN

Two camera enthusiasts were discussing their hobby. "This morning," said one, "I saw an old lady huddled beneath rags. She was hungry and homeless. She told me she came from a prominent family but had lost her wealth."

"The poor thing," said the other photographer. "What did you give her?"

"Well, it was sunny," the first replied, "so I gave her f.11 at 1/100th."

WE OFTEN FISH

Maj. Gen. Wilton B. Persons, White House aid, recently joined Gerald D. Morgan, special counsel to President Eisenhower, for a week-end.

"Any fishing around here?" Persons asked a Marylander during a morning walk which brought him to a stream in the countryside.

"Some," was the curt answer.

"What do you catch?"

"You said fishin' not ketchin'."

NOT YET, BUT SOON

A young Texan grade-school teacher was filling out a health questionnaire for the coming term. Weary after a difficult first semester, she was ready for the query, "Have you ever had a nervous breakdown?" In big letters she wrote: "NOT YET, BUT WATCH THIS SPACE FOR DEVELOPMENTS."

SCARED

A teen-ager asked George Gobel whether he put anything on his crew cut to make it stand up so straight. Said George: "Man, no; I'm just scared all the time!"

OFTEN TRUE

In a school essay on "Parents," one little girl wrote: "We get our parents when they are so old it is hard to change their habits."

HE WAS STUCK WITH IT

Willy came home from school and breathlessly called: "Ma, isn't that hair tonic in the yellow bottle on the shelf?"

"No," answered his mother. "That's glue."

Willy sighed disgustedly. "No wonder I couldn't get my hat off in school."

ONE FOLLOWER

A father wrote to a college about the possibility of his son attending it. "Frankly," he wrote, "Henry may not be much of a leader, but he gets along well with everyone."

"Send him along," replied the dean, "we need him. We now have 985 leaders in our freshman class, and we do need a follower."

WHEN NOBODY'S LISTENING

When two gentlemen bump into each other in an elevator or revolving door, one will say, "I beg your pardon." The other will say, "Excuse me, please."

But when these same "gentlemen" get behind the wheel of a high-powered car, their word exchanges are more apt to be like this: "Get out of the way, you road hog!" and "Who do you think you are?"

DO IT YOURSELF

A do-it-yourselfer fixed a cuckoo clock, and now it backs out and says: "What time is it?"

AN HONEST DEBT

Supreme Court justice Tom Clark recalls that in his days of practicing before the Texas bar he defended a man in a civil action who was notorious for slowness in paying his debts. The client never paid until he was sued and judgment was entered against him. In the course of the trial the client, protesting poverty, was examined by the judge about his assets and refused to answer.

The exchange between the judge and the client became quite heated, though Clark did all he could to offset it. Finally the judge roared:

"I fine you $100 for contempt of this court!"

The client dug into his pocket, pulled out a huge roll, peeled off $100 in bills and said: "It's a just debt; I'll pay it."

WE CERTAINLY DO

Every restaurant operator is familiar with the patrons who ask that the steak leavings be put in a bag "for the dog."

Recently, where we were eating, the small boy in the family involved piped up in a shrill and excited voice, "Oh boy, now we gotta get a dog!"

LOST IN THOUGHT

Former Sen. Eugene D. Millikin of Colorado was a man of devastating wit. Although he was mild in manner and seldom given to speech, none of his colleagues cared to cross words with him in debate.

He once destroyed a fellow senator, who had been heckling him, with the remark: "The distinguished senator has made it abundantly clear to all that he couldn't even entertain a doubt."

On another occasion he deflated a pompous orator with the observation: "If the distinguished senator will allow me, I shall try to extricate him from his thoughts."

QUIETLY

A man doesn't mind a wife's reading him like a book if she doesn't insist on doing it aloud.

HE WANTS TO BE SHOWN

A small boy with a penny clutched in his hand entered a toy shop. The proprietor, driven almost to distraction after showing him nearly all the toys in stock, said, "Look here, my boy, what do you want to buy for a penny, the world with a fence around it?"

"Let's see it," replied the small boy.

EXPENSIVE CHAIR

"That chair," a salesman told a client, "is worth $5,000."

"How could a chair like that be worth $5,000?" scoffed the client.

"That's what it cost me last year," the salesman explained. "Sitting in it instead of going out after business."

SHE REALLY MOVES

A figure of speech from George Gobel: "When Alice starts spending money she moves faster than a penguin with a hot herring in his cummerbund."

VANITY

A friend of Robert Q. Lewis was bragging about his gay new car.
"What color is it?" asked Lewis.
"Black," said the guy.
"Show-off," sneered Lewis.

WORST JOKE

A theater manager was questioning a hypnotist about his act.

"When you hypnotized people during the Summer months," the manager said, "they stayed in a trance for long periods of time. Now that the weather has grown cooler, however, your subjects remain in a trance for much shorter periods. Why is this?"

"There's nothing surprising about it," the hypnotist replied. "You have to expect the daze to be shorter from now on."

HE STILL HAD A PROBLEM

A sad-looking character was shown into the office of a prominent psychiatrist.

"I've lost all desire to go on, Doctor. Life has become too hectic, too confused."

"Yes," said the doctor, sympathetically, "I understand. We all have our problems. You'll need a year or two of treatment at $50 a week."

There was a pause. "Well, that solves your problem, Doc. Now what about mine?"

WRITE THEM

Wife: "John, I'm ashamed of the way we live. Mother pays our rent. Father pays for our car and its upkeep. Aunt Martha buys our clothes; my sister sends us money for food. I don't like to complain but I'm sorry we can't do better than that."

Husband: "You should be. You've got two uncles who don't send us a dime."

WHAT YOU DON'T KNOW

Deep in the swamps of southern Louisiana three men stopped their car and watched a small boy fishing in a roadside lake. One of the men said, "Boy, are there any snakes in this water?"

"Naw, suh, they sure ain't," replied the lad slowly

The three men left their clothes on the bank and all had a refreshing swim. After dressing, one of the men asked the boy, "How come there aren't any snakes in this lake?"

"The alligators et 'em," replied the boy.

WHO CAN TELL

A mother, annoyed because her 14-year-old daughter had been calling her boy friend too frequently, took a tip from a former wartime advertisement and posted a sign over the telephone: IS THIS CALL NECESSARY?

Next day there appeared, pencilled on the card, a brief but logical reply: HOW CAN I TELL TILL I'VE MADE IT?

YOU'LL BE SORRY

The new recruit didn't salute the colonel. "Do you realize who I am?" asked the officer. "I run this entire camp. I'm in charge of 25,000 soldiers."

"You got a good job," said the private, "don't louse it up."

CHARGE IT OFF

A school inspector entered a classroom while the Scripture lesson was in progress, and decided to ask the children some questions. Calling on one small boy, he asked, "Who broke down the walls of Jericho?" The boy answered, "Not me, sir." The inspector turned to the teacher and asked, "Is this the usual standard in this class?" The teacher replied, "The boy is usually quite honest, and I believe him."

Leaving the room in disgust, the inspector sought out the headmaster and explained what had transpired. The headmaster said, "I've known both teacher and boy concerned for several years, and I'm sure that neither of them would do a thing like that."

By this time the inspector was furious and reported the incident to the Director of Education. The Director said, "I feel, y'know, that we are making a mountain out of a molehill in this case. I suggest that we pay the bill and write the sum off."

SEEMS LOGICAL

A man on the parkway stood beside an upside down foreign car. Asked if he had been hurt, he replied: "No, I always turn it on its back whenever I have to change a tire."

NO RAIN

A Navajo Indian attended a dinner in Phoenix and happened to hear a speaker whose main asset was high volume. "Ugh," said the Indian, appropriately enough. "Big wind, loud thunder, no rain."

SOUNDS RIGHT

A Hollywood blonde has a Chinese restaurant named after her. It's called "Low I. Queue."

LAZY

Pat MacCaffrie knows a poultry farmer out in McHenry county who has a rooster so lazy that when the others crow he just nods his head.

HE HAD HER THERE

A medium was bringing people back from the other world. A nine-year-old insisted, "I want to talk to Grandpa."

"Quiet!" hushed the medium, quite annoyed.

"I want to talk to Grandpa," repeated the child.

"Very well, little boy," said the medium, making a few hocus-pocus passes. "Here he is."

"Grandpa," said the little boy, "what are you doing up there? You ain't dead."

AMBITION

It is the ambition of most young couples to own a good home—and a good car in which to get away from it.

SMART BOY

Proud parent: "My son is only three and he can spell his name backwards."

Skeptical Neighbor: "That's interesting. What's his name?"

Parent: "Otto."

OR HIS NERVE

A man called a dozen of his creditors together to tell them that he was about to go into bankruptcy.

Man: "I owe you over $100,000 and my assets aren't enough to pay you 5 cents on the dollar. So I guess it will be impossible for

you to get anything—unless (with a feeble smile) you want to cut
me up and divide me among you."

One creditor: "Say, Mr. Chairman, I move we do it. I'd like to
have his gall."

HE WINS

Banker's son: "My father makes $50 an hour just sitting at a desk."

Lawyer's son: "My father talks for an hour and makes $100."

Minister's son: "That's nothing. My father preaches for an hour,
and it takes four men to collect the money."

TRADE STORY

On Ad Row they're now telling the one about the two advertising
agency executives who ran into each other one day while walking down
Madison Avenue. "Have you heard about poor old Rubicall?" asked
one. "Why no I haven't," came the answer, "what about poor old
Rubicall?" . . . "Well, the poor fellow died last week." "Oh, that's
too bad. What did he have?" "Well, let's see," said the first ad
man, "he had Rinso, RCA Victor, Lucky Strike. . . ."

HONEST

"Have a good night?" the hostess asked sweetly of the house guest
who had slept on a couch.

"Fairly good," he answered. "I got up from time to time and
rested."

ANOTHER MATTER

Judge: "Have you ever been in trouble before?"

Gangster: "Only once, your honor, when I robbed my kid brother's
bank."

Judge: "Well, now, that couldn't have been too serious."

Policeman: "I'd better explain, your honor, that his younger
brother is president of the Reliable National Bank."

HARD ADVICE

At the urging of his wife, Brownie went to see the president of
his company for advice on achieving success. The boss gave him
the old, tried, and true formula: "Get in early. Work hard on the
job assigned to you. Do more than is expected of you. Don't
hesitate to work overtime. Study hard." And so on.

That night his wife asked him how he made out. "He said I should kill myself," Brownie replied.

IS THAT CLEAR?

Conversation overheard in a store:
"Do you have any four-volt, two-watt bulbs?"
"For what?" asked the clerk.
"No, two."
"Two what?"
"Yes."
"No."

WAITING FOR THE WAITER

Man in restaurant to waiter: "What's our offense? We've been on bread and water for almost an hour."

THEY OFTEN DO

A little girl was showing her playmate her new home. "This is daddy's den," she explained as they entered one room. "Does your daddy have a den?"
"No," was the answer, "my pop just growls all over the house."

ODD HOURS

A burglar's wife was badgering him for money. "Okay, okay, stop nagging," grumbled the man. "I'll get you some as soon as the bank closes!"

MORE DIFFICULT

"After all, you can't take it with you," said the exasperated salesman who was trying without success to sell a grand piano to a wealthy old lady.
She replied: "Well, I think I can take it with me easier than I can a grand piano."

IN THE BLOOD

Gen. Alfred M. Gruenther, head of the American Red Cross, tells of an ailing woman, who needed blood. It was found that the only other one of her blood type in her small town was the village miser.
After the first pint the woman mailed the miser $50. After the second she sent a check for $25. After the third she sent a brief note of thanks.

TERRIBLE

Wife to husband: "You mean the bank saves all my checks and then sends them to you?   What a nasty thing to do."

JUST A LITTLE

Wife to husband: "I scratched the front fender a little, dear.   If you want to look at it, it's in the back seat."

GOOD QUESTION

Reporter: "The name of that man on the west side who was struck by lightning is Brzinslatowskiwicz."

City Editor: "What was his name before he was struck by lightning?"

IT REALLY PAYS

One of two women riding on a bus suddenly realized she had failed to pay her fare.   "I'll go right up and pay it," she declared.

"Why bother?" her friend replied.   "You got away with it—so what?"

"I've found that honesty always pays," said the first woman virtuously, and went up to pay the driver.   When she returned to her seat, she exclaimed, "See, I told you honesty pays: I handed the drived a quarter and he gave me change for 50 cents."

THAT'S TELLING HER

In a suburban area where houses were fairly close together, one resident heard a man's voice from inside the next house: "I want a little consideration around here.   I want some kindness.   I want respect and I'm telling you I want plenty of hot water.   I won't wash dishes in cold water for no woman."

BE CAREFUL

Driving along a lonely road a man saw a woman looking helplessly at a flat tire.   He stopped and changed the tire and as he picked up the tools the lady said: "Please let the jack down easy.   My husband is asleep in the back seat."

IT ISN'T EASY

A motorist charged with speeding through a red light at an intersection, explained to the judge:

"I always hurry through intersections to get out of the way of the reckless drivers."

RETIRED

When the late Calvin Coolidge sent his annual dues to the National Press Club, he had to fill out the usual card giving his name, address, and occupation, just to keep the records straight. His occupation, he wrote, was "retired."

The remaining few lines, invitingly blank, were headed "Remarks," and Mr. Coolidge, who made remarks with impunity now that the government was off his shoulders, wrote, "Glad of it."

EXCITING

The train stopped for fifteen minutes at a large station in western Canada, and two elderly American ladies stepped out onto the platform to stretch a bit.

"What place is this?" one of them asked a man lounging against a baggage truck.

"Saskatoon, Saskatchewan," he replied.

As they turned away, one whispered to the other, "Isn't it exciting? They don't speak English here."

NO SUBSTITUTIONS

It actually happened in a restaurant in Jersey City. A matronly-type told the waiter, "Look, on the special blue-plate, instead of the carrots and peas, I'd like spinach and instead of the lamb chops, I'd like the roast beef. Oh yes, for dessert instead of the ice cream I'll have pinapple."

"Certainly," returned the waiter, "and instead of ME, I'll send you the manager."

ECONOMY

"If there's anything you want," the landlady told him, "just let me know and I'll show you how to get along without it."

AN INDIAN CHIEF ON URANIUM

"Couple of hundred years ago white man came to north shore of Lake Superior. He take all the fur and give Indian string of beads. Then, a few years later, he come and cut down all the trees and build lumber mills. Soon all the big trees gone; he go away. Few years later he came back and cut down all the small trees. Now nothing on north short but rock. Now, by gosh, he come back for rock!"

A REFUGEE

Judge: "So you left your wife. Do you realize you are a deserter?"
Accused: "Well, your Honor, maybe you're right. But if you knew my wife, you wouldn't call me a deserter, but a refugee."

HOW, CHIEF!

Sandy McPherson had just started to write a telegram to his wife when he was told there was no charge for the name. Putting down his pencil, he said, "I may not look it, but I am an Indian, and my name is 'I-won't-be-home-until-Saturday-night.'"

MARRIAGE

Marriage entitles women to the protection of strong men who steady the stepladder for them while they paint the kitchen ceiling.

ORATORICAL OBSERVATION

A speech that's full of sparkling wit will keep its hearers grinning, provided that the end of it is close to the beginning!

WE UNDERSTAND

The 1939 dollar was worth $1. But the dollar now is worth 48½ cents. Which reminds me of something apropos and apocryphal overheard at a recent wedding. Ushers started passing the plates, and one whispered, "Yes, Ma'am, it is rather unusual, but the father of the bride requested it." *Oren Arnold*

DRY ENOUGH

The building committee of the church was discussing plans for the new addition to the present edifice when the matter of an appropriate cornerstone came under discussion. One member thought that the minister's dedicatory sermon should be placed in the cavity of the stone. To this all agreed, the minister adding that it would be necessary to enclose a certain chemical to keep it dry. Whereupon one of the older members, with a straight face, added, "I don't think the chemical will be necessary."

NOT SO FAST

The crystal-gazer collected $25 for a reading and told the visitor: "This entitles you to ask me two questions."

"Isn't that a lot of money for only two questions?" the startled visitor asked.

"Yes, madam, it is," answered the fortune teller gravely. "And now, what is your second question?"

MODERN COOK

Housewife to prospective cook: "And what wages do you expect here?"

"That depends, ma'am," said the woman. "Do you peel or do you unfreeze?"

SHE REALLY TOLD HIM

Secretary of the Interior Fred Seaton tells of the henpecked husband who was advised by his drinking pal to go home and assert himself. Fortified by spirituous courage the husband flung open the door of his home and told his waiting wife:

"From now on, you're taking orders from me, see. You're going to rustle up a snack and then you're going to draw my bath and lay out my clothes. I'm going out on the town tonight and who do you think is going to dress me in my tuxedo and black tie?"

"The undertaker," the wife snapped.

SOUNDS PROBABLE

Johnny Carson likes the story about the billy goat at the movie studio that found a can of film and devoured it.

"How did you like it?" asked a nanny.

"It was all right," the goat replied, "but I liked the book better."

HE TOLD HIM

"Sir, you must be a new member here," said a golf-club member to a golfer. "You should know you can't take your first shot eight feet ahead of the marker."

The golfer ignored the member and continued to address the ball. "Sir," pursued the other, "I must remind you to go back to the marker." The golfer continued to ignore the member.

"Sir, I am chairman of the 'greens' and I will have to report you to the board!" angrily said the member.

Finally the golfer looked up and replied, "Sir, in the first place I
am not a new member.   In the second place, I have been a member
of this club for nearly a year and you are the first person who has
spoken to me.   In the third place, this is my second shot."

KEEP QUIET

Sen. Thomas J. Dodd reports that at a recent meeting of the
politburo, Russian Premier Nikita S. Khrushchev ended a long tirade
against the west by turning on deputy Premier A. I. Mikoyan.
"What right have you to argue with me?" Khrushchev demanded.
"I never said a word," Mikoyan protested.
"Never mind, you were listening in a very aggressive manner."

HE REALLY CAN'T REMEMBER

Secretary of the Interior Fred A. Seaton told of the harassed man
who entered the office of a psychiatrist.
"Doctor, I can't remember a thing from one minute to the next."
"Since when has this been going on?" asked the psychiatrist.
"Since when has what been going on?"

INADEQUATE

Two cows were grazing alongside a highway when a milk truck
went by.   On the side of the truck were the words "Pasteurized,
Homogenized, Standardized, Vitamin A added."   One cow turned
to the other and said, "Makes you feel sort of inadequate, doesn't it?"

IT COULDN'T BE THAT BAD

A young spring poet sent some verses to the editor of a magazine.
The verses were entitled, "Why do I live?"   It is reported the editor's reply was as follows: "You live just because you happened to
send your poem by mail instead of bringing it in person."

STRUCK THE PROFESSOR DUMB

A college professor of logic was attempting to teach his young
son the principles of clear thinking and the necessity for defining all
terms.   He pointed to a wall clock which had just struck.
"Now, if I were to take a hammer and smash the clock," he
queried, "could I be arrested for killing time?"
The lad hesitated a moment.   "No," he said, "it'd be self-defense."
The professor frowned.   "How do you figure that out?"
"Because," answered the boy, "the clock struck first."

EASY TRIP

The teacher was explaining the wondrous things which science has discovered about the universe. "Just think!" she exclaimed. "The light we need comes all the way from the sun at a speed of 186,000 miles per second. Isn't that almost unbelievable?"

"Aw, I dunno," retorted one unimpressed youngster. "After all, it's downhill all the way."

SUBSTITUTE YOUR OWN CITIES

Sales Manager: "I'm starting a wonderful sales contest. I won't give you all the details at this time, but there are lots of valuable prizes. For instance, whoever wins Second Prize gets an expense-paid trip to Winnipeg."

Salesman: "What's First Prize, Chief?"

Sales Manager: "The man winning that doesn't HAVE to go to Winnipeg."

THAT'S DIFFERENT

Senator Clint Anderson says a small, shy man entered a swank Washington restaurant and ordered a dozen oysters and a dozen clams, cream of chicken soup, a fillet of sole amandine, duck a la orange, an avocado salad, and pie a la mode topped with chocolate sauce. A man at an adjacent table couldn't contain himself.

"Boy! You sure love food."

"Oh, it isn't that. You see I'm terribly fond of bicarbonate of soda."

OF COURSE

When the man answered his telephone one evening, a woman asked him if he had his television set on. He replied that he did, and the caller asked if anyone else was in the room. "Yes," he replied, "my wife is." The surveyor then asked, "What are you listening to?" "My wife," he answered.

HIS EXCUSE

Two men, fishing on a Sunday morning, were feeling pretty guilty. One said to the other:

"I suppose we should have gone to church."

To which the second angler replied lazily, "I couldn't have gone to church anyway.   My wife is sick in bed."

AT LEAST IT BALANCED

The woman had spent the whole afternoon trying to balance her checkbook.   When her husband came home, she handed him four neatly typed sheets, with items and costs in their respective columns. He read them over carefully:

"Milkman, $1.25; cleaners, $4.67, etc."   Everything was clear except one item reading ESP, $24.49.

Warily, he asked, "What does ESP mean?"

"Error some place," she explained.

NOT SO FAST

Teacher: "We will have only a half day of school this morning." Class: "Hurrah!"

Teacher: "We'll have the other half this afternoon."

TIME FLIES

The old storekeeper, who also was the community's postmaster, was a real go-getter.   He had no helper, and when he had to leave his store to meet the mail train, he was tormented by thoughts of tourists stopping for gas and soft drinks, and finding him gone and his store closed.

Finally he hit upon a shrewd solution.   He printed a sign in bold letters which explained everything during his enforced absences:

BACK IN 15 MINUTES

ALREADY BEEN GONE 10

HAPPY BIRTHDAY

Elder daughter Judy O'Reilly was putting my three-year-old granddaughter Robin to bed after a big birthday celebration, but Robin wouldn't let her stay to hear her prayers.   Judy eavesdropped and heard this: "Thank you, God, for the happy birthday.   Let's have another one soon, hunh, shall we, hunh?"   *Oren Arnold*

HE DOES

The parson phoned the local board of health to ask that a dead mule be removed from in front of his house.

The young clerk who answered thought he'd be smart. "I thought you ministers took care of the dead," he remarked.

"We do," answered the parson, "but first we get in touch with their relatives."

LITTLE THINGS

It's the little things that bother us, and keep us on the rack; we can sit upon a mountain, but not upon a tack!

NO VACANCY

A San Antonio newspaper featured this ad in its classified column recently: "Wanted, big executive, from 22 to 80. To sit with feet on desk from 10 to 4:30 and watch other people work. Must be willing to play golf every afternoon. Salary to start: $500 a week. We don't have this job open, you understand. We just thought we'd like to see in print what everybody is applying for."

TWO CAMPS

In addressing the Friendly Sons of St. Patrick at a dinner visited by President Eisenhower and President Sean O'Kelly of Ireland on St. Patrick's Day, Senator Barry Goldwater began: "Tonight the world is divided into two camps, and I do not refer to the east and west, but to those who are Irish and those who would like to be."

COOPERATION

Father: "Did you children help your mother today?"
First Child: "Yes, Daddy. I washed the dishes."
Second Child: "I dried them."
Third Child: "I picked up the pieces."

NOW FOR THE SHOPPING

At a 57th Street art gallery in New York, a tall, rugged Texan and his pretty wife dropped in and within a period of a half-hour bought up all the Van Goghs, Picassos, El Grecos, Gauguins, Monets, etc., in the place.

"There, honey," beamed the man with a relieved sigh, "that takes care of the Christmas cards. Now let's get started on our shopping."

SAY THAT AGAIN

Wife (trying on a new hat): "Isn't it just too sweet, dear?"
Husband (firmly): "No, it's just too dear, sweet."

ON A PARTIAL DIET

"Just look at this expense account!" roared the sales manager. "How is it humanly possible for you to spend $11 for food in one day in Podunk, Mass.?"

"Easy," answered the salesman. "Skip breakfast."

TEACHER STANDS CORRECTED

Teacher: "Willie, correct this sentence: 'Girls is naturally better looking than boys.'"

Willie: "Girls is artificially better looking than boys."

SMART GUY

It was in a lawyer's office, and the bereaved but expectant relatives were all waiting for the reading of Uncle Jeffrey's will.

The lawyer read: "Being of sound mind, I spent all my money."

SHE KNEW HOW

John Doremus tells about the little girl who was asked how she went about drawing a picture. "First I think," she said, "and then I put a line around it."

NO LUCK

The late Joe Frisco spent his life in need of money because of a love for the race track. In addition to his own betting, he used to pass out racing tips to anyone he met. He started giving this "inside" information to the bank teller who cashed his checks. The teller soon was deep in the hole, but Frisco advised, "Just keep doubling your bets and sooner or later you are bound to catch up with things." "Sure enough," Frisco told a friend one day, "a horse I told him about came in first and paid 50 to 1!"

"Did that make the teller even?"

"No," admitted Frisco, "the Warden wouldn't let him use the phone."

DEEP ROOT

Discussing people's feelings about various events, William A. McDonnell, former president of the U. S. Chamber of Commerce, told the story about a nervous patient in a dental chair.

The dentist was striving to extract a tooth, but every time he got ready to proceed he clamped his jaws. At last, he took his assistant

aside and told her at the very moment he poised the forceps, to give
the patient's hip a vicious pinch.

The pinch was administered, the nervous patient's mouth flew open,
and the tooth was easily removed.

"Didn't hurt, did it?" asked the dentist.

"Not much," replied the patient, "but who would have thought
the root went that deep?"

FAME

Lt. Gen. Arthur G. Trudeau told this story of the Wright brothers
coming home for Christmas to emphasize the fact that the public is
not always impressed by scientific accomplishment.

After Wilbur and Orville made their history making flight at Kitty
Hawk, N. C., on Dec. 17, 1903, they wrote home about it and added
they'd be home in a few days.   Their letter reached a Dayton newspaper which headlined the story, "Prominent Local Bicycle Mer-
chants to Be Home for Christmas."

SALESMANSHIP

Said the clerk, "How can I stop women customers from talking
about the low prices in the good old days?"

The floorwalker suggested, "Act surprised, and tell them you didn't
think they were old enough to remember them."

EXAMPLE

A little boy of six was invited to lunch at a neighbor's home.   As
soon as all were seated, the food was served, and they started to eat.

The little boy was puzzled.   He had been trained to say grace at the
table.   With his boyish frankness he asked, "Don't you say a prayer
before you eat?"

The host was uncomfortable, and mumbled, "No, we don't take
time for that."

The boy was quiet for a moment, then said, "You're just like my
dog—start right in eatin'."

I HOPE NOT

Inviting a friend to his wedding anniversary, an Irishman explained: "We're on the seventh floor, apartment D.   Just touch the
button with your elbow."

"And why should I use my elbow?"

"For goodness' sake, man, you're not coming empty-handed, I hope!"

DIPLOMACY

"Pa," said Hector, looking up from the book he was reading, "what is meant by 'diplomatic phraseology'?"

"Well," replied Pa, "if you were to say to a homely girl, 'Your face would stop a clock,' that would be stupidity, but if you said to her, "When I look into your eyes, time stands still," that would be diplomatic phraseology."

A CONCRETE PROBLEM

When the mother found her infant daughter eating handfuls of sand from the sandbox she was frantic. She rushed the child into the house and made her drink lots of water then called the doctor.

After explaining what had happened and what she had done, she asked the doctor what she should do next.

"Just don't give her any cement," the doctor admonished.

DECISIVE

Psychiatrist: "Do you have trouble making up your mind?"
Patient: "Well—yes and no."

NICE GUY

Two men were discussing their new boss. "You can't help liking the guy," said one. "If you don't, he fires you."

PATIENT

A young man was hauled into court for fighting. "Tell your side of the story," said the Judge.

"Well, I was in the phone booth talkin' to my girl when this guy wants to use the phone. He opened the door, grabs me by the neck and tosses me out of the booth."

"Then you got angry?" asked the Judge.

"No," the young man replied, "I really didn't get mad 'til he grabbed my gal an' threw her out, too!"

THEY NEEDED A NEW ONE

Eddie Hubbard knows a couple planning to buy a new TV set because they've seen everything on the old one at least twice.

OUCH

The fat man and his wife were returning to their seats in the theater after the intermission.

"Did I step on your toes as I went out?" he asked a man at the end of the row.

"You did," replied the other grimly, expecting an apology.

The fat man turned to his wife: "All right, Mary," he said, "this is our row."

WORDS

George Gobel notes: "One picture is worth 10,000 words—but for some reason most women prefer to use 10,000 words."

SORRY

Telegram received by a hotel: "Do you have suitable accommodations where I can put up with my wife?"

QUESTION

Sunday School Teacher: "Remember, children, you were put into this world to help others."

Small Boy: "And what are the others here for?"

SUCCESS

Walter Slezak tells about the little boy who was all thumbs. Yet, he grew up to be successful. He became a butcher.

SAFETY

There's a line on the ocean where by crossing you can lose a day. There's one on the highway where you can do even better.

LIFE

Some men work hard and save money so their sons won't have the problems that made men of their fathers.

MEXICAN RADIO ANNOUNCER

"At the sound of the tone, the time will be exactly 9 o'clock—or maybe 9:15."

TEXAS

A Texas billionaire lost all his money and couldn't afford to have his new Cadillac air-conditioned. So, to keep up appearances, he rode all summer with the windows closed.

And there's another one about the tear-stained Texas eyes peering wistfully through the windshield of last year's Cadillac.

HARD TO BELIEVE

One day when Herbert Hoover was the chief tenant of the White House, he invited a business friend to lunch. The friend asked whether he could bring his son, who was seeing the capital during a private school vacation. Mr. Hoover was aware that the luncheon would be the highlight of the young man's trip, so he instructed the cook to have fried chicken and ice cream. Among the vegetables, the cook included spinach.

A few days later Mr. Hoover received a letter from his young guest, who is today a prominent industrialist, saying that his schoolmates refused to believe he had lunched at the White House because of the spinach. Each and every one of his fellow scholars insisted, the youth wrote, that the President of the United States would not have to eat spinach, and that therefore it would not be found on the White House menu. The youngster begged Mr. Hoover to confirm the menu.

Mr. Hoover summoned White House Secretary Larry Ritchie and ordered him to bring some parchment and the seal of the United States. Whereupon Mr. Hoover solemnly proclaimed that the White House had served spinach at luncheon to its honored guest.

AROUND THE CORNER

George Gobel says it is a mistake to outlaw billboards on federal highways. After all, if they take down the billboards, where will the traffic cops hide?

HOW TO DOUBLE YOUR MONEY

Fold it over once and put it back in your pocket.

DON'T FENCE ME IN

Eli Wallach tells about the Texas wife who complained that she wanted to get out and see the world.

"I'm tired of riding from one end of the ranch to the other," she moaned. "All I see is Mexico, then Canada, and then back to Mexico again."

SEEMS LIKELY

"These lovely soft hands," he whispered. "That hair. And those beautiful eyes! Where did you get those beautiful eyes?"
"They came with the head," the girl replied.

SIGNS OF THE TIMES

Sign in Detroit: Volkswagen and Renault, go home.

TIT FOR TAT

The man was more than a little annoyed when a neighbor telephoned at 3 a.m. and complained, "Your dog is barking so loudly that I can't sleep." The neighbor hung up before he could protest.
The following morning at 3 a.m. he called his neighbor and said: "I don't have a dog."

SOUNDS LIKE TWO POLITICIANS

Senator James O. Eastland summed up the relationship of Soviet Russia and Communist Yugoslavia as similar to that of the lonely small boy who was approached by a genial old gentleman.
"Why aren't you playing?" the man asked. "Haven't you got any friends?"
"I have a friend," the boy answered, "but I hate him."

NOT SO DUMB

A six-year-old boy, separated from his mother in a supermarket, began to call frantically for "Martha! Martha! Martha!"
That was his mother's name and she came running to him quickly. "But, honey," she admonished, "you shouldn't call me Martha. I'm 'Mother' to you."
"Yes, I know," he answered, "but this store is full of mothers, and I want mine."

HE FIXED OUR CAR

Two garage mechanics were overheard to say:
"What kind of upholstery do you like best?" one asked. "Fabric or leather?"

The other replied, "Fabric. Leather is too slick to wipe your hands on."

TEXAS AGAIN

Robert Q. Lewis tells the sad story of a little boy in Texas whose father couldn't get him a set of electric trains: The New York Central wouldn't sell!

RULES FOR SUCCESS

Hitch your wagon to a star; keep your nose to the grindstone; put your shoulder to the wheel; keep an ear to the ground; and watch the handwriting on the wall.

TOYS

The child had every toy his father wanted. *Robert E. Whitten*

GOOD WIFELY ADVICE

The belligerent husband demanded, "I want to know once and for all who is the boss in this house."

His wife replied, "You'll be happier if you don't try to find out."

OF COURSE

Mrs. Thornton went into a photographer's studio and asked him to enlarge a picture of her late husband. She gave explicit instructions and concluded by saying, "And, for goodness' sake, take off that awful-looking straw hat."

The photographer considered for a moment and then commented, "Hmmm, I think I can do that. What color hair did he have, and what side did he part it on?"

Mrs. Thornton thought a bit, then smiled and said, "I can't quite remember, but when you take off his hat you can see for yourself!"

HE WAS TRYING

A small boy sat on a fence eyeing the luscious-looking apples hanging from the branches of a nearby tree. Suddenly the farmer appeared. "Sonny," he demanded sternly, "are you trying to steal those apples?"

"No, sir," answered the boy, "I'm trying not to."

GETTING INCREASED MILEAGE

A man recently bought a foreign-made automobile, and after careful computation came to the conclusion that he was not getting the phenomenally high gasoline mileage so often credited to such cars.

He took it to a local mechanic, who after checking it thoroughly pronounced it in perfect condition.

"But isn't there something I can do to increase the mileage per gallon of gasoline?" the owner asked.

"You can do the same as most foreign-car owners do," replied the mechanic. "You can fib about it."

SORRY

The choir boys of the church were organizing a baseball team, and being short of equipment and money, decided to ask the pastor for assistance. The leading choir boy was authorized to contact the parson. He did, by means of this short note: "We would be glad for any financial aid you could give us. Also, could we please have the use of the bats that the sexton says you have in your belfry?"

THAT'S WHAT HURT

An old gent was passing a bus intersection when a large St. Bernard brushed against him and knocked him down. An instant later a foreign sports car skidded around the corner and inflicted more damage.

A bystander helped him up and asked him if the dog had hurt him.

"Well," he answered, "the dog didn't hurt so much, but that tin can tied to his tail nearly killed me!"

IT COULD BE

A cynical woman was complaining about the ineffectiveness of her hearing aid.

"Why not get a new one?" her son inquired.

"The kind I'd want," she said, "would cost three hundred dollars."

"Well, get it," said the son.

"No," she replied wistfully. "I'm not going to pay that for one. There isn't that much worth hearing!"

A PROBLEM

Bank Teller: "So you wish to open a joint account with your husband? A checking account, I suppose?"

Mrs. B.: "A checking account for me, yes, and just a deposit account for my husband."

SALESMANSHIP

The best salesman we ever heard of was the one who sold two milking machines to a farmer who had only one cow. Then this salesman helped finance the deal by taking the cow as down payment on the two milking machines.

IS THAT FAIR?

Boy: "In the old days did the knights fight with battleaxes?"

Father: "Well, the married ones did."

THAT'S NOTHING

The braggart was letting everybody know that he could bend a horseshoe with his bare hands. One farmer had had enough.

"That ain't anything to brag about," he said, "my wife can tie up 10 miles of telephone wire with her chin."

ELECTRIC IMPULSE

Asked to write a brief essay on the life of Benjamin Franklin, one little girl wrote this gem of a paragraph:

"He was born in Boston, traveled to Philadelphia, met a lady on the street, she laughed at him, he married her, and discovered electricity."

FAIR DEAL

A young man wrote to a prominent business firm, ordering a razor: "Dear Sirs: Please find enclosed fifty cents for one of your razors as advertised. P.S. I forgot to enclose the fifty cents, but no doubt a firm of your high standing will send the razor anyway."

The firm addressed thus replied: "Dear Sir: Your most valued order received the other day and we are sending the razor as per request, and hope it will prove satisfactory. P.S. We forgot to enclose the razor, but no doubt a man with your cheek will have no need of it."

A GOOD QUESTION

While a coalman and his helper were carrying bags of coal to a five-story tenement in Edinburgh, Scotland, a voice called, "Bring three bags of coal up to Mrs. Brown!" After delivering them to the bin outside her door on the fourth floor, they knocked on the door and asked for payment. "But," said Mrs. Brown, "I never ordered coal!" "Oh, yes, you did—you called from the window," said the boss. So she paid him.

When her husband came home, Mrs. Brown told what had happened. "It would be that parrot," he replied. With that he picked up the parrot, gave it a good shaking. The parrot ran under the bed in the next room. At that moment the cat was passing and Mr. Brown gave it a kick, saying, "And that goes for you too!" The cat also ran under the bed. The parrot looked up and said, "You here too? How many bags did you order?"

IT GENERALLY DOES

A motorist was driving through a remote section of the country, and after stopping in a small village for something to eat, noticed that his wrist watch had stopped. As he paused on the porch of the small cafe he turned to a native lounging nearby and said:

"I wonder if you could tell me what time it is?"

"It's twelve o'clock," drawled the other.

"Only twelve o'clock?" questioned the traveler. "I thought it was much more than that."

"It's never more than that around this part of the country," replied the native. "It goes up to twelve o'clock and then starts all over again."

LOOKING AHEAD

"Tell me what you eat and I'll tell you what you are," said a lunch-counter philosopher.

Whereupon a meek little man, sitting a few stools away, called to the waitress: "Cancel my order for shrimp salad, please."

DISCOURAGING

John: "I hear your wife is a finished singer."
Tom: "Not yet, but the neighbors almost got her last night."

CORRECT

The reporter was sent to get the story of the charity ball. The editor called him in.

"Look here," he demanded, "what do you mean by this? 'Among the most beautiful girls was Henry Lewis Bottomley.' Why, you crazy idiot! Old Bottomley isn't a girl—and besides, he's one of our main stockholders."

"I can't help that," replied the reporter. "That's where he was."

EFFECTIVE

A man received from the tax office a "Second Notice" that his tax payment was overdue, carrying with it dire threats as to what would be done if it was not immediately forthcoming. Hastening to the collector's office, the man paid up and said, "I would have paid this before, but I didn't get your first notice."

"Oh," replied the clerk, "we've run out of first notices, and we find that the second notices are much more effective."

ECONOMICAL TOO

"We got plenty good doctors in China," the saffron sage replied. "Hang Chang is best. He saved my life."

"How was that?" asked the tourist.

"Me velly sick, call Dr. Hang Kin. He give medicine make me sicker. Call Dr. San Sing. Give more medicine make more sick. I feel gonna die. Bimeby call Dr. Hang Chang. He gone somewhere else. No come. Save my life."

RATHER DULL

Mrs. Brown: "Is Mrs. Jones an active member of your sewing club?"

"Mrs. Smith: "Oh, dear, no. She never has a word to say—just sits there and sews all the time."

WE PLAYED IN THAT BAND

The village band just finished a vigorous and not over-harmonious selection. As the perspiring musicians sank to their seats after acknowledging the enthusiastic applause, the trombonist asked, "What's the next number?"

The leader, consulting his program, announced, "Washington Post March."

"Oh, no!" exclaimed the trombonist. "I just got through playing that!"

AN ASSORTMENT

A tourist, entering a village store, asked, "Whaddya got in the shape of automobile tires?"

Replied the storekeeper, "In the shape of automobile tires? Well, we've got funeral wreaths, life preservers, invalid cushions, and fresh doughnuts."

A PRACTICAL CHEMIST

Professor: "Give the chemical formula for water."

Student: "H I J K L M N O."

Professor: "Are you trying to be funny, young man?"

Student: "No. That's what you told us: 'Water is H to O.'"

LOTS OF STARS

An American and a Dutchman were talking. "What does your flag look like?" asked the American.

"It has three stripes," replied the Dutchman, "red, white and blue. We say they have a connection with our taxes—we get red when we talk about them, white when we get our tax bills, and we pay them until we're blue in the face."

"With us," replied the American, "we see stars, too."

THESE QUIPS DON'T DIE EITHER

Old gardeners never die; they just spade away.

ADVICE FOR SUCCESS

"Integrity and wisdom are essential to success in every business," said the boss to a new employee. "By integrity I mean that when you promise a customer something, we must keep that promise even if we lose money."

"And what is wisdom?" asked the new man.

"Don't make such fool promises."

MAYBE

A father said to his son: "I'd like to know what would have happened to me if I'd asked as many questions when I was a boy."

"Maybe you'd have been able to answer some of mine," suggested the son.

ECONOMY

A millionaire was being interviewed on how he became so rich.

"It's a long story," the wealthy one said, "and while I'm telling it we might as well turn off the lights and save on electricity."

"You don't have to tell me the story," said the interviewer. "I know it already."

WHY?

A panhandler asked for a nickel for a cup of coffee.

"A nickel?" said the man who was approached. "Where can you get coffee for a nickel?"

"And why," asked the loafer, "should I let you in on a good thing?"

A LONG LUNCHEON

Henry Cooke overheard a man in a restaurant say to his luncheon partner: "I've got to get back to the office or I'll be late for closing time."

8 ✦✦✦

Biographical, Inspirational and Other Practical Material for the Toastmaster

ACHIEVEMENT

When the great doctor-missionary, Albert Schweitzer, announced at the age of thirty his decision to study medicine and enter the African mission field, his dismayed family and friends protested strongly. He was already renowned throughout Europe as a musician, philosopher, and theologian. It was almost beyond belief that such a man, established in a distinguished career and in the late days of his youth, should enter medical school as a freshman, and then bury himself in the jungle.

But Albert Schweitzer replied, "I can do it—I must do it." Today the world recognizes him as one of its greatest men. *Jack Kytle*

MAKING A BETTER WORLD

When "Boss" Kettering, for years vice president of General Motors and director of their research laboratories, was just beginning his inventive career in Ashland, Ohio, he worked out a central battery telephone exchange which did away with the nuisance of cranking the phone in rural communities. It seemed like a huge success but at one point it was in danger of being scrapped because for about two hours every afternoon the whole thing went dead. Kettering worked frantically for several weeks to locate the trouble. He finally discovered that out on one of the farms a certain grandfather had the habit of laying his spectacles on top of the telephone box every afternoon while he took a nap, thus short-circuiting the system.

In a measure that is a picture of the world into which the graduates of today are moving. A world of unbelievable wonders—wonders in atomic science, medicine, industrial management and political organization, but so many short circuits because some oldsters in my generation and those ahead of us have gone to sleep and laid down our aids to living at the wrong places. A large part of your opportunity in the years that lie ahead is to discover the cause of those short circuits, and to clear the lines of communication to make the world today a better world tomorrow. *W. Ralph Ward, Jr., Vital Speeches*

SELLING

Bruce Barton once made a great speech pointing out how Joseph grew to be a foremost figure in ancient Egypt, only to die, and how Exodus reports "there arose in Egypt a new king who knew not Joseph." This story led Bruce Barton to a conclusion: "A good product, a good service, a good organization, a good individual, or a good idea must be sold all the time. Because every day Joseph dies and there arise new 'kings which know not Joseph.' " *Kenneth McFarland*

LONELINESS

Shakespeare, Leonardo da Vinci, Benjamin Franklin, and Lincoln never saw a movie, heard a radio or looked at TV. They had "loneliness" and knew what to do with it. They were not afraid of being lonely because they knew that was when the creative mood in them would work. *Carl Sandburg*

AMBITION

Shakespeare's Macbeth is a young man going places. He is already a success . . . and greedy of greater success. Any man going ahead is in danger, if he has strong ambition without strong principles. . . . Macbeth is evil, not in ambition, but in the willingness to pay too great a price. He does not know how to put first things first. *Ernest Marshall Howse*

OUR PRAYERS

Before all else we seek, upon our common labor as a nation, the blessings of Almighty God. And the hopes in our hearts fashion the deepest prayers of our whole people.

May we pursue the right—without self-righteousness.

May we know unity—without conformity.

May we grow in strength—without pride in self.

May we, in our dealings with all peoples of the earth, ever speak truth and serve justice. . . .

May the light of freedom, coming to all darkened lands, flame brightly—until at last the darkness is no more.

May the turbulence of our age yield to a true time of peace, when men and nations shall share a life that honors the dignity of each, the brotherhood of all. *Dwight D. Eisenhower, Second Inaugural Address*

BIGNESS

By faith Abraham . . . went out, not knowing whither he went. This ancient and dim figure of Abraham leads a procession which in some measure we all join. It is the Big Parade of our time, indeed, of every time. We are conscripted into an expedition beyond familiar landmarks, a thrust outward into new and uncharted territory. . . . Harold Lamb's life of Alexander the Great . . . describes memorably the consternation which came upon the Greek army following Alexander across Asia Minor, when they discovered that they had marched clear off the map. The only maps they had were Greek maps, showing only a part of Asia Minor. The rest was blank space . . . our world has marched off many maps, and new ones must be drawn . . . more true to the realities of the present situation. *Halford E. Luccock*

BOOKS

The man who does not read good books has no advantage over the man who can't read them. *Mark Twain*

CONVERSATIONS WITH THE GREAT

Reading good books is like having a conversation with the highly worthy persons of the past who wrote them; indeed, it is like having a prepared conversation in which those persons disclose to us only their best thinking. *Descartes*

MANKIND'S DIARY

A great library contains the diary of the human race. *George Dawson*

RAPID CHANGES

From Exurbia come words of an alarming sequence. A housewife in a supermarket was overheard to wail: "They went from Episcopalians to Unitarians—and from Republicans to Democrats—all in one week." *John G. Fuller*

ELECTRIC TRAINS

No man is really depraved who can spend half an hour by himself on the floor playing with his little boy's electric train. *Simeon Strunsky*

GRANDCHILDREN

When grandchildren visit their grandparents, it is the happiest day in the grandparents' lives. The only day that is happier is when they go home. *Sir Frederick Messer*

THE EARLY CHURCH

The early vigorous church was essentially a working, serving, and forward-looking church . . . the young church did not have much chance of becoming self-satisfied and complacent. *J. B. Phillips*

ON THE TEAM

A high-school coach spoke at our church's Men's Club this week: "Some people refuse to go to church," he said, "because, they say, they're better than a lot of folks who do. Maybe they are. But a star basket-ball player can do a lot more for the game if he's on the team." *Burton Hillis, Better Homes & Gardens*

THE RESPONSIBILITY OF PARENTS

The parents of America can strike a most effective blow against the forces which contribute to juvenile delinquency, if our mothers and fathers will take their children to Sunday school and church regularly. *J. Edgar Hoover*

NO ONE BUT GOD

Whether a man lives or dies in vain can be measured only by the way he faces his own problems, by the success or failure of the inner conflict within his own soul. And of this no one may know save God. *James Conant*

FREE GOVERNMENT

The very essence of a free government consists in considering offices as public trusts, bestowed for the good of the country, and not for the benefit of an individual or a party. *John C. Calhoun*

KNOWLEDGE

No wonder colleges are reservoirs of knowledge. The freshman brings a little in, and the seniors take none away, and knowledge accumulates. *Abbott Lawrence Lowell*

COMMUNISM

The cure for communism lies in a more effective Christianity. Communism is the devil's latest substitute for the Christian concept of the Kingdom of God. Christianity is based on love and is distinguished by stewardship. In the Christian context, we must provide for all mankind a better measure of security, without robbing them of their freedom. Clear thinking, forthright action, and sacrificial living will be required. *Frederick H. Olert*

COMMUNISM FAILS

Communism comes in the wake of . . . disillusionment and offers some kind of faith and some kind of discipline. To some extent it fills the vacuum. It succeeds in some measure in giving a content to man's life. But, in spite of its apparent success, it fails—partly because of its rigidity but even more so because it ignores certain essential needs of human nature . . . It's supervision of individual freedom brings about powerful reactions. Its contempt for what might be called the moral and spiritual side of life not only ignores something that is basic in man, but also deprives human behavior of standards and values. Its unfortunate association with violence encourages a certain evil tendency in human beings. . . . Even if it does not indulge normally in physical violence, its language is that of violence, its thought is violent and it does not seek to change by persuasion or peaceful democratic pressures but by coercion and, indeed, by destruction and extermination. . . . Violence cannot possibly lead today to a solution of any major problem, because violence has become much too terrible and destructive. *Jawaharlal Nehru, The New Leader*

CONTENT

I am always content with that which happens, for I think that which God chooses is better than what I choose.   *Epictetus*

COOPERATION

No one can whistle a symphony.   It takes an orchestra to play it. *Halford E. Luccock*

COURAGE

Never give in!   Never give in!   Never, never, never.   Never—in nothing great or small, large or petty—never give in except to convictions of honor and good sense.   *Winston Churchill*

CRITICISM

If I were to try to read, much less answer, all the attacks made on me, this shop might as well be closed for any other business.   I do the very best I know how—the very best I can; and I mean to keep doing so until the end.   If the end brings me out all right, what is said against me won't amount to anything.   If the end brings me out wrong, ten angels swearing I was right would make no difference. *Abraham Lincoln*

CRIME

The cure of crime is not the electric chair, but the high chair. *J. Edgar Hoover*

CRISIS

Crises refine life.   In them you discover what you are.   *Allan Knight Chalmers*

LIFE

The greatest of men stand but a heartbeat from the grave.   *Charles Templeton*

DEATH

Death is not the enemy of life, but its friend, for it is the knowledge that our years are limited which makes them so precious.   It is the truth that time is but lent to us which makes us, at our best, look upon our years as a trust handed into our temporary keeping. *Joshua Loth Liebman*

DEMOCRACY

In a democracy, the votes of the vicious and stupid count. On the other hand, in any other system, they might be running the show. *Boston Globe*

DEMOCRACY AND THE BIBLE

Democracy is nothing but an attempt to apply the principles of the Bible to a human society. *Wallace C. Speers*

THESE ARE DIFFICULT

There are three things difficult: to keep a secret, to suffer an injury, to use leisure. *Voltaire*

A DEDICATED LIFE

No horse gets anywhere till he is harnessed. No steam or gas ever drives anything until it is confined. No Niagara is ever turned into light and power until it is tunneled. No life ever grows great until it is focused, dedicated, disciplined. *Harry Emerson Fosdick*

EASTER

Far be it from me to preach to you, but as a long-time usher and greeter, I suggest that if you begin attending church regularly about now, you won't feel like such a total stranger there on Easter. *Burton Hillis*

CONVINCING EVIDENCE

To this day, the most convincing evidence for the resurrection of Christ is men and women whose lives bear witness to His living reality . . . *John S. Bonnell*

ECONOMICS

Like theology, and unlike mathematics, economics deals with matters which men consider very close to their lives. *Kenneth Galbraith*

EDUCATION

Education means teaching people to behave as they do not behave. *John Ruskin*

PRAYER

Prayer . . . the very highest energy of which the mind is capable. *Samuel Taylor Coleridge*

CIVILIZATION

Civilizations come to birth in environments that are unusually difficult and not unusually easy.   *Arnold J. Toynbee*

ERROR

Men in high places in industry, government, radio, press, etc., can often spread enough error in a day to keep the forces of enlightenment busy for a year.   *Glenn D. Hoover*

EXAMPLE

Everyone's portrait of Jesus is incomplete.   Did someone see Jesus in you today?   Did they see enough?   *J. Willis Hamblin*

No man can bring another man closer to Christ than he is himself. *Dwight L. Moody*

Example is not the main thing in life—it is the only thing.   *Albert Schweitzer*

EXPERIENCE

Experience is remolding us every moment, and our mental reaction on any given thing is really a resultant of our experience of the whole world up to that date.   *William James*

Experience does not allow a gross lie to have a long life; it challenges it with constant contradictions.   *M. C. D'Arcy*

FINDING GOD

I have never known a worthwhile man who has not had . . . doubts and . . . spiritual lapses.   But I am not disturbed because I know this: sooner or later every man needs God.   The stronger and more male the man, the surer he is to need Him, and to need Him is to find Him.   *Mary Roberts Rinehart*

CHRISTIAN FAITH

It is now obvious that for a number of generations we have been attempting to hold on to Christian practices without possessing Christian beliefs.   But Christian behavior, which is not supported by

Christian faith, is a wasting asset, as we have discovered to our great dismay. *Arnold J. Toynbee*

A LIFE-GIVING FAITH

It is easy to achieve emancipation from false and little faiths. It is quite another thing to come to a large and life-giving faith. Yet this is what we all need. *Nathan M. Pusey*

FATHER

Build me a son, O God, who will be strong enough to know when he is weak and brave enough to face himself when he is afraid; one who will be proud and unbending in honest defeat, but humble and gentle in victory. Build me a son whose wishes will not replace his actions —a son who will know Thee, and that to know himself is the foundation stone of knowledge. Send him, I pray, not in the path of ease and comfort but the stress and spur of difficulties and challenge; here let him learn to stand up in the storm, here let him learn compassion for those who fail.

Build me a son whose heart will be clear, whose goal will be high; a son who will master himself before he seeks to master others; one who will learn to laugh, yet never forget how to weep; one who will reach into the future, yet never forget the past, and after all these things are his, this I pray, enough sense of humor that he may always be serious yet never take himself too seriously. Give him humility so that he may always remember the simplicity of true greatness, the open mind of true wisdom, the meekness of true strength; then I, his father, will dare to whisper, "I have not lived in vain." *General MacArthur, "Father's Prayer"*

SIN

Sin is anything that separates us from God. If we are so good that we don't feel any need for God's mercy, then our goodness is sin. *Alexander Purdy*

THE FLAG

The question has been raised in a recent news story . . . as to how big is a big flag. There is no standard-size American flag. The main criterion is that the flag's width be two-thirds of the length. We think that there are certain general dimensions, however, that should be observed.

A flag is a symbol, of course, and as such it should represent the qualities for which it stands.   Consequently it can be large or small.   It should be large enough to deserve respect and allegiance wherever it is flown.   But it should not be so big that it can serve as a ready shield for scoundrels, the intemperate or the ignoble.   It must not be so small that it is easily forgotten in the times or places where liberty is a dim and distant thing.   It must be large enough to win a place dear to hearts of its sons and daughters.   But it should not be so big that its sight strikes terror and fear where it is shown.

It should be large enough to cover all its people, not just the few. It should not be so small that it is easily waved in moments of wild, careless enthusiasm for causes that in a more sober, reflective moment would be rejected as unworthy.   It matters little if a flag's history is long or short, its colors bright or pale, its design simple or complex. What matters is that where the banner waves, those who live under it dwell in peace, in liberty and in justice.   *The New York Times*

MANY OF US DO NOT

God has tried again and again to speak to me, but I wouldn't listen. *Oliver Wendell Holmes*

GENIUS

When a man of genius appears in the world, it is immediately recognized by the fact that all the blockheads join forces against him. *Jonathan Swift*

Common sense is instinct, and enough of it is genius.   *George Bernard Shaw*

CHARITY

God loves a cheerful giver, but we settle for a grudging one.   *Mildred McAfee Horton*

HOW TO LIVE

The only way to compel men to speak good of us is to do it.   *Voltaire*

THE BEST IS AHEAD

If the passing of the years brings anything to the soul, it is the richer experiences, the deeper truths, the surer hopes, the better attainments. Always the best is yet ahead.   Hence, why fret because the step is a little less agile, or the vision a little dimmer, or the mind less keen, or the locks are white?   If the soul is growing, you are traveling toward the heights.   Each year is bringing you closer to the best that is to be.

Consider the physical side:

Bismarck, who died at 83, did his greatest work after he was seventy.

Titian, the celebrated painter, lived to be 99, painting until he died. Some of his finest work was done after he had reached the zenith of life.

Von Goethe died at 83, and finished his Faust only a few years earlier.

Gladstone took up a new language when he was 70.

Commodore Vanderbilt increased the mileage of his lines from 100 to more than 10,000 between his 70th birthday and his death at 83.

Laplace, the astronomer, was still at work when death caught up with him at 78.   He died crying, "What we know is nothing; what we do not know is immense."

As long as man can keep himself in the attitude of growing, he is still young.   *Sunshine Magazine*

GRATITUDE

Gratitude is not a virtue that comes easy to the human race.   *W. Somerset Maugham*

To receive a present handsomely and in the right spirit, even when you have none to return, is to give one in return.   *Leigh Hunt*

THE POWER OF PRAYER

Let the divine mind flow through your own mind, and you will be happier.   I have found the greatest power in the world is the power of prayer.   There is no shadow of doubt of that.   I speak from my own experience.   *Cecil B. DeMille*

HAPPINESS

Happiness is a hard thing because it is achieved only by making others happy.   *Stuart Cloete*

We have no more right to consume happiness without producing it than to consume wealth without producing it.   *Bernard Shaw, Candida*

LOVE

Hatred toward any human being cannot exist in the same heart as love to God.   *Dean Inge*

HOME

The most influential of all educational factors is the conversation in a child's home.   *William Temple*

By profession I am a soldier and take pride in that fact.   But I am prouder to be a father.   My hope is that my son, when I am gone, will remember me not from battle, but in the home, repeating with him one simple prayer, "Our Father which art in heaven."   *General Douglas MacArthur*

We must stride to overcome the apathy, ignorance and guile which nourish the twin enemies of our freedom—crime and communism. Let us never forget that strength and good character, like charity, begins at home.   So long as the American home is nurtured by the spirit of our Father in heaven and is a center of learning and living, America will remain secure.   *J. Edgar Hoover*

IMMORTALITY

There is only one way to get ready for immortality, and that is to love this life and live it as bravely and faithfully and cheerfully as we can.   *Henry van Dyke*

What a man believes about immortality will color his thinking in every area of life.   *John Sutherland Bonnell*

INTELLIGENCE QUOTIENT

I. Q. could mean internal quality.   *Elmaar Bakken*

HUMOR

Men show their characters in nothing more clearly than in what they think laughable.   *Goethe*

A GREATER KING

In an old church in England, there is a striking epitaph, honoring a Cavalier soldier who had sold much of his property and given a great deal of his money to the Royalist cause.   When he was killed in a battle against the Roundheads, his friends paid him tribute in these words: "He served King Charles with a constant, dangerous, and expensive loyalty."

It is to the same kind of service that we are called in this place, in these days of dread and opportunity. But we are called for a cause and by a King greater by far. *Arthur R. McKay*

MORE FOR ALL

Frequently we hear people ask: "What does labor want? What is labor looking for?" The most direct answer to such questions can be summed up in one word: "More." But let me make it clear that we want more not only for ourselves, but for all Americans—for the farmers and the businessmen as well as for wage-earners.

When we fight for a higher standard of living, we are helping all workers, not only union members. We are also helping employers and farmers, who must depend upon the high purchasing power of city workers to buy their products. When we campaign for legislation to build better schools, to erase slums, to broaden and improve social security and to provide national health insurance, every American family, not only the families of union members, stands to benefit. *George Meany*

LIFE

The life of every man is a diary in which he means to write one story and writes another; and his humblest hour is when he compares the volume as it is with what he vowed to make. *J. M. Barrie*

A FLAMING TORCH

A young Burmese came to our Ashram group and, when he went away, he said so simply and sincerely, "I came here a flickering torch, but I go away a flaming torch." This must happen to people as they come to our churches. *E. Stanley Jones*

MAKE BIG PLANS

Make no little plans. They have no magic to stir men's blood. Make big plans: aim high in hope and work. *D. H. Burnham*

TROUBLE

Nothing brings out the best in men like trouble. *Hal Boyle*

MISTAKES

A mistake is evidence that somebody has tried to accomplish something.   *John E. Babcock*

AN ORPHAN

On Mother's Day one of the girls in the House of Neighborly Service in California was pinning red carnations on the children. Said one little girl: "You'd better give me a white one. As far as church is concerned, I'm an orphan. Mother and Daddy never come with me." *Annual Report Presbyterian Board of National Missions*

TEACHER AND STUDENT

I put the relation of a fine teacher to a student just below the relation of a mother to a son, and I don't think I could say more than this. *Thomas Wolfe*

PRAYER

Prayer is not using God; it is more often to get us in a position where God can use us. I watched the deck hands on the great liner *United States,* as they docked that ship in New York Harbor. First, they threw out a rope to the men on the dock. Then inside the boat the great motors went to work and pulled on the great cable. But oddly enough, the pier wasn't pulled out to the ship; but the ship was pulled snugly up to the pier. Prayer is the rope that pulls God and man together. But it doesn't pull God down to us: it pulls us to Him. We must learn to say with Christ, the master of the art of praying, "Not my will; but thine be done." *Billy Graham*

PRAYER STRENGTHENS

Personal prayer, it seems to me, is one of the simple necessities of life, as basic to the individual as sunshine, food and water—and at times, of course, more so. By prayer I believe we mean an effort to get in touch with the Infinite. We know that our prayers are imperfect. Of course they are. We are imperfect human beings. A thousand experiences have convinced me beyond room of doubt that prayer multiplies the strength of the individual and brings within the scope of his capabilities almost any conceivable objective. *Dwight D. Eisenhower*

IN HASTE

The days in which we live are shot through with the spirit of haste. Everyone is in a hurry. The man of the hour is the man out of breath. The quick lunch and the short story, the swift flight—all these are thoroughly characteristic of the life we live. Half the people you meet are just in the act of leaving something half done in order to rush ahead to tackle something else which will be left half done. "In quietness and confidence shall be your strength." *Charles R. Brown*

RIGHT

Always do right; this will gratify some people and astonish the rest. *Mark Twain*

THE PERPETUAL STRUGGLE

There are times when our children, perhaps unconsciously, see into the heart of life, after the fashion of the little girl who remarked: "Mother, I've had such a happy time today." "Really," her mother answered. "What made today different from yesterday?" The child thought a moment and responded, "Yesterday my thoughts pushed me around and today I pushed my thoughts around."

Those perceptive words of a child picture life as it is, a perpetual struggle between the things that push us around and the inner resources that enable us to push our lives where they ought to go. *Harold Blake Walker*

TROUBLE WITH HIMSELF

I have had more trouble with myself than with any other man. *Dwight L. Moody*

UNDOING TROUBLE

Sure the world is full of trouble, but as long as we have people undoing trouble we have a pretty good world. *Helen Keller*

TWO TRAGEDIES

In this world there are only two tragedies. One is not getting what one wants, and the other is getting it. The last is much the worse; the last is the real tragedy. *Oscar Wilde*

LINCOLN, THE UNDERPRIVILEGED

Former Governor Henry J. Allen of Kansas recently made a statement that makes such good sense that it should be more widely disseminated.   Said the Governor:

"Had Abraham Lincoln been living today, the Rotary Club would supply him with a set of books; the Lions Club with a good reading lamp; the Cosmopolitan Club with writing equipment; and the Kiwanis Club with a wooden terrazzo for the cabin.

"He would have the protection of child labor insurance.   A kindly philanthropist would send him to college with a scholarship.

"Incidentally, a case worker would see that his father received a monthly check from the county.   He would receive a subsidy for rail splitting, another one for raising a crop he was going to raise anyway, and still another subsidy for not raising a crop he had no intention of raising.

"Result: There would have been no Abraham Lincoln!"

TOO SACRED TO BE SOLD

I was born with music in my system.   It was a gift of God.   I did not acquire it.   So I do not even deserve thanks for the music. Music is too sacred to be sold, and the outrageous prices charged by musical celebrities today are truly a crime against society.

I never look upon the money I earn as my own.   It is public money.   It is only a fund entrusted to me for proper disbursement. I am constantly endeavoring to reduce my needs to the minimum.   I feel morally guilty in ordering a costly meal, for it deprives someone else of a slice of bread; some child, perhaps, of a bottle of milk.

My beloved wife feels exactly as I do about these things.   In all these years of my so-called success in music we have not built a house for ourselves.   Between it and us stand all the homeless in the world.
Fritz Kreisler

A MAN OF SENSIBILITY

Sir Ian Fraser, of Manchester, England, perhaps the best known of the new peers, is blind.   He lost his sight on the Somme.   He was once asked how one should treat a blind man.   He replied, "Instead of passing him by, pass the time of day with him.   A man of sensibility, like Sir Winston Churchill, always touches me on the arm when he passes me. He says, 'Ian, this is Winston,' and has a word or two to pass on to me."

CERTAIN HE WOULD FAIL

Tennyson's grandfather gave the lad ten shillings for writing an elegy about his grandfather. Handing it to the happy boy, he commented: "There, that's the first money you ever earned by your poetry, and, take my word for it, it will be the last!" *Sunshine Magazine*

COUNT HIM IN

Former Senator Ashurst was one of a group of Democratic senators who lived at the Wardman Park hotel, now the Sheraton Park. This group was given to sitting on the porch in summer afternoons in the 1930s to ponder and complain about the way President Franklin Delano Roosevelt put them thru the political jumps to get relief and public works funds. The late Senator Ellison D. (Cotton Ed) Smith of South Carolina was dozing as Ashurst defended the President.

"I say F.D.R. is his own worst enemy," Ashurst opined.

With that Smith struggled thru the descending curtains of sleep, like a swimmer breasting the surf. He struggled to his feet and roared:

"Not while I'm alive, he ain't."

NO INTRODUCTION

Ogden Nash was once asked to write an introduction to an anthology of bits and pieces by P. G. Wodehouse. He wrote it. The introduction, unabridged and without footnotes, read, if memory serves, as follows: "The work of P. G. Wodehouse needs no introduction." *Charles Poore in The New York Times*

THE PRICE

A young man came to Dwight L. Moody and said, "Mr. Moody, I want to be a Christian, but must I give up the world?" Moody characteristically replied, "Young man, if you live the out-and-out Christian life, the world will soon give *you* up."

WHAT DO YOU EXPECT?

Ambassador Robert Hill in Mexico was touring the countryside when he came upon a familiar sight south of the border—a man was riding a burro and his wife trudged along at his side.

"Why does your wife walk while you ride?" Hill asked in Spanish. "She doesn't own a burro," the Mexican replied.

A SPLENDID TORCH

I am of the opinion that my life belongs to the whole community, and as long as I live, it is my privilege to do for it whatsoever I can. I want to be thoroughly used up when I die, for the harder I work, the more I live. I rejoice in life for its own sake. Life is no "brief candle" for me. It is a sort of splendid torch which I have got hold of for a moment, and I want to make it burn as brightly as possible before handing it on to the future generations. *George Bernard Shaw, Irish dramatist and wit (1856–1950)*

THESE THINGS ARE PASSED AWAY

And God shall wipe away all tears from their eyes; and there shall be no more death, neither sorrow nor crying, neither shall there be any more pain, for the former things are passed away. *Revelation xxi, 4*

COURAGE

The essence of courage is not that your heart should not quake, but that nobody else should know that it does. *E. F. Benson*

ON CROWDS

Here are many different people
All roaring with one voice.
Beware!
Go not too near!
Or you will lose your voice
And roar with them. *T. W. Earp*

I do not believe in the collective wisdom of individual ignorance. *Thomas Carlyle*

Intellectually I have an inclination for democratic institutions, but I am an aristocrat by instinct—that is to say I despise and fear the mob. *De Tocqueville*

DEATH

The Angel of Death has been abroad throughout the land; you may almost hear the beating of his wings. *John Bright (in the House of Commons)*

HAPPINESS OR POWER

"If I could but show you the cabbages which I have planted here with my own hands, you would not urge me to relinquish the joys of happiness for the pursuit of power." *Diocletian (to his former co-emperor Maximilian)*

EARLY RISER

I am not an early riser.   The self-respect which other men enjoy in rising early I feel due to me for waking up at all.   *William Gerhardi*

HAPPINESS

Before we set our hearts too much upon any thing, let us examine how happy those are who already possess it.   *La Rochefoucauld*

NATURE

Great things are done when men and mountains meet
This is not done by jostling in the street.   *William Blake*

A MOTHER'S ADVICE TO HER SON

In 1781 Andrew Jackson, then a boy of fourteen, enlisted in the American army.   Before long he was captured by the enemy and thrown into prison, where he contracted smallpox, relates *The New Age*.   His mother, Elizabeth Hutchinson Jackson, arranged for his release and nursed him back to health.

When he had recovered, she responded to urgent appeals from some neighbors to go to Charleston and nurse the sick on board a British hospital ship.   This errand of mercy cost Elizabeth Jackson her life, for she contracted yellow fever in Charleston and died.

Before leaving her home, she spoke these words to her son Andrew:

Andrew, if I should not see you again, I wish you to remember and treasure up some things I have learned in life: In this world you will have to make your own way.   To do that, you must have friends. You can make friends by being honest, and you can keep them by being steadfast.   You must keep in mind that friends worth having will in the long run expect as much from you as they give to you.

To forget an obligation or to be ungrateful for a kindness is a base crime—not merely a fault or a sin, but an actual crime.   Men guilty of it sooner or later must suffer the penalty.

In personal conduct always be polite, but never fawning.   None will respect you more than you respect yourself.

Avoid quarrels as long as you can without yielding to imposition, but sustain your manhood always.   Never bring a suit in law for assault and battery, or for defamation.   The law affords no remedy for such outrages that can satisfy the feelings of a true man.

Never wound the feelings of others.   Never brook wanton outrage upon your own feelings.   If you ever have to vindicate your feelings, or defend your honor, do it calmly.   If angry at first, wait till your wrath cools before you proceed.   *Sunshine Magazine*

THREE PRECIOUS THINGS

I have three precious things which I hold fast and prize.   The first is gentleness; the second is frugality; the third is humility, which keeps me from putting myself before others.   Be gentle and you can be bold; be frugal and you can be liberal; avoid putting yourself before others and you can become a leader among men.   *Tao-tze, Chinese philosopher (6th century B. C.)*

WHAT HIS MOTHER TAUGHT

It was my sainted mother who taught me a devotion to God and a love of country, which have ever sustained me in many lonely and bitter moments of decision in distant lands.   To her I yield anew a son's reverent thanks for her guidance on a path of duty as God gave me the light to see that duty.   *General Douglas MacArthur*

WRAPPED UP IN HIMSELF

A wise man pasted this in his hat to serve as a reminder along the way of life:

"Any man can spoil himself for himself.   He can allow himself to grow so sensitive that he lives in constant pain.   He can nurse his grudges until they are an intolerable burden.   He can think himself insulted until he is apt to be.   He can believe the world's against him until it is.   He can imagine troubles until they are real.   He can hold so many under suspicion that no one believes in him.   He can insult his friends until they are no longer friends.   He can think himself so important that no one else does.   He can have such a good opinion of himself that no one else enjoys his friendship.   He can become so wrapped up in himself that he becomes very small.   *Sunshine Magazine*

SEEING MORE

I find that with the passing years my pace is just a little slowed; I may not go so far so fast, but I see more along the road. *Sunshine Magazine*

THE ACHIEVEMENTS OF AGE

Howdy, old-timer.   I hear tell you are "getting old," sir.   Fact is, I hear it from you—and I'm getting bored with it.   You keep mumbling that you are not much good for anything any more, just because there is snow on your roof.   Well, let me tell you a thing or two about old age.

Vanderbilt at eighty added more than $100 million to his fortune. Thiers at seventy-three established the French Republic and became its first president.   Gladstone became Premier of England for the fourth time at age eighty-three.   Wordsworth earned the laureateship at seventy-three.   Verdi wrote "Falstaff" at eighty.   Stradivari made his first violin after the age of sixty.   At fifty-five Sir Walter Scott was $600,000 in debt, but through his own efforts he paid that amount in full and built a lasting reputation.

Now shake hands and refocus your attention and get on back to work for the Kingdom, and stay with it one way or another until the day you die. *Oren Arnold*

WHEN WE PLAY THE FOOL

But when we play the fool, how wide
The theatre expands!   beside,
How long the audience sits before us!
How many prompters!   what a chorus! *Landor*

9 ❖❖❖

Business Quotations

THE RIGHTS OF MAN

America is not a mere body of traders; it is a body of free men. Our greatness is built upon our freedom—is moral, not material. We have a great ardor for gain; but we have a deep passion for the rights of man. *Woodrow Wilson*

HUMAN DIGNITY

The meaning of our word America flows from one pure source. Within the soul of America is the freedom of mind and spirit in man. Here alone are the open windows through which pours the sunlight of the human spirit.   Here alone human dignity is not a dream but a major accomplishment. *Herbert C. Hoover*

THINGS THAT ARE BAD

Things that are bad for business are bad for the people who work for business. *Thomas E. Dewey*

BIGNESS

Without big business great accumulations of capital cannot be mobilized from investors to buy the tools and equipment necessary for technological advance and a reduction in the price of goods to the people. *Margaret Chase Smith*

THE TEST

You are not going to be barred from the contest . . . and you are not going to be penalized because you are big and strong, but you are going to be made to observe the rules of the track and not get in anybody's way except as you can keep ahead of him by having more vigor and skill than he has. *Woodrow Wilson*

BIG BUSINESS AND SMALL BUSINESS

America can no more survive and grow without big business than it can survive and grow without small business. Every fact of our economic and industrial life proves that the two are interdependent. You cannot strengthen one by weakening the other; and you cannot add to the stature of a dwarf by cutting off the leg of a giant. . . . The American industrial machine is a unit, just like an automobile. It is made of big parts and little parts, each of which does its own particular job and all of which are intricately fitted together. You may think that it would be fun to sort them all out into neat piles according to size to please the statisticians. You could even pass a law declaring that all the parts must be the same size; and the theorists, no doubt, would be delighted. But when you get through, your automobile won't run—and neither will American industry. *Benjamin Fairless*

PARSIMONY

Parsimony, and not industry, is the immediate cause of the increase of capital. Industry, indeed, provides the subject which parsimony accumulates. But whatever industry might acquire, if parsimony did not save and store up, the capital would never be the greater. *Adam Smith*

YOU HAVE TO SAVE

You cannot take a whiff of "Free enterprise" or a "Way of life" and start a factory with it. To start a factory and provide jobs, you have to have money—capital. *Eric Johnston*

GOVERNMENT CAPITAL

"Government" capital is a deceptive phrase. It does not come from savings or from efficiency; it is the product of taxes or deficits.

Employed on a large scale, it demands politically distasteful imposts or enormously increasing debts. *Henry M. Wriston*

CAPITAL

That men who are industrious and sober and honest in the pursuit of their own interests should after a while accumulate capital, and after that should be allowed to enjoy it in peace, and also if they should choose, when they have accumulated it, to use it to save themselves from actual labor, and hire other people to labor for them, is right. In doing so, they do not wrong the man they employ, for they find men who have not their own land to work upon, or shops to work in, and who are benefited by working for others—hired laborers, receiving their capital for it. Thus a few men that own capital hire a few others, and these establish the relation of capital and labor rightfully—a relation of which I make no complaint. *Abraham Lincoln, September 17, 1859*

CAPITALISM

Industrial crisis, unemployment, waste, widespread poverty, these are the incurable diseases of capitalism. *Joseph Stalin*

CIVILIZATION

Civilization is order and freedom promoting cultural activity. . . . Civilization begins with order, grows with liberty and dies with chaos. *Will Durant*

WHERE THE RESPONSIBILITY RESTS

Our American heritage is threatened as much by our own indifference as it is by the most unscrupulous office or by the most powerful foreign threat. The future of this republic is in the hands of the American voter. *Dwight D. Eisenhower*

CHANGE

The world hates change, yet it is the only thing that has brought progress. *Charles F. Kettering*

EMPLOYERS AND EMPLOYEES

Our employers can no more afford to be absolute masters of their employees than they can afford to submit to the mastery of their

employees. Bluff and bluster have no place here. The spirit must
be "Come, let us reason together." *Louis D. Brandeis*

COLLECTIVE BARGAINING

We will have to distinguish more sharply, and especially in collective bargaining, between genuine questions of principle and matters
which are really just questions of advantage. We should not wrap
ourselves in a banner of so-called principle when we are really concerned only with economic advantage. And we should be prepared,
on questions of genuine principle, to stand firm against the heaviest
economic pressure. *John L. McCaffrey*

BUSINESS

Business is a public trust and must adhere to national standards in
the conduct of its affairs. *Harry S. Truman*

The great menace to the life of an industry is industrial self-
complacency. *David Sarnoff*

Executive ability is deciding quickly and getting somebody else to
do the work. *J. P. Pollard*

If you are ready to give up everything else—to study the whole history and background of the market and all the principal companies
whose stocks are on the board as carefully as a medical student studies
anatomy—if you can do all that, and, in addition, you have the cool
nerves of a great gambler, the sixth sense of a clairvoyant, and the
courage of a lion, you have a ghost of a chance. *Bernard Baruch*

FORCE

The Communists . . . declare that their ends can be attained only
by the forcible overthrow of all existing social conditions. *Karl Marx
and Friedrich Engels*

CAPITALISM AND SOCIALISM

It is necessary to use any ruse, evasion, cunning, unlawful methods,
concealment of the truth. . . . As long as capitalism and socialism
exist, we cannot live in peace. *V. I. Lenin*

THE DREAM OF COMMUNISM

The dream of communism lurks in every modern society as a racial
memory of a simpler and more equal life; and where inequality or
insecurity rises beyond sufferance, men welcome a return to a condi-

tion which they idealize by recalling its equality and forgetting its poverty. *Will Durant, Our Oriental Heritage*

STRONG MASTERS

Communism is based on the belief that man is so weak and inadequate that he is unable to govern himself, and therefore requires the rule of strong masters. *Harry S. Truman*

MAN'S WANTS

The most important law in the whole of political economy is the law of "variety" in human wants; each separate want is soon satisfied, and yet there is no end to wants. *W. S. Jevons*

THE CONSUMER'S POWER

Every human being has a vote every time he makes a purchase. No one is disenfranchised on account of age, sex, race, religion, education, length of residence, or failure to register. Every day is election day. . . . Moreover, minorities count. *W. T. Foster and W. Catchings*

COST

Which of you, intending to build a tower, sitteth not down first and counteth the cost, whether he have sufficient to finish it? *Luke 14:28*

DEBTS

Any government, like any family, can for a year spend a little more than it earns. But you and I know that continuance of that habit means the poorhouse. *Franklin D. Roosevelt*

CONTINUING DEFICITS

If the Nation is living within its income, its credit is good. If, in some crisis, it lives beyond its income for a year or two, it can usually borrow temporarily at reasonable rates. But, if, like a spendthrift, it throws discretion to the winds, and is willing to make no sacrifice at all in spending; if it extends its taxing to the limit of the people's power to pay, and continues to pile up deficits, it is on the road to bankruptcy. *Franklin D. Roosevelt*

PRESERVING DEMOCRACY

It is harder to preserve than to found a Democracy. To preserve it we must prevent the poor from plundering the rich; we must not exhaust the public revenues by giving pay for the performance of public duties; we must prevent the growth of a pauper class. *Aristotle*

DEMOCRATIC IDEAS

Russia has only one opponent: the explosive power of democratic ideas and the inborn urge of the human race in the direction of freedom. *Karl Marx*

NO ONE TO BE LEFT BEHIND

Democracy is a method of our getting ahead without leaving any of us behind. *T. V. Smith*

DEPRESSION

Economists are almost invariably engaged in defeating the last slump. *Stuart Chase*

No one has yet found a sure way of bringing about just a little depression. *Allan Sproul*

EFFICIENCY

The efficiency of most workers is beyond the control of the management and depends more than has been supposed upon the willingness of men to do their best. *Sumner H. Slichter*

EXPERIENCE

Don't, like the cat, try to get more out of an experience than there is in it. The cat, having sat upon a hot stove lid, will not sit upon a hot stove lid again. Nor upon a cold stove lid. *Samuel L. Clemens (Mark Twain)*

FREEDOM

No man, who knows aught, can be so stupid to deny that all men naturally were born free, being the image and resemblance of God himself, and were by privilege above all the creatures, born to command and not to obey. *John Milton*

Those who expect to reap the blessings of freedom must, like men, undergo the fatigue of supporting it. *Thomas Paine*

There are more instances of the abridgement of the freedom of the people by gradual and silent encroachments of those in power than by violent and sudden usurpation. *James Madison*

If a nation expects to be ignorant and free, in a state of civilization, it expects what never was and never will be. *Thomas Jefferson*

FANATICISM

Fanaticism consists in redoubling your efforts when you have forgotten your aim. *George Santayana*

FUTURE

We should all be concerned about the future because we will have to spend the rest of our lives there. *Charles F. Kettering*

GOVERNMENT

The office of government is not to confer happiness, but to give men opportunity to work out happiness for themselves. *William Ellery Channing*

GOVERNMENT OWNERSHIP

I am firmly opposed to the Government entering into any business the major purpose of which is competition with our citizens. . . . I hesitate to contemplate the future of our institutions, of our Government, and of our country if the preoccupation of its officials is no longer the promotion of justice and equal opportunity but is devoted to barter in the market. That is not liberalism; it is degeneration. *Herbert Hoover*

GOVERNMENT SPENDING

Government spending as a permanent policy cannot fail to develop into governmental planning of investment. In fact, its failure to do so would be quite uneconomical. If government expenditure is to be the pivot of the economic process it stands to reason that the productive efforts propelled by that expenditure will in the end have to be directed by public authority. *Joseph A. Schumpeter*

IN THE LONG RUN

There are men regarded today as brilliant economists, who deprecate saving and recommend squandering on a national scale as the way of economic salvation; and when anyone points to what the consequences of these policies will be in the long run, they reply flippantly, as might the prodigal son of a warning father: "In the long run we are all dead." *Henry Hazlitt*

LIBERALISM

The first principle of liberalism . . . is that the market must be preserved and protected as the prime regulator of the division of labor. . . . The liberal philosophy is based on the conviction that, except in emergencies and for military purposes, the division of labor cannot be regulated successfully by coercive authority . . . and that . . . the true line of progress is not to impair or abolish the market. *Walter Lippmann*

A liberal is a man who is willing to spend somebody else's money. *Carter Glass*

Liberal: a person with a high pressure feeling, low pressure thinking and a constant urge to give away what belongs to somebody else. *Anonymous*

MINORITIES

The thing we have to fear in this country, to my way of thinking, is the influence of the organized minorities, because somehow or other the great majority does not seem to organize. They seem to feel that they are going to be effective because of their known strength, but they give no expression of it. *Alfred E. Smith*

INNOCENT EMPLOYMENT

There are few ways in which a man can be more innocently employed than in getting money. *Samuel Johnson*

PRINCIPLE OR MONEY

When a fellow says it hain't the money but the principle o' the thing, it's th' money. *Abe Martin (Frank McKinney Hubbard)*

OBSOLESCENCE

Obsolescence is a factor which says that the new thing I bring you is worth more than the unused value of the old thing. *Charles F. Kettering*

Prosperity and obsolescence are absolutely tied together, and obsolescence makes prosperity. A research organization is the originator of obsolescence. *Charles F. Kettering*

PLANNED ECONOMY

No country in the world, so far as I know, has yet succeeded in carrying through a planned economy without compulsion of labour. *Sir Stafford Cripps*

MAN'S NATURAL RIGHT

The right of private property, the fruit of labor or industry, or of concession or donation by others, is an incontrovertible natural right; and everybody can dispose reasonably of such property as he thinks fit. *Oliver Wendell Holmes*

PROGRESS

All progress is based upon the universal innate desire on the part of every organism to live beyond its income. *Samuel Butler*

POVERTY

Poverty is the parent of revolution and crime. *Aristotle*

It's no disgrace to be poor, but it might as well be. *Abe Martin (Frank McKinney Hubbard)*

The American people have decided that poverty is just as wasteful and just as unnecessary as preventable disease. We have pledged our common resources to help one another in the hazards and struggles of individual life. *Harry S. Truman*

HUMAN AND PROPERTY RIGHTS

Cynics who continually attack businessmen as greedy monsters camouflage such attacks by a professed desire to preserve human rights as against property rights. They would have you believe that there is an eternal conflict between human rights and property rights. . . .

There can be—there is—no conflict between human rights and property rights when exercised by men dedicated to our American ideals.

Under the Bill of Rights of our Constitution, the right to hold and use property is clearly recognized as a human right.

This isn't my own private interpretation. It's right there in the Constitution. It says the people shall not "be deprived of life, liberty or property, without due process of law." . . .

You don't have to be a lawyer to understand that. It simply means that the ownership and use of property is a human right indivisible from the other basic human rights of life and liberty. *Morris R. Sayre*

PUBLIC DEBT

When national debts have once been accumulated to a certain degree, there is scarce, I believe, a single instance of their having been fairly and completely paid. The liberation of the public revenue, if it has even been brought about at all has always been brought about by a bankruptcy; sometimes by an avowed one, but always by a real one, though frequently by a pretended one. *Adam Smith*

RESEARCH

A research laboratory is not simply a building that contains apparatus for conducting experiments. I contend that it is a state of mind. . . . The research man ought to be thought of as the fellow you keep up in the crow's-nest to see beyond your horizon, to tell you where there is another prize ship to be taken or a man-o'-war to be avoided. *Charles F. Kettering*

WHAT IS RESEARCH

Research is an organized method for keeping you reasonably dissatisfied with what you have. *Charles F. Kettering*

Research is an organized method of finding out what you are going to do when you can't keep on doing what you are doing now. *Charles F. Kettering*

A SOFT SECURITY

A people bent on a soft security, surrendering their birthright of individual self-reliance for favors, voting themselves into Eden from a supposedly inexhaustible public purse, supporting everyone by soaking a fast-disappearing rich, scrambling for subsidy, learning the arts of political log-rolling and forgetting the rugged virtues of the pioneer, will not measure up to competition with a tough dictatorship. *Dr. Vannevar Bush*

A SOCIALIST

A young man who isn't a Socialist hasn't got a heart; an old man who is a Socialist hasn't got a head. *Variously attributed*

A GOOD QUESTION

How can you have states' rights when you keep running to Washington for money?   *Bernard Baruch*

IMPOSSIBLE

According to the theory of aerodynamics, as may be readily demonstrated through wind tunnel experiments, the bumblebee is unable to fly.   This is because the size, weight and shape of his body in relation to the total wingspread make flying impossible.

But the bumblebee, being ignorant of these scientific truths, goes ahead and flies anyway—and makes a little honey every day.   *Sign in a General Motors Corporation plant*

THE GROWTH OF UNIONS

The growth of unions means far more than the substitution of collective bargaining for individual bargaining.   It means that the United States is gradually shifting from a capitalistic community to a laboristic one—that is, to a community in which employees rather than business men are the strongest single influence.   *Sumner H. Slichter*

ADVERTISING

Advertising may be described as the science of arresting the human intelligence long enough to get money from it.   *Stephen Leacock*

Advertising is the principal reason why the business man has come to inherit the earth.   *James R. Adams*

Advertising created in the consumer an insatiable desire for goods, and the installment plan gave him the immediate means to satisfy his desires.   *Henry Morton Robinson*

Of what value would mass production be without mass consumption?   How could we stimulate mass consumption without mass merchandising?   And how could we have mass merchandising without mass advertising?   *Paul Garrett*

Advertising promotes that divine discontent which makes people strive to improve their economic status.   *Ralph Starr Butler*

A hundred years ago, Ralph Waldo Emerson wrote, "If a man has good corn, or wood, or boards, or pigs to sell, or can make better chairs or knives, crucibles or church organs than anybody else, you will find a broad, hard-beaten road to his house, though it be in the woods."

That's the origin of the much more familiar "If you build a better mousetrap" proverb that has long been cited to prove that action is more important than advertising. But the adapter of Emerson's words forgot the sentence just before that quoted above: "I trust a good deal to common fame, as we all must." For "common fame" read "advertising" and you will see that the better mousetrap theory doesn't hold much water. Nobody's going into the woods after mousetraps unless he knows why he's going. *Daily Idahonian*

EXPANDING THE NATION'S WEALTH

In our kind of society the expansion of the nation's wealth can best be gained by the voluntary efforts of its citizens. America cannot be governed into perpetual prosperity. Rather, national economic policy must be based on incentives for individual effort which open the way for every individual to be somebody and to have something. *Gabriel Hauge*

FREEDOM AND TRADE

The only type of economic structure in which government is free and in which the human spirit is free is one in which commerce is free. *Thurman Arnold*

Perfect freedom is as necessary to the health and vigor of commerce, as it is to the health and vigor of citizenship. *Patrick Henry*

COMPETITION

Anybody can win unless there happens to be a second entry. *George Ade*

We believe in competition, in the excitement of conflict and the testing of man against man in a fair fight. *Felix Frankfurter*

I am firmly opposed to the Government entering into any business the major purpose of which is competition with our citizens. *Herbert Hoover*

The idea of imposing restrictions on a free economy to assure freedom of competition is like breaking a man's leg to make him run faster. *M. R. Sayre*

Competition is the keen cutting edge of business, always shaving away at costs.   *Henry Ford II*

Of all human powers operating on the affairs of mankind, none is greater than that of competition.   *Henry Clay*

The purpose of our competitive system . . . is to maintain that degree of competition which induces progress and protects the consumer.   *Herbert Hoover*

The best of truth is the power of the thought to get itself accepted in the competition of the market.   *O. W. Holmes, Jr.*

A BALANCED BUDGET

A balanced budget is no summum bonum of fiscal policy.   It is, however, a useful instrument of self-discipline, to keep government from expanding without the people's express consent.   Deficits will appear, of course, when recession shrinks revenues.   But deficit financing cannot in good conscience be carried over into the good years, when we should generate a surplus to pay down the recession-created increase in the national debt.   To hear voices inventing specious reasons why we need not live within our means, even in prosperous times, is dismaying, but a challenge we must deal with.   *Gabriel Hauge*

COMPETITION IN ECONOMIC POLICY

One of the costliest heritages of the Depression Decade of the thirties is the disposition to abridge competition and to defend departures from it as necessary in the national interest.   Certainly some of these interventions had a valid basis and some still do.   But, by and large, our profession of belief in a competitive economy tends to outrun our performance.   We need to remind ourselves of this fact, for, in terms of economic theology, there is probably a bit of the monopolist in us all.   *Gabriel Hauge*

CREDIT

There is no power to compel a nation to pay its just debts.   Its credit depends on its honor.   *R. B. Hayes*

As William James said of the boarder: "It is much more important for the landlady to know his philosophy than his income."   *Harry Scherman*

Creditors have a better memory than debtors, and creditors are a superstitious sect, great observers of set days and fines. *B. Franklin*

EXCHANGE

Commerce is the great civilizer. We exchange ideas when we exchange fabrics. *R. G. Ingersoll*

FREE ENTERPRISE

The private enterprise system really consists of harnessing men, money and ideas, and the genius of inventors and technologists with the savings of the thousands. *Malcolm Muir*

The free enterprise system is a way of economic life, open to hope— an economy open to new ideas, new products, new jobs, new men. *W. B. Benton*

The very survival of free enterprise depends upon a rising standard of living and an expanding economy. *H. S. Truman*

Essential to a system of free enterprise is a climate in which new, small, and independent business can be conceived and born, can grow and prosper. *W. B. Benton*

WHAT WE BELIEVE

As business leaders, we believe that the operation of a free, competitive private enterprise system is the most productive and fruitful economic system the world has known and that its benefits are more widely distributed to more people than under any other system. As citizens, we believe that our system of democratic government with the protection of individual freedom is the most satisfying social and political system that man has been able to devise. We believe that both our economic and political systems must be grounded on integrity, honesty and the recognition of the rights and the dignity of the individual human being. *A. L. M. Wiggins, Chairman of the Board, Atlantic Coast Line Railroad Company and Louisville and Nashville Railroad Company*

10 •••

Quotations from Modern Sources

ACTION

The judgment of the world has been that Pilate did not do enough. There is no vigor in expressing an opinion and then washing your hands. *Heywood Broun*

We may believe that our words—which we assume to express our principles—represent us more truly even than our actions, but to outsiders it is the actions that are more eloquent than the words. *H. S. Commager*

Nothing, says Goethe, is so terrible as activity without insight. Look before you leap is a maxim for the world. *E. P. Whipple*

AGE

Anyone who stops learning is old, whether this happens at twenty or eighty. Anyone who keeps on learning not only remains young, but becomes constantly more valuable regardless of physical capacity. *Harvey Ullman*

You can take no credit for beauty at sixteen. But if you are beautiful at sixty, it will be your own soul's doing. *Marie Stopes*

You take all the experience and judgment of men over 50 out of the world and there wouldn't be enough left to run it. *Henry Ford*

As one grows into one's middle sixties death seems more reasonable than it does in childhood and youth. *William Allen White*

AMERICA

I am certain that, however great the hardships and the trials which loom ahead, our America will endure and the cause of human freedom will triumph.   *Cordell Hull*

Our America is Here, is Now, and beckons on before us, and this glorious assurance is not only our living hope, but our dreams to be accomplished.   *Thomas Wolfe*

There is nothing wrong with America that the faith, love of freedom, intelligence and energy of her citizens cannot cure.   *Dwight D. Eisenhower*

In America with a stubborn world to conquer . . . unremitting labor was the price of survival.   *Stuart Chase*

America is not a mere body of traders; it is a body of free men. *Woodrow Wilson*

In the United States there is more space where nobody is than where anybody is.   This is what makes America what she is.   *Gertrude Stein*

One of the things that is wrong with America is that everybody who has done anything at all in his own field is expected to be an authority on every subject under the sun.   *Elmer Davis*

The problems of America are the family problems multiplied a million-fold.   *President Eisenhower*

For any American who had the great and priceless privilege of being raised in a small town there always remains with him nostalgic memories of those days.   And the older he grows the more he senses what he owed to the simple honesty and neighborliness, the integrity that he saw all around him in those days. . . .   *President Eisenhower*

I know that Americans everywhere are the same, in their longing for peace, a peace that is characterized by justice, by consideration for others, by decency, above all by its insistence on respect for the individual human being as a child of his God.   *President Eisenhower*

ANCESTORS

Remember, remember always, that all of us, and you and I especially, are descended from immigrants and revolutionists.   *Franklin D. Roosevelt*

ARMED FORCES

When we are wrong, make us easy to change,
When we are right, make us easy to live with.   *General Alfred Gruenther*

ART

For art, if it is to be reckoned with as one of the great values of life, must teach man humility, tolerance, wisdom and magnanimity.   The value of art is not beauty, but right action.   *W. Somerset Maugham*

There is no such thing as modern art.   There is art—and there is advertising.   *Albert Sterner*

The most immoral and disgraceful and dangerous thing that anybody can do in the arts is knowingly to feed back to the public its own ignorance and cheap tastes.   *Edmund Wilson*

Whenever an artist thinks that the community does not sufficiently appreciate him, he takes an appeal to posterity.   I wonder where his notion comes from, that posterity is equipped with superior judgment and wisdom?   *Heywood Broun*

All the really good ideas I ever had came to me while I was milking a cow.   *Grant Wood*

I am the most curious of all to see what will be the next thing that I do.   *Jacques Lipchitz, sculptor*

AUTHORS

I am one of those curious persons who cannot make up their minds about anything.   I read and read . . . But I find that one history contradicts another, one philosopher drives out another.   *Theodore Dreiser*

If you steal from one author, it's plagiarism; if you steal from many, it's research.   *Wilson Mizner*

He . . . with all indications of a fine talent, wrote two or three intelligently amusing comedies, went to Hollywood, and, like so many others, died there.   *George Jean Nathan*

One of the amusements of being old is that I have no illusions about my literary position.   I have been taken very seriously, but I have also seen essays by clever young men on contemporary fiction who would never think of considering me.   I no longer mind what people think. On the whole, I have done what I set out to do. Now, my age makes everyone take me very seriously. If you are a writer, live a long time. I have found that longevity counts more than talent. *W. Somerset Maugham*

Literary awards usually come late in life when the recipient is well established. It's like throwing a lifebelt to a shipwrecked man after he has reached safety. *Ernest Hemingway*

An archaeologist is the best husband any woman can have: the older she gets, the more interested he is in her. *Agatha Christie*

Pain makes man think. Thought makes man wise. Wisdom makes life endurable. *John Patrick*

All my major works have been written in prison. . . . I would recommend prison not only to aspiring writers but to aspiring politicians, too. *Prime Minister Nehru of India*

BEST

Only a mediocre person is always at his best. *Somerset Maugham*

BROTHERHOOD

Brotherhood is not just a Bible word. Out of comradeship can come and will come the happy life for all. *Heywood Broun*

Humanity cannot go forward, civilization cannot advance, except as the philosophy of force is replaced by that of human brotherhood. *F. B. Sayre*

Grant us brotherhood, not only for this day but for all our years— a brotherhood not of words but of acts and needs. *Stephen V. Benet*

BUSINESS

Before you can get action, you've got to have a crisis. And in any crisis, someone's nerve has got to crack. I always bet that I can hold out longer than the government or the operators. *John L. Lewis*

All the problems of the world could be settled easily if men were only willing to think. The trouble is that men very often resort to all sorts of devices in order not to think, because thinking is such hard work. *Thomas J. Watson*

A man's worth is counted in the things he creates for the betterment of his fellow men. *Harry Morrison*

Whenever I think, I make a mistake. *Roger Stevens*

When I've had a rough day, before I go to sleep I ask myself if there's anything more I can do right now. If there isn't, I sleep sound. *L. L. Colbert, President, Chrysler Corporation*

Well, yes. You could say we have independent means. *John D. Rockefeller III*

CAPACITY

One can no more develop capacity by resting on his job than he can learn to spell by sitting on a dictionary. *Arthur Dean*

CAPITALISM

The dynamo of our economic system is self-interest which may range from mere petty greed to admirable types of self-expression. *Felix Frankfurter*

What we mean when we say we are for or against capitalism is that we like or dislike a certain civilization or scheme of life. *J. A. Schumpeter*

Our capitalism in the '80's and '90's was a buccaneer capitalism, and our labor leaders during the formative years of the American Federation of Labor were primitive tribal chieftains, each craft a tribe, who fought back with desperate guerilla tactics. *Benjamin Stolberg*

CHANGE

There is a New America every morning when we wake up. It is upon us, whether we will it or not. The New America is the sum of many small changes—a new subdivision here, a new school there, a new industry where there had been swampland—changes that add up to a broad transformation of our lives. Our task is to guide these changes. For, though change is inevitable, change for the better is a full-time job. *Adlai Stevenson*

In times of change and danger when there is a quicksand of fear under men's reasoning. *John Dos Passos*

With me, a change of trouble is as good as a vacation. *David Lloyd George*

CHILDREN

Children are a great comfort in your old age—and they help you reach it faster, too. *Lionel M. Kauffman*

CIVILIZATION

When men are brought face to face with their opponents, forced to listen and learn and mend their ideas, they cease to be savages and begin to live like civilized men. *Walter Lippmann*

A civilization is not destroyed by barbarian invasion from without; it is destroyed by barbarian multiplication within. *Will Durant*

The individual contribution, the work of any single generation, is infinitesimal: the power and the glory belong to human society at large, and are the long result of time. *Lewis Mumford*

I wonder if we have really grown to the point where the size of a house in which a person lives will have little interest to his neighbors, but what he contributes in mind and character to the community will bring him respect and admiration. *Eleanor Roosevelt*

I'd like some of it (money) to go where it would undo two great American falsities—that making money is distinguished and important and that motor cars and lavatories have anything to do with what is called civilization. *Louis Bromfield*

COMPLACENCY

Just the minute you get satisfied with what you've got, the concrete has begun to set in your head. *C. F. Kettering*

CONCEIT

He (Bernard Shaw) had discovered himself and gave ungrudgingly of his discovery to the world. *Saki*

Tell me, George (Gershwin), if you had to do it all over, would you fall in love with yourself again? *Oscar Levant*

. . . the deepest urge in human nature is the desire to be important. *John Dewey*

CONSERVATIVE

A conservative is a man who does not think that anything should be done for the first time. *Frank Vanderlip*

A conservative is a man with two perfectly good legs who, however, has never learned to walk. *Franklin D. Roosevelt*

COUNTRIES

God is good to the Irish, but no one else is: not even the Irish. *Austin O'Malley*

. . . there is nothing on earth more depressing on earth than an Englishman feeling inferior.   *Robert Forsythe*

China colors all seas that wash her shores.   *Madame Chiang Kai-shek*

Finland, a country which sophisticated Europeans even today barely consider civilized, especially for its queer custom of paying its debts.   *E. T. Bell*

COURAGE

Courage is almost a contradiction in terms.   It means a strong desire to live taking the form of readiness to die.   *G. K. Chesterton*

CRITICISM

There are some literary critics . . . who remind me of a gong at a grade crossing clanging loudly and vainly as the train roars by. *Christopher Morley*

CRITICS

When a playwright tells you that the reviews of his new show were "mixed," he means they were "good and rotten."   *George S. Kaufman*

CYNIC

Never, never, never be a cynic, even a gentle one.   Never help out a sneer, even at the devil.   *Vachel Lindsay*

DEATH

Whatever the state of the dead, they are not divided by prejudice of race or nationality.   To them, at least, all things are common.   *Heywood Broun*

A feeling of the huge and nameless death that waits around the corner for all men, to break their backs and shatter instantly the blind and pitiful illusions of their hope.   *Thomas Wolfe*

He who looks life squarely in the face sees death, which is the great condition of living.   *Isaac Goldberg*

The goal of all life is death.   *Sigmund Freud*

DEFINITIONS

Life is something like this trumpet.   If you don't put anything in it you don't get anything out.   And that's the truth.   *W. C. Handy*

An egghead is one who stands firmly on both feet in mid-air on both sides of an issue.   *Senator Homer Ferguson*

An elder statesman is somebody old enough to know his own mind and keeps quiet about it.   *Bernard Baruch*

DEMOCRACY

My political ideal is democracy.   Everyone should be respected as an individual, but no one idolized.   *Albert Einstein*

. . . we may conclude from the close relationship of democracy and Christianity not that they will disappear together but that they will survive together.   *Thomas Mann*

The measure of a democracy is the measure of the freedom of its humblest citizens.   *John Galsworthy*

Democracy has not failed; the intelligence of the race failed before the problems the race has raised.   *Robert M. Hutchins*

The greatest destroyer of democracy in the world is war itself.
Harry Emerson Fosdick

The future belongs to a socialistic democracy.   I hope—and am convinced—that Russia will become more democratic while the west will become more socialistic.   *Thomas Mann*

Parliaments, which were originally set up to limit the profligacy of the ruling powers, have by evolution become less apt to limit than to increase expenditures.   *Andre Tardieu*

All the ills of democracy can be cured by more democracy.   *Alfred E. Smith*

I believe in democracy because it releases the energies of every human being.   *Woodrow Wilson*

Democracy is based upon the conviction that there are extraordinary possiblities in ordinary people.   *Harry Emerson Fosdick*

While democracy must have its organization and controls, its vital breath is individual liberty. *Charles Evans Hughes*

Democracy is a method of our getting ahead without leaving any of us behind. *T. V. Smith*

On the whole, with scandalous exceptions, Democracy has given the ordinary worker more dignity than he ever had. *Sinclair Lewis*

The beauty of democracy is that you never can tell when a youngster is born what he is going to do with you, and that, no matter how humble he is born . . . he has got a chance to master the minds and lead the imaginations of the whole country. *Woodrow Wilson*

DESIRE

Any time you don't want anything, you get it. *Calvin Coolidge*

DISILLUSIONMENT

Wisdom comes by disillusionment. *George Santayana*

DOUBT

The heart-breaking hesitation of Lincoln, the troublesome doubts and perplexed questionings, reveal as nothing else could the simple integrity of his nature. *Vernon Louis Parrington*

EDUCATION

It is nonsense to talk of the college years as only a preparation for life. They are part of life, just as much as any other four-year period. *Paul Swain Havens*

One thing you learn very quickly in teaching students at the loftiest levels of education is that they cannot read. *Robert Maynard Hutchins*

The scholar must from time to time return to the people and learn their life, that he may continue to live himself. *Alvin Johnson*

Why in every other field of human activity is the goal of utility stressed while in education it seems to be held in contempt? *Henry Noble McCracken*

The most conservative persons I ever met are college undergraduates. *Woodrow Wilson*

Education is not salesmanship. No genuine teacher is trying to put something over. *Alexander Meiklejohn*

Part of the American myth is that people who are handed the skin of a dead sheep at graduation time think that it will keep their minds alive forever.   *John Mason Brown*

I am surprised that in my later life I should have become so experienced in accepting honorary university degrees when, as a schoolboy, I was so bad at passing examinations.   In fact, one might say that no one ever passed so few examinations and received so many degrees! *Winston Churchill*

There are obviously two educations.   One should teach us how to make a living and the other how to live.   *James Truslow Adams*

The true business of liberal education is greatness.   *Dr. Nathan Pusey*

If the schools cannot or do not send the colleges properly qualified students, the whole fabric of higher education becomes a bridge built on rotten pilings.   *Dr. Whitney Griswold*

If a man has good manners and is not afraid of other people, he will get by—even if he is stupid.   *Sir David Eccles, Look*

While I am not in favor of maladjustment, I view this cultivation of neutrality, this breeding of mental neuters, this hostility to eccentricity and controversy with grave misgiving.   One looks back with dismay at the possibility of a Shakespeare perfectly adjusted to bourgeois life in Stratford, a Wesley contentedly administering a country parish, George Washington going to London to receive a barony from George III, or Abraham Lincoln prospering in Springfield with nary a concern for the preservation of the crumbling Union.   *Adlai Stevenson*

EXECUTIVES

Executive ability is deciding quickly and getting somebody else to do the work.   *J. G. Pollard*

EXPERIENCE

In youth we learn how little we can do for ourselves; in age how little we can do for others.   The wisdom of experience is incommunicable.   *Isabel Paterson*

A prudent person profits from personal experience, a wise one from the experience of others.   *Dr. Joseph Collins*

FACTS

Every man has a right to his opinion, but no man has a right to be wrong in his facts.   *Bernard M. Baruch*

It is a strange fact that the impractical among mankind are remembered.   *Hans Zinsser*

The basic fact is economic insecurity.   The correlative fact is the mind's despair.   *Samuel D. Schmalhausen*

The fact that man possessed the capacity to rise from bestial savagery to civilization, at a time when it had never before been done, is the greatest fact in the history of the universe as known to us.   *James H. Breasted*

Some people have a peculiar faculty for denying facts.   *G. D. Prentice*

You can't put the facts of experience in order while you are getting them, especially if you are getting them in the neck.   *Lincoln Steffens*

FAILURE

When I was a young man I observed that nine out of every ten things I did were failures.   I didn't want to be a failure.   So I did ten times more work.   *George Bernard Shaw*

FAITH

It is the children of little faith who are easily scared.   *Lin Yutang*

Death and sorrow will be the companions of our journey; hardship our garment; constancy and valor our only shield.   *Winston Churchill*

Faith is not contrary to reason, but rather "reason grown courageous."   *Sherwood Eddy*

To be thoroughly religious, one must, I believe, be sorely disappointed.   One's faith in God increases as one's faith in the world decreases.   The happier the man, the farther he is from God.   *George Jean Nathan*

FEAR

Don't be afraid to take a big step if one is indicated. You can't cross a chasm in two small jumps. *Lloyd George*

The basest of all things is to be afraid. *William Faulkner*

I learned that fear was inspired in men and women who could not reconcile themselves to the possibility that hardship and sacrifice might confront them in battling for the right. *George W. Norris*

Don't be afraid! Fear means destruction. It makes the hand tremble and the mind waver. *Frank Crane.*

If a man harbors any sort of fear, it percolates through all his thinking, damages his personality, makes him landlord to a ghost. *Lloyd Douglas*

FONDER OF HIMSELF

People always get tired of one another. I grow tired of myself whenever I am left alone for ten minutes, and I am certain that I am fonder of myself than anyone can be of another person. *Bernard Shaw*

FOOD

Vegetarianism is harmless enough, although it is apt to fill a man with wind and self-righteousness. *R. M. Hutchinson*

Success may go to one's head, but the stomach is where it gits in its worst work. *Kin Hubbard*

FREEDOM

If I were a dictator, the first book I would exterminate would be the Bible. I would destroy it because I realize that our whole concept of democracy came from the Book.

In the Bible, and particularly in Jesus' spiritual concepts of God and man, all men can find the key to victory, not only over one evil system, but in the greater crusade against all falsehood. Mankind, however, appears to come slowly to the realization that Freedom is not won and held solely by material means. *Admiral Arthur Radford*

When liberty destroys order, the hunger for order will destroy liberty. *Will Durant*

No amount of political freedom will satisfy the hungry masses.
Nikolai Lenin

FRIENDS

That fellow certainly knows how to pick his friends—to pieces.
Dennis O'Keefe

If you wish to make a man your enemy, tell him simply, "You are wrong." This method works every time. *Henry C. Link*

GOD

Men talk of "finding God," but no wonder it is difficult; He is hidden in that darkest hiding-place, your own heart. You yourself are a part of Him. *Christopher Morley*

It is hard to believe in God, but it is far harder to disbelieve in Him.
H. E. Fosdick

The existence of God means that we are living in a moral order, and in a moral order we can no more sin and get away with it than we can break all physical laws and escape the penalty. *H. E. Fosdick*

GOVERNMENT

There is no question in my mind that the government, acting on behalf of all the people, must assume the ultimate responsibility for the economic health of the nation. *Harry S. Truman*

For three long years I have been going up and down this country preaching that government . . . costs too much. I shall not stop that preaching. *Franklin D. Roosevelt: 1932*

Very few established institutions, governments and constitutions . . . are ever destroyed by their enemies until they have been corrupted and weakened by their friends. *Walter Lippmann*

You can't run a government solely on a business basis. . . . Government should be human. It should have a heart. *Herbert H. Lehman*

If people do not possess the capacity to govern themselves, they are inevitably governed by others. *Felix Morley*

The function of Government must be to favor no small group at the expense of its duty to protect the rights of personal freedom and of private property of all its citizens. *Franklin D. Roosevelt*

Every form of government tends to perish by excess of its basic principles. *Will Durant*

Good government is not a substitute for self-government. *Dwight Morrow*

Good government, and especially the government of which every American citizen boasts, has for its objects the protection of every person within its care in the greatest liberty consistent with the good order of society, and his perfect security in the enjoyment of his earnings with the least possible diminution for public needs. *Grover Cleveland*

Experience teaches us to be most on our guard to protect liberty when the government's purposes are beneficent. *Louis D. Brandeis*

It is one thing to recognize evil as a fact. It is another thing to take evil to one's breast and call it good. *John Foster Dulles*

Neighborly love, in political action, means loving others, based on the brotherhood that was created with God as the Father of all. It means that the political power of any government must be considered an opportunity, not to favor individuals but to do well for all. *John Foster Dulles*

Production is the goose that lays the golden egg. Payrolls make consumers. *George Humphrey*

We women don't care too much about getting our pictures on money as long as we can get our hands on it. *Ivy Baker Priest, United States Treasurer*

. . . Old reformers never die. They get thrown out. *Herbert Hoover*

Conferences at the top level are always courteous. Name-calling is left to the Foreign Ministers. *Averell Harriman*

HAPPINESS

Everybody is looking for happiness, and only succeeds in finding death. Is it in death then, or beyond death, that happiness is to be found? *Maurice Maeterlinck*

Happiness is possible even in pain and suffering. But pleasure alone can never create happiness. *Paul Tillich*

There is no record in history of a happy philosopher: they exist only in romantic legends. *H. L. Mencken*

HEALTH

Illness is a great leveler. At its touch, the artificial distinctions of society vanish away. People in a hospital are just people. *Max Thorek*

A minor operation is one that was performed on the other fellow. *Russell Pettis Askue*

When envy, hate, fear are habitual they are capable of starting genuine diseases. *Dr. Alexis Carrel*

HISTORY

The history of the world is the record of a man in quest of his daily bread and butter. *Hendrik Van Loon*

History repeats itself, that's one of the things that's wrong with history. *Clarence Darrow*

Any event, once it has occurred, can be made to appear inevitable by a competent historian. *Lee Simonson*

HOLLYWOOD

I don't know how much I'm making, but I have a faint idea of how much I'm spending, and it's more than I can afford. *Broderick Crawford, actor, New York Journal-American*

Hollywood is the town where inferior people have a way of making superior people feel inferior. *Dudley Field Malone*

. . . one of the charms of Hollywood is that almost nothing they do is real or true or practical or anything resembling life. . . . *Frank Case*

HOW TO FAIL

The surest way to be a failure as a writer is to set out with the determination to please everyone. *Herbert Bayard Swope*

HUMILITY

When I feel like finding fault I aways begin with myself and then I never get any further. *David Grayson*

You grow up the day you have your first real laugh—at yourself.
Ethel Barrymore

HUNGER

God Himself dare not appear to a hungry man except in the form of bread. *Mahatma Gandhi*

We can plant wheat every year, but people who are starving die only once. *Fiorello H. La Guardia*

When one is really hungry he asks very few questions about source of supply, sanitation or purity. *C. C. & S. M. Furnas*

Hunger does not breed reform; it breeds madness, and all the ugly distempers that make an ordered life impossible. *Woodrow Wilson*

IDEALISM

Words without actions are the assassins of idealism. *Herbert Hoover*

IDEALS

To live is nothing, but to sacrifice his life for an ideal is the only thing which gives man his true quality. *Auguste Rodin*

IDEAS

New ideas can be good or bad, just the same as old ones. *Franklin D. Roosevelt*

If you want to get across an idea, wrap it up in a person. *Ralph Bunche*

The old ideas are the ancestors of our own; we build up on the sunken piers of obsolete wisdom. *Donald Culross Peattie*

Man's fear of ideas is probably the greatest dike holding back human knowledge and happiness. *Morris L. Ernst*

An idea isn't responsible for the people who believe in it. *Don Marquis*

For an idea ever to be fashionable is ominous, since it must afterwards be always old-fashioned. *George Santayana*

The policy of repression of ideas cannot work and never has worked. *Robert M. Hutchins*

The kind of man who demands that government enforce his ideas is always the kind whose ideas are idiotic. *H. L. Mencken*

An idea that is not dangerous is unworthy of being called an idea at all. *Elbert Hubbard*

In many ways ideas are more important than people—they are much more permanent. *C. F. Kettering*

IGNORANCE

Any frontal attack on ignorance is bound to fail because the masses are always ready to defend their most precious possession—their ignorance. *Hendrik Van Loon*

The compounding of individual ignorances in masses (cannot) produce a continuous directing force in public affairs. *Walter Lippmann*

Genuine ignorance is . . . profitable because it is likely to be accompanied by humility, curiosity, and open-mindedness; whereas ability to repeat catch-phrases, cant terms, familiar propositions, gives the conceit of learning and coats the mind with varnish waterproof to new ideas. *John Dewey*

In order to have wisdom we must have ignorance. *Theodore Dreiser*

Where ignorance is bliss it's foolish to borrow your neighbor's newspaper. *Kin Hubbard*

The older we grow the greater becomes our wonder at how much ignorance one can contain without bursting one's clothes. *Mark Twain*

Everybody is ignorant, only on different subjects. *Will Rogers*

The trouble with most folks isn't so much their ignorance, as knowing so many things that ain't so. *Josh Billings*

IMMIGRANTS

They (immigrants to the United States) came to us speaking many tongues—but a single language, the universal language of human aspiration. . . . *Franklin D. Roosevelt*

IMPORTANT

There are two kinds of people in one's life—people whom one keeps waiting—and the people for whom one waits. . . . *S. N. Behrman*

INDIVIDUALISM

No one ever heard of state freedom, much less did anyone ever hear of state morals. Freedom and morals are the exclusive possession of individuals. *H. M. Wriston*

Individualism may be regarded . . . as the system in which human stupidity can do the least harm. *J. M. Clark*

As we teach a young person it is not enough to teach him to "be himself." We must teach him to "be himself in an organized society." *A. Meiklejohn*

More than ever before, in our country, this is the age of the individual. *D. D. Eisenhower*

The free individual has been justified as his own master; the state as his servant. *D. D. Eisenhower*

INFLATION

Inflation is repudiation. *Calvin Coolidge*

No civilized country in the world has ever voluntarily adopted the extreme philosophies of either fascism or communism, unless the middle class was first liquidated by inflation. *H. W. Prentis*

The first panacea for a mismanaged nation is inflation of the currency; the second is war. Both bring a temporary prosperity; both bring a permanent ruin. *Ernest Hemingway*

INSULT

There are two insults which no human will endure: the assertion that he hasn't a sense of humor, and the doubly impertinent assertion that he has never known trouble. *Sinclair Lewis*

INTELLIGENCE

In any argument the man with the greater intelligence is always wrong, because he did not use his intelligence to avoid the argument in the first place. *Anonymous*

JOURNALISM

These pallid days upon which we have fallen do not recall the blithe gay years when reporting was combined with foot-racing, mayhem, ground and lofty tumbling, buck and wing dancing, and assault with intent to kill.   *William Allen White*

The American country paper rests entirely upon the theory of the dignity of the human spirit.   It is democracy embodied.   It emphasizes the individual.   *William Allen White*

JUSTICE

Justice, though due to the accused, is due to the accuser also.   The concept of fairness must not be strained till it is narrowed to a filament.   We are to keep the balance true.   *Benjamin N. Cardozo*

Unless justice be done to others it will not be done to us.   *Woodrow Wilson*

All things come to him who waits—even justice.   *Austin O'Malley*

Justice is the tolerable accommodation of the conflicting interests of society.   *Learned Hand*

Injustice is relatively easy to bear; what stings is justice.   *H. L. Mencken*

KINDERGARTEN

The world is a kind of spiritual kindergarten where bewildered infants are trying to spell God with the wrong blocks.   *E. A. Robinson*

KNOWLEDGE

To the small part of ignorance that we arrange and classify we give the name knowledge.   *Ambrose Bierce*

We do not need more knowledge, we need more character!   *Calvin Coolidge*

In whatever direction the future moves, whether the earthquake is long in coming or not, we must from now onward learn to live and act in the knowledge that we are all responsible to and for one another, because we have one common eternal destiny and because we are dependent on the one Father, who made brothers of us all.   *Pierre Van Paassen*

The best corrective of American provincialism is not merely a knowledge of Europe, but also a richer knowledge of the struggle of the republic to become what it has dreamt of becoming. *Howard Mumford Jones*

Fullness of knowledge always means some understanding of the depths of our ignorance; and that is always conducive to humility and reverence. *R. H. Millikan*

LAUGHTER

All that a comedian has to show for his years of work and aggravation is the echo of forgotten laughter. *Fred Allen*

LAW

The law and the stage—both are a form of exhibitionism. *Orson Welles*

To have convicted the innocent is horrible. For the innocent to have been irresponsibly charged with a serious violation of law, is but little less so: The power to prosecute can be the power to destroy. *Jerome Frank*

The trouble with law and government is lawyers. *Clarence Darrow*

LAZINESS

People who throw kisses are mighty near hopelessly lazy. *Bob Hope*

Some folks can look so busy doing nothin' that they seem indispensable. *Kin Hubbard*

LIAR

A man who won't lie to a woman has very little consideration for her feelings. *Olin Miller*

LIBERTY

The notion of liberty on which the Republic was founded, the spirit of America that animated Emerson and Whitman, is vividly alive today only in the unassimilated foreigner, in that pathetic pilgrim to a forgotten shrine. *Ludwig Lewisohn*

The foundation stone of democracy, indeed of all our liberties, is the free enterprise system; we cannot long enjoy political and religious liberty unless we likewise possess economic liberty. *H. F. Byrd*

The greatest dangers to liberty lurk in insidious encroachment by men of zeal, well-meaning but without understanding. *Louis D. Brandeis*

The history of liberty is a history of resistance. The history of liberty is a history of limitations of governmental power, not the increase of it. *Woodrow Wilson*

LIFE

We live as fully as we can the fragment of life that is our own life. *Max Ascoli*

I see life—for most at least—as a very grim and dangerous contest, relieved . . . by a sense or by an illusion of pleasure, which is the bait, and the lure for all in this internecine contest. *Theodore Dreiser*

Only a blind man would deny that characteristic traits of present life are a mad scramble for material commodities, a devotion to attainment of external power, and an insensate love of foolish luxuries and idle display. *John Dewey*

Every life is a march from innocence, through temptation, to virtue or to vice. *Lyman Abbott*

Life is work, and everything you do is so much more experience. *Henry Ford*

Born in throes, 'tis fit that man should live in pains and die in pangs. *Herman Melville*

Life is like a cash register, in that every account, every thought, every deed, like every sale, is registered and recorded. *Fulton J. Sheen*

In spite of everything, life is good. *H. W. Van Loon*

Life consists not simply in what heredity and environment do to us but in what we make out of what they do to us. *H. E. Fosdick*

A little work, a little sleep, a little love and it is all over. *Mary Roberts Rinehart*

I don't want to own anything that won't fit into my coffin. *Fred Allen*

I am very grateful for the opportunity to have lived. I know the world is full of sin, trouble, pain, and sorrow, but it is a very interesting world. *William Lyon Phelps*

We are all eavesdroppers, peering through a keyhole, and minding other people's business. *Robert Edmond Jones*

The significant questions of human destiny are not to be approached with a smile. God, misery, and salvation are no joke. *Irwin Edman*

LISTENING

Most of the successful people I've known are ones who do more listening than talking. If you choose your company carefully, it's worth listening to what they have to say. You don't have to blow out the other fellow's light to let your own shine. *Bernard Baruch*

LONELINESS

The whole conviction of my life now rests upon the belief that loneliness, far from being a rare and curious phenomenon, peculiar to myself and to a few other solitary men, is the central and inevitable fact of human existence. *Thomas Wolfe*

. . . like most self-sufficient men, he was a lonesome man. It is the dependent people who find friends. *Arthur Hopkins*

LOVE

. . . the unity that binds us all together, that makes this earth a family, and all men brothers and the sons of God, is love. *Thomas Wolfe*

MAN

Men will often say that they have "found themselves" when they have really been worn down into a groove by the brutal and compulsive force of circumstance. *Thomas Wolfe*

Perhaps man, having remade his environment, will turn around at last and begin to remake himself? *Will Durant*

First time you buy a house you see how pretty the paint is and buy it. The second time you look to see if the basement has termites. It's the same with men. *Lupe Velez*

The man of creative imagination pays a ghastly price for all his superiorities and immunities. . . . *H. L. Mencken*

MANNERS

Having many servants, though it makes a man a master, does not make him a gentleman. . . . *George Santayana*

I like him. He is every other inch a gentleman. *Noel Coward*

. . . the rich can be as dull or insolent as the most obscure village boor . . . *Ilka Chase*

We always deeply resent the person at a party who, while he speaks with us, keeps his eyes roving around the room as if in search of someone bigger and better to talk to. *Dorothy Walworth*

He's the kind of a bore who's here today and here tomorrow. *Binnie Barnes*

Apologize—to lay the foundation for a future offence. . . . *Ambrose Bierce*

MARRIAGE

Woman knows what Man has too long forgotten, that the ultimate economic and spiritual unit of any civilization is still the family. . . . *Clare Booth Luce*

Married life hain't so bad after you git so you kin eat th' things your wife likes. *Kin Hubbard*

The feller that puts off marryin' till he can support a wife ain't very much in love. *Kin Hubbard*

If it were not for the Presents, an Elopement would be Preferable. *George Ade*

It isn't tying himself to one woman that a man dreads when he thinks of marrying; it's separating himself from all the others. *Helen Rowland*

Marriage is the only known example of the happy meeting of the immovable object and the irresistible force. *Ogden Nash*

A chap ought to save a few of the long evenings he spends with his girl till after they're married. *Kin Hubbard*

It takes a man twenty-five years to learn to be married; it's a wonder women have the patience to wait for it. *C. B. Kelland*

MATHEMATICS

How can it be that mathematics, being after all a product of human thought independent of experience, is so admirably adapted to the objects of reality? *Albert Einstein*

MEDICINE

There are no such things as incurables, there are only things for which man has not found a cure. *Bernard Baruch*

MIDDLE AGE

One of the many things nobody ever tells you about middle age is that it's such a nice change from being young. *Dorothy Canfield Fisher*

MONEY

The notion of making money by popular work, and then retiring to do good work on the proceeds, is the most familiar of all the devil's traps for the artist. *Logan Pearsall Smith*

The first panacea for a mismanaged nation is inflation of the currency. *Ernest Hemingway*

. . . a man's treatment of money is the most decisive test of his character—how he makes it and how he spends it. *James Moffatt*

When a fellow says it hain't the money but the principle o' the thing, it's th' money. *Kin Hubbard*

Bad money, even in small doses, is poison to the economic system. *W. Randolph Burgess*

What this country needs is a good five-cent nickel. *Ed Wynn*

Money is the only substance which can keep a cold world from nicknaming a citizen "Hey, you!" *Wilson Mizner*

Nobody works as hard for his money as the man who marries it. *Kin Hubbard*

Broadway is a place where people spend money they haven't earned to buy things they don't need to impress people they don't like. *Walter Winchell*

MONOTONY

Monotony is the awful reward of the careful.   *A. G. Buckham*

MORALS

The whistling loafer, the irresponsible wit, have a lesson to teach the grave deacons of contemporary thought.   *Irwin Edman*

. . . it is amazing how many reasons we can give to justify our habits of behavior.   *Henry C. Link*

MUSIC

We depend largely on tricks, we writers of songs.   There is no such thing as a new melody.   *Irving Berlin*

Oh, the kinda singing I do, you can't hurt your voice.   *Bing Crosby*

The history of a country is written in its popular songs.   *Sigmund Spaeth*

To me, "God Bless America" was not just a song but an expression of my feeling toward the country to which I owe what I have and what I am.   *Irving Berlin*

NEW YORK

One hears the hoarse notes of the great ships in the river, and one remembers suddenly the princely girdle of proud, potent tides that bind the city, and suddenly New York blazes like a magnificent jewel in its fit setting of sea, and earth, and stars.   *Thomas Wolfe*

Why, if you're not in New York you are camping out.   *Thomas W. Dewing*

Coney Island, where the surf is one-third water and two-thirds people.   *John Steinbeck*

PEACE

World peace means a peace of bread.   *Herbert Hoover*

PERSONALITIES

Age is only a number, a cipher for the records.   A man can't retire his experience.   He must use it.   Experience achieves more with less energy and time.   *Bernard Baruch*

PESSIMISM

Idealists maintain that all nations should share the atomic bomb.
Pessimists maintain that they will.   *Punch (London)*

A pessimist is a man who thinks everybody as nasty as himself, and
hates them for it.   *George Bernard Shaw*

There is no sadder sight than a young pessimist, except an old optimist.   *Mark Twain*

PITY

Let no one underestimate the need of pity.   We live in a stony universe whose hard, brilliant forces rage fiercely.   *Theodore Dreiser*

For pity, more than any other feeling, is a "learned" emotion; a
child will have it least of all.   *Thomas Wolfe*

POETS

Poets are terribly sensitive people and one of the things they are
most sensitive about is cash.   *Robert Penn Warren*

POLITICS

Politics—a strife of interests masquerading as a contest of principles.   The conduct of public affairs for private advantage . . .
Ambrose Bierce
Imposter—a rival aspirant to public honors.   *Ambrose Bierce*
Conservative—a statesman who is enamored of existing evils, as
distinguished from the Liberal, who wishes to replace them with
others. . . .   *Ambrose Bierce*
Adherent—a follower who has not yet obtained all that he expects
to get . . . *Ambrose Bierce*
Alliance—in international politics, the union of two thieves who
have their hands so deeply inserted in each other's pocket that they
cannot separately plunder a third. . . .   *Ambrose Bierce*
How a minority, reaching majority, seizing authority, hates a minority.   *L. H. Robbins*

POPULARITY

Popularity is exhausting.   The life of the party almost always winds
up in a corner with an overcoat over him.   *Wilson Mizner*

PREJUDICE

Bigot—one who is obstinately and zealously attached to an opinion that you do not entertain. . . . *Ambrose Bierce*

THE PRESS

I am always in favor of the free press but sometimes they say quite nasty things. *Sir Winston Churchill*

I have never discovered a genius who spoke of talent. Or even of inspiration. Only brutal work. So, if you or I or my children don't succeed, might it not be more fitting to blame it, perhaps, on a measure of laziness rather than lack of talent? *Wilfred Funk*

PRIDE

The proud ones who boast and threaten and lust for power must watch the split seconds on the stopwatch of time. *Heywood Broun*

In the institution as in the individual, complacency and self-righteousness are the seeds of decline and fall. *George Fort Milton*

Lack of something to feel important about is almost the greatest tragedy a man may have. *Dr. Arthur E. Morgan*

PRINCIPLE

We should not wrap ourselves in a banner of so-called principle when we are really concerned only with economic advantage. *J. L. McCaffrey*

PROGRESS

Men have learned to travel farther and faster, though on errands not conspicuously improved. This, I believe, is called progress. *Willis Fisher*

PSYCHOANALYSIS

A wonderful discovery—psychoanalysis. Makes quite simple people feel they're complex. *S. N. Behrman*

QUOTATIONS FROM WINSTON CHURCHILL

I always avoid prophesying beforehand, because it is much better policy to prophesy after the event has already taken place.

I never take pleasure in human woe.

Personally I am always ready to learn, although I do not always like being taught.

I was once asked to devise an inscription for a monument in France. I wrote "In war, Resolution. In defeat, Defiance. In victory, Magnanimity. In Peace, Goodwill." The inscription was not accepted.

The night was chilly. Colonel Byng and I shared a blanket. When he turned over I was in the cold. When I turned over I pulled the blanket off him and he objected. He was the Colonel. It was not a good arrangement.

I am without an office, without a seat, without a party, and without an appendix.

This was a memorable occasion in my life. On my right sat the President of the United States, on my left the master of Russia. Together we controlled a large preponderance of the naval and three-quarters of all the air forces in the world, and could direct armies of nearly twenty millions of men, engaged in the most terrible of wars that had yet occurred in human history.

Be on your guard! I am going to speak in French—a formidable undertaking and one which will put great demands upon your friendship for Great Britain.

He can best be described as one of those orators who, before they get up, do not know what they are going to say; when they are speaking, do not know what they are saying; and, when they have sat down, do not know what they have said.

All social reform . . . which is not founded upon a stable medium of internal exchange becomes a swindle and a fraud.

I would make boys all learn English; and then I would let the clever ones learn Latin as an honour and Greek as a treat. But the only thing I would whip them for is not knowing English. I would whip them hard for that.

The story of the human race is War. Except for brief and precarious interludes, there has never been peace in the world.

Only faith in a life after death in a brighter world where dear ones will meet again—only that and the measured tramp of time can give consolation.

We must beware of trying to build a society in which nobody counts for anything except a politician or an official, a society where enterprise gains no reward and thrift no privileges.

I admire men who stand up for their country in defeat, even though I am on the other side.

There is a precipice on either side of you—a precipice of caution and a precipice of over-daring.

Young people at universities study to achieve knowledge and not to learn a trade.   We must all learn how to support ourselves, but we must also learn how to live.   We need a lot of engineers in the modern world, but we do not want a world of modern engineers.

Science burrows its insulated head in the filth of slaughterous inventions.

Man in this moment of his history has emerged in greater supremacy over the forces of nature than has ever been dreamed of before. . . . There lies before him, if he wishes, a golden age of peace and progress. All is in his hand.   He has only to conquer his last and worst enemy—himself.

History with its flickering lamp stumbles along the trail of the past, trying to reconstruct its scenes, to revive its echoes, and kindle with pale gleams the passion of former days.

The truth is incontrovertible.   Panic may resent it; ignorance may deride it; malice may distort it, but there it is.

The farther backward you can look, the farther forward you are likely to see.

RADICAL

A radical is a man with both feet firmly planted—in the air.   *Franklin D. Roosevelt*

Radicalism—the conservatism of tomorrow injected into the affairs of today . . . *Ambrose Bierce*

RECOMMENDATIONS

It was a wise man that recommended men, for their souls' good, to do each day two things they disliked.   And it is a precept that I have followed scrupulously: for every day I have got up and I have gone to bed.   *W. Somerset Maugham*

RELIGION

I could prove God statistically.   Take the human body alone—the chance that all the functions of the individual would just happen is a statistical monstrosity.   *George Gallup*

The Church after all is not a club of saints; it is a hospital for sinners. *George Craig Stewart*

Theologians have exalted God so much and debased men so far that it has become almost impossible for them to believe that men are truly the children of God, sons of God. *Edward S. Ames*

We have made a discovery that surprises and horrifies us . . . Sin and guilt are not merely words and empty symbols . . . but terrible matters of fact and reality . . . Wherefore let us now call ourselves to repentance. *Pastor Martin Niemoeller*

The primary movement in religious thinking—so clear that even the hasty runner can read, is the movement from more or less man-centered faith to a God-centered faith. *Halford E. Luccock*

Only through love can we attain to communion with God. *Dr. Albert Schweitzer*

Prayer, our deepest source of power and perfection, has been left miserably undeveloped. *Dr. Alexis Carrel*

Often the feeling is reflected that conventional religious belief is too superficial, too much a comfortable support for the well-fed to face the ugly realities of the world. *Halford E. Luccock*

There are no atheists in fox holes. *Father William T. Cummings*

There never was such a stupendous event as that which introduced the ideal of Jesus into the world. *John H. Dietrich*

Life is full of big and small Pilates. "The crucifixion of Christ" can never be accomplished without their help. *P. D. Ouspensky*

Religion may be the most immoral thing in the world. It is, when it is a religion which brings comfort without rebuke, when it gives satisfaction without conviction of sin. *Halford E. Luccock*

It was not the outer grandeur of the Roman but the inner simplicity of the Christian that lived on through the ages. *Colonel Charles Lindbergh*

I feel it is time that I also pay tribute to my four writers, Matthew, Mark, Luke, and John. *Bishop Fulton Sheen, New York World-Telegram & Sun*

I propose that God should be openly and audibly invoked at the United Nations in accordance with any one of the religious faiths which are represented here. I do so in the conviction that we cannot make the United Nations into a successful instrument of God's peace without God's help—and that with His help we cannot fail. To this end I propose that we ask for that help. . . . *Henry Cabot Lodge, Jr., chief U. S. delegate to the UN*

REPUTATION

Whatever reputation I have is due to the fact that I never open my mouth unless I have something to say. *George Bernard Shaw*

RICH

People who are hard, grasping . . . and always ready to take advantage of their neighbors, become very rich. *George Bernard Shaw*

Philanthropist—a rich (and usually bald) old gentleman who has trained himself to grin while his conscience is picking his pocket. . . . *Ambrose Bierce*

SATIRE

Satire is a lonely and introspective occupation, for nobody can describe a fool to the life without much patient self-inspection. *Frank Moore Colby*

SCIENCE

Science keeps on assiduously transforming the world, and trusts to luck that the transformation will be benign, beneficial to the majority. *Henry A. Wallace*

Science, which was to be the midwife of progress, became the angel of death, killing with a precision and a rapidity that reduced the wars of the middle ages to the level of college athletics. *Will Durant*

SOCIALISM

In a country where the sole employer is the State, opposition means death by slow starvation. The old principle: who does not work shall not eat, has been replaced by a new one: who does not obey shall not eat. *L. Trotsky*

Collective ideologists—those professional intellectuals who revel in decimals and polysyllables. *Winston Churchill*

SOCIETY

In Europe the poor envy the rich. In America the poor expect to be rich. There are no horizontal inherited barriers of caste to put a remorseless ceiling on a man's future. *Hans Bendix*

No social system will bring us happiness, health, and prosperity unless it is inspired by something greater than materialism. *Clement R. Attlee*

SPECULATION

A man cannot administer great corporations which employ armies of men and serve large communities if his judgment is diluted and distracted by huge speculative transactions. . . . A man cannot be a good doctor and keep telephoning to his broker between visits to his patients, nor a good lawyer with one eye on the ticker. *Walter Lippmann*

SPEECH

It is impossible to defeat an ignorant man in argument. *William G. McAdoo*

STATESMAN

A statesman is a politician who is held upright by equal pressure from all directions. *Eric A. Johnston*

SUCCESS

I dread success. To have succeeded is to have finished one's business on earth. *George Bernard Shaw*

Achievement—the death of endeavor and the birth of disgust. . . . *Ambrose Bierce*

The price of greatness is responsibility. *Winston Churchill*

THEATRE

Some actors think they are elevating the stage when they're merely depressing the audience. *George A. Posner*

Audiences? No, the plural is impossible. Whether it is in Butte, Montana, or Broadway, it's an audience. The same great hulking monster with four thousand eyes and forty thousand teeth. . . . *John Barrymore*

A fan club is a group of people who tell an actor he's not alone in the way he feels about himself. *Jack Carson*

Has anybody ever seen a dramatic critic in the daytime? Of course not. They come out after dark, up to no good. *P. G. Wodehouse, London Punch*

THOUGHT

People like to imagine that because all our mechanical equipment moves so much faster, that we are thinking faster, too. *Christopher Morley*

We have lost confidence in reason because we have learned that man is chiefly a creature of habit and emotion.   *John Dewey*

Where all think alike, no one thinks very much.   *Walter Lippmann*

Folks that blurt out just what they think wouldn't be so bad if they thought.   *Kin Hubbard*

If you make people think they're thinking, they'll love you; but if you really make them think, they'll hate you.   *Don Marquis*

An Englishman thinks seated; a Frenchman, standing; an American, pacing; an Irishman, afterward.   *Austin O'Malley*

TIME

Don't let yesterday use up too much of today!   *Will Rogers*

TOASTMASTER

. . . the obvious duty of a toastmaster is to be so infernally dull that the succeeding speakers will appear brilliant by contrast.   *Clarence Budington Kelland*

TRAVEL

In America there are two classes of travel—first class and with children.   *Robert Benchley*

Too often travel, instead of broadening the mind, merely lengthens the conversation.   *Elizabeth Drew*

TRUTH

As scarce as truth is, the supply has always been in excess of the demand.   *Josh Billings*

Truth is such a precious article let us all economize in its use.   *Mark Twain*

It is hard to believe that a man is telling the truth when you know that you would lie if you were in his place.   *H. L. Mencken*

UNITED NATIONS

. . . The United Nations was not set up to be a reformatory.   It was assumed that you would be good before you got in and not that being in would make you good.   *John Foster Dulles*

VICE-PRESIDENT

The vice-president of the United States is like a man in a cataleptic state; he cannot speak; he cannot move; he suffers no pain; and yet

he is perfectly conscious of everything that is going on about him.
Thomas R. Marshall

. . . once there were two brothers.   One ran away to sea, the other
was elected vice-president, and nothing was ever heard of either of
them again.   *Thomas R. Marshall*

VICTORY

Nothing in history has turned out to be more impermanent than
military victory.   *Harry Emerson Fosdick*

VIRTUE

Every vice was once a virtue, and may become respectable again,
just as hatred becomes respectable in wartime.   *Will Durant*

WAR

From time immemorial wars have been, especially for noncom-
batants, the supremely thrilling excitement.   *William James*

War comes as the great failure of man, out of fear, lust for power,
injustice, or misery left unrectified.   *Cordell Hull*

Certainly there is no hunting like the hunting of man; and those
who have hunted armed men long enough and like it, never really care
for anything else thereafter.   *Ernest Hemingway*

There is no such thing as civilized warfare.   *William Allen White*

. . . never think that war, no matter how necessary, nor how
justified, is not a crime.   Ask the infantry and ask the dead.   *Ernest
Hemingway*

WEALTH

A rich man is nothing but a poor man with money.   *W. C. Fields*

. . . there is nothing more demoralizing than a small but adequate
income.   *Edmund Wilson*

The concentration of wealth is made inevitable by the natural inequality of men.   *Will Durant*

WISDOM

Sometimes one pays most for the things one gets for nothing.   *Albert Einstein*

No man really becomes a fool until he stops asking questions.
Charles P. Steinmetz

WOMAN

Any girl can be glamorous. All you have to do is stand still and look stupid. *Hedy Lamarr*

Actually most women keep secrets as well as men. It just takes more women. *Lt. Clyde Melton, Jr.*

Being a woman is a terribly difficult task, since it consists principally in dealing with men. *Joseph Conrad*

A capacity for self-pity is one of the last things that any woman surrenders. *Irvin S. Cobb*

WORK

Work is the greatest thing in the world, so we should always save some of it for tomorrow. *Don Herold*

The world is full of willing people; some willing to work, the rest willing to let them. *Robert Frost*

I have succeeded in getting my actual work down to thirty minutes a day. That leaves me eighteen hours for engineering. *Charles Steinmetz*

Heaven is blessed with perfect rest but the blessing of earth is toil. *H. Van Dyke*

WORRY

Worry is a thin stream of fear trickling through the mind. If encouraged, it cuts a channel into which all other thoughts are drained. *Arthur Somers Roche*

WRITERS

Only a mediocre writer is always at his best. *W. Somerset Maugham*

11 •••

Proverbs of Many Nations

ABUNDANCE

Abundance, like want, ruins man.   *Franklin*

ACHE

The tongue ever turns to the aching tooth.

ADVERSITY

Adversity makes a man wise, not rich.
There is no education like adversity.   *Disraeli*

Adversity has no friends.   *Tacitus*

ADVICE

Fools need Advice most, but wise Men only are the better for it.
Franklin

Less advice and more hands.   *German*

Hazard not your wealth on a poor man's advice.   *Spanish*

When the rabbit has escaped comes advice.   *Spanish*

AGE

All would live long, but none would be old.   *Franklin*

Many foxes grow gray, but few grow old.   *Franklin*

286

Youth is a blunder; manhood a struggle; old age a regret. *Disraeli*

When old men are not upright, they teach their sons to be rogues.
Chinese

The old forget, the young don't know. *German*

Old age and the wear of time teach many things. *Sophocles*

The old age of an eagle is better than the youth of a sparrow.
Greek

ALMS

Alms never make poor. *Italian*

ALONE

Better be alone than in bad company.
A wise man is never less alone than when alone. *Latin*

AMBITION

Ambition obeys no law but its own appetite.
. . . fling away ambition:
By that sin fell the angels. *Shakespeare*

Ambition destroys its possessor. *Hebrew*

AMUSEMENT

Amusement is the happiness of those who cannot think. *Pope*

ANGER

Let not the sun go down upon your wrath. *Ephesians*
A man in a passion rides a mad horse.
Anger is never without a Reason, but seldom with a good One.
Franklin
Anger punishes itself.
The greatest remedy for anger is delay. *Seneca*

APPETITE

Poor men want meat for their stomachs, rich men stomachs for
their meat.
A stomach that is seldom empty despises common food. *Horace*

ARGUMENT

A noisy man is always in the right.
You have not converted a man because you have silenced him.
Anonymous

ASPIRATION

No bird soars too high if he soars with his own wings. *Blake*

Too low they build, who build beneath the stars. *Young*

ATHEISM

The fool hath said in his heart, There is no God. *Psalms*
Some are atheists only in fair weather. *Anonymous*

AVARICE

A covetous man does nothing well till he dies.
Avarice, the spur of industry. *Hume*

The more a man has, the more he desires. *Italian*

He who covets is always poor. *Latin*

BEAUTY

Everything has its beauty but not everyone sees it. *Confucius*

All heiresses are beautiful.
Beauty and folly are old companions.
What is beautiful is good, and who is good will soon also be beautiful. *Sappho*

When the candles are out all women are fair. *Plutarch*

Beauty and wisdom are rarely conjoined. *Petronius*

BIOGRAPHY

Biography is the only true history. *Carlyle*

Biography—one of the new terrors of death. *Arbuthnot*

BOOK

A book may be as great a thing as a battle. *Disraeli*

A good book is the precious life-blood of a master spirit . . . *Milton*

Books are ships which pass through the vast seas of time. *Bacon*

Books, the children of the brain.

That is a good book which is opened with expectation and closed with profit. *A. B. Alcott*

Word by word the great books are written. *Voltaire*

A room without books is a body without a soul. *Latin*

BORROW

The borrower is the servant of the lender. *Proverbs*
Creditors have better memories than debtors.
Let us . . . live within our income, even if we have to borrow the money to do it. *Art. Ward*

BREAD

Cast thy bread upon the waters: for thou shalt find it after many days. *Ecclesiastes*
Man shall not live by bread alone. *Matthew*
What man is there of you, whom if his son ask bread, will he give him a stone. *Matthew*
His bread is buttered on both sides. *Anonymous*

BRIBE

Few men have virtue to withstand the highest bidder. *Washington*

Honesty stands at the gate and knocks, and bribery enters in. *Anonymous*

CHARACTER

A man shows his character by what he laughs at. *German*

There is a great deal of unmapped country within us.
No man can climb out beyond the limitations of his own character. *J. Morley*

It matters not what you are thought to be, but what you are. *Latin*

CHARITY

He that gives to be seen will relieve none in the dark.
The living need charity more than the dead.
Do good and ask not for whom. *Yiddish*

DEATH

The Lord gave, and the Lord hath taken away; blessed be the name of the Lord. *Job*

Yet a little sleep, a little slumber, a little folding of the hands to sleep. *Proverbs*

As soon as a man is born he begins to die.

Men may live fools, but fools they cannot die.

To live in hearts we leave behind is not to die.

It is uncertain where death may await thee, therefore expect it everywhere. *Latin*

Pale Death, with impartial step, knocks at the poor man's cottage and at the palaces of kings. *Horace*

DEED

A noble deed is a step toward God.

How far that little candle throws his beams!
    So shines a good deed in a naughty world. *Shakespeare*

DEMOCRACY

Democracy substitutes election by the incompetent many for appointment by the corrupt few. *G. B. Shaw*

Democracy becomes a government of bullies tempered by editors. *Emerson*

DUTY

Duty is what one expects from others. *O. Wilde*

EDUCATION

Only the educated are free. *Greek*

There is no royal road to geometry. *Euclid*

ELOQUENCE

Eloquence is the child of knowledge.

He is eloquent enough for whom truth speaks. *Latin*

It is the heart which makes men eloquent. *Latin*

FACT

Facts do not cease to exist because they are ignored.

You can't alter facts by filming them over with romance. *Anonymous*

FAILURE

Give me the heart to fight and lose.

They went forth to battle but they always fell. *Ossian*

FEAR

Fear is the offspring of ignorance.

Our fears always outnumber our dangers. *Latin*

If the thunder is not loud, the peasant forgets to cross himself.
Russian

FRIEND

If you have one true friend, you have more than your share.

The wretched have no friends.

Prosperity makes friends and adversity tries them. *Latin*

GENIUS

Genius is mainly an affair of energy.

Genius is nothing but labor and diligence. *Anonymous*

GIVING

He that gives his heart will not deny his money.

He who gives fair words feeds you with an empty spoon. *Anonymous*

GOD

God often visits us, but most of the time we are not at home.
French

God sends nothing but what can be borne. *Italian*

If God be with us, who shall stand against us? *Latin*

GOVERNMENT

The whole of government consists in the art of being honest. *Jefferson*

Every country has the government it deserves. *French*

GREAT

Towers are measured by their shadows and great men by their calumniators. *Chinese*

Great hopes make great men.
Great men have great faults.
Great men will always pay deference to greater. *Lander*

Great men's vices are esteemed as virtues.
No really great man ever thought himself so. *Hazlitt*

To be great is to be misunderstood. *Emerson*

HASTE

A hasty man drinks his tea with a fork. *Chinese*

HEART

Where there is room in the heart there is room in the house. *Danish*

Every heart hath its own ache.
He wears his heart on his sleeve.
When the heart is on fire, some sparks fly out of the mouth.
The heart has reasons which reason does not know. *Pascal*

When the heart is full, the eyes overflow. *Yiddish*

HEAVEN

Earth has no sorrow that Heaven cannot heal.
He will never get to heaven that desires to go thither alone.
No man must go to heaven who hath not sent his heart thither before. *Anonymous*

HISTORY

History is lies agreed upon.
Sin writes histories, goodness is silent. *Goethe*

HONESTY

An honest man does not make himself a dog for the sake of a bone.
Danish

An honest man's the noblest work of God. *Pope*

They are all honest men, but my cloak is not to be found. *Spanish*

HONOR

The louder he talked of his honor, the faster we counted our spoons. *Emerson*

> When faith is lost, when honor dies,
> The man is dead! *Whittier*

HOPE

Hope is the poor man's income. *Danish*

Great hopes make great men.
Hope is a good breakfast but a bad supper.
> The heart bowed down by weight of woe
> To weakest hope will cling. *Bunn*

> The miserable have no medicine
> But only hope. *Shakespeare*

Who lives by hope will die of hunger. *Anonymous*

HUMILITY

The boughs that bear most hang lowest.
There is no true holiness without humility. *Anonymous*

HUSBAND

The more a wife loves her husband, the more she corrects his faults. *Chinese*

A good husband makes a good wife.
A good wife makes a good husband. *Anonymous*

IGNORANCE

He who knows nothing is confident of everything.
Ignorance is a voluntary misfortune. *Anonymous*

IMMORTALITY

> Dust thou art, to dust returnest,
> Was not spoken of the soul. *Longfellow*

JUSTICE

Justice is truth in action.　*Joubert*
Justice is half religion.　*Turkish*

KNOWLEDGE

Knowledge in youth is wisdom in age.
He who knows nothing never doubts.　*Italian*

LABOR

Be the first in the field and the last to the couch.　*Chinese*

The gods will sell us all good things at the price of labor.　*Greek*

He who would eat the kernel must crack the shell.　*Latin*

LATE

A little too late is much too late.　*German*

LAUGH

And if I laugh at any mortal thing,
　'Tis that I may not weep.　*Byron*

Our sincerest laughter
　With some pain is fraught.　*Shelley*

LAW

He who goes to law for a sheep loses his cow.　*German*

There is no law without a loophole for him who can find it.　*German*

Laws were made that the stronger might not in all things have his way.　*Latin*

LEISURE

A life of leisure and a life of laziness are two things.
He was never less at leisure than when at leisure.　*Latin*

LEND

Great spenders are bad lenders.

LIFE

I wept when I was born, and every day shows why.
Learn that the present hour alone is man's.
Life's a long headache in a noisy street. *Masefield*

Life is a loom, weaving illusion.
Plain living and high thinking . . . *Wordsworth*

Most men employ the earlier part of life to make the other part
miserable. *French*

LOSE

Better lose the anchor than the whole ship. *Dutch*

Losers are always in the wrong. *Spanish*

If you've nothing to lose, you can try everything. *Yiddish*

MAN

Good men and bad men are each less so than they seem.
Man, an animal that makes bargains. *Adam Smith*

Man is Nature's sole mistake.
Man is the miracle in nature.
Man is the only animal that blushes. Or needs to. *Mark Twain*

No man is born wise or learned.
    Though every prospect pleases,
        And only man is vile. *Heber*
Man is but a reed, the weakest in nature, but he is a thinking reed.
Pascal

MANNERS

Everyone thinks himself well-bred.
Good breeding consists in concealing how much we think of ourselves and how little we think of the other person. *Mark Twain*

MARRIAGE

To marry once is a duty, twice a folly, thrice is madness. *Dutch*

Every woman should marry, and no man. *Disraeli*

Marriage halves our griefs, doubles our joys, and quadruples our expenses.

Marriage is the only venture open to the cowardly.   *Voltaire*

Marriages are made in heaven and consummated on earth.   *French*

I never married and I wish my father never had.   *Greek*

MISFORTUNE

We all have sufficient strength to bear other people's misfortunes. *La Rochefoucauld*

Misfortune is friendless.   *Greek*

MONEY

Money is a good servant but a bad master.

   Money is honey, my little sonny,
     And a rich man's joke is always funny.

The love of money and the love of learning seldom meet.

When money speaks, truth keeps silent.   *Russian*

MOTHER

Mother is the name for God in the lips and hearts of little children. *Thackeray*

Simply having children does not make mothers.   *Anonymous*

NECESSITY

Necessity makes even the timid brave.   *Latin*

Necessity urges desperate measures.   *Spanish*

NOBLE

There is nothing noble in being superior to some other man.   True nobility is in being superior to your former self.   *Hindu Proverb*

OPPORTUNITY

   There is a tide in the affairs of men
     Which taken at the flood leads on to fortune.   *Shakespeare*

PATIENCE

He preacheth patience that never knew pain.

Patience is the art of hoping.   *French*

PEACE

When a man finds no peace within himself, it is useless to seek it elsewhere. *French*

PEOPLE

The mob has many heads but no brains.
No man who depends upon the caprice of the ignorant rabble can be accounted great. *Cicero*

Nothing is so uncertain as the judgments of the mob. *Latin*

PHILANTHROPY

The most acceptable service of God is doing good to man. *Franklin*

I am a man, and nothing human can be indifferent to me. *Terence*

POOR

Whoso stoppeth his ear at the cry of the poor, shall cry himself and not be heard. *Hebrew*

Not he who has little, but he who wishes for more, is poor. *Latin*

POVERTY

He can give little to his servant that licks his knife.
Poverty is no vice—but an inconvenience.
Poverty is the mother of all the arts.
Poverty—the mother of temperance. *Greek*
No man should praise poverty but he who is poor. *St. Bernard*

There are many things which ragged men dare not say. *Latin*

There are only two families in the world, the Haves and the Have-Nots. *Cervantes*

PRAISE

He who praises everybody praises nobody.
Our praise are our wages.
Self-praise is no recommendation. *Anonymous*

PRAYER

And Satan trembles when he sees
  The weakest saint upon his knees. *Cowper*

God warms his hands at man's heart when he prays. *Masefield*

Who goes to bed, and doth not pray,
  Maketh two nights to every day.
Who rises from prayer a better man, his prayer is answered. *Meredith*

If you pray for another, you will be helped yourself. *Yiddish*

PRIDE

Pride is at the bottom of all great mistakes.
Pride may lurk under a threadbare cloak. *Anonymous*

PROSPERITY

Prosperity is a great teacher; adversity, a greater.
Prosperity makes friends, adversity tries them. *Latin*

The prosperous man is never sure that he is loved for himself. *Latin*

QUARREL

Those who in quarrels interpose
  Must often wipe a bloody nose.

READING

I love to lose myself in other men's minds. *Lamb*

Let blockheads read what blockheads wrote.
The art of reading is to skip judiciously. *Anonymous*

REVENGE

The noblest vengeance is to forgive.
To forget a wrong is the best revenge. *Anonymous*

RICH

To gain wealth is easy; to keep it, hard. *Chinese*
  But Satan now is wiser than of yore,
    And tempts by making rich, not making poor. *Pope*

Ill fares the land, to hastening ills a prey,
 Where wealth accumulates, and men decay.   *Goldsmith*

I never knew a silent rich man.   *French*
The richest man carries nothing away with him but his shroud.
French

RUSSIAN PROVERBS

When you meet a man, you judge him by his clothes; when you
leave, you judge him by his heart.
An old friend is better than two new ones.

Give your children too much freedom and you lose your own.

If everyone gives one thread, the poor man will have a shirt.

Someone else's calamity doesn't add to your own wisdom.

Tears come more often from the eyes than from the heart.

Do not wish for any other blessing than a good wife and rich soup.

SAVING

For age and want save while you may:
 No morning sun lasts a whole day.   *Anonymous*

SCHOLAR

The scholar who cherishes the love of comfort is not fit to be deemed
a scholar.   *Confucius*

SELF-LOVE

To love oneself is the beginning of a life-long romance.   *O. Wilde*

Self-love is the greatest of all flatterers.   *La Rochefoucauld*

SERVICE

They serve God well who serve his creatures.

SICKNESS

The chamber of sickness is the chapel of devotion.
In time of sickness the soul collects itself anew.   *Latin*

Sickness shows us what we are.   *Latin*

SILENCE

It is sad when men have neither wit to speak, nor judgment to hold their tongues. *French*

SIN

Every man carries the bundle of his sins upon his own back.
I am a man more sinned against than sinning. *Shakespeare*

Some rise by sin, and some by virtue fall. *Shakespeare*

The cat shuts its eyes while it steals cream.
Sin writes histories; goodness is silent. *Goethe*

Who is not ashamed of his sins, sins double. *German*

There is a sin of omission as well as of commission. *Greek*
Who sins and mends, commends himself to God. *Spanish*

SOLITUDE

Solitude is the best nurse of wisdom.
I am never less alone than when alone. *Latin*

The strongest man in the world is he who stands alone. *Ibsen*

SORROW

Earth has no sorrow that Heaven cannot heal.
The longest sorrow finds at last relief.
   When sorrows come, they come not single spies,
      But in battalions. *Shakespeare*

SPEECH

Blessed is the man who, having nothing to say, abstains from giving us wordy evidence of the fact. *George Eliot*

Discretion of speech is more than eloquence.
He that speaks much is much mistaken.
The true use of speech is to conceal our thoughts.
One speaks little when vanity does not make one speak. *La Rochefoucauld*

SUCCESS

Nothing is so impudent as success.
Success makes a fool seem wise.
Everything is subservient to success. *French*

TALK

So much they talked, so very little said.
He who talks much is sometimes right. *Spanish*

THOUGHT

If men would think more, they would act less.
The profound thinker always suspects that he may be superficial.
Disraeli

TIME

Nought treads so silent as the foot of time.
All the treasures of earth cannot bring back one lost moment.
French
Time is a river of passing events—a rushing torrent. *Greek*

TRAVEL

It is not worth while to go around the world to count the cats in
Zanzibar. *Thoreau*
Traveling makes a man wiser, but less happy.
If a goose flies across the sea, there comes back a quack-quack.
German
See one mountain, one sea, one river—and see all. *Greek*
He who never leaves his country is full of prejudices. *Italian*

TRUTH

When in doubt, tell the truth. *Mark Twain*
Individuals may perish; but truth is eternal. *French*
To fool the world, tell the truth. *Bismarck*

TYRANT

Tyranny is a lovely eminence, but there is no way down from it.
Solon

UNDERSTANDING

What we do not understand we do not possess. *Goethe*

VICE

Never open the door to a little vice lest a great one enter with it.
The virtues of society are the vices of the saints. *Emerson*

VIRTUE

Virtue is always in a minority. *French*

Virtue has no greatei enemy than wealth. *Italian*

Virtue unites man with God. *Latin*

WANT

Man wants but little here below, nor wants that little long.

He that wants the kernel must crack the nut. *French*

To have no wants is divine . . . *Socrates*

WAR

Force and fraud are in war the two cardinal virtues. *Hobbes*

War never leaves where it found a nation. *Burke*

In war it is not permitted to make a mistake twice. *Greek*

War loves to seek its victims in the young. *Greek*

WEALTH

A man's wealth is his enemy.

WIFE

He that tells his wife news is but newly married.
The wife that loves the looking-glass hates the saucepan.
A virtuous wife rules her husband by obeying him. *Latin*

WISE

What's the good of being wise when foolishness serves? *Yiddish*

WIT

Wit does not take the place of knowledge.
Wit is the salt of conversation, not the food. *Anonymous*

WOMAN

A handsome woman is always right. *German*

Silence gives grace to a woman. *Sophocles*

It is a sad house where the hen crows louder than the cock. *Italian*

Kind words and few are a woman's ornament.   *Danish*

The three virtues of a woman: Obey the father, obey the husband, obey the son.   *Chinese*

WORK

Blessed is he who has found his work; let him ask no other blessedness.   *Carlyle*

YOUTH

The majority of men employ the first portion of their life in making the other portion miserable.   *La Bruyere*

Youth holds no society with grief.   *Aristotle*

Whilst the morning shines, gather the flowers.   *Latin*

12 •••

Material for Special Occasions

BIRTHDAY

Monday's child is fair in face,
Tuesday's child is full of grace,
Wednesday's child is full of woe,
Thursday's child has far to go,
Friday's child is loving and giving,
Saturday's child works hard for its living;
And a child that's born on Christmas Day,
Is fair and wise, and good and gay. *J. O. Halliwell-Phillips*

What hath this day deserv'd?   What hath it done,
That it in golden letters should be set
Among the high tides in the calendar?   *Shakespeare*

Oh! be thou blest with all that Heaven can send,
Long health, long youth, long pleasure—and a friend.   *Pope*

CHRISTMAS

A young Frenchman was applying for inclusion in his country's quota of immigrants to America.   A member of the board asked him why he wanted to go to America.

The young man earnestly replied, "I want to go to America because—" he paused and then continued with a rush "—because in America, it's Christmas every day." *Chain Gang*

304

When we were children we were grateful to those who filled our stockings with toys at Christmastide. Why are we not grateful to God for filling our stockings with legs? *G. K. Chesterton*

He who has no Christmas in his heart will never find Christmas under a tree. *Roy L. Smith, Methodist Christian Advocate*

I sometimes think we expect too much of Christmas Day. We try to crowd into it the long arrears of kindliness and humanity of the whole year. *David Grayson*

CHRISTMAS PRAYER

May the forgiving spirit of Him to whom we dedicate this season prevail again on earth.

May hateful persecution and wanton aggression cease.

May man live in freedom and security, worshipping as he sees fit, loving his fellow man.

May the sanctity of the home be ever preserved.

May peace, everlasting peace, reign supreme. *Sunshine Magazine*

People say that Christmas today is too commercialized. But I have never found it that way. If you spend money to give people joy, you are not being commercial. It is only when you feel obliged to do something about Christmas that the spirit is spoiled. *Eleanor Roosevelt*

> O little town of Bethlehem,
>   How still we see thee lie!
> Above thy deep and dreamless sleep
>   The silent stars go by. *Phillips Brooks*

What babe new born is this that in a manger cries?
Near on her lowly bed his happy mother lies.
Oh, see the air is shaken with white and heavenly wings—
This is the Lord of all the earth, this is the King of Kings.
                                                    Richard Watson Gilder

> There's a song in the air!
> There's a star in the sky!
> There's a mother's deep prayer
>   And a Baby's low cry!
> And the star rains its fire where the
>   Beautiful sing,

For the manger of Bethlehem cradles a King. *Josiah Gilbert
Holland*

I heard the bells on Christmas Day
Their old, familiar carols play,
   And wild and sweet
   The words repeat
Of peace on earth, good-will to men! *Henry Wadsworth
Longfellow*

Heap on more wood!—the wind is chill;
But let it whistle as it will,
We'll keep our Christmas merry still. *Sir Walter Scott*

It came upon the midnight clear,
   That glorious song of old,
From angels bending near the earth
   To touch their harps of gold;
"Peace on the earth, good will to men
   From Heaven's all-gracious King"—
The world in solemn stillness lay
   To hear the angels sing. *Edmund Hamilton Sears*

Christmas is coming, the geese are getting fat,
Please to put a penny in the old man's hat;
If you haven't got a penny, a ha'penny will do,
If you haven't got a ha'penny, God bless you! *Unknown
Beggar's Rhyme*

Hark the herald angels sing,
Glory to the new-born King;
Peace on earth, and mercy mild,
God and sinners reconciled! *Charles Wesley*

God rest you merry, gentlemen,
   Let nothing you dismay,
For Jesus Christ, our Saviour,
   Was born upon this day. *Anonymous Old Carol*

It is good to be children sometimes, and never better then at Christmas when its mighty Founder was a child Himself. *Dickens*

Let Christmas be a bright and happy day; but let its brightness come from the radiance of the star of Bethlehem, and its happiness be found in Christ, the sinner's loving Saviour. *H. G. Den*

God rest ye, little children; let nothing you affright,
For Jesus Christ, your Saviour, was born this happy night;
Along the hills of Galilee the white flocks sleeping lay,
When Christ, the Child of Nazareth, was born on Christmas day.
Diana Mulock Craik

At Christmas play, and make good cheer,
For Christmas comes but once a year. *Thomas Tusser*

Be merry all, be merry all,
With holly dress the festive hall;
Prepare the song, the feast, the ball,
To welcome merry Christmas. *W. R. Spencer*

No Santa Claus! Thank God, he lives, and he lives forever. A thousand years from now, Virginia, nay, ten times ten thousand years from now, he will continue to make glad the heart of childhood. *Francis P. Church*

DECORATION DAY

The passions of the titanic struggle will finally enter upon the sleep of oblivion, and only its splendid accomplishments for the cause of human freedom and a united nation, stronger and richer in patriotism because of the great strife, will be remembered. *General James Longstreet*

Here sleeps heroic dust! It is meet that a redeemed nation should come, to pay it homage at such tombs, wreathing the memory of its patriot dead in the emblems of grateful affection. These grass-grown mounds, these flower-decked graves, awake the memories of the past, and the history of our nation's perils and its triumphs comes crowding on us here. *American Wesleyan*

EASTER

Tomb, thou shalt not hold Him longer;
Death is strong, but Life is stronger;
Stronger than the dark, the light;
Stronger than the wrong, the right;
Faith and Hope triumphant say
Christ will rise on Easter Day. *Phillips Brooks*

"Christ the Lord is risen to-day,"
Sons of men and angels say:
Raise your joys and triumphs high;
Sing, ye heavens, and earth, reply. *Charles Wesley*

If someone asks you for the best recipe for drawing a cross, the best answer is this: Write a capital "I" and then scratch it out. *Telescope-Messenger*

God expects from men something more at such times, and that it were much to be wished for the credit of their religion as well as the satisfaction of their conscience that their Easter devotions would in some measure come up to their Easter dress. *South*

The Easter story is the story of the fundamental fight between life and death, between hope and despair. *Heywood Broun*

At Easter let your clothes be new
Or else be sure you will it rue. *Old English Rhyme*

FOURTH OF JULY

We, therefore, the representatives of the United States of America, in General Congress assembled, appealing to the Supreme Judge of the world for the rectitude of our intentions, do, in the name and by the authority of the good people of these colonies, solemnly publish and declare that these United Colonies are, and of right ought to be, free and independent states. *Declaration of Independence*

That which distinguishes this day from all others is that then both orators and artillerymen shoot blank cartridges. *John Burroughs*

MARRIAGE

Every man who is high up loves to think that he has done it all himself; and the wife smiles, and lets it go at that. *J. M. Barrie*

There is only one thing for a man to do who is married to a woman who enjoys spending money, and that is to enjoy earning it. *Edgar W. Howe*

No man likes to live under the eye of perpetual disapprobation. *Dr. Samuel Johnson*

NEW YEAR

The special insecurity in which we now live in an age in which one civilization is dying and another is powerless to be born is typical of the insecurity in which the children of man have always lived. Each New Year is an adventure into which we must, as did Abraham of old, go out, not knowing whither we go. *Reinhold Niebuhr*

And as the Old Year slips away,
He kindly with him takes
The pages we have blurred and marred
With failure and mistakes.
The blighted hopes and needless fears
Are gone beyond recall.
And ours once more the fair, clean page
The New Year brings to all. *Marion Sanford Sunshine Magazine*

Ring out the old, ring in the new,
Ring, happy bells, across the snow;
The year is going, let him go;
Ring out the false, ring in the true. *Alfred Tennyson*

No one ever regarded the first of January with indifference. It is the nativity of our common Adam. *Charles Lamb*

THANKSGIVING

The first Thanksgiving Proclamation was made by Governor Bradford three years after the Pilgrims settled at Plymouth:
"To all ye Pilgrims:
"Inasmuch as the great Father has given us this year an abundant harvest of Indian corn, wheat, peas, beans, squashes, and garden vegetables, and has made the forests to abound with game and the sea with fish and clams, and inasmuch as he has protected us from the ravages of the savages, has spared us from pestilence and disease, has granted us freedom to worship God according to the dictates of our own conscience; now I, your magistrate, do proclaim that all ye Pilgrims, with your wives and ye little ones, do gather at ye meeting house, on ye hill, between the hours of 9 and 12 in the day time, on Thursday, November ye 29th, of the year of our Lord one thousand six hundred and twenty-three, and the third year since ye Pilgrims landed on ye Pilgrim Rock, there to listen to ye pastor and render thanksgiving to ye Almighty God for all his blessings. William Bradford, Ye Governor of Ye Colony."

We Americans are, on the whole, a generous people. . . . But let us take care that we do not fail to be as generous in thanking God as we are in sharing with others the gifts He has shared with us. Thanksgiving Day? No, rather three hundred and sixty-five "Thanksgiving Days" a year—every year! *Indiana Catholic and Record*

Truly, this is God's country. Nothing can destroy it unless we become unthinkably weak—too weak to lift our hearts to heaven in gratitude for its uncounted blessings. *Burton Hillis*

So once in every year we throng
　　Upon a day apart,
To praise the Lord with feast and song
　　In thankfulness of heart. *Arthur Guiterman*

It is a good thing to give thanks unto the Lord. *Psalms XCII, 1*

O give thanks unto the Lord, for he is good: for his mercy endureth forever. *Psalms CVII, 1*

Let never day nor night unhallow'd pass,
But still remember what the Lord hath done. *Shakespeare*

Now thank we all our God,
　　With heart and hand and voices
Who wondrous things hath done,
　　In whom His world rejoices. *Catherine Winkworth*

Almighty God, Father of all mercies, we, thine unworthy servants, do give thee most humble and hearty thanks for all thy goodness and loving-kindness to us, and to all men. *The Book of Common Prayer*

Some people always sigh in thanking God. *E. B. Browning*

SPRING

The flowers appear on the earth; the time of the singing of birds is come, and the voice of the turtle is heard in our land. *Solomon's Song II, 12*

Now every field is clothed with grass, and every tree with leaves; now the woods put forth their blossoms, and the year assumes its gay attire. *Virgil*

SUMMER

Summer is the mother of the poor. *Italian Proverb*

The Autumn with its fruits provides disorders for us, and the Winter's cold turns them into sharp diseases, and the Spring brings flowers to strew our hearse, and the Summer gives green turf and brambles to bind upon our graves. *Jeremy Taylor*

Sing a song of seasons;
  Something bright in all;
Flowers in the Summer;
  Fires in the Fall.   *R. L. Stevenson*

AUTUMN

There is a harmony
In Autumn, and a lustre in its sky,
Which thro' the Summer is not heard or seen.   *P. B. Shelley*

The melancholy days are come, the saddest of the year,
Of wailing winds, and naked woods, and meadows brown and
  sear.   *W. C. Bryant*

Earth's crammed with Heaven,
And every common bush afire with God.   *E. B. Browning*

WINTER

From Winter, plague, and pestilence, good Lord, deliver us!
Thomas Nashe

If Winter comes, can Spring be far behind?   *P. B. Shelley*

Every Winter,
When the great sun has turned his face away,
The earth goes down into a vale of grief,
And fasts, and weeps, and shrouds herself in sables.   *Charles
Kingsley*

Oh, the long and dreary Winter!
Oh, the cold and cruel Winter!   *H. W. Longfellow*

13 •••

Humorous Definitions

Absurdity: A statement or belief manifestly inconsistent with one's own opinion. *Ambrose Bierce*

Acquaintance: A person whom we know well enough to borrow trom, but not well enough to lend to. *Ambrose Bierce*

Admiration: Our polite recognition of another's resemblance to ourselves. *Ambrose Bierce*

Adult Western: One in which the plot is more than 20 years old.

Adversity: A medicine people recommend as good for the neighbors.

Advertising agency: Eighty-five per cent confusion and fifteen per cent commission. *Fred Allen*

After dinner speaker: Someone who knows how to dilute a two minute idea into a two hour speech.

Agriculturist: A farmer who owns a station wagon.

Alimony: The billing without the cooing.

America: The country where you buy a lifetime supply of aspirin for one dollar, and use it up in two weeks. *John Barrymore*

American university: Defined by a Chinese student as a vast athletic association where, however, some studies are maintained for the benefit of the feeble-minded. *Indiana Telephone News*

Amnesty: The state's magnanimity to those offenders whom it would be too expensive to punish. *Ambrose Bierce*

Amusement: The happiness of those that cannot think. *Pope*

Anger: A condition where the tongue works faster than the mind.

Antique furniture: Furniture found in the homes of the rich and in homes with a number of children. A piece of furniture that is paid for.

Apologize: To lay the foundation for a future offense. *Ambrose Bierce*

Applause: The echo of a platitude. *Ambrose Bierce*

Auctioneer: The man who proclaims with a hammer that he has picked a pocket with his tongue. *Ambrose Bierce*

Auto thief: A person who steals automobiles and known in Texas as a Cadillac Rustler.

Bachelor: A man who shirks responsibilities and duties. *George Bernard Shaw*

Bachelor girl: Girl looking for a bachelor.

Ballet teacher: A teacher who criticizes her students in order to keep them on their toes.

Beard: A thing you need to wear with gift neckties.

Biography: One of the new terrors of death. *John Arbuthnot*

Biped: Anything that goes on two feet, for instance a pair of socks.

Bore: A person who talks about himself in contrast to a brilliant person who talks about you.

Bore: A person who talks when you wish him to listen. *Ambrose Bierce*

Braggart: A person who enters a conversation feat first.

Bridegroom: Something they use at weddings.

Budget: The family's attempt to live below its yearnings.

Calamities: Misfortune to ourselves, and good fortune to others. *Ambrose Bierce*

Calendar: Something that goes in one year and out the other.

California: A fine place to live in—if you happen to be an orange. *Fred Allen*

Camel: A race horse designed by a committee.

Capital punishment: When the government taxes you to get capital, in order to go into business in competition with you, and then taxes the profits on your business in order to pay its losses.

Car sickness: The feeling you get when the monthly installment comes due.

Civilization: A system under which a man pays a quarter to park his car so he won't be fined a dollar while spending a dime for a nickel cup of coffee.

Coeducational college: A match factory.

Cold war: A period when nations flex their missiles.

Comedian: A fellow who finds other comedians too humorous to mention. *Jack Herbert*

Commendation: The tribute that we pay to achievements that resemble, but do not equal, our own. *Ambrose Bierce*

Committee: A group of the unfit, appointed by the unwilling, to do the unnecessary. *Henry Cooke*

Communist: A man who has given up hope of becoming a capitalist.

Conference: A gathering of important people who singly can do nothing, but together can decide that nothing can be done. *Fred Allen*

Conference: A place where you talk about doing something instead of doing it.

Conference: A place where conversation is substituted for the dreariness of labor and the loneliness of thought.

Confidence: The feeling you have before you know better.

Conservative: A statesman who is enamored of existing evils, as distinguished from the liberal who wishes to replace them with others. *Ambrose Bierce*

Consultant: A man who knows less about your business than you do and gets more for telling you how to run it than you could possibly make out of it even if you ran it right instead of the way he tells you.

Courtesy: Smiling while your departing guest holds the screen door open and lets the flies in.

Coward: One who in a perilous emergency thinks with his legs. *Ambrose Bierce*

Criticism: What we say about other people who don't have the same faults we have.

Cynic: A blackguard whose faulty vision sees things as they are, not as they ought to be. *Ambrose Bierce*

Diaphragm: A muscular partition separating disorders of the chest from disorders of the bowels. *Ambrose Bierce*

Diplomacy: The patriotic art of lying for one's country. *Ambrose Bierce*

Disc jockey: A person who lives on spins and needles.

Duty: Something we look forward to with distaste, do with reluctance, and boast about forever after.

Education: That which discloses to the wise and disguises from the foolish their lack of understanding. *Ambrose Bierce*

Efficiency: Using instant coffee to dawdle away an hour.

Egotist: A person of low taste, more interested in himself than in me. *Ambrose Bierce* A stupid fool who thinks he knows as much as you do.

Eiffel Tower: The Empire State Building after taxes.

Enough: What would satisfy us if the neighbors didn't have more.

Etc.: A sign used to make people believe you know more than you are telling them.

Eulogy: Praise of a person who has either the advantages of wealth and power, or the consideration to be dead. *Ambrose Bierce*

European trip: A trip you enjoy after you have rested a month at home.

Failure: The line of least persistence.

Fame: The advantage of being known to those who do not know us. *Nicholas Chamfort*

Farmer: A man who is outstanding in his field.

Fashion: A despot whom the wise ridicule and obey. *Ambrose Bierce*

Forger: A man who makes a name for himself.

Free speech: The right to argue about issues you don't understand.

Garden: A thing of beauty and a job forever.

Genealogist: Someone who traces your family tree back as far as your money will go.

Generalities: The substance of most uninteresting conversation.

Gentleman: A person who has had the same operation but says nothing.

Golf: A game in which you drive hard to get to the green and then wind up in the hole.

Good neighbor: A fellow who smiles at you over the back fence but doesn't climb over it. *Arthur (Bugs) Baer*

Good sermon: One that goes over your head—and hits one of your neighbors.

Gossip: What no one claims to like but everybody enjoys. *Joseph Conrad*

Grade crossing: A place where headlights and light heads meet.

Grapefruit: A fruit that succeeds in getting into the public eye.

Hangover: The thing that occupies the head you didn't use the night before.

Hard work: An accumulation of easy things you didn't do when you should have.

Henpecked husband: A man who gives his wife the best ears of his life.

Highbrow: A person educated beyond his intelligence. *Brander Matthews*

Hollywood: A place where people from Iowa mistake each other for movie stars. *Fred Allen*

Hollywood: A place where you can see many a famous movie star skate down Sunset Boulevard on a pair of sports cars.

Home: Where a woman puts up with her husband.

Honest politician: One who when he is bought will stay bought. *Simon Cameron*

Hospitality: The virtue which induces us to feed and lodge certain persons who are not in need of food and lodging. *Ambrose Bierce*

Hypocrisy: The homage which vice pays to virtue. *La Rochefoucauld*

Ignorance: The thing that causes a lot of interesting arguments.

Income tax: The fine you pay for thriving too fast.

Insomniac: A guy who keeps sheep jumping over a fence all night just because he can't sleep.

Insurance: An ingenious modern game of chance in which the player is permitted to enjoy the comfortable conviction that he is beating the man who keeps the table. *Ambrose Bierce*

Jaywalking: A bad habit that may give you that run-down feeling.

Joint checking account: A handy little device that permits your wife to beat you to the draw.

Jury: Twelve people of average ignorance.

Kangeroo. A large economy size grasshopper.

Kindergarten teacher: A woman who makes the little things in life count.

Knowledge: The small part of ignorance that we arrange and classify. *Ambrose Bierce*

Law and equity: Two things which God hath joined, but which man has put asunder. *Charles Caleb Colton*

Lawyer: A learned gentleman who rescues your estate from your enemies and keeps it himself. *Henry Brougham*

Lawyers: The only persons in whom ignorance of the law is not punished. *Jeremy Bentham*

Laziness: An overwhelming love for physical calm.

Lecturer: One with his hand in your pocket, his tongue in your ear, and his faith in your patience. *Ambrose Bierce*

Liar: A man who won't lie to a woman and so has very little consideration for her feelings.

Liberal: A man who is willing to spend somebody else's money. *Carter Glass*

Litigant: A person about to give up his skin for the hope of retaining his bones. *Ambrose Bierce*

Luck: When a man marries a girl who will help with the dishes.

Market: A place set apart where men may deceive each other. *Anacharsis*

Marriage: A legalized way of suppressing free speech.

Mausoleum: The final and funniest folly of the rich. *Ambrose Bierce*

Medicine: The only profession that labours incessantly to destroy the reason for its own existence. *James Bryce*

Middle age: When you begin to exchange your emotions for symptoms. *Irvin S. Cobb* When you are too young to take up golf and too old to rush up to the net. *Franklin Pierce Adams*

Mixed greens: An assortment of fives, tens and twenties.

Modern wife: A woman who knows what her husband's favorite dishes are and the restaurants that serve them.

Money: A commodity that won't buy everything, but it keeps you from being more than moderately sullen and depressed.

Mosquito: One of the few indestructible objects in the world.

Newspaper: A circulating library with high blood pressure. *Arthur (Bugs) Baer*

Nickel: What this country needs—a good five cent one.

Old age: A period in life when you bend over once to pick up two things.

Old-timer: Someone who remembers when people who wore jeans worked. A person who drives into a gas station and says, "Fill her up." A person who can remember when a baby-sitter was called mother.

Opportunity: A favorable occasion for grasping a disappointment. *Ambrose Bierce*

Optimism: The noble temptation to see too much in everything. *Gilbert Keith Chesterton*

Optimist: A guy that has never had much experience. *Don Marquis* One who proclaims that we live in the best of all possible worlds, and the pessimist fears this is true. *James Branch Cabell*

Oratory: The art of making deep noises from the chest sound like important messages from the brain. *H. I. Phillips*

Organ recital: Two persons discussing their operations.

Paris: A city of gaieties and pleasures where four-fifths of the inhabitants die of grief. *Nicholas Chamfort*

Parking space: The area that disappears while you are making a U-turn.

Patience: A minor form of despair, disguised as a virtue. *Ambrose Bierce*

Pauper: A poor fish without a fin.

Piccolo: The smallest instrument a musician may play in public and still maintain his self-respect. *Emile Gauvreau*

Plagiarists: Those who are suspicious of being stolen from. *Samuel Taylor Coleridge*

Politician: A person who shakes your hand before election and your confidence afterwards.

Positive: Being mistaken at the top of one's voice. *Ambrose Bierce*

Posterity: What an author writes for after the publishers turn him down.

Professor: One who talks in someone else's sleep. *Wystan Hugh Auden*   A scholar who is paid to study the sleeping habits of students.

Psychiatrist: A mind sweeper.   A guy who convinces you that your parents were failures because you turned out to be such a louse.

Public speaker: A person whose mind sits down when he stands up.

Puritan: A person who pours righteous indignation into the wrong things. *Gilbert Keith Chesterton*

Quiet: What home would be without children.

Quotation: The act of repeating erroneously the words of another. *Ambrose Bierce*

Raving beauty: A girl who finishes last in a beauty contest.

Repartee: What you wish you'd said. *Heywood Broun*

Romance: The only sport in which the animal that gets caught has to buy the license.

Rumor: A favorite weapon of the assassins of character. *Ambrose Bierce*

Russia: A riddle wrapped in a mystery inside an enigma. *Winston Churchill*

Satire: A lonely and introspective occupation, for nobody. *Frank Moore Colby*

Secret: Something that's not worth keeping or too good to keep. Something you tell to only one person at a time.

Self-esteem: The most voluble of the emotions. *Frank Moore Colby*

Selfishness: That detestable vice which no one will forgive in others and no one is without in himself. *Henry Ward Beecher*

Shakespeare: A dramatist of note who lived by writing things to quote. *Henry Cuyler Bunner*

Silence: The unbearable repartee. *Gilbert Keith Chesterton*

Skiing: A winter sport that people learn in several sittings.

Society: Two great classes: those who have more dinners than appetite, and those who have more appetite than dinners. *Nicholas Chamfort*

Suburbanite: A man who hires someone to mow his lawn so he will have time to play golf for exercise.

Tact: Knowing how far we may go too far. *Jean Cocteau* The ability to close your mouth before somebody else wants to.

Taxation: Plucking the goose so as to obtain the largest amount of feathers with the least amount of hissing. *Jean Baptiste Colbert*

Texan: A wealthy man who has ranch to ranch carpeting.

Thomas Edison: The man who did not invent the first talking machine.   He invented the first one you could turn off.

Toothache: A pain that drives you to extraction.

Traffic light: A device that helps you get halfway across the street safely.

Travel: Activity that broadens the mind, flattens the traveler, and lengthens conversation.

Truth: The object of philosophy, but not always of philosophers. *John Churton Collins*

Turkey: An old bird that strutted and got caught.

TV western actor: Someone who is quick on the drawl.

Vacation: A period of travel and relaxation when you take twice the clothes and half the money you need.

Washington, D. C.: A place where they take the taxpayer's shirt and have a bureau in which to put it.

Wife: A woman who keeps breaking things, like fives, tens and twenties.

Yawn: A silent shout. *Gilbert Keith Chesterton*

14 •••

Quotations and Materials for Vocations and Professions

ARCHITECTS

Old houses mended,
Cost little less than new before they're ended. *Colley Cibber*

Ah, to build, to build!
That is the noblest of all the arts. *Longfellow*

ARTISTS

A poet or a painter or a musician does not say to himself, "I will make a million first, and then I will write poetry or paint pictures or compose music." His art is life itself, the best of life, for the genuine artist. *James Truslow Adams*

Every artist dips his brush in his own soul, and paints his own nature into his pictures. *Henry Ward Beecher*

Artists must be sacrificed to their art. Like bees, they must put their lives into the sting they give. *Ralph Waldo Emerson*

None of the best head work in art, literature, or science, is ever paid for. How much do you think Homer got for his *Iliad*? or Dante for his *Paradise*? Only bitter bread and salt, and going up and down other people's stairs. *John Ruskin*

The true artist will let his wife starve, his children go barefoot, his mother drudge for her living at seventy, sooner than work at anything but his art. *George Bernard Shaw*

It is the artist only who is the true historian. *W. G. Simms*

Of all men the artist has been perhaps the most insecure. *Leo Gurko*

Every artist writes his own autobiography. *H. Ellis*

AUTHORS

The author who speaks about his own books is almost as bad as a mother who talks about her own children. *Benjamin Disraeli*

Talent alone cannot make a writer. There must be a man behind the book. *Ralph Waldo Emerson*

No author is a man of genius to his publisher. *Heinrich Heine*

There is probably no hell for authors in the next world . . . they suffer so much from critics and publishers in this. *Christian Nestell Bovee*

But words are things, and a small drop of ink,
Falling, like dew, upon a thought produces
That which makes thousands, perhaps millions think. *George Gordon, Lord Byron*

I never saw an author in my life, saving perhaps one, that did not purr as audibly as a full-grown domestic cat on having his fur smoothed the right way by a skilful hand. *Oliver Wendell Holmes*

A bad book is as much of a labour to write as a good one; it comes as sincerely from the author's soul. *Aldous Huxley*

I would rather be attacked than unnoticed. For the worst thing you can do to an author is to be silent as to his works. *Samuel Johnson*

He was a one-book man. Some men have only one book in them; others, a library. *Sydney Smith*

Authors are judged by strange capricious rules,
The great ones are thought mad, the small ones fools. *Alexander Pope*

The pen is the tongue of the mind. *Cervantes*

The ink of the scholar is more sacred than the blood of the martyr. *Mohammed*

The Great Author of All made everything out of nothing, but many a human author makes nothing out of everything. *G. D. Prentice*

The only happy author in this world is he who is below the care of reputation. *Washington Irving*

A writer who attempts to live on the manufacture of his imagination is continually coquetting with starvation. *E. P. Whipple*

To produce a mighty book, you must choose a mighty theme. No great and enduring volume can ever be written on the flea, though many there be that have tried it. *Herman Melville*

In the main, there are two sorts of books: those that no one reads and those that no one ought to read. *H. L. Mencken*

That is a good book which is opened with expectation and closed with profit. *A. B. Alcott*

Books are not men and yet they are alive. *Stephen V. Benet*

A good many young writers make the mistake of enclosing a stamped, self-addressed envelope, big enough for the manuscript to come back in. This is too much of a temptation to the editor. *Ring Lardner*

In Hollywood the woods are full of people that learned to write, but evidently can't read. If they could read their stuff, they'd stop writing. *Will Rogers*

There seems to be no physical handicap or change of environment that can hold a real writer down. *Kathleen Norris*

Writers seldom write the things they think. They simply write the things they think other folks think they think. *Elbert Hubbard*

You must write to the human heart, the great consciousness that all humanity goes to make up. *Willa Cather*

The problems of the human heart in conflict with itself alone can make good writing because only that is worth writing about, worth the agony and the sweat. *William Faulkner*

The chief glory of a country, says Johnson, arises from its authors. But this is only when they are oracles of wisdom. Unless they teach virtue they are more worthy of a halter than of the laurel. *Jane Porter*

Every author in some degree portrays himself in his works, even if it be against his will. *Goethe*

Satire lies about men of letters during their lives, and eulogy after their death. *Voltaire*

BANKERS

A million in the hands of a single banker is a great power; he can at once loan it where he will, and borrowers can come to him, because they know or believe that he has it. But the same sum scattered in 10s and 50s through a whole nation has no power at all; no one knows where to find it or whom to ask for it. *Walter Bagehot, London, 1873*

The borrower is servant to the lender. *Proverbs XXII, 7*

Neither a borrower nor a lender be;
For loan oft loses both itself and friend,
And borrowing dulls the edge of husbandry. *Shakespeare*

BUSINESSMEN

The crossroads of trade are the meeting place of ideas, the attrition ground of rival customs and beliefs; diversities beget conflict, comparison, thought; superstitions cancel one another, and reason begins. *Will Durant*

Commerce is of trivial import; love, faith, truth of character, the aspiration of man, these are sacred. *Ralph Waldo Emerson*

Don't let business interfere with your civic enterprise. *Richard King Mellon*

The propensity to truck, barter, and exchange one thing for another . . . is common to all men, and to be found in no other race of animals. *Adam Smith*

The best investment a young man starting out in business could possibly make is to give all his time, all his energies to work, just plain, hard work. *C. M. Schwab*

If small business goes, big business does not have any future except to become the economic arm of a totalitarian state. *P. D. Reed*

It is very easy to manage our neighbor's business, but our own sometimes bothers us. *Josh Billings*

No business is above Government; and Government must be empowered to deal adequately with any business that tries to rise above Government. *Franklin D. Roosevelt*

There is a sense in which the business men of America represent America, because America has devoted herself time out of mind to the arts and achievements of peace, and business is the organization of the energies of peace. *Woodrow Wilson*

One of the rarest phenomena is a really pessimistic businessman. *Miriam Beard*

Seest thou a man diligent in his business? He shall stand before kings; he shall not stand before mean men. *Proverbs, XXII, 29*

The market is a place set apart where men may deceive each other. *Greek*

Everyone lives by selling something.

The most sensible people to be met with in society are men of business and of the world, who argue from what they see and know, instead of spinning cobweb distinctions of what things ought to be. *William Hazlitt*

There are geniuses in trade as well as in war, or the state, or letters; and the reason why this or that man is fortunate is not to be told. It lies in the man: that is all anybody can tell you about it. *R. W. Emerson*

My own business always bores me to death; I prefer other people's. *Oscar Wilde*

I hold it to be our duty to see that the wage-worker, the small producer, the ordinary consumer, shall get their fair share of the benefit of business prosperity. But it either is or ought to be evident to everyone that business has to prosper before anybody can get any benefit from it. *Theodore Roosevelt*

Business underlies everything in our national life, including our spiritual life. Witness the fact that in the Lord's Prayer, the first petition is for daily bread. No one can worship God or love his neighbor on an empty stomach. *Woodrow Wilson*

In thousands of years there has been no advance in public morals, in philosophy, in religion or in politics, but the advance in business has been the greatest miracle the world has ever known. *E. W. Howe*

CRITICS

A drama critic is a person who surprises the playwright by informing him what he meant. *Wilson Mizner*

Nature, when she invented, manufactured, and patented her authors, contrived to make critics out of the chips that were left. *O. W. Holmes*

A wise scepticism is the first attribute of a good critic. *J. R. Lowell*

DIPLOMATS

Ambassadors are the eye and ear of states. *Francesco Guicciardini*

Diplomacy is to do and say
The nastiest thing in the nicest way. *Isaac Goldberg*

It is fortunate that diplomats generally have long noses, since usually they cannot see beyond them.   *Unknown*

A diplomat is a man who remembers a lady's birthday but forgets her age.   *Anonymous*

When a diplomat says yes he means perhaps; when he says perhaps he means no; when he says no he is no diplomat.   *Anonymous*

An Ambassador is a man of virtue sent to lie abroad for his country; a news-writer is a man without virtue who lies at home for himself. *Sir Henry Wotton*

DOCTORS

Surgery does the ideal thing—it separates the patient from his disease.   *Logan Clendening*

Sometimes give your services for nothing, calling to mind a previous benefaction or present satisfaction.   And if there be an opportunity of serving one who is a stranger in financial straits, give full assistance to all such.   For where there is love of man, there is also love of the art. For some patients, though conscious that their condition is perilous, recover their health simply through their contentment with the goodness of the physician.   And it is well to superintend the sick to make them well, to care for the healthy to keep them well, but also to care for one's own self, so as to observe what is seemly.   *Hippocrates*

No physician, in so far as he is a physician, considers his own good in what he prescribes, but the good of his patient; for the true physician is also a ruler having the human body as a subject, and is not a mere money-maker. *Plato*

A good surgeon must have an eagle's eye, a lion's heart, and a lady's hand.   *Proverb*

The best doctors in the world are Doctor Diet, Doctor Quiet, and Doctor Merryman.   *Jonathan Swift*

Honour a physician with the honor due unto him for the uses which ye may have of him: for the Lord hath created him.   For of the most High cometh healing, and he shall receive honour of the king.   The skill of the physician shall lift up his head: and in the sight of great men he shall be in admiration.   *Apocrypha: Ecclesiasticus, xxxviii, 1–3*

Now when a doctor's patients are perplexed,
A consultation comes in order next—
You know what that is?   In a certain place
Meet certain doctors to discuss a case

And other matters, such as weather, crops,
Potatoes, pumpkins, lager-beer, and hops. *Oliver Wendell Holmes*

As a physician, I have seen men, after all other therapy had failed, lifted out of disease and melancholy by the serene effort of prayer. *Dr. Alexis Carrel*

What I mean is this—all good doctors must be primarily enthusiasts. They must have, like writers and painters, and priests, a sense of vocation—a deep-rooted, unsentimental desire to do good. *Noel Coward*

Physician—one upon whom we set our hopes when ill and our dogs when well. *Ambrose Bierce*

Doctors are men who prescribe medicines of which they know little, to cure diseases of which they know less, in human beings of whom they know nothing. *Voltaire*

I firmly believe that if the whole materia medica as now used, could be sunk to the bottom of the sea, it would be all the better for mankind and all the worse for the fishes. *Holmes*

FARMERS

The farmer is covetous of his dollar, and with reason . . . He knows how many strokes of labor it represents. His bones ache with the day's work that earned it. *Ralph Waldo Emerson*

The agricultural population, says Cato, produces the bravest men, the most valiant soldiers, and a class of citizens the least given of all to evil designs. *Pliny The Elder*

And he gave it for his opinion . . . that whoever could make two ears of corn, or two blades of grass, to grow upon a spot of ground where only one grew before, would deserve better of mankind, and do more essential service to his country, than the whole race of politicians put together. *Jonathan Swift*

Those who labor in the earth are the chosen people of God, if ever He had a chosen people. Corruption of morals in the mass of cultivators is a phenomenon of which no age or nation has furnished an example. *Thomas Jefferson*

When tillage begins, other arts follow. The farmers therefore are the founders of human civilization. *Daniel Webster*

One good thing about living on a farm is that you can fight your wife without being heard. *Kin Hubbard*

Burn down your cities and leave our farms, and your cities will spring up again as if by magic; but destroy our farms and the grass will grow in the streets of every city in the country.   *W. J. Bryan*

The first farmer was the first man; and all historic nobility rests on possession and use of land.   *Ralph Waldo Emerson*

FISHERMEN

There are more fish taken out of a stream than ever were in it. *Oliver Herford*

There is no use in your walking five miles to fish when you can depend on being just as unsuccessful near home.   *Mark Twain*

GARDENERS

God Almighty first planted a garden.   And, indeed, it is the purest of human pleasures.   *Francis Bacon*

Authorities differ as to the best way of hoeing up a garden. . . . All agree that it is impossible to avoid walking for a week afterwards as if you were imitating an old colored waiter with lumbago.   *Robert Benchley*

One is nearer God's heart in a garden than anywhere else on earth. *Dorothy Frances Gurney*

Many things grow in the garden, that were never sowed there. *Proverb*

In order to live off a garden, you practically have to live in it.   *Kin Hubbard*

What a man needs in gardening is a cast-iron back with a hinge in it. *C. D. Warner*

JOURNALISTS

The freedom of the press is one of the greatest bulwarks of liberty. *George Mason*

Three hostile newspapers are more to be feared than a thousand bayonets.   *Napoleon Bonaparte*

We live under a government of men and morning newspapers. *Wendell Phillips*

Who would not be an editor?   To write
The magic *we* of such enormous might;

To be so great beyond the common span
It takes the plural to express the man.   *John Godfrey Saxe*

Get your facts first, and then you can distort 'em as much as you please.   *Mark Twain*

A would-be satirist, a hired buffoon,
A monthly scribbler of some low lampoon,
Condemn'd to drudge, the meanest of the mean,
And furbish falsehoods for a magazine.   *George Gordon, Lord Byron*

I believe it has been said that one copy of the (London) *Times* contains more useful information than the whole of the historical works of Thucydides.   *Richard Cobder*

Journalism has become . . . the most important function in the community.   *Henry George*

It is the newspaper owner's business to sell information and not advice nor propaganda.   *Walter B Pitkin*

Journalism is organized gossip.   *Edward Eggleston*

Journalism consists in buying white paper at two cents a pound and selling it at ten cents a pound.   *Charles A. Dana*

What is the difference between journalism and literature: Oh! Journalism is unreadable, and literature is not read.   That is all.   *Oscar Wilde*

Skin a hard-boiled journalist and you find a thwarted idealist.   *Russell Green*

Writing good editorials is chiefly telling the people what they think, not what you think.   *Arthur Brisbane*

JUDGES

A judge is a law student who marks his own examination papers.   *H. L. Mencken*

The jurists of today . . . insist upon study of the actual social effects of legal institutions and legal doctrines.   *Roscoe Pound*

Judges are apt to be naive, simple-minded men, and they need something of the Mephistopheles.   *O. W. Holmes, Jr.*

When a court decides a case upon grounds of public policy, the judge becomes, in effect, a legislator.   The question then involved is no longer one for lawyers only.   *Louis D. Brandeis*

The average man's judgment is so poor, he runs a risk every time he uses it.   *E. W. Howe*

LAWYERS

Every man should know something of law; if he knows enough to keep out of it, he is a pretty good lawyer.   *Josh Billings*

When there's a rift in the lute, the business of the lawyer is to widen the rift and gather the loot.   *A. G. Hays*

If a man dies and leaves his estate in an uncertain condition, the lawyers become his heirs.   *E. W. Howe*

The trouble with law is lawyers.   *Clarence Darrow*

You cannot live without the lawyers and certainly you cannot die without them.   *Joseph H. Choate*

It is the trade of lawyers to question everything, yield nothing, and to talk by the hour.   *Thomas Jefferson*

I know that whenever the medicos are bankrupt as to source of cure of a disease they give it a long Latin name, just as we lawyers bandy around words like "certiorari" and "hereditament" whenever clients catch on to the credited mysteries of the law.   *Morris L. Ernst*

It is a feature of nearly every Utopia, that there has been no place in it for lawyers.   *Benjamin Cardozo*

If there were no bad people there would be no good lawyers. *Charles Dickens*

Adversaries in law strive mightily, but eat and drink as friends. *Shakespeare*

Accuracy and diligence are much more necessary to a lawyer than great comprehension of mind, or brilliancy of talent.   His business is to refine, define, split hairs, look into authorities, and compare cases. A man can never gallop over the fields of law on Pegasus, nor fly across them on the wing of oratory.   If he would stand on terra firma, he must descend.   If he would be a great lawyer, he must first consent to become a great drudge.   *Daniel Webster*

Most good lawyers live well, work hard, and die poor.   *Daniel Webster*

I know you lawyers can with ease
Twist words and meanings as you please.   *Gay*

A lawyer's opinion is worth nothing unless paid for.   *English Proverb*

"Virtue in the middle," said the Devil, when he sat down between two lawyers.   *Danish*

The Law is the true embodiment
Of everything that's excellent.
It has no kind of fault or flaw,
And I, my Lords, embody the Law.   *W. S. Gilbert*

Necessity has no law; I know some attorneys of the same.   *Franklin, Poor Richard's Almanac*

A lawyer must first get on, then get honor, and then get honest.
Anonymous

LEGISLATORS

No legislator is qualified to vote on or propose measures designed to affect the destinies of millions of social units until he masters all that is known of the science of society.   *Lester Ward*

Every true legislator must be a sociologist.   *Lester Ward*

Now and then an innocent man is sent to the legislature.   *Kin Hubbard*

LIBRARIANS

There are seventy million books in American libraries, but the one you want to read is always out.   *Tom Masson*

A library is but the soul's burial ground.   *H. W. Beecher*

Shelved around me lie the mummied authors.   *Bayard Taylor*

MINISTERS

I do not envy a clergyman's life as an easy life, nor do I envy the clergyman who makes it an easy life.   *Samuel Johnson*

The Christian ministry is the worst of all trades, but the best of all professions.   *John Newton*

In pulpit eloquence, the grand difficulty is, to give the subject all the dignity it deserves without attaching any importance to ourselves.
Colton

"Three things," says Luther, "make a Divine—prayer, meditation, and trials."   These make a Christian; but a Christian minister needs three more, talent, application, and acquirements.   *C. Simmons*

If a minister takes one step into the world, his hearers will take two.
Cecil

The preaching that comes from the soul, most works on the soul.
Fuller

I have heard many great orators, said Louis XIV to Massilon, and have been highly pleased with them; but whenever I hear you, I go away displeased with myself. This is the highest encomium that could be bestowed on a preacher. *C. Simmons*

The minister is to be a real man, a live man, a true man, a simple man, great in his love, in his life, in his work, in his simplicity, in his gentleness. *John Hall*

The life of a pious minister is visible rhetoric. *Hooker*

Do as we say, and not as we do. *Boccaccio*

The test of a preacher is that his congregation goes away saying, not What a lovely sermon, but, I will do something! *St. Francis de Sales*

Who is he that can twice a week be inspired, or has eloquence always on tap? *Lowell*

His preaching much but more his practice wrought
A living sermon of the truths he taught. *Dryden*

He was of that stubborn crew
Of errant saints whom all men grant
To be the true Church Militant. *Butler*

MUSICIANS

No musician is any good to me unless he's a good musician. You work with a man because he's a good man—that's all. *Benny Goodman*

Please do not shoot the pianist. He is doing his best. *Oscar Wilde*

The requisites of a singer—a big chest, a big mouth, 90 per cent memory, 10 per cent intelligence, lots of hard work, and something in the heart. *Enrico Caruso*

POLITICIANS

An honest politician is one who, when he is bought, will stay bought. *Simon Cameron*

The most successful politician is he who says what everybody is thinking most often and in the loudest voice. *Theodore Roosevelt*

A politician is like quicksilver; if you try to put your finger on him, you will find nothing under it. *Austin O'Malley*

The statesman shears the sheep, the politician skins them. *Austin O'Malley*

I'm not a politician and my other habits are good. *Artemus Ward*
We cannot safely leave politics to politicians, or political economy to
college professors. *Henry George*
You cannot adopt politics as a profession and remain honest. *Louis Untermeyer*
Politics is the art by which politicians obtain campaign contributions
from the rich and votes from the poor on the pretext of protecting each
from the other. *Oscar Ameringer*

Politics is the art of looking for trouble, finding it everywhere, diag-
nosing it wrongly, and applying unsuitable remedies. *Sir Ernest Benn*

A successful politician is a person who can take a popular economic
fallacy and make a major plank for his party. *Herbert V. Prochnow*

"You can't fool all of the people all of the time," observed a veteran
of the political wars. "Besides, once every four years is enough."

> I always voted at my party's call,
> And never thought of thinking for myself at all!
> I thought so little, they rewarded me
> By making me the ruler of the Queen's navee! *W. S. Gilbert*

Some people put themselves above politics, saying, "Politics is dirty,"
or "I have no patience with politics." In the name of all that's American, how can any good citizen feel superior to politics? We achieved
our independence by politics. We freed the slaves by politics. We
are taxed by politics. Our businesses flourish or wither by politics.
Charles Edison

He serves his party best who serves the country best. *Rutherford B. Hayes*

PREACHERS

Billy Sunday once said: "Here is my first rule in homiletics: Never
preach to the intellectual giraffes in your congregation. And the second . . . Always leave some cookies on the bottom shelf." *Charles F. Hall*

"What do they do when they install a minister, Papa? Do they put
him in a stall and feed him?"
"Oh, no, Son, they hitch him to a church and expect him to pull it."
George B. Gilbert

I'd rather see a sermon than hear one any day; I'd rather one should walk with me than merely tell the way. *Edgar Guest*

PROFESSORS

Surely the nation which has built palaces for libraries, laboratories and students will not permanently ignore the professor who is in truth the institution itself. *Abraham Flexner*

SALESMEN

His name was George F. Babbitt, and . . . he was nimble in the calling of selling houses for more than people could afford to pay. *Sinclair Lewis*

SCIENTISTS

Look at those cows and remember that the greatest scientists in the world have never discovered how to make grass into milk. *Michael Pupin*

One humiliating thing about science is that it is gradually filling our homes with appliances smarter than we are. *Oskaloosa (Iowa) Herald*

There is only one proved method of assisting the advancement of pure science—that of picking men of genius, backing them heavily and leaving them to direct themselves. *Dr. James B. Conant*

A contemporary historian, speaking on our scientific advances, expresses the choice before us: "If things go well, the epitaph of history may run: 'Here lie the technicians, who united mankind.' And if things go badly: 'Here lie the technicians, who exterminated the human race.'" *Christian Century*

SOLDIERS

The nation which forgets its defenders will be itself forgotten. *Calvin Coolidge*

> For it's Tommy this, an' Tommy that,
> an'
> "Chuck 'im out, the brute!"
> But it's the "Saviour of 'is country"
> when the guns begin to shoot. *Rudyard Kipling*

But in a larger sense, we cannot dedicate, we cannot consecrate, we cannot hallow this ground. The brave men living and dead, who struggled here, have consecrated it far above our poor power to add or detract.   The world will little note, nor long remember, what we say here, but it can never forget what they did here.   *Abraham Lincoln*

Let it be your pride, therefore, to show all men everywhere not only what good soldiers you are, but also what good men you are.   *Woodrow Wilson*

SPEAKERS—TOASTMASTERS

Eloquence is the child of Knowledge.   *Benjamin Disraeli*

There is no eloquence without a man behind it.   *Ralph Waldo Emerson*

Eloquence is the power to translate a truth into language perfectly intelligible to the person to whom you speak.   *Ralph Waldo Emerson*
Honesty is one part of eloquence.   We persuade others by being in earnest ourselves.   *William Hazlitt*

In a country and government like ours, eloquence is a powerful instrument, well worthy of the special pursuit of our youth.   *Thomas Jefferson*

As the grace of man is in the mind, so the beauty of the mind is eloquence.   *Proverb*

It is the heart which makes men eloquent.   *Quintilian*

When I had spoken half an hour I had told them everything I knew in the world!   *Agassiz*

Another flood of words!   a very torrent!   *B. Jonson*

No, never say nothin' without you're compelled tu.
An' then don't say nothin' thet you can be held tu.   *Lowell*

  I am no orator as Brutus is,
But, as you know me all, a plain blunt man.   *Shakespeare*

Into the question whether the ability to express ourselves in articulate language has been productive of more good or evil, I shall not here enter at large.   *Lowell*

  Set up an hour-glass; he'll go on until
The last sand make his period.   *W. Cartwright*

STATESMEN

In statesmanship get the formalities right, never mind about the moralities.   *Mark Twain*

A statesman is a successful politician who is dead.   *Thomas Buchanan Reed*

A ginooine statesman should be on his guard,
Ef he must hev beliefs, not to b'lieve 'em tu hard.   *James Russell Lowell*

TEACHERS

A teacher affects eternity; he can never tell where his influence stops.   *Henry Adams*

It is the supreme art of the teacher to awaken joy in creative expression and knowledge.   *Albert Einstein*

Let our teaching be full of ideas.   Hitherto it has been stuffed only with facts.   *Anatole France*

There, in his noisy mansion, skill'd to rule,
The village master taught his little school;
A man severe he was, and stern to view,—
I knew him well, and every truant knew.   *Oliver Goldsmith*

I can easier teach twenty what were good to be done, than be one of the twenty to follow my own teaching.   *William Shakespeare*

Those having torches will pass them on to others.   *Plato*

A teacher who is attempting to teach without inspiring the pupil with a desire to learn is hammering on cold iron.   *Horace Mann*

The one exclusive sign of a thorough knowledge is the power of teaching.   *Aristotle*

I put the relation of a fine teacher to a student just below the relation of a mother to a son, and I don't think I could say more than this.   *Thomas Wolfe*

More people than ever before are graduated but not educated.   *Robert G. Gunderson*

Last fall a youngster who had done pre-nursery and nursery school went to real school for the first time.   He came home downcast and said glumly, "I'm tired of being teached to play.   I want to be teached to learn."   *Robert Sylvester, The Chicago Tribune*

You cannot teach old dogs new tricks.   *Anonymous*

Our American professors like their literature clear, cold, pure, and very dead.   *Sinclair Lewis*

Base men by his endowments are made great.   *Shakespeare*

Index

Mark Twain (Samuel Langhorne Clemens), 113, 118, 131–132, 136, 138, 139, 141, 144, 145, 146, 148, 149, 152, 156, 157, 218, 230, 242, 267, 276, 283, 295, 301, 327, 328, 335
Markham, Edwin, 141
Marmion, 127
Marquis, Don, 137, 266, 283, 317
Marriage, 39, 52–53, 146, 160–161, 166–167, 171, 172, 174, 178, 182, 189, 195, 197, 200, 201, 202, 206, 209, 211, 273, 295–296, 308
Marshall, Thomas R., 284
Marshall Plan, 77
Martial, 143
Martin, Abe, 244, 245
Martin, Joseph W., Jr., 42–43
Martino, Al, 177
Marx, Groucho, 181
Marx, Karl, 124, 240, 242
Mary and the Lamb (story), 50
Masefield, John, 151, 295, 298
Mason, George, 23–24, 327
Massieu, J. B., 136
Masson, Tom, 330
Mathematics, 274
Matthews, Brander, 316
Maugham, W. S., 124, 226, 253–254, 279, 285
Maximilian, 234
Maybe (story), 214–215
A Meaningful Life (speech), 90–91
Meany, George, 228
Mechanization of agriculture, 109–110 *see also* Farmers and farming
Medicine, 29–30, 49, 213, 274
Meeting, running of, 2–3
Meiklejohn, Alexander, 259, 268
Melbourne, Viscount, 108–109
Mellon, Richard King, 323
Melton, Lt. Clyde, Jr., 285
Melville, Herman, 121, 271, 322
Memory (quotations on), 147
Mencken, H. L., 265, 267, 269, 273, 283, 322, 328
Menjou, Adolphe, 38
Meredith, George, 158
Meredith, Owen *see* Bulwer-Lytton
Messer, Sir Frederick, 219
Methodist Christian Advocate, 305
Mexican Radio Announcer (story), 206
Meyers, Helen G., 47
Michael Angelo, 115
Middle age, 274
Mikoyan, A. I., 199
Mill, John Stuart, 57, 133, 137
Miller, Olin, 270
Millikan, Robert A., 141, 270
Millikin, Eugene D., 189

Milton, George Fort, 277
Milton, John, 115, 158, 242, 288
Ministers, 330
Minorities, 244
Misery (quotations on), 147
Misfortune, proverbs, 296
Missiles, 35
Mistakes, 229
Mitchell, James P., 88–89
Mizner, Wilson, 253, 274, 276, 324
Moby Dick, 121
Modern Cook (story), 198
Modern Farming (story), 44–45
Modern sources, (quotations), 251–285
Modern Youth (story), 180
Moffatt, James, 274
Mohammed, 321
Moliere, 132
Mollenhoff, Clark, 92–93
Monarchies, 152
Money, 147, 274, 296
Monotony, 275
Montague, C. E., 157
Montaigne, 156
Montesquieu, 150, 152
Moody, Dwight L., 223, 230, 232
Moore, George, 159
Moore, Thomas, 128–129, 147, 153
Morals, 275
Moran, Dr. William E., 183
More difficult (story), 194
More Than He Thought (story), 177
More Than Satisfied (story), 179
Morgan, Dr. Arthur E., 277
Morgan, Gerald D., 187
Morgan, Henry, 39
Morley, Christopher, 257, 263, 282
Morley, Felix, 263
Morley, J., proverb, 289
Moron story, 45
Morrill, J. L., 19–20, 101–102
Morrison, Harry, 254
Morrow, Dwight W., 35, 264
Moscow, Russia, 27, 87–88, 105, 107
Most of Us Do (story), 182
Mothers, 147–148, 296 *see also* Parents
Muir, Malcolm, 250
Muller, Philip, 98
Mumford, Lewis, 256
Murphy, Howard D., 15–16, 20–21, 23–24, 31
Museums (quotation on), 148
Music and musicians, 148, 231, 275, 331
Muss, Alfred de, 98
Musset, A. de, 130
My Get Up and Go (story), 34

NATO, 27
Napoleon, 123, 138

Volume B

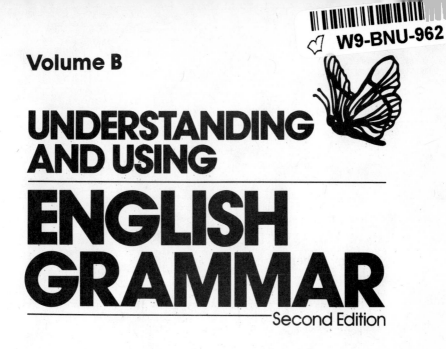

UNDERSTANDING AND USING
ENGLISH GRAMMAR

Second Edition

Distance Learning
Video Check out.

Betty Schrampfer Azar

PRENTICE HALL REGENTS
Upper Saddle River, NJ 07458

Library of Congress Cataloging-in-Publication Data

Azar, Betty Schrampfer, (date)
    Understanding and using English grammar / by Betty Schrampfer
Azar. -- 2nd ed.
      p. cm.
    Includes index.
    ISBN 0-13-943663-4 (v. A). -- ISBN 0-13-943671-5 (v. B)
    1. English language--Textbooks for foreign speakers. 2. English
language--Grammar--1950- I. Title.
PE1128.A97 1989b
428.2'4--dc19   88-37396
                                                            CIP

To my mother,
FRANCES NIES SCHRAMPFER
and my father,
WILLIAM H. SCHRAMPFER

Editorial/production supervision and
   interior design: *Ros Herion Freese*
Cover design : *Joel Mitnick Design*
Manufacturing buyer: *Laura Crossland*
Publisher: *Tina B. Carver*
Managing editor, production: *Slyvia Moore*

Published by Prentice-Hall, Inc.
A Simon & Schuster Company
Upper Saddle River, New Jersey 07458

Printed in the United States of America
10 9 8 7

ISBN 0-13-943614-6

ISBN 0-13-943663-4   {VOL A}

ISBN 0-13-943671-5   {VOL B}

Prentice-Hall International (UK) Limited, *London*
Prentice-Hall of Australia Pty. Limited, *Sydney*
Prentice-Hall Canada Inc., *Toronto*
Prentice-Hall Hispanoamericana, S.A., *Mexico*
Prentice-Hall of India Private Limited, *New Delhi*
Prentice-Hall of Japan, Inc., *Tokyo*
Simon & Schuster Asia Pte. Ltd., *Singapore*
Editora Prentice-Hall do Brasil, Ltda., *Rio de Janeiro*

Contents

Preface to the
Second Edition

The second edition of *Understanding and Using English Grammar* contains changes directed primarily toward clarification of structure presentations in the charts and improvements in the exercises. The revisions are based in large part upon the many wonderful and graciously offered suggestions from teachers and students familiar with the original text. A few new short grammar units have been included. One grammar area (comparisons) has been moved from *Understanding and Using English Grammar* to the second edition of *Fundamentals of English Grammar*. Additional notes on structure differences between American and British English have been included in the second edition.

The text remains a developmental skills text for students of English as a second or foreign language. While focusing on grammar, it promotes the development of all language skills in a variety of ways.

As in the original edition, the charts consist of examples accompanied by explanations and are intended to be easily understood by the students. Terminology is kept to a minimum.

The exercises reflect an eclectic approach, not only because there are many effective ways of teaching language, but also because certain structures simply tend to lend themselves to one approach rather than another. The exercises may be directed toward listening skills, oral production, writing skills, or reading comprehension—or any combination thereof. Some of the exercises have a straightforward, controlled concentration on form and meaning. These are followed by other more complicated and challenging exercises that engender creative, independent use of target structures. The exercise contexts reflect realistic, typical language use and are relevant to the students' concerns, daily lives, and life experiences. Items in the exercises are variously designed to encourage students to talk about themselves and their activities, to promote vocabulary development, to be informative, to engender cross-cultural comparisons, to be thought-provoking, to cause a smile or a chuckle, or to stimulate short discussions on a variety of topics.

In order to meet the needs of different teachers in different teaching situations, the revision of *Understanding and Using English Grammar* is available in two formats: in a single volume or in split volumes. The restructuring of the organization was designed principally to accommodate splitting the text into two volumes, with Volume A focusing on verb forms and Volume B focusing on complex structures. As in the original edition, each chapter is a self-contained unit; the teacher may present the chapters in the given order or rearrange the order of presentation to suit his/her needs and purposes.

Appendix 1 (*Supplementary Grammar Units*) has been expanded and now includes exercises. Information about parts of speech and basic structures such as questions and negatives is in the appendix so that students may have these units available whether using the single-volume text or the split volumes. The teacher can fit these units in as s/he deems appropriate in the syllabus. A teacher may, for example, choose to teach the question unit either prior to or in the course of teaching the verb tense chapter, may teach it in conjunction with the noun clause chapter, or may simply refer to it as needed in connection with tenses, modals, the passive, or any other unit. Much of the material in Appendix 1 is review from the other two texts in the series, but not all. As with any other grammar units in the text, the Appendix 1 material seeks to consolidate previous understandings as the basis upon which to expand usage ability.

Understanding and Using English Grammar (blue cover) is intended for upper-level students. It is part of a series of three grammar books. *Fundamentals of English Grammar* (black) is directed toward mid-level students, and *Basic English Grammar* (red) is designed for lower-level students.

WORKBOOKS

The second edition is accompanied by student workbooks: *Understanding and Using English Grammar—Workbooks A and B*. They contain not only Self-study Practices (answers given) for independent out-of-class work by the students, but also Guided Study Practices (answers not given) for classwork, homework, and individualized instruction as the teacher sees the need. In addition, there are suggestions for oral and/or writing activities, an emphasis on vocabulary development, and two practice tests for each chapter.

TEACHER'S GUIDE

The second edition of *Understanding and Using English Grammar* is also accompanied by a much expanded *Teacher's Guide* that contains: presentation suggestions; specific techniques for handling the varied types of exercises; background grammar notes; item notes on cultural content, vocabulary, and structure usage; problems to anticipate; suggestions for oral and written student-centered activities; and answers to the exercises.

ACKNOWLEDGMENTS

First of all, I would like to express my appreciation to Donald A. Azar for his irreplaceable encouragement, partnership, good humor, and computer expertise. He is the co-author of the *Workbooks* and also has served as an advisor on the revision. A person of myriad skills, he has eased the way through a demanding project during a busy time in our lives, making the work I enjoy even more enjoyable.

I wish also to express my great appreciation to Barbara Matthies, the writer of the accompanying *Teacher's Guide,* for her continuing support both as a colleague and a friend—and for a wonderful time in Kathmandu, where we spent hours tossing around ideas. To me, there is nothing better than a good friend/colleague who likes to talk about English grammar and the teaching of ESL/EFL.

I wish to express my gratitude to the following colleagues for their suggestions, interest, keen perceptions, and cheerful repartee: Irene Juzkiw, Rachel Spack (Shelley) Koch, Jeanie Francis, Susan Jamieson, Phyllis Mithin, Larry Francis, Barbara Leonhard, Nancy Price, Maureen Burke, Steve Molinsky, Bill Bliss, and Candace Matthews. An additional special thanks goes to Shelley, Jeanie, Susan, and Barbara Andrews for their wonderful contributions to and interest in the workbook project.

The many other colleagues I have spoken with about the revision are too numerous to name, but I thank all of them for sharing their ideas with me. I would like to say a special thank you to the teachers I met in Puerto Rico. And to all of those who so conscientiously and scrupulously responded to the questionnaire on revising the text, my heartfelt thanks.

The reviewers of the revised manuscript have been exceptionally helpful. In particular, I wish to thank Mr. Richard Eisman; Ms. J. Rajah; Ms. Mohana K. Nambiar; Dr. Dagmar Buhring Acuna, Universidad Interamericana de Puerto Rico; Mr. James E. Purpura, Institute for North American Studies, Barcelona, Spain; Ms. Teresa Pica, University of Pennsylvania, Graduate School of Education; Prof. Habibah HJ. Ashari, Coordinator, TESL Program, Center of Preparatory Education, MARA Institute of Technology, Malaysia; Mr. Richard L. Coe, State University of New York at Buffalo, Cooperative Education Program in Malaysia; Ms. Lynne Sarkisan Cresitello; Mr. Nicholas J. Dimmitt, University of Bahrain, Isa Town, Bahrain; Ms. Cheryl Engber, Indiana University; Ms. Linda A. Moody, Associate Director, The English Center for International Women, Mills College; Mr. William R. Slager, Department of English, University of Utah; and Ms. Shirley Wu, Singapore.

I must say a special thank you to Lilian and Leonard Feinberg, who graciously made available to me language teaching materials they had written. They are much appreciated as friends and mentors.

My gratitude also goes to Tina Carver, editor and friend, and to Ed Stanford, Andy Martin, Gil Muller, Noel Carter, Ros Herion Freese, Sylvia

Moore, Don Martinetti, and all of the others with Prentice Hall Regents who made this project possible and enjoyable.

I wish to thank Chelsea Parker for her willing, cheerful, and able office assistance. She is also a great joy and delight in my life.

Finally, I thank my mother for inputting and editing, my father for being a veritable wellspring of ideas for entries, and both of them for helping with the tedious job of reading proof. Throughout my life, they have been and still are ever ready to assist me in my various endeavors—for which I am truly grateful.

BETTY S. AZAR
Langley, Washington

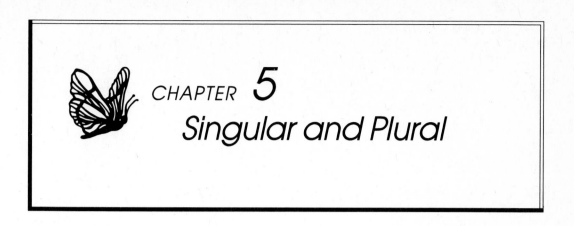

CHAPTER *5*

Singular and Plural

☐ **EXERCISE 1:** In the following sentences, add final *-s/-es* where necessary. Discuss why you need to add *-s/-es*. Do not change or omit any other words in the sentences. All of the sentences are SIMPLE PRESENT.

                         pens
1. I have two pen. (***pens*** = *a plural noun*)

2. Tom work hard every day.

3. Our solar system consist of nine planet.

4. The earth rotate around the sun.

5. All animal need water.

6. A dog need fresh water every day.

7. Student take test.

8. Hawaii has beautiful sunset.

9. A library contain a lot of book.

10. Encyclopedia contain information about many thing.

11. Butterfly are beautiful.

12. Martha watch TV every evening.

13. Alex almost never change his mind.

5–1 FINAL -S/-ES

(a) NOUN + **-S**: ***Friends*** are important. NOUN + **-ES**: I like my ***classes***.	A final **-s** or **-es** is added to a noun to make a noun plural. ***friend*** = *a singular noun* ***friends*** = *a plural noun*

(b) VERB + **-S**:   John ***works*** at the bank.
 VERB + **-ES**:   She ***watches*** birds.
	A final **-s** or **-es** is added to a simple present verb when the subject is a singular noun or third person singular pronoun.*
	    John works = *singular* ***The students work*** = *plural*
	    He works = *singular* ***They work*** = *plural*

SPELLING: FINAL -S vs. -ES (c) sing → *sings* song → *songs*	For most words (whether a verb or a noun), simply a final **-s** is added to spell the word correctly.

(d) wash → *washes*
     watch → *watches*
     class → *classes*
     buzz → *buzzes*
     box   → *boxes*
	Final **-es** is added to words that end in **-sh**, **-ch**, **-s**, **-z**, and **-x**.

(e) toy   → *toys*
     buy   → *buys*
 (f) baby → *babies*
     cry   → *cries*
	For words that end in **-y**:
	 In (e): If **-y** is preceded by a vowel, only **-s** is added.
	 In (f): If **-y** is preceded by a consonant, the **-y** is changed to **-i** and **-es** is added.

*A singular noun = *Mary, my father, the machine.*
A third person singular subject pronoun = *she, he, it.*

☐ **EXERCISE 2:** Add **-s** or **-es** to the following words to spell them correctly.

1. passenger ___s___
2. tax ___es___
3. talk _____
4. blush _____
5. discover _____
6. develop _____
7. season _____
8. flash _____
9. hall _____
10. touch _____
11. sketch _____
12. press _____
13. method _____

14. mix _____
15. try _____
16. tray _____
17. ferry _____
18. guy _____
19. enemy _____
20. pry _____
21. pray _____

□ **EXERCISE 3—ORAL:** Practice pronouncing the following words. Say the final *-s/-es* sounds loudly and clearly.

GROUP A: Final *-s* is pronounced /s/ after voiceless sounds.

Examples: seats = seat + /**s**/
ropes = rope + /**s**/
backs = back + /**s**/

1. hats
2. hates
3. sleeps
4. trips
5. books

6. unlocks
7. sniffs
8. laughs
9. asks

GROUP B: Final *-s* is pronounced /z/ after voiced sounds.

Examples: seeds = seed + /**z**/
robes = robe + /**z**/
bags = bag + /**z**/
sees = see + /**z**/

10. feeds
11. lids
12. robs
13. grabs
14. homes
15. occurs

16. fills
17. miles
18. rugs
19. days
20. pies
21. agrees

GROUP C: Final *-es* and *-s* are pronounced /əz/ after *-sh, -ch, -s, -z,* and *-ge/dge* sounds.

Examples: dishes = dish + /əz/   mixes = mix + /əz/
catches = catch + /əz/   prizes = prize + /əz/
kisses = kiss + /əz/   edges = edge + /əz/

22. wishes
23. ashes
24. matches
25. sandwiches
26. guesses
27. courses
28. faces
29. fixes

30. relaxes
31. quizzes
32. sizes
33. rises
34. pages
35. judges
36. arranges

☐ **EXERCISE 4—ORAL:** Practice the pronunciation of final *-s/-es* by reading the following sentences aloud.

1. The teacher encourages the students to speak freely.
2. Chickens, ducks, and turkeys lay eggs.
3. He possesses many fine qualities.
4. My wages are low, but my taxes are high.
5. The cafeteria serves good sandwiches.
6. He coughs, sneezes, and wheezes.
7. People come in many shapes and sizes.
8. She scratches her chin when it itches.
9. He practices pronunciation by reading sentences aloud.
10. She bought some shirts, shoes, socks, dresses, slacks, blouses, earrings, and necklaces.

☐ **EXERCISE 5—ORAL (BOOKS CLOSED):** What do the following people or things do? Follow the pattern in the example. Say final *-s/-es* sounds loudly and clearly.

Example: bird watcher
Response: A bird watcher watches birds.

1. stamp collector
2. animal trainer
3. bank robber
4. dog catcher
5. book publisher
6. tax collector
7. ticket taker
8. fire extinguisher
9. mind reader
10. bullfighter
11. wage earner
12. storyteller

☐ **EXERCISE 6—ORAL (BOOKS CLOSED):** What do the following people, animals, and things do? Respond in complete sentences. Say the final *-s/-es* sounds loudly and clearly.

Example: bird
Response: A bird flies (sings, builds nests, etc.).

1. baby
2. telephone
3. star
4. dog
5. duck
6. ball
7. heart
8. river
9. cat
10. door
11. clock
12. airplane
13. doctor
14. teacher
15. psychologist

5-2 IRREGULAR PLURAL NOUNS

The nouns in (a) have irregular plural forms:			
(a) *man–men*	*child–children*	*mouse–mice*	*foot–feet*
woman–women	*ox–oxen*	*louse–lice*	*goose–geese*
			tooth–teeth

Some nouns that end in *-o* add *-es* to form the plural:

(b) *echoes*　　　　　*heroes*　　　　　*potatoes*　　　　　*tomatoes*

Some nouns that end in *-o* add only *-s* to form the plural:

(c) *autos*　　　　*photos*　　　　*solos*　　　　*tatoos*
　　kilos　　　　*pianos*　　　　*sopranos*　　　*videos*
　　memos　　　　*radios*　　　　*studios*　　　　*zoos*

Some nouns that end in *-o* add either *-es* or *-s* to form the plural:

(d) *mosquitoes/mosquitos*　　　　　*volcanoes/volcanos*
　　tornadoes/tornados　　　　　　*zeroes/zeros*

Some nouns that end in *-f* or *-fe* are changed to *-ves* in the plural:

(e) *calf–calves*　　　*leaf–leaves*　　　*self–selves*　　　*wolf–wolves*
　　half–halves　　　*life–lives*　　　*shelf–shelves*　　*scarf–scarves/scarfs*
　　knife–knives　　*loaf–loaves*　　*thief–thieves*

Some nouns that end in *-f* simply add *-s* to form the plural:

(f) *belief–beliefs*　　　*chief–chiefs*　　　*cliff–cliffs*　　　*roof–roofs*

Some nouns have the same singular and plural form: (e.g., One deer is . . . . Two deer are . . . .)

(g) *deer*　　　*fish*　　　*means*　　　*series*　　　*sheep*　　　*species*

Some nouns that English has borrowed from other languages have foreign plurals:

(h) *criterion–criteria*　　　(k) *analysis–analyses*　　　(m) *bacterium–bacteria*
　　phenomenon–phenomena　　　　*basis–bases*　　　　　　　*curriculum–curricula*
　　　　　　　　　　　　　　　　　　crisis–crises　　　　　　　　*datum–data*
(i) *cactus–cacti/cactuses*　　　　*hypothesis–hypotheses*　　　*medium–media*
　　stimulus–stimuli　　　　　　　*oasis–oases*　　　　　　　　*memorandum–memoranda*
　　syllabus–syllabi/syllabuses　　*parenthesis–parentheses*
　　　　　　　　　　　　　　　　　　thesis–theses

(j) *formula–formulae/formulas*　　(l) *appendix–appendices/appendixes*
　　vertebra–vertebrae　　　　　　　*index–indices/indexes*

☐ **EXERCISE 7:** Write the plural form of the following nouns.

1. child ＿＿＿*children*＿＿＿　　　7. fox ＿＿＿＿＿＿＿＿

2. zero ＿＿＿*zeros/zeroes*＿＿＿　　8. goose ＿＿＿＿＿＿＿

3. mouse ＿＿＿＿＿＿＿＿　　　　　9. sheep ＿＿＿＿＿＿＿

4. monkey ＿＿＿＿＿＿＿＿　　　　10. series ＿＿＿＿＿＿＿

5. industry ＿＿＿＿＿＿＿＿　　　11. belief ＿＿＿＿＿＿＿

6. woman ＿＿＿＿＿＿＿＿　　　　12. leaf ＿＿＿＿＿＿＿＿

13. self _____   17. hypothesis _____

14. echo _____   18. curriculum _____

15. photo _____   19. phenomenon _____

16. analysis _____   20. stimulus _____

5–3 POSSESSIVE NOUNS

(a) **SINGULAR NOUN**	**POSSESSIVE FORM**	To show possession, add an apostrophe (') and -s to a singular noun: The **girl's** book is on the table.
the girl	*the girl's*	
Tom	*Tom's*	
my wife	*my wife's*	If a singular noun ends in -s, there are two possible forms:
a lady	*a lady's*	(1) Add an apostrophe and -s: **Thomas's** book.
Thomas	*Thomas's/Thomas'*	(2) Add only an apostrophe: **Thomas'** book.
(b) **PLURAL NOUN**	**POSSESSIVE FORM**	Add only an apostrophe to a plural noun that ends in -s: The **girls'** books are on the table.
the girls	*the girls'*	
their wives	*their wives'*	
the ladies	*the ladies'*	Add an apostrophe and -s to plural nouns that do not end in -s: The **men's** books are on the table.
the men	*the men's*	
my children	*my children's*	

☐ **EXERCISE 8:** Complete the sentences with the possessive form of the nouns in parentheses.

1. (*Mrs. Smith*)   ___Mrs. Smith's___ husband often gives her flowers.

2. (*boy*)   The _____ hat is red.

3. (*boys*)   The _____ hats are red.

4. (*children*)   The _____ toys are all over the floor.

5. (*child*)   I fixed the _____ bicycle.

6. (*baby*)   The _____ toys are in her crib.

7. (*babies*)   The _____ toys are in their cribs.

8. (*wives*)   Tom and Bob are married. Their _____

names are Cindy and Jane, respectively.

9. (*wife*)   That is my _____ coat.

10. (*Sally*)   _____ last name is White.

11. (*Phyllis*)   _____ last name is Young.

12. (*boss*)	That's my _____ office.
13. (*bosses*)	Those are my _____ offices.
14. (*woman*)	This is a _____ purse.
15. (*women*)	That store sells _____ clothes.
16. (*sister*)	Do you know my _____ husband?
17. (*sisters*)	Do you know my _____ husbands?
18. (*yesterday*)	Did you read _____ newspaper?
19. (*today*)	There are many problems in _____ world.
20. (*month*)	It would cost me a _____ salary
	to buy that refrigerator.

5-4 USING NOUNS AS MODIFIERS

(a) The soup has vegetables in it. It is *vegetable soup*. (b) The building has offices in it. It is an *office building*.	Notice: When a noun is used as a modifier, it is in its singular form.
(c) The test lasted two hours. It was a *two-hour test*. (d) Her son is five years old. She has a *five-year-old son*.	When a noun used as a modifier is combined with a number expression, the noun is singular and a hyphen (-) is used.

☐ **EXERCISE 9:** Use the italicized noun or noun phrase in the first sentence as a modifier in the second sentence.

1. My garden has *flowers* in it. It is _____ *a flower garden.* _____

2. That handbook is for *students*. It is _____

3. Their baby is *ten months old*. They have _____

4. Our trip lasted for *three days*. We took _____

5. She is a psychologist for *children*. She is _____

6. I wrote a check for *fifty dollars*. I wrote _____

7. I will get *three credits* for that course. It is _____

8. Their house has *nine rooms*. It is _____

9. That food is for *dogs*. It is _____

10. That room is for *guests*. It is _____

11. The professor asked us to write a paper of *five pages*. She asked us to

    write _____

12. I have a sister who is *ten years old* and a brother who is *twelve years old*. I

    have _____

5–5 COUNT AND NONCOUNT NOUNS

(a) I bought *a chair*. Sam bought *three chairs*.	*Chair* is a count noun; chairs are items that can be counted.
(b) We bought *some furniture*. INCORRECT: *We bought a furniture.* INCORRECT: *We bought some furnitures.*	*Furniture* is a noncount noun. In grammar, furniture cannot be counted.

	SINGULAR	PLURAL	
COUNT NOUN	a chair one chair	chairs two chairs some chairs a lot of chairs many chairs★	A count noun: (1) may be preceded by *a/an* in the singular; (2) takes a final *-s/-es* in the plural.
NONCOUNT NOUN	furniture some furniture a lot of furniture much furniture★		A noncount noun: (1) is not immediately preceded by *a/an*; (2) has no plural form; does not take a final *-s/-es*.

★See Chart 5-8 for other expressions of quantity that are used with count and noncount nouns.

☐ **EXERCISE 10:** Look at the italicized nouns in the following sentences. Write ''**C**'' above the count nouns and ''**NC**'' above the noncount nouns.

                C   C   C
1. I bought some *chairs*, *tables*, and *desks*. In other words, I bought some

     NC
    furniture.

2. I have some *pennies*, *nickels*, and *dimes* in my pocket. In other words, I

    have some *money* in my pocket.

3. Ann likes to wear *jewelry*. Today she is wearing four *rings*, six *bracelets*,

    and a *necklace*.

4. We saw beautiful *mountains*, *fields*, and *lakes* on our trip. In other words,

    we saw beautiful *scenery*.

5. Would you like some *food*? How about a *sandwich* and an *apple*?

6. We had *meat, rice, bread, butter, cheese, fruit, vegetables*, and *tea* for dinner.

7. *Gold* and *iron* are metals.

8. I used an *iron* to press my shirt because it was wrinkled.

9. I wish you *happiness, health*, and *luck* in your life.

10. Tom is studying *chemistry, history*, and *English*.

11. In the United States, *baseball* is called the national pastime. To play it, you need a *baseball* and a bat.

12. My hometown has *rain, thunder, fog, sleet*, and *snow* in the winter months. In other words, it has bad *weather*.

13. Ed has black *hair* and brown *eyes*.

5-6 NONCOUNT NOUNS

Notice in the following: Most noncount nouns refer to a "whole" that is made up of different parts.	
(a) I bought some chairs, tables, and desks. In other words, I bought some **furniture**.	In (a): **furniture** represents a whole group of things that is made up of similar but separate items.
(b) I put some **sugar** in my **coffee**.	In (b): **sugar** and **coffee** represent whole masses made up of individual particles or elements.*
(c) I wish you **luck**.	In (c): **luck** is an abstract concept, an abstract "whole." It has no physical form; you can't touch it. You can't count it.
(d) **Sunshine** is warm and cheerful.	In (d): Phenomena of nature, such as **sunshine**, are frequently used as noncount nouns.
(e) NONCOUNT: Ann has brown **hair**. COUNT: Tom has *a hair* on his jacket.	Many nouns can be used as either noncount or count nouns, but the meaning is different; e.g., **hair** in (e) and **light** in (f).
(f) NONCOUNT: I opened the curtains to let in some **light**. COUNT: Don't forget to turn off the **lights** before you go to bed.	(Dictionaries written especially for learners of English as a second language are a good source of information on count/noncount usages of nouns.)

*To express a particular quantity, some noncount nouns may be preceded by unit expressions: e.g., *a spoonful of sugar, a glass of water, a cup of coffee, a quart of milk, a loaf of bread, a grain of rice, a bowl of soup, a bag of flour, a pound of meat, a piece of furniture, a piece of paper, a piece of jewelry*.

5-7 SOME COMMON NONCOUNT NOUNS

The following are typical of nouns that are commonly used as noncount nouns. Many other nouns can be used as noncount nouns. This list serves only as a sample.

(a) WHOLE GROUPS MADE UP OF SIMILAR ITEMS: *baggage, clothing, equipment, food, fruit, furniture, garbage, hardware, jewelry, junk, luggage, machinery, mail, makeup, money/cash/change, postage, scenery, traffic*

(b) FLUIDS: *water, coffee, tea, milk, oil, soup, gasoline, blood, etc.*

(c) SOLIDS: *ice, bread, butter, cheese, meat, gold, iron, silver, glass, paper, wood, cotton, wool, etc.*

(d) GASES: *steam, air, oxygen, nitrogen, smoke, smog, pollution, etc.*

(e) PARTICLES: *rice, chalk, corn, dirt, dust, flour, grass, hair, pepper, salt, sand, sugar, wheat, etc.*

(f) ABSTRACTIONS:
—*beauty, confidence, courage, education, enjoyment, fun, happiness, health, help, honesty, hospitality, importance, intelligence, justice, knowledge, laughter, luck, music, patience, peace, pride, progress, recreation, significance, sleep, truth, violence, wealth, etc.*
—*advice, information, news, evidence, proof*
—*time, space, energy*
—*homework, work*
—*grammar, slang, vocabulary*

(g) LANGUAGES: *Arabic, Chinese, English, Spanish, etc.*

(h) FIELDS OF STUDY: *chemistry, engineering, history, literature, mathematics, psychology, etc.*

(i) RECREATION: *baseball, soccer, tennis, chess, bridge, poker, etc.*

(j) GENERAL ACTIVITIES: *driving, studying, swimming, traveling, walking (and other gerunds)*

(k) NATURAL PHENOMENA: *weather, dew, fog, hail, heat, humidity, lightning, rain, sleet, snow, thunder, wind, darkness, light, sunshine, electricity, fire, gravity*

□ **EXERCISE 11:** Complete the sentences with the given nouns. Add final *-s/-es* if necessary. Use each noun only one time.

advice	information	screwdriver
✔ change	junk	stuff
city	luggage/baggage	thunder
garbage	music	traffic
hardware	progress	traveling
homework	✔ river	trip

1. I have some coins in my pocket. In other words, I have some

   _____*change*_____ in my pocket.

2. The Mississippi, the Amazon, and the Nile are well-known

   _____*rivers*_____ in the world.

3. I like to listen to operas, symphonies, and folk songs. I enjoy

   _____.

4. Since I came to the United States, I have visited Chicago, New York, and Miami. I want to visit other _____ before I return to my country.

5. The street is full of cars, trucks, and buses. This street always has heavy _____, especially during rush hour.

6. In the last couple of years, I've gone to France, India, and the Soviet Union. I like to take _____. In other words, _____ _____ is one of my favorite activities.

7. I put some banana peels, rotten food, and broken bottles in the waste can. The can is full of _____.

8. They have a rusty car without an engine, broken chairs, and an old refrigerator in their front yard. Their yard is full of _____.

9. Paul has books, pens, papers, notebooks, a clock, scissors, a tape recorder, and some other things on his desk. He has a lot of _____ on his desk.*

10. The children got scared when they heard _____ during the storm.

11. Tools that are used to fasten screws into wood are called _____ _____.

12. I went to the store to get some nails, hammers, and screws. In other words, I bought some _____.

13. Tonight I have to read 20 pages in my history book, do 30 problems in algebra, and write a composition for my English teacher. In other words, I have a lot of _____ to do tonight.

14. Ann took three suitcases, a shoulder bag, and a cosmetics case. In other words, she took a lot of _____ on her trip.

---

*As a noncount noun, **stuff** usually means "a group of various things." It is an inexact term used primarily in very informal spoken English. (*Junk* sometimes has the same meaning.)
Examples: I keep a lot of stuff in my desk drawers.
      Look at all the stuff in this room.

15. Toronto is 356 ft./109 m above sea level. The average annual precipitation in Toronto is 32 in./81 cm. The population of the metropolitan area is over 3,000,000. I found (*this, these*) _____ in the encyclopedia.

16. I didn't feel good. Ann said, "You should see a doctor."

    Tom said, "You should go home and go to bed."

    Martha said, "You should drink fruit juice and rest."

    I got _____ from three people.

17. My English is slowly getting better. My vocabulary is increasing. It's getting easier for me to write and I make fewer mistakes. I can often understand people even when they talk fast. I'm satisfied with the _____ I have made in learning English.

☐ **EXERCISE 12:** Add final *-s/-es* to the nouns in italics if necessary. Do not add or change any other words.

1. I had *chicken* and *rice* for dinner last night. (*no changes*)

2. Mary always has fresh *egg* available because she raises *chicken* in her yard.

   eggs   **chickens**

3. Outside my window, I can see a lot of *tree, bush, grass, dirt*, and *flower*.

4. Tom gave me some good *advice*. Milly also gave me some good *suggestion*.

5. Yoko learned several new *word* today. She increased her *vocabulary* today.

6. I drank two *glass* of *water*.

7. *Window* are made of *glass*.

8. Jack wears *glass* because he has poor *eyesight*.

9. It took me a lot of *time* to finish my *homework*. I had a lot of *assignment*.

10. I have been in Mexico three *time*. I've spent a lot of *time* there.

11. There are *typewriter, copier, telephone*, and *stapler* in a typical business office. A business office needs a lot of *equipment*.

12. The *air* is full of *smoke, dust*, carbon *monoxide*, and many other harmful *substance*. We must seek to reduce air *pollution*.

13. I like to read good *literature*. I especially like to read *novel, poetry*, and *essay*. My favorite *poet* are Longfellow and Wordsworth. I have always liked their *poem*.

14. You can find a lot of time-saving *machine* in a modern *factory*. Modern *factory* need modern *machinery*.

15. There are more *star* in the universe than there are *grain* of *sand* on all the beaches on earth.

☐ **EXERCISE 13—PRETEST:** Before you look at Chart 5-8, try this exercise. Draw a line through the expressions that *cannot* be used to complete the sentence correctly.

Example: I bought _____ furniture.
    a. some
    b. a couple of
    c. several
    d. too much
    e. too many

1. I received _____ letters.
    a. two
    b. a couple of
    c. both
    d. several
    e. some
    f. a lot of
    g. plenty of
    h. too many
    i. too much
    j. a few
    k. a little
    l. a number of
    m. a great deal of
    n. hardly any
    o. no

2. I received _____ mail.
    a. two
    b. a couple of
    c. both
    d. several
    e. some
    f. a lot of
    g. plenty of
    h. too many
    i. too much
    j. a few
    k. a little
    l. a number of
    m. a great deal of
    n. hardly any
    o. no

5–8 EXPRESSIONS OF QUANTITY

> An expression of quantity (e.g., **one**, **several**, **many**, **much**) may precede a noun. *Notice below*: Some expressions of quantity are used only with count nouns; some only with noncount nouns; some with either count or noncount nouns.

EXPRESSIONS OF QUANTITY	USED WITH COUNT NOUNS	USED WITH NONCOUNT NOUNS
one each every	*one apple* *each apple* *every apple*	Ø* Ø Ø
two both a couple of three, etc. a few several many a number of	*two apples* *both apples* *a couple of apples* *three apples* *a few apples* *several apples* *many apples* *a number of apples*	Ø Ø Ø Ø Ø Ø Ø Ø
a little much a great deal of	Ø Ø Ø	*a little rice* *much rice* *a great deal of rice*
not any/no some a lot of lots of plenty of most all	*not any/no apples* *some apples* *a lot of apples* *lots of apples* *plenty of apples* *most apples* *all apples*	*not any/no rice* *some rice* *a lot of rice* *lots of rice* *plenty of rice* *most rice* *all rice*

*Ø = "not used." For example, you can say "*I ate one apple*" but NOT "*I ate one rice.*"

☐ **EXERCISE 14:** Draw a line through the expressions that *cannot* be used to complete the sentence correctly.

1. Isabel has _____ assignments.
   a. three
   b. several
   c. some
   d. a lot of
   e. too much
   f. too many
   g. a few
   h. a little
   i. a number of
   j. a great deal of
   k. hardly any
   l. no

2. Jake has _____ homework, too.
   a. three
   b. several
   c. some
   d. a lot of
   e. too much
   f. too many
   g. a few
   h. a little
   i. a number of
   j. a great deal of
   k. hardly any
   l. no

3. Ann is wearing _____ rings.
   a. four
   b. several
   c. some
   d. lots of
   e. too many
   f. too much
   g. a few
   h. a little
   i. hardly any
   j. no

4. Sue is wearing _____ jewelry.
   a. four
   b. several
   c. some
   d. lots of
   e. too many
   f. too much
   g. a few
   h. a little
   i. hardly any
   j. no

☐ **EXERCISE 15—ORAL (BOOKS CLOSED):** Use *many* or *much** with the following words, changing the words to plural if necessary. Pronounce final *-s/-es* loudly and clearly.

Examples: sentence → *many sentences*
water → *much water*
thief → *many thieves*

1. furniture
2. desk
3. branch
4. equipment
5. machinery
6. machine
7. woman
8. piece
9. mouse
10. advice
11. sheep
12. homework
13. prize
14. goose
15. music
16. progress
17. race
18. knowledge
19. marriage
20. information
21. luck
22. hypothesis
23. mail
24. office
25. slang
26. roof
27. phenomenon
28. human being
29. shelf
30. tooth

*You may want to practice using some of these words in sentences. **Much** is usually not used in affirmative sentences; instead, *a lot of* or *a great deal of* is frequently used. **Much** is used primarily in negative sentences and questions.

5-9 USING *A FEW* AND *FEW*; *A LITTLE* AND *LITTLE*

a few a little	(a) She has been here only two weeks, but she has already made *a few friends*. *(Positive idea: She has made some friends.)* (b) I'm very pleased. I've been able to save *a little money* this month. *(Positive idea: I have saved some money instead of spending all of it.)*	*A few* and *a little** give a positive idea; they indicate that something exists, is present, as in (a) and (b).
few little	(c) I feel sorry for her. She has *(very) few friends*. *(Negative idea: She does not have many friends; she has almost no friends.)* (d) I have *(very) little money*. I don't even have enough money to buy food for dinner. *(Negative idea: I do not have much money; I have almost no money.)*	*Few* and *little* (without *a*) give a negative idea; they indicate that something is largely absent. *Very* (+ *few/little*) makes the negative idea stronger, the number/amount smaller.

*A few and *few* are used with plural count nouns. *A little* and *little* are used with noncount nouns.

☐ **EXERCISE 16:** Complete the sentences with *a few, (very) few, a little,* or *(very) little*.

1. Do you have _____*a few*_____ minutes? I'd like to ask you _____*a few*_____ questions. I need _____*a little*_____ more information.

2. Ann's previous employer gave her a good recommendation because she makes __*(very) few*__ mistakes in her work.

3. After Rodney tasted the soup, he added _____ salt to it.

4. I don't like a lot of salt on my food. I add _____ salt to my food.

5. The professor lectured very clearly. As a result, _____ students had questions at the end of the class period.

6. I like music. I like to listen to _____ music after dinner before I begin studying.

7. Jim is having a lot of trouble adjusting to eighth grade. He seems to be unpopular. Unfortunately, he has _____ friends.

8. I have to go to the post office because I have _____ letters to mail.

9. Every day Max goes to his mailbox, but it is usually empty. He gets _____ mail.

10. We're looking forward to our vacation. We're planning to spend _____ days with my folks and then _____ days with my husband's folks. After that, we're going to go to a fishing resort in Canada.

11. Driving downtown to the stadium for the baseball game was easy. We got there quickly because there was _____ traffic.

12. My friend arrived in the United States _____ months ago.

13. I think you could use some help. Let me give you _____ advice.

14. Because the family is very poor, the children have _____ clothes.

15. A: Are you finished?

    B: Not yet. I need _____ more minutes.

16. A: Are you finished?

    B: Not yet. I need _____ more time.

17. _____ days ago I met a very interesting person.

18. Into each life, _____ rain must fall. (*a saying*)

19. I was hungry, so I ate _____ nuts.

20. Margaret likes sweet tea. She usually adds _____ honey to her tea. Sometimes she adds _____ milk, too.

21. Has anyone ever called you on the phone and tried to sell you something you didn't want? I have _____ patience with people who interrupt my dinner to try to sell me a magazine.

22. He's a lucky little boy. Because his parents have taken good care of him, he has had _____ problems in his young life.

5-10 USING *OF* IN EXPRESSIONS OF QUANTITY

MOST* + NONSPECIFIC NOUN** (a) ***Most books are interesting.	In (a): The speaker is not referring to specific books. The speaker is not referring to "those books" or "your books" or "the books written by Mark Twain." The noun "books" is nonspecific.
(b) *INCORRECT: Most of books are interesting.*	In (b): The word *of* is not added to an expression of quantity (e.g., ***most***) if the noun it modifies is nonspecific.
MOST* + *OF* + SPECIFIC NOUN** (c) *Most* ***of *those* books are mine. (d) *Most* ***of*** *my* books are in English. (e) *Most* ***of*** *the* books on that table are mine.	A noun is specific when it is preceded by: —***this***, ***that***, ***these***, ***those***, as in (c); OR —***my***, ***John's***, ***their*** (any possessive) as in (d); OR —***the***, as in (e). When a noun is specific, ***of*** is used with an expression of quantity.★

EXPRESSIONS OF QUANTITY FOLLOWED BY *OF* + A SPECIFIC NOUN
all, most, some/any + ***of*** + specific plural *count* noun or *noncount* noun, as in (f) ***many, (a) few, several, both, two, one*** + ***of*** + specific plural *count* noun, as in (g) ***much, (a) little*** + ***of*** + specific *noncount* noun, as in (h)

(f) *count:* ***Most of those chairs*** are uncomfortable. *noncount:* ***Most of that furniture*** is uncomfortable. (g) *count:* ***Many of those chairs*** are uncomfortable. (h) *noncount:* ***Much of that furniture*** is uncomfortable.

*NOTE: *of* is always a part of the following expressions of quantity, whether the noun is nonspecific or specific: ***a lot of, lots of, a couple of, plenty of, a number of, a great deal of***.
   NONSPECIFIC: I've read *a lot of books*.   SPECIFIC: I've read *a lot of those books*.

☐ **EXERCISE 17:** Add *of* if necessary. Write Ø if *of* is not necessary.

1. I know several ___*of*___ Jack's friends.

2. I've made several ___Ø___ friends lately.

3. Some _____ students are lazy, and some _____ students are hard-working.

4. Some _____ the students in Mrs. Gray's class are a little lazy.

5. Most _____ books have an index.

6. Most _____ Ali's books are written in Arabic.

7. I bought a few _____ books yesterday.

8. I've read a few _____ those books.

9. I'm new here. I don't know many _____ people yet.

10. I've just moved into a new apartment. I don't know many _____ my neighbors yet.

11. Have you taken any _____ trips lately?

12. Sam hasn't met any _____ the students in the other class.

13. I usually get a lot _____ mail.

14. A lot _____ the mail I get is junk mail.

15. Our class has 30 students. Mr. Freeman's class has 25 students. Ms. North's class has 20 students. Of the three classes, our class has the most _____ students.*

16. Most _____ the students in our class are very smart.*

17. Out of all the students, Ali usually asks the most _____ questions during class. Most _____ his questions are about grammar.

18. Most _____ people need six to eight hours of sleep every night.

19. Most _____ the people in this class always hand in their assignments on time.

20. China has the most _____ people of any country in the world.

□ **EXERCISE 18:** Study the examples.

(a) CORRECT: ***All of the students*** in my class are here. (b) CORRECT: ***All the students*** in my class are here.	When a noun is specific (*e.g., the students*), using ***of*** after ***all*** is optional.
(c) CORRECT: ***All students*** must have an I.D. card. (d) *INCORRECT:* *All of students must have an I.D. card.*	When a noun is nonspecific, ***of*** does NOT follow ***all***.
(e) I know ***both (of) those men.***	Similarly, using ***of*** after ***both*** is optional when the noun is specific.

_____

*COMPARE:
    (1) ***The most*** = superlative. The superlative is used to compare three or more persons or things. ***The most*** is never immediately followed by *of*. *Example: Out of all the boys, Tom ate* ***the most food***.
    (2) ***Most*** (not preceded by ***the***) = an expression of quantity whose meaning ranges from "over fifty percent" to "almost all." *Example:* ***Most of the food*** *at that restaurant is good, but not all of it.*

*Notice that **of** is not necessary in any of the following sentences. However, if it is possible to use **of**, write (of) in the blank. If **of** is not possible because the noun is nonspecific, write Ø.*

1. All _____(of)_____ the children listened to the story.

2. Almost all _____Ø_____ children like fairy tales.

3. Both _____ those books are mine.

4. I bought two books. Both _____ books were expensive.

5. Almost all _____ students study hard for exams.

6. All _____ the students in my class are studying English.

7. I have two brothers. Both _____ my brothers are in school.

8. Do you know all _____ the people in your biology class?

9. Not all _____ people are friendly, but most _____ people have kind hearts.

10. All _____ birds have wings, but not all _____ birds can fly.

5–11 SINGULAR EXPRESSIONS OF QUANTITY: ONE, EACH, EVERY

(a) **One student** was late to class. (b) **Each student** has a schedule. (c) **Every student** has a schedule.	**One**, **each**, and **every** are followed immediately by *singular count nouns* (never plural nouns, never noncount nouns).
(d) **One of the students** was late to class. (e) **Each (one) of the students** has a schedule. (f) **Every one of the students** has a schedule.	**One of**, **each of**, and **every one of*** are followed by *specific plural count nouns* (never singular nouns, never noncount nouns).

*COMPARE:
    Every one (spelled as two words) is an expression of quantity; e.g., *I have read **every one** of those books.*
    Everyone (spelled as one word) is an indefinite pronoun; it has the same meaning as **everybody**; e.g.,
    Everyone/Everybody has a schedule.
NOTE: **Each** and **every** have essentially the same meaning.
    Each is used when the speaker is thinking of one person/thing at a time: *Each student has a schedule. = Mary has a schedule. John has a schedule. Hiroshi has a schedule. Carlos has a schedule. Sabrina has a schedule. (etc.)*
    Every is used when the speaker means "all." *Every student has a schedule. = All of the students have schedules.*

☐ **EXERCISE 19:** Complete the sentences with the correct form, singular or plural, of the noun in parentheses.

1. There is only one _____girl_____ on the sixth-grade soccer team. (*girl*)

2. Only one of the _____ in the sixth grade is on the soccer team. (*girl*)

3. Mrs. Hoover gave a present to each _____. (*child*)

4. Each of the _____ got a present. (*child*)

5. We invited every _____ of the club. (*member*)

6. Every one of the _____ came. (*member*)

☐ **EXERCISE 20—ERROR ANALYSIS:** Some (but not all) of the following sentences contain errors. Find and correct the errors.

                                            student

1. It's important for every students to have a book.

2. Each of the students in my class has a book.

3. Spain is one of the country I want to visit.

4. The teacher gave each of students a test paper.

5. Every student in the class did well on the test.

6. Every furniture in that room is made of wood.

7. One of the equipment in our office is broken.

8. I gave a present to each of the woman in the room.

9. One of my favorite place in the world is an island in the Caribbean Sea.

10. Each one of your suitcases will be checked when you go through customs.

11. It's impossible for one human being to know every languages in the world.

12. I found each of the error in this exercise.

☐ **EXERCISE 21—PRETEST:** Choose the correct answer in parentheses.

1. The weather in the southern states (*gets, get*) very hot during the summer.

2. The results of Dr. Noll's experiment (*was, were*) published in a scientific journal.

3. Bob and his friend (*is, are*) coming to the anniversary party tomorrow night.

4. Every man, woman, and child (*is, are*) protected under the law.

5. Washing the dishes (*is, are*) the children's job.

6. A lot of the students (*is, are*) already here.

7. Some of the furniture in our apartment (*is, are*) secondhand.

8. Some of the desks in the classroom (*is, are*) broken.

9. At least three-quarters of that book on famous Americans (*is, are*) about people who lived in the nineteenth century.

10. One of the countries I would like to visit (*is, are*) Italy.

11. Some of the cities I would like to visit (*is, are*) Rome and Venice.

12. Each student in the class (*has, have*) to have a book.

13. Each of the students (*has, have*) a notebook.

14. None of the students (*was, were*) late today.

15. The number of students in this room right now (*is, are*) twenty.

16. A number of students in the class (*speaks, speak*) English very well.

17. There (*is, are*) some interesting pictures in today's paper.

18. There (*is, are*) an incorrect statement in that newspaper article.

19. The United States (*is, are*) located in North America.

20. Economics (*is, are*) Don's favorite subject.

21. Ten minutes (*is, are*) more than enough time to complete this exercise.

22. Most people (*likes, like*) to go to the zoo.

23. The police (*is, are*) coming. I've already called them.

24. Japanese (*is, are*) very difficult for English speakers to learn.

25. The Japanese (*has, have*) a long and interesting history.

26. The old in my country (*is, are*) cared for by their children and grandchildren.

27. This exercise on singular–plural agreement of subjects and verbs (*is, are*) easy.

5–12 BASIC SUBJECT–VERB AGREEMENT

SINGULAR VERB	PLURAL VERB	
(a) My *friend* **lives** in Boston.	(b) My *friends* **live** in Boston.	*verb* + **-s/-es** = third person singular in the simple present tense *noun* + **-s/-es** = plural
(c) That *book* on political parties **is** interesting.	(d) The *ideas* in that book **are** interesting.	A prepositional phrase that comes between a subject and a verb does not affect the verb.
	(e) My *brother and sister* **live** in Boston.	Two (or more) subjects connected by **and** take a plural verb.
(f) *Every man, woman, and child* **needs** love. (g) *Each book and magazine is* listed in the card catalog.		EXCEPTION: **Every** and **each** are always followed immediately by singular nouns. In this case, even when there are two (or more) nouns connected by **and**, the verb is singular.
(h) *Growing* flowers **is** her hobby.		A gerund used as the subject of a sentence takes a singular verb.

☐ **EXERCISE 22:** Choose the correct answer in parentheses.

1. The extent of Jane's knowledge on various complex subjects (*astounds, astound*) me.
2. The subjects you will be studying in this course (*is, are*) listed in the syllabus.
3. Massachusetts and Connecticut (*is, are*) located in New England.
4. Only the black widow spider, of all the spiders in the United States, (*has, have*) caused death among human beings.
5. Oranges, tomatoes, fresh strawberries, cabbage, and green lettuce (*is, are*) rich in vitamin C.
6. The professor and the student (*agrees, agree*) on that point.
7. Almost every professor and student at the university (*approves, approve*) of the choice of Dr. Brown as the new president.
8. Each girl and boy in the sixth-grade class (*has, have*) to do a science project.
9. Making pies and cakes (*is, are*) Mrs. Reed's specialty.
10. Getting to know students from all over the world (*is, are*) one of the best parts of my job.
11. Annie had a hard time when she was coming home from the store because the bag of groceries (*was, were*) too heavy for her to carry.

12. Where (*does, do*) your parents live?
13. Why (*was, were*) Susan and Alex late for the meeting?
14. (*Is, Are*) having the responsibility for taking care of pets good for young children?

5–13 SUBJECT–VERB AGREEMENT: USING EXPRESSIONS OF QUANTITY

SINGULAR VERB	PLURAL VERB	
(a) *Some of the book is* good. (c) *A lot of the equipment is* new. (e) *Two-thirds of the money is* mine.	(b) *Some of the books are* good. (d) *A lot of my friends are* here. (f) *Two-thirds of the pennies are* mine.	The verb is determined by the noun (or pronoun) that follows *of* in most expressions of quantity. Notice in (a) and (b): **some of** + *singular noun* + *singular verb* **some of** + *plural noun* + *plural verb*
(g) *One of my friends is* here. (h) *Each of my friends is* here. (i) *Every one of my friends is* here.		EXCEPTIONS: **One of, each of,** and **every one of** take singular verbs. **one of** **each of** }+ *plural noun* + *singular verb* **every one of**
(j) *None of the boys is* here.	(k) *None of the boys are* here. *(informal)*	Subjects with **none of** are considered singular in very formal English, but plural verbs are often used in informal speech and writing.
(l) *The number of students* in the class *is* fifteen.	(m) *A number of students were* late for class.	COMPARE: In (l): **The number** is the subject. In (m): **A number of** is an expression of quantity meaning "a lot of." It is followed by a plural noun and a plural verb.

☐ **EXERCISE 23:** Choose the correct answer in parentheses.

1. Some of the fruit in this bowl (*is*, *are*) rotten.
2. Some of the apples in that bowl (*is*, *are*) rotten.
3. Half of the students in the class (*is*, *are*) from Arabic-speaking countries.
4. Half of this money (*belongs*, *belong*) to you.
5. A lot of the students in the class (*is*, *are*) from Southeast Asia.
6. A lot of clothing in those stores (*is*, *are*) on sale this week.
7. One of my best friends (*is*, *are*) coming to visit me next month.
8. Each boy in the class (*has*, *have*) his own notebook.
9. Each of the boys in the class (*has*, *have*) his own notebook.
10. Every one of the students (*is*, *are*) required to take the final test.
11. None of the animals at the zoo (*is*, *are*) free. All of them (*is*, *are*) in enclosures.
12. A number of students (*is*, *are*) absent today.

13. The number of students at that university (*is, are*) approximately 10,000.
14. One of the chief materials in bones and teeth (*is, are*) calcium.
15. (*Does, Do*) all of the children have their books?
16. (*Does, Do*) all of this homework have to be finished by tomorrow?
17. Why (*was, were*) some of the students excused from the examination?
18. Why (*was, were*) one of the students excused from the examination?
19. What percentage of the earth's surface (*is, are*) covered by water?
20. What percentage of the people in the world (*is, are*) illiterate?
21. (*Does, Do*) any of you know the answer to that question?

5–14 SUBJECT–VERB AGREEMENT: USING *THERE* + *BE*

SINGULAR VERB	PLURAL VERB	
(a) There ***is*** *a book* on the shelf.	(b) There ***are*** *some books* on the shelf.	The subject follows ***be*** when ***there*** is used.* In (a): The subject is *book*. In (b): The subject is *books*.

*In the structure ***there*** + ***be***, ***there*** is called an *expletive*.

☐ **EXERCISE 24:** Choose the correct answer in parentheses.

1. There (*isn't, aren't*) any letters in the mail for you today.
2. There (*isn't, aren't*) any mail for you today.
3. There (*is, are*) a lot of problems in the world.
4. There (*is, are*) a fly in this room. Where's the flyswatter?
5. There (*is, are*) over 600,000 kinds of insects in the world.
6. How many kinds of birds (*is, are*) there in the world?
7. Why (*isn't, aren't*) there a hospital close to those villages?
8. There (*is, are*) a green pen on Tim's desk.
9. There (*is, are*) a blue pen and a yellow notebook on Sue's desk.*
10. There (*is, are*) some pens and notebooks on Jack's desk.

---

*Sometimes in informal English, a singular verb is used after ***there*** when the first of two subjects connected by ***and*** is singular. For example:
    *Formal: There **are** a book and a pen on the desk.*
    *Informal: There **is** a book and a pen on the desk.*

5–15 SUBJECT–VERB AGREEMENT: SOME IRREGULARITIES

SINGULAR VERB

(a) *The news **is*** interesting. (b) *The United States **is*** big. (c) *The Philippines **consists*** of more than 7,000 islands. (d) *The United Nations **has*** its headquarters in New York City. (e) *Sears **is*** a department store. (f) *Mathematics **is*** easy for her. *Physics **is*** easy for her, too.	Sometimes a noun that ends in *-s* is singular. Notice the examples: If the noun is changed to a pronoun, the singular pronoun *it* is used (not the plural pronoun *they*) because the noun is singular. In (a): *news* = *it* (not *they*). In (b): *the United States* = *it* (not *they*). Note: Fields of study, as in (f), that end in *-ics* take singular verbs.
(g) *Eight hours* of sleep **is** enough. (h) *Ten dollars **is*** too much to pay. (i) *Five thousand miles **is*** too far to travel.	Expressions of *time, money,* and *distance* usually take a singular verb.

PLURAL VERB

(j) *Those people **are*** from Canada. (k) *The police **have*** been called.	***People*** and **police*** do not end in *-s* but are plural nouns and take plural verbs.

SINGULAR VERB   **PLURAL VERB**

(l) *English **is*** spoken in many countries. (n) *Chinese **is*** his native language.	(m) *The English **drink*** tea. (o) *The Chinese **have*** an interesting history.	In (l): ***English*** = language. In (m): *the English* = people from England. Some nouns of nationality that end in *-sh*, *-ese*, and *-ch* can mean either language or people; e.g., *English, Spanish, Chinese, Japanese, Vietnamese, Portuguese, French.*
	(p) *The poor **have*** many problems. (q) *The rich **get*** richer.	A few adjectives can be preceded by *the* and used as a plural noun (without final *-s*) to refer to people who have this quality. Other examples: *the young, the old, the living, the dead, the blind, the deaf, the handicapped.*

*The word ***people*** has a final *-s* (*peoples*) only when it is used to refer to nations or ethnic groups: *All the peoples of the world desire peace.*

☐ **EXERCISE 25:** Choose the correct answer in parentheses.

1. The United States (*has, have*) a population of around 250 million.
2. The news about Mr. Hogan (*is, are*) surprising.

3. Massachusetts (*is, are*) a state in the northeastern part of the United States.
4. Physics (*seeks, seek*) to understand the mysteries of the physical world.
5. Statistics (*is, are*) a branch of mathematics.
6. The statistics in that report on oil production (*is, are*) incorrect.*
7. Fifty minutes (*is, are*) the maximum length of time allowed for the exam.
8. Twenty dollars (*is, are*) an unreasonable price for the necklace.
9. Many people in the world (*does, do*) not have enough to eat.
10. The police (*is, are*) prepared in case there is a riot.
11. The English (*is, are*) proud, independent people.
12. English (*is, are*) not my native language.
13. Many Japanese (*commutes, commute*) to their places of work.
14. Portuguese (*is, are*) somewhat similar to Spanish, (*isn't, aren't*) it?
15. The poor (*is, are*) helped by government programs.
16. The effect of a honeybee's sting on a human being (*depends, depend*) on that person's susceptibility to the bee's venom. Most people (*is, are*) not in danger if they are stung, but there (*has, have*) been instances of allergic deaths from a single honeybee sting.

☐ **EXERCISE 26—ORAL (BOOKS CLOSED):** Respond with *is* or *are*.

Examples: Some of my classmates....　Some of that information....
Response: ...are　...is

1. His idea....
2. His ideas....
3. People....
4. Each of the students....
5. Most of the fruit....
6. Most of the students....
7. The United States....
8. The news in this morning's paper....
9. One of the girls....
10. French....
11. The Vietnamese....
12. Two-thirds of the food....
13. The number of students....
14. Some of the people....
15. Ninety-three million miles....
16. The story about his adventures....
17. A lot of the chairs....
18. A lot of the furniture....
19. Everyone in the English classes....
20. The clothes in that store....
21. Most of the information in those books....
22. The news from home....
23. Fifty percent of the people in the world....

Statistics is singular when it refers to a field of study: e.g., ***Statistics is*** *an interesting field of study.* When it refers to particular numbers, it is used as a count noun: *singular = one statistic (no final -s); plural = two statistics.* For example: ***This statistic is*** *correct.* ***Those statistics are*** *incorrect.*

24. Fifty percent of the world's population....
25. The clothing in those stores....
26. Her husband's relatives....
27. Over half of the books by that author....
28. A million dollars....
29. The rich....

30. His method of doing things....
31. A number of people....
32. Most of the stores in this city....
33. Mathematics....
34. The police....
35. Everybody in the whole world....

☐ **EXERCISE 27:** Write the correct form of the given verb. Use only the SIMPLE PRESENT.

1. My alarm clock _____rings_____ at seven every morning. (*ring*)

2. There _____are_____ a lot of sheep in the field. (*be*)

3. One of my friends _____ a goldfish bowl on her kitchen table. (*keep*)

4. Sensitivity to other people's feelings _____ him a kind and understanding person. (*make*)

5. Each penny, nickel, dime, and quarter _____ counted carefully by the bank teller. (*be*)

6. My driver's license _____ in my wallet. (*be*)

7. _____ John's uncle live in the suburbs? (*do*)

8. _____ most of the students live in the dormitories? (*do*)

9. An orange and black bird _____ sitting in that tree. (*be*)

10. An orange bird and a black bird _____ sitting in that tree. (*be*)

11. The insurance rates on our car _____ high because we live in a city. (*be*)

12. _____ January and February the coldest months of the year? (*be*)

13. Almost two-thirds of the land in the southwestern areas of the country _____ unsuitable for farming. (*be*)

14. The economic and cultural center of the United States _____ New York City. (*be*)

15. Two hours of skiing _____ plenty of exercise. (*provide*)

16. In many respects, this magazine article on wild animals in North America _____ the very real danger of extinction that many species face. (*oversimplify*)

17. A car with poor brakes and no brake lights ＿＿＿＿＿＿ dangerous. (*be*)

18. A number of people from the company ＿＿＿＿ to attend the conference. (*plan*)

19. Most of the news on the front pages of both daily newspapers ＿＿＿＿＿ the progress of the peace conference. (*concern*)

20. The northernmost town in the forty-eight contiguous states ＿＿＿＿ Angle Inlet, Minnesota. (*be*)

21. The number of human skeletons found at the archaeological site ＿＿＿＿ seven. (*be*)

22. Almost all the information in those texts on the Aztec Indians and their civilization ＿＿＿＿＿＿ to be well researched. (*appear*)

23. Every day there ＿＿＿＿ more than a dozen traffic accidents in the city. (*be*)

24. No news ＿＿＿＿＿＿ good news. (*be*)

25. Every member of this class ＿＿＿＿＿＿＿ English very well. (*speak*)

□ **EXERCISE 28—WRITTEN/ORAL:** Complete the following sentences with your own words. Use only present tenses.

Examples: One of my . . . *teachers knows Chinese.*
Some of my . . . *friends are coming to visit me.*

1. All of the rooms in . . . .
2. In my country, there . . . .
3. A lot of . . . .
4. The people in my country . . . .
5. The number of students . . . .
6. A number of students . . . .
7. Each of . . . .
8. The United States . . . .
9. The English language . . . .
10. The English . . . .
11. English . . . .
12. One of my . . . .
13. Most of the food . . . .
14. Most of my classmates . . . .
15. Linguistics . . . .
16. Linguists . . . .

5–16 PERSONAL PRONOUNS: AGREEMENT WITH NOUNS

(a) **A student** walked into the room. **She** was looking for the teacher. (b) **A student** walked into the room. **He** was looking for the teacher. (c) **Some students** walked into the room. **They** were looking for the teacher.	A singular pronoun is used to refer to a singular noun, as in (a) and (b). A plural pronoun is used to refer to a plural noun, as in (c).
(d) **A student** should always do **his** assignments. (e) **A student** should always do **his/her** assignments. **A student** should always do **his or her** assignments.	With a "generic noun"* (e.g, in (d): *a student = anyone who is a student*) a singular masculine pronoun has been used traditionally, but many English speakers now use both masculine and feminine pronouns, as in (e).

*A generic noun does not refer to any person or thing in particular; rather, it represents a whole group. (See Appendix 1, Chart D-1, *Basic Article Usage.*)

5–17 PERSONAL PRONOUNS: AGREEMENT WITH INDEFINITE PRONOUNS

The following are indefinite pronouns:				
	everyone	*someone*	*anyone*	*no one*
	everybody	*somebody*	*anybody*	*nobody*
	everything	*something*	*anything*	*nothing*

(f) **Somebody** left **his** book on the desk. (g) **Everyone** has **his or her** own ideas.	A singular personal pronoun is used in formal English to refer to an indefinite pronoun, as in (f) and (g).
(h) INFORMAL: **Somebody** left **their** book on the desk. **Everyone** has **their** own ideas.	In everyday informal English, a plural personal pronoun is often used to refer to an indefinite pronoun, as in (h).

☐ **EXERCISE 29:** Complete the sentences with pronouns. In some of the blanks there is more than one possibility. Choose the appropriate singular or plural verb in parentheses where necessary.

    1. When a student wants to study, _*s/he; he or she; he*_ should try to find a quiet place.*

---

*Notice in 1 through 4: The problem of masculine/feminine pronouns can be avoided if a plural instead of singular generic noun is used.

2. A citizen has two primary responsibilities. _____ should vote in every election, and _____ should willingly serve on a jury.

3. Each student in Biology 101 has to spend three hours per week in the laboratory, where _____ (*does, do*) various experiments by following the directions in _____ lab manual.

4. A pharmacist fills prescriptions, but _____ (*is, are*) not allowed to prescribe medicine. By law, only a doctor can prescribe medicine.

5. Anyone can learn how to dance if _____ (*wants, want*) to.

6. Hmmm. Someone forgot _____ umbrella. I wonder whose it is.

7. Everyone who came to the picnic brought _____ own food.

8. A: Is that your notebook?

   B: No. It belongs to one of the other students.

   A: Look on the inside cover. Did _____ write _____ name there?

9. A dog makes a good pet if _____ (*is, are*) properly trained.

10. Tom's cat is named Maybelle Alice. _____ is very independent. _____ obeys Tom only if _____ feels like it.★

5–18 PERSONAL PRONOUNS: AGREEMENT WITH COLLECTIVE NOUNS

The following are examples of collective nouns:			
audience	couple	family	public
class	crowd	government	staff
committee	faculty	group	team

(a) **My family** is large. **It** is composed of nine members.	When a collective noun refers to a single impersonal unit, a singular pronoun (**it, its**) is used, as in (a).
(b) **My family** is loving and supportive. **They** are always ready to help me.	When a collective noun refers to a collection of various individuals, a plural pronoun (**they, them, their**) is used, as in (b).★

*NOTE: When the collective noun refers to a collection of individuals, the verb may be either singular or plural: My family **is** OR **are** loving and supportive. A singular verb is generally preferred in American English. A plural verb is used more frequently in British English, especially with the words government and public. (American: **The government is** planning many changes. British: **The government are** planning many changes.)*

---

*If the sex of a particular animal is known, usually **she** or **he** is used instead of **it**.

☐ **EXERCISE 30:** Complete the sentences with pronouns. In some of the sentences, there is more than one possibility. Choose the appropriate singular or plural verb in parentheses where necessary.

1. I have a wonderful family. I love _____*them*_____ very much, and
   _____*they love*_____ (*loves, love*) me.

2. I looked up some information about the average American family. I
   found out that _____ (*consists, consist*) of 2.3 children.

3. The soccer team felt unhappy because _____ had lost in the
   closing moments of the game.

4. A basketball team is relatively small. _____ (*doesn't, don't*)
   have as many members as a baseball team.

5. The audience clapped enthusiastically. Obviously _____
   had enjoyed the concert.

6. The audience filled the room to overflowing. _____ (*was,
   were*) larger than I had expected.

7. The crowd became more and more excited as the premier's motorcade
   approached. _____ began to shout and wave flags in the air.

8. The crowd at the soccer game was huge. _____ exceeded 100,000
   people.

9. The office staff gave _____ boss a gold watch when she retired.

10. The office staff isn't large. _____ (*consists, consist*) of a
    secretary, a file clerk, and a receptionist.

11. The young couple finally saved enough money to make a downpayment
    on _____ own house.

12. The class is planning a party for the last day of school. _____
    (*is, are*) going to bring many different kinds of food and invite some of
    _____ friends to celebrate with _____.

13. The class is too small. _____ (*is, are*) going to be cancelled.

5–19 USING REFLEXIVE PRONOUNS

The following are reflexive pronouns:		
	myself	*ourselves*
	yourself	*yourselves*
	himself, herself, itself	*themselves*

(a) ***He*** looked at ***himself*** in the mirror.	A reflexive pronoun usually refers to the subject of a sentence. In (a): ***he*** and ***himself*** refer to the same person.
(b) ***He himself*** answered the phone, not his secretary. (c) ***He*** answered the phone ***himself***.	Sometimes reflexive pronouns are used for emphasis, as in (b) and (c).
(d) She lives ***by herself***.	The expression ***by*** + *a reflexive pronoun* usually means "alone," as in (d).

☐ **EXERCISE 31**: Complete the following by using appropriate reflexive pronouns.

1. I can't help you, Bob. You'll have to solve your problem by _yourself_.

2. Jane did not join the rest of us. She sat in the back of the room by

   _____.

3. You may think Stan is telling the truth, but I _____ don't

   believe him.

4. It is important for all of us to be honest with _____.

5. Now that their children are grown, Mr. and Mrs. Grayson live by

   _____.

6. You _____ have to make that decision, Ann. No one can

   make it for you.

7. I don't know what to tell you, Sue and Jack. You will have to take care of

   that problem _____.

8. When everybody else forgot his birthday, Ralph decided to give

   _____ a birthday present. He bought a new shirt for

   _____.

☐ **EXERCISE 32:** Complete the sentences by using a word or expression from the given list and an appropriate reflexive pronoun.

angry at	*introduced*	*promised*
enjoy	*killed*	*proud of*
entertained	*laugh at*	*talking to*
feeling sorry for	*pat*	✔ *taught*

1. Karen Williams never took lessons. She ___*taught herself*___ how to play the piano.

2. Did Hank have a good time at the party? Did he _____?

3. All of you did a good job. You should be _____.

4. You did a good job, Barbara. You should _____ on the back.

5. A man down the street committed suicide. We were all shocked by the news that he had _____.

6. The children played very well without adult supervision. They _____ by playing school.

7. I had always wanted to meet Mr. Anderson. When I saw him at a party last night, I walked over and _____ to him.

8. Yesterday Fred's car ran out of gas. Fred had to walk two miles to a gas station. He is still _____ for forgetting to fill the tank.

9. Nothing good ever comes from self-pity. You should stop _____, George, and start doing something to solve your problems.

10. Carol made several careless mistakes at work last week, and her boss is getting impatient with her. Carol has _____ to do better work in the future.

11. People might think you're a little crazy, but _____ _____ is one way to practice using English.

12. Humor can ease the trials and tribulations of life. Sometimes we have to be able to _____.

5-20 USING *YOU* AND *ONE* AS IMPERSONAL PRONOUNS

(a) **One** should always be polite. (b) How does **one** get to 5th Avenue from here?	In (a) and (b): **one** means "any person, people in general." In (c) and (d): **you** means "any person, people in general." **One** is more formal than **you**. Impersonal **you**, rather than **one**, is used more frequently in everyday English.
(c) **You** should always be polite. (d) How do **you** get to 5th Avenue from here?	
(e) **One** should take care of **one's** health. **One** should take care of **his** health. **One** should take care of **his or her** health.	In (e): Notice the pronouns that may be used in the same sentence to refer back to **one**.

☐ **EXERCISE 33—ERROR ANALYSIS:** All the following have errors. Make the pronoun usage in the following consistent and correct.

1. One should always try to be friendly to your neighbors.
   *One should always try to be friendly to **one's** neighbors (OR **his or her** neighbors).*
   *You should always try to be friendly to **your** neighbors.*
   *People should always try to be friendly to **their** neighbors.*
   *A person should always try to be friendly to **his or her** neighbors.*

2. One can't know what he can actually do until you try.

3. It is important for a person to listen to your conscience.

4. You can get to the airport by taxi or by bus. People can catch the airport bus at the hotel.

5. Self-esteem is important to one's mental health. It is important for you to like yourself.

6. It is important for one to take care of their health. For example, you should not smoke. Smoking has been shown to cause various life-threatening diseases. One should also be careful to get plenty of exercise. Adequate rest is important, too. People can't be their best if one is tired all the time. We also need to eat a wide variety of food to make sure you get all the nutrients your body needs.

5-21 FORMS OF *OTHER*

	ADJECTIVE	PRONOUN	
singular: *plural:*	**another book** (is) **other books** (are)	**another** (is) **others** (are)	Forms of **other** are used as either adjectives or pronouns. Notice: A final **-s** is used only for a plural pronoun (**others**).
singular: *plural:*	**the other book** (is) **the other books** (are)	**the other** (is) **the others** (are)	

(a) The students in the class come from many countries. One of the students is from Mexico. **Another student is** from Iraq. **Another is** from Japan. **Other students are** from Brazil. **Others are** from Algeria.	The meaning of **another**: *one more in addition to the one(s) already mentioned.* The meaning of **other/others** (without *the*): *several more in addition to the one(s) already mentioned.*
(b) I have three books. Two are mine. **The other book** is yours. (**The other** is yours.) (c) I have three books. One is mine. **The other books** are yours. (**The others** are yours.)	The meaning of **the other(s)**: *all that remains from a given number; the rest of a specific group.*
(d) We write to **each other** every week. (e) We write to **one another** every week.	**Each other** and **one another** indicate a reciprocal relationship. In (d) and (e): I write to him every week, and he writes to me every week.
(f) Please write on **every other** line. (g) I see her **every other** *week*.	**Every other** can give the idea of "alternate." In (f): Write on the first line. Do not write on the second line. Write on the third line. Do not write on the fourth line. (etc.)
(h) I will be here for **another three years**. (i) I need **another five dollars**. (j) We drove **another ten miles**.	**Another** is used with expressions of time, money, and distance, even if these expressions contain plural nouns.

☐ **EXERCISE 34:** Supply a form of **other** in the following.

1. I got three letters. One was from my father. ____*Another*____ one was from my sister. ____*The other*____ letter was from my girlfriend.

2. Look at your hand. There is a total of five fingers. One is your thumb. _____ is your index finger. _____ one is your middle finger. _____ finger is your ring finger. And _____ finger (the last of the five) is your little finger.

3. Look at your hands. One is your right hand. _____ is your left hand.

4. I invited five people to my party. Out of those five people, only John and Mary can come. _____ can't come.

5. I invited five people to my party. Out of those five people, only John and Mary can come. _____ people can't come.

6. I would like some more books on this subject. Do you have any _____ that you could lend me?

7. I would like to read more about this subject. Do you have any _____ books that you could lend me?

8. There are many means of transportation. The airplane is one means of transportation. The train is _____.

9. There are many means of transportation. The airplane is one. _____ are the train, the automobile, and the horse.

10. There are two women standing on the corner. One is Helen Jansen and _____ is Pat Hendricks.

11. Alice reads *The New York Times* every day. She doesn't read any _____ newspapers.

12. Some people prefer classical music, but _____ prefer rock music.

13. Mr. and Mrs. Jay are a happily married couple. They love _____. They support _____. They like _____.

14. He will graduate in _____ two years.

15. I'm almost finished. I just need _____ five minutes.

☐ **EXERCISE 35:** Supply a form of *other* in the following.

1. One common preposition is *from*. _____ common one is *in*. _____ are *by*, *for*, and *of*. The most frequently used prepositions in English are *at*, *by*, *for*, *from*, *in*, *of*, *to*, and *with*. What are some _____ prepositions?

2. Two countries border on the United States. One is Canada. _____ is Mexico.

3. One of the countries I would like to visit is Sweden. _____ is Mexico. Of course, besides these two countries, there are many _____ places I would like to see.

4. They have three children. One has graduated from college and has a job.

_____ is in school at the University of Arkansas. _____

_____ is still living at home.

5. Thank you for inviting me to go on the picnic. I'd like to go with you, but

I've already made _____ plans.

6. Most of the guests have already arrived, and I'm sure that all of _____

_____ will be here soon.

7. Some people are tall; _____ are short. Some people are fat;

_____ are thin. Some people are nearsighted; _____

people are farsighted.

8. That country has two basic problems. One is inflation, and _____

is the instability of their government.

9. I have been in only three cities since I came to the United States. One is

New York, and _____ are Washington, D.C., and Chicago.

10. When his alarm went off this morning, he shut it off, rolled over, and

slept for _____ twenty minutes.

11. Louis and I have been friends for a long time. We've known _____

_____ since we were children.

12. Individual differences in children must be recognized. Whereas one

child might have a strong interest in mathematics and science,

_____ child might tend toward more artistic endeavors.

13. It's a long trip. I'm getting tired of riding in the car, but we still have

_____ two hundred miles to go.

14. In just _____ three weeks, he will be a married man.

15. Prices continually rise. Next year a new car will cost _____

three or four hundred dollars.

☐ **EXERCISE 36—ORAL (BOOKS CLOSED):** Complete the sentences, using an appropriate form of ***other***.

Example: There are two books on the desk. One is . . . .
Response: (One is . . .) mine, and the other is yours.
(One is . . .) red. The other is blue.

1. I speak two languages. One is . . . .
2. I speak three languages. One is . . . .
3. I lost my textbook, so I had to buy . . . .
4. Some people have straight hair, but . . . .
5. I'm still thirsty. I'd like . . . .
6. George Washington is one American hero. Abraham Lincoln . . . .
7. I have two books. One is . . . .
8. Some TV programs are excellent, but . . . .
9. Some people need at least eight hours of sleep each night, but . . . .
10. Only two of the students failed the quiz. All of . . . .
11. Mary and John are in love. They love . . . .
12. There are three colors that I especially like. One is . . . .
13. I have two candy bars. I want only one of them. Would you like . . . .
14. I'm still hungry. I'd like . . . .
15. There are three places in particular that I would like to visit while I am in (*the United States*). One is . . . .

□ **EXERCISE 37—ERROR ANALYSIS:** The following sentences are adapted from student writing and contain typical errors. Test your skill by finding and correcting these errors.

1. That book contain many different kind of story and article.

2. There is a lot of differences between United States and my country.

3. The English is one of the most important language in the world.

4. She is always willing to help her friends in every possible ways.

5. I don't have enough time to make all of my homeworks.

6. He succeeded in creating one of the best army in the world.

7. There are many equipments in the research laboratory, but undergraduates are not allowed to use them.

8. All of the guest enjoyed themself at the reception.

9. I have a five years old daughter and a three years old son.

10. I am not accustomed to a cold weather.

11. Each states in the country have a different language.

12. Most of people in my apartment building is friendly.

13. A political leader should have the ability to adapt themselves to a changing world.

14. In my opinion, a foreign student should live in a dormitory because they will meet many people and can practice their English every day. Also, if you live in a dormitory, your food is provided for you.

15. When I lost my passport, I had to apply for the another one.

16. When I got to class, all of the others students were already in their seats.

☐ **EXERCISE 38—PREPOSITIONS:** Supply an appropriate preposition for each of the following.

1. Do you believe _____ ghosts?

2. Anthony is engaged _____ my cousin.

3. Ms. Ballas substituted _____ our regular teacher yesterday.

4. I can't distinguish one twin _____ the other.

5. Did you forgive him _____ lying to you?

6. Children rely _____ their parents for food and shelter.

7. Tim wore sunglasses to protect his eyes _____ the sun.

8. Chris excels _____ sports.

9. Andrea contributed her ideas _____ the discussion.

10. I hope you succeed _____ your new job.

11. I'm very fond _____ their children.

12. The firefighters rescued many people _____ the burning building.

13. I don't care _____ spaghetti. I'd rather eat something else.

14. Charles doesn't seem to care _____ his bad grades.

15. Sometimes Bobby seems to be jealous _____ his brother.

☐ **EXERCISE 39—PHRASAL VERBS:** Supply appropriate prepositions for the following two-word or three-word verbs.

1. A: Omar, would you please pass these papers _____ to the rest of the class?

   B: I'd be happy to.

2. A: When are we expected to be at the hotel?

   B: According to our reservation, we are supposed to check _____ the hotel before 6 P.M. Monday and check _____ before noon Tuesday.

3. A: How do you get _____ with your roommate?

   B: Fine. He's a nice guy.

4. A: Thanks for the ride. I appreciate it.

   B: Where should I drop you _____?

   A: The next corner would be fine.

5. A: I'm going to be out of town for a couple of days. Would you mind looking _____ my cat?

   B: Not at all. I'd be happy to. Just tell me what I'm supposed to do.

6. A: I think I'm going to turn _____ now. Good night.

   B: 'Night. See you in the morning. Sleep well.

7. A: Don't you think it's hot in here?

   B: Not especially. If you're hot, why don't you take your sweater _____?

8. A: How do you spell ''occasionally''?

   B: I'm not sure. You'd better look it _____ in your dictionary.

9. A: How much lettuce should we get?

   B: I think we could use two heads. Pick _____ two that feel fresh and firm.

10. A: Why are you sniffling?

    B: I had a cold last week, and I can't seem to get _____ it.

CHAPTER *6*

Adjective Clauses

6–1 ADJECTIVE CLAUSES: INTRODUCTION

Terms:	**clause:**	A *clause* is a group of words containing a subject and a verb.
	independent clause:	An *independent clause* is a complete sentence. It contains the main subject and verb of a sentence. (It is also called *a main clause*.)
	dependent clause:	A *dependent clause* is not a complete sentence. It must be connected to an independent clause.
	adjective clause:	An *adjective clause* is a dependent clause that modifies a noun. It describes, identifies, or gives further information about a noun. (An adjective clause is also called *a relative clause*.)

6–2 USING SUBJECT PRONOUNS: *WHO, WHICH, THAT*

I thanked the woman. **She** helped me. ↓ (a) I thanked the woman **who** *helped me.* (b) I thanked the woman **that** *helped me.*	In (a): *I thanked the woman* = an independent clause *who helped me* = an adjective clause The adjective clause modifies the noun *woman*.
	In (a): **who** is the subject of the adjective clause. In (b): **that** is the subject of the adjective clause. Note: (a) and (b) have the same meaning.
The book is mine. **It** is on the table. ↓ (c) The book **which** *is on the table* is mine. (d) The book **that** *is on the table* is mine.	**who** = used for people **which** = used for things **that** = used for both people and things

☐ **EXERCISE 1—ORAL:** Combine the two sentences. Use the second sentence as an adjective clause.

1. I saw the man. He closed the door. →

   I saw the man $\left\{ \begin{array}{l} who \\ that \end{array} \right\}$ *closed the door.*

2. The girl is happy. She won the race.
3. The student is from China. He sits next to me.
4. The students are from China. They sit in the front row.
5. We are studying sentences. They contain adjective clauses.
6. I am using a sentence. It contains an adjective clause.
7. Algebra problems contain letters. They stand for unknown numbers.
8. The taxi driver was friendly. He took me to the airport.

6–3 USING OBJECT PRONOUNS: *WHO(M), WHICH, THAT*

1. PRONOUN USED AS THE OBJECT OF A VERB
 	
The man was Mr. Jones.
I saw **him**.
 	
(e) The man   **who(m)**   *I saw*   was Mr. Jones.
(f) The man   **that**   *I saw*   was Mr. Jones.
(g) The man   Ø   *I saw*   was Mr. Jones.
 	
    The movie wasn't very good.
    We saw **it** last night.
 	
(h) The movie   **which**   *we saw last night*   wasn't very good.
(i) The movie   **that**   *we saw last night*   wasn't very good.
(j) The movie   Ø   *we saw last night*   wasn't very good.
	Notice in the examples: The adjective clause pronouns are placed at the *beginning* of the clause. (General guideline: Place an adjective clause pronoun as close as possible to the noun it modifies.)

	In (e): **who** is usually used instead of **whom**, especially in speaking. **Whom** is generally used only in very formal English.
	In (g) and (j): An object pronoun is often omitted from an adjective clause. (A subject pronoun, however, may not be omitted.)
	who(m) = used for people **which** = used for things **that** = used for both people and things

☐ **EXERCISE 2—ORAL:** Combine the sentences, using the second sentence as an adjective clause. Give all the possible patterns.

1. The book was good. I read it.
2. I liked the woman. I met her at the party last night.
3. I liked the composition. You wrote it.
4. The people were very nice. We visited them yesterday.

2. PRONOUN USED AS THE OBJECT OF A PREPOSITION	In very formal English, the preposition comes at the beginning of the adjective clause, as in (k) and (o). Usually, however, in everyday usage, the preposition comes after the subject and verb of the adjective clause, as in the other examples.

She is the woman.
I told you *about her*.

(k) She is the woman	*about whom*	I told you.
(l) She is the woman		*who(m)*	I told you *about*.
(m) She is the woman		*that*	I told you *about*.
(n) She is the woman		Ø	I told you *about*.

The music was good.
We listened *to it* last night.

(o) The music	*to which*	we listened	last night	was good.
(p) The music	*which*	we listened *to*	last night	was good.
(q) The music	*that*	we listened *to*	last night	was good.
(r) The music	Ø	we listened *to*	last night	was good.

Note: If the preposition comes at the beginning of the adjective clause, only *whom* or *which* may be used. A preposition is never immediately followed by *that* or *who*.

☐ **EXERCISE 3—ORAL:** Combine the sentences, using the second sentence as an adjective clause. Give all the possible patterns.

1. The meeting was interesting. I went to it.
2. The man was very kind. I talked to him yesterday.
3. I must thank the people. I got a present from them.
4. The picture was beautiful. She was looking at it.
5. The man is standing over there. I was telling you about him.

6–4 USING *WHOSE*

I know the man.
His bicycle was stolen.

(s) I know the man *whose bicycle* was stolen.

The student writes well.
I read *her composition*.

(t) The student *whose composition I read* writes well.

Whose is used to show possession. It carries the same meaning as other possessive pronouns used as adjectives: *his*, *her*, *its*, and *their*. Like *his*, *her*, *its*, and *their*, *whose* is connected to a noun:

his bicycle → *whose bicycle*
her composition → *whose composition*

Both *whose* and the noun it is connected to are placed at the beginning of the adjective clause. *Whose* cannot be omitted.

Mr. Catt has a painting. *Its value* is inestimable.
(u) Mr. Catt has a painting *whose value* is inestimable.

Whose usually modifies "people," but it may also be used to modify "things," as in (u).

☐ **EXERCISE 4—ORAL:** Combine the two sentences, using the second sentence as an adjective clause.

1. I apologized to the woman. I spilled her coffee.
2. The man called the police. His wallet was stolen.
3. I met the woman. Her husband is the president of the corporation.
4. The professor is excellent. I am taking her course.
5. Mr. North teaches a class for students. Their native language is not English.
6. I come from a country. Its history goes back thousands of years.
7. The people were nice. We visited their house.
8. I live in a dormitory. Its residents come from many countries.
9. I have to call the man. I accidentally picked up his umbrella after the meeting.
10. The man poured a glass of water on his face. His beard caught on fire when he lit a cigarette.

☐ **EXERCISE 5:** Identify the adjective clause in each sentence. Then give the other possible patterns, if any.

1. The dress which she is wearing is new. →
   Adjective clause: *which she is wearing*
   Other possible patterns: The dress $\begin{Bmatrix} that \\ \emptyset \end{Bmatrix}$ *she is wearing is new.*
2. The doctor who examined the sick child was very gentle.
3. The people I was waiting for were late.
4. The term paper David is writing must be finished by Friday.
5. The man whose opinions I respect most is my father.
6. Did I tell you about the woman I met last night?

7. Did you hear about the earthquake that occurred in California?

8. The woman I was dancing with stepped on my toe.

□ **EXERCISE 6:** Combine the following sentences. Use sentence (b) as an adjective clause. Give all the possible adjective clause patterns.*

1. (a) The scientist is well-known for her research. (b) We met her yesterday. →

   The scientist $\begin{cases} \varnothing \\ who(m) \\ that \end{cases}$ *we met yesterday is well-known for her research.*

2. (a) She lectured on a topic. (b) I know very little about it.

3. (a) The students missed the assignment. (b) They were absent from class.

4. (a) Yesterday I ran into an old friend. (b) I hadn't seen him for years.

5. (a) I explained my absence to the teacher. (b) I had missed his class.

6. (a) The young women are all from Japan. (b) We met them at the meeting last night.

7. (a) I am reading a book. (b) It was written by Jane Austen.

8. (a) The man gave me good advice. (b) I spoke to him.

9. (a) The instructor gives difficult tests. (b) I failed her course.

10. (a) I returned the money. (b) I had borrowed it from my roommate.

11. (a) The dogcatcher caught the dog. (b) It bit my neighbor's daughter.

12. (a) The people are very kind. (b) I am staying at their house.

---

*In everyday usage, often one pattern is used more commonly than another:
   (1) As a subject pronoun, **who** is more common than **that**.
   (2) As a subject pronoun, **that** is more common than **which**.
   (3) Object pronouns are usually omitted.

6–5 USING *WHERE*

	The building is very old. He lives *there* (*in that building*).			*Where* is used in an adjective clause to modify a place (*city, country, room, house, etc.*).
(a) The building	*where*	*he lives*	is very old.	If *where* is used, a preposition is not included in the adjective clause. If *where* is not used, the preposition must be included.
(b) The building	*in which*	*he lives*	is very old.	
The building	*which*	*he lives in*	is very old.	
The building	*that*	*he lives in*	is very old.	
The building	Ø	*he lives in*	is very old.	

☐ **EXERCISE 7—ORAL:** Combine the sentences, using the second sentence as an adjective clause.

1. The city was beautiful. We spent our vacation there (in that city).
2. That is the restaurant. I will meet you there (at that restaurant).
3. The town is small. I grew up there (in that town).
4. That is the drawer. I keep my jewelry there (in that drawer).

6–6 USING *WHEN*

	I'll never forget the day. I met you *then* (*on that day*).		*When* is used in an adjective clause to modify a noun of time (*year, day, time, century, etc.*)
(c) I'll never forget the day	*when*	*I met you.*	The use of a preposition in an adjective clause that modifies a noun of time is somewhat different from that in other adjective clauses: A preposition is used preceding *which*, as in (d). Otherwise, the preposition is omitted.
(d) I'll never forget the day	*on which*	*I met you.*	
(e) I'll never forget the day	*that*	*I met you.*	
(f) I'll never forget the day	Ø	*I met you.*	

☐ **EXERCISE 8—ORAL:** Combine the sentences, using the second sentence as an adjective clause.

1. Monday is the day. We will come then (on that day).
2. 7:05 is the time. My plane arrives then (at that time).
3. 1960 is the year. The revolution took place then (in that year).
4. July is the month. The weather is usually the hottest then (in that month).

□ **EXERCISE 9—ORAL (BOOKS CLOSED):** Begin your response with "That is . . . ." Use *where* in an adjective clause.

Example: You were born in *that* city.
Response: That is *the* city where I was born.

1. We have class in that room.
2. We ate dinner at that restaurant.
3. He works in that building.
4. He lives on that street.
5. You eat lunch at that cafeteria.
6. You keep your money at that bank.
7. You do your grocery shopping at that store.
8. You spent your vacation on that island.
9. You went swimming in that lake.
10. You grew up in that town.
11. The examination will be given in that room.
12. The earthquake occurred in that country.
13. Your sister went to graduate school at that university.
14. We are going to have a picnic at that park.
15. You lived in that city until you were ten years old.

□ **EXERCISE 10—ORAL (BOOKS CLOSED):** Begin your response with "Did she tell you about . . . ?" (*To the teacher: Write "Did she tell you about . . . ?" on the board.*)

Example: She wrote *a* letter.
Response: Did she tell you about *the* letter she wrote?

1. She wrote a report.
2. She got a letter.
3. She went to a party.
4. She met some people.
5. She took a trip.
6. She went to a movie.
7. She saw a program on TV.
8. She took a test.
9. She read a book.
10. She bought some furniture.
11. She saw an accident.
12. She met a man.
13. She talked to a woman.
14. She had a problem.
15. She took a physics course.

□ **EXERCISE 11—ORAL (BOOKS CLOSED):** Begin your response with "She told me about . . . ."

Example: Did she write *a* letter to her parents yesterday?
Response: Yes. She told me about *the* letter she wrote to her parents yesterday.

1. Did she write a letter to the President of the United States?
2. Did she get a letter from her brother yesterday?
3. Did she go to a party yesterday?
4. Did she meet some people at that party?

5. Did she take a trip to Mexico last summer?
6. Did she have some experiences in Mexico?
7. Did she use to live in a small town?
8. Did she get some presents for her birthday?
9. Did she do an experiment in chemistry lab yesterday?
10. Did she have to write a term paper for her English course?
11. Did she take an American history course last semester?
12. Is she reading a science fiction book?

☐ EXERCISE 12—ORAL (BOOKS CLOSED):

Example: You read *a* book. Was it interesting?
Response: Yes, *the* book I read was interesting.

Example: You drank *some* tea. Did it taste good?
Response: Yes, *the* tea I drank tasted good.

1. You are sitting in a chair. Is it comfortable?
2. You saw a man. Was he wearing a brown suit?
3. You talked to a woman. Did she answer your question?
4. You had some meat for dinner last night. Was it good?
5. You bought a coat. Does it keep you warm?
6. You went to a soccer game. Was it exciting?
7. You watched a TV program last night. Was it good?
8. You are wearing boots/tennis shoes/loafers. Are they comfortable?
9. You stayed at a hotel. Was it in the middle of the city?
10. You eat at a cafeteria. Does it have good food?
11. You got a package in the mail. Was it from your parents?
12. You are doing an exercise. Is it easy?

☐ EXERCISE 13—ORAL (BOOKS CLOSED):

Example: A stranger gave you directions to the post office. Did she speak too fast?
Response: Yes, the stranger who gave me directions to the post office spoke too fast.

1. A waiter served you at a restaurant. Was he polite?
2. A barber cut your hair. Did he do a good job?
3. A clerk cashed your check. Did he ask for identification?
4. A man stopped you on the street. Did he ask you for directions?
5. A student stopped you in the hall. Did she ask you for the correct time?

6. A woman stepped on your toe. Did she apologize?
7. A car drove through a red light. Did it hit another car?
8. Some students took a test. Did most of them pass?
9. Some students are sitting in this room. Can all of them speak English?
10. A woman shouted at you. Was she angry?

11. A police officer helped you. Did you thank her? (*Yes, I thanked* . . . .)
12. A person is sitting next to you. Do you know him/her?
13. A professor teaches Chemistry 101. Do you like him?
14. A taxi driver took you to the bus station. Did you have a conversation with her?
15. A woman came into the room. Did you recognize her?
16. A man opened the door for you. Did you thank him?
17. A student is wearing a (*blue shirt/blouse*). Are you sitting next to him/her?
18. Some students were sitting on the grass outside the classroom building. Did you join them?
19. You were reading a book. Did you finish it?
20. You went to a party last night. Did you enjoy it?
21. You were looking for a book. Did you find it?
22. (. . .) told a story. Did you believe it?
23. (. . .) gave you a present. Did you open it?
24. You borrowed a pen from (. . .). Did you return it?
25. (. . .) told a joke. Did you laugh at it?

☐ **EXERCISE 14—ORAL (BOOKS CLOSED):** Follow the pattern and supply your own completion.

Example: You spoke to a woman.
Response: The woman I spoke to . . . (was Mrs. Jones/was very kind/etc.).

1. You are looking at a person.
2. You are sitting at a desk.
3. This book belongs to a student.
4. You are interested in a field of study.
5. (. . .) and you listened to some music.
6. (. . .) went to a movie last night.
7. (. . .) was talking about a movie.
8. The police are looking for a man.
9. (. . .) is married to a man/woman.
10. You are living in a city/town.
11. You waited for a person.
12. You are studying at a school.
13. You got a letter from a person.
14. You grew up in a city/town.
15. I am pointing at a person.
16. (. . .) spoke to some people.
17. You are living with some people.
18. You went to a doctor to get some medicine.

☐ **EXERCISE 15—ORAL (BOOKS CLOSED):** You are in a room full of people. You are speaking to a friend. You are identifying various people in the room for your friend. Begin your response with "There is . . . ."

Example: That man's wife is your teacher.
Response: There is the man whose wife is my teacher.

1. That woman's husband is a football player.
2. That boy's father is a doctor.
3. That girl's mother is a dentist.
4. That person's picture was in the newspaper.
5. That man's dog bit you.
6. That man's daughter won a gold medal at the Olympic Games.
7. That woman's car was stolen.
8. You borrowed that student's lecture notes.
9. You found that woman's keys.
10. You are in that teacher's class.
11. You read that author's book.
12. We met that man's wife.

☐ **EXERCISE 16—ORAL (BOOKS CLOSED):** Use *whose* in the response.

Example: Dr. Jones is a professor. You are taking his course.
Response: Dr. Jones is the professor whose course I am taking.

1. (. . .) is a student. You found his/her book.
2. (. . .) is a student. You borrowed his/her dictionary.
3. Mark Twain is an author. You like his books best.
4. You used a woman's phone. You thanked her.
5. You broke a child's toy. He started to cry.
6. You stayed at a family's house. They were very kind.
7. A woman's purse was stolen. She called the police.
8. (*Name of a famous singer*) is a singer. You like his/her music best.
9. A girl's leg is in a cast. She has trouble climbing stairs.
10. Everyone tried to help a family. Their house had burned down.

☐ **EXERCISE 17—ORAL (BOOKS CLOSED):** Begin your response with either "I'll never forget . . ." or "I'll always remember . . . ."

Example: trip
Response: I'll never forget the trip . . . (I took to France).

1. trip
2. experiences
3. day
4. first day
5. time
6. first time
7. person
8. people
9. woman
10. man
11. house
12. story
13. accident
14. wonderful food
15. room
16. friends

☐ EXERCISE 18—ORAL (BOOKS CLOSED):

(To the teacher: Use the questions to elicit information from someone in the class. Then ask another student to summarize this information in one sentence beginning with "The . . . .")

Example:	Who got a letter yesterday?
Response:	I did.
	Who was it from?
Response:	My brother.
(to another student):	Can you summarize this information? Begin with "the."
Response:	The letter (*Ali*) got yesterday was from his brother.

1. Who got a letter last week?
   Where was it from?

2. Who is wearing earrings?
   What are they made of?

3. Who lives in an apartment?
   Is it close to school?

4. Pick up something that doesn't belong to you.
   Whose is it?

5. Who grew up in a small town?
   In what part of the country is it located?

6. Who has bought something recently?
   What did you buy?
   Was it expensive?

7. Hold up a book.
   What is the title?

8. Who went to a bar/restaurant last night?
   Was it crowded?

9. What did you have for dinner last night?
   Was it good?

10. Who watched a TV program last night?
    What was it about?

11. Who has borrowed something recently?
    What did you borrow?
    Who does it belong to?

12. Who shops for groceries?
    What is the name of the store?

13. Who eats lunch away from home?
    Where do you usually eat?
    Does it have good food?

14. Who took the bus to class today?
    Was it late or on time?

15. Who read a newspaper yesterday?
    Which newspaper?

16. Point at a person.
    Who is s/he pointing at?

6–7 USING ADJECTIVE CLAUSES TO MODIFY PRONOUNS

(a) There is **someone** *(whom) I want you to meet.* (b) **Everything** *he said* was pure nonsense. (c) **Anybody** *who wants to come* is welcome.	Adjective clauses can modify indefinite pronouns (e.g., *someone, everybody*). Object pronouns (e.g., *whom, which*) are usually omitted in the adjective clause.
(d) Paula was **the only one** *I knew at the party.* (e) Scholarships are available for **those** *who need financial assistance.*	Adjective clauses can modify **the one(s)** and **those.***
(f) It is **I** *who am responsible.* (g) **He** *who laughs last* laughs best.	Adjective clauses rarely modify personal pronouns. (f) is very formal and uncommon. (g) is a well-known saying in which "he" is used as an indefinite pronoun (meaning "anyone," "any person").

*An adjective clause with **which** can also be used to modify the pronoun **that**. For example:
  We sometimes fear **that which** *we do not understand.*
  The bread my mother makes is much better than **that which** *you can buy at a store.*

□ **EXERCISE 19:** Complete the sentences with adjective clauses.

1. Ask Jack. He's the only one ___*who knows the answer.*___

2. I have a question. There is something _____

3. He can't trust anyone. There's no one _____

4. I'm powerless to help her. There's nothing _____

5. I know someone _____

6. Susan makes a good first impression. She charms everyone _____

7. What was Mrs. Wood talking about? I didn't understand anything _____

   _____

8. I listen to everything _____

9. You can believe him. Everything _____

10. All of the students are seated. The teacher is the only one _____

11. The test we took yesterday was easier than the one _____

12. The courses I'm taking this term are more difficult than the ones _____

   _____

13. The concert had already begun. Those _____

   had to wait until intermission to be seated.

14. The class was divided in half. Those _____

    were assigned to Section A. Those _____

    were assigned to Section B.

6–8 PUNCTUATION OF ADJECTIVE CLAUSES

General guidelines for the punctuation of adjective clauses:
  (1) DO NOT USE COMMAS IF the adjective clause is necessary to identify the noun it modifies.*
  (2) USE COMMAS IF the adjective clause simply gives additional information and is not necessary to identify the noun it modifies.**

(a) **The professor** *who teaches Chemistry 101* is an excellent lecturer.	In (a): No commas are used. The adjective clause is necessary to identify which professor is meant.
(b) **Professor Wilson**⊙ *who teaches Chemistry 101*⊙ is an excellent lecturer.	In (b): Commas are used. The adjective clause is not necessary to identify who Professor Wilson is. We already know who he is: he has a name. The adjective clause simply gives additional information.
(c) **Hawaii**⊙ *which consists of eight principal islands*⊙ is a favorite vacation spot.	Guideline: Use commas, as in (b), (c), and (d), if an adjective clause modifies a proper noun. (A proper noun begins with a capital letter, not a small letter.)
(d) **Mrs. Smith**⊙ *who is a retired teacher*⊙ does volunteer work at the hospital.	Note: A comma reflects a pause in speech.
(e) **The man** $\left\{ \begin{matrix} who(m) \\ that \\ \emptyset \end{matrix} \right\}$ *I met* teaches chemistry.	In (e): If no commas are used, any possible pronoun may be used in the adjective clause. Object pronouns may be omitted.
(f) **Mr. Lee**⊙ *whom I met yesterday*⊙ teaches chemistry.	In (f): When commas are necessary, the pronoun **that** may not be used (only **who**, **whom**, **which**, **whose**, **where**, and **when** may be used), and object pronouns cannot be omitted.
COMPARE THE MEANING	
(g) We took some children on a picnic. **The children**⊙ **who wanted to play soccer**⊙ ran to an open field as soon as we arrived at the park.	In (g): The use of commas means that *all* of the children wanted to play soccer and all of the children ran to an open field. The adjective clause is used only to give additional information about the children.
(h) We took some children on a picnic. **The children who wanted to play soccer** ran to an open field as soon as we arrived at the park. The others played a different game.	In (h): The lack of commas means that *only some* of the children wanted to play soccer. The adjective clause is used to identify which children ran to the open field.

*Adjective clauses that do not require commas are called "essential" or "restrictive" or "identifying."
**Adjective clauses that require commas are called "nonessential" or "nonrestrictive" or "nonidentifying."
Note: Nonessential adjective clauses are more common in writing than in speaking.

□ **EXERCISE 20:** Add commas where necessary. Change the adjective clause pronoun to *that* if possible.

1. Alan and Jackie , who did not come to class yesterday , explained their absence to the teacher. (*Commas necessary; "who" cannot be changed to "that."*)

2. The students who did not come to class yesterday explained their absence to the teacher. (*No commas; "who" can be changed to "that."*)

3. The geologist who lectured at Browning Hall last night predicted another earthquake.

4. Dr. Fields who lectured at Browning Hall last night predicted another earthquake.

5. Only people who speak Russian should apply for the job.

6. Matthew who speaks Russian applied for the job.

7. The rice which we had for dinner last night was very good.

8. Rice which is grown in many countries is a staple food throughout much of the world.

9. I have fond memories of my hometown which is situated in a valley.

10. I live in a town which is situated in a valley.

11. The Mississippi River which flows south from Minnesota to the Gulf of Mexico is the major commercial river in the United States.

12. A river which is polluted is not safe for swimming.

13. Mr. Brown whose son won the spelling contest is very proud of his son's achievement. The man whose daughter won the science contest is also very pleased and proud.

14. Goats which were first tamed more than 9,000 years ago in Asia have provided people with milk, meat, and wool since prehistoric times.

15. Mrs. Clark has two goats. She's furious at the goat which got on the wrong side of the fence and is eating her flowers.

☐ **EXERCISE 21:** Circle the correct explanation (a. or b.) of the meaning of each sentence.

1. The teacher thanked the students, who had given her some flowers.
   a. The flowers were from *only some* of the students.
   b. The flowers were from *all* of the students.

2. The teacher thanked the students who had given her some flowers.
   a. The flowers were from *only some* of the students.
   b. The flowers were from *all* of the students.

3. There was a terrible flood. The villagers who had received a warning of the impending flood escaped to safety.
   a. *Only some* of the villagers had been warned; only some escaped.
   b. *All* of the villagers had been warned; all escaped.

4. There was a terrible flood. The villagers, who had received a warning of the impending flood, escaped to safety.
   a. *Only some* of the villagers had been warned; *only some* escaped.
   b. *All* of the villagers had been warned; *all* escaped.

5. Tom stood under the oak tree which was near the house.
   a. There was *only one* oak tree in the yard.
   b. There were *more than one* oak trees in the yard.

6. Tom stood under the oak tree, which was near the house.
   a. There was *only one* oak tree in the yard.
   b. There were *more than one* oak trees in the yard.

Discuss the differences in meaning in the following pairs of sentences.

7. He reached in the basket and threw away the apples that were rotten.
8. He reached in the basket and threw away the apples, which were rotten.
9. The students who had done well on the test were excused from class early.
10. The students, who had done well on the test, were excused from class early.
11. Cindy was delighted when she opened the present, which was from her grandmother.
12. Cindy was delighted when she opened the present that was from her grandmother.
13. The teacher pointed to the maps that were hanging on the rear wall of the classroom.
14. The teacher pointed to the maps, which were hanging on the rear wall of the classroom.

□ **EXERCISE 22:** Add commas where necessary.

1. We enjoyed the city where we spent our vacation.
2. We enjoyed Mexico City where we spent our vacation.
3. An elephant which is the earth's largest land mammal has few natural enemies other than human beings.
4. One of the elephants which we saw at the zoo had only one tusk.
5. At the botanical gardens, you can see a Venus's-Flytrap which is an insectivorous plant.
6. In Venezuela, there are plants which eat insects with their roots.
7. One of the most useful materials in the world is glass which is made chiefly from sand, soda, and lime.
8. Glaciers which are huge masses of ice that flow slowly over land form in the cold polar regions and in high mountains.
9. A rebel is a person who resists or fights against authority.
10. Petroleum which some people refer to as black gold is one of the most valuable resources in the world today.
11. You don't need to take heavy clothes when you go to Bangkok which has one of the highest average temperatures of any city in the world.
12. A political party is an organized group of people who control or seek to control a government.
13. Child labor was a social problem in late eighteenth-century England where employment in factories became virtual slavery for children.
14. We had to use a telephone, so we went to the nearest house. The woman who answered our knock listened cautiously to our request.
15. According to a newspaper article which I read, the police arrested the man who had robbed the First National Bank. The man who was wearing a plaid shirt and blue jeans was caught shortly after he had left the bank.
16. I watched a scientist conduct an experiment on bees. The research scientist who was well protected before she stepped into the special chamber holding the bees was not stung. A person who was unprotected by the special clothing could have gotten 300–400 bee stings within a minute.

6-9 USING EXPRESSIONS OF QUANTITY IN ADJECTIVE CLAUSES

In my class there are 20 students. *Most of **them*** are from the Far East. (a) In my class there are 20 students, *most of **whom*** are from the Far East.	An adjective clause may contain an expression of quantity with ***of***: *some of, many of, most of, none of, two of, half of, both of, neither of, each of, all of, several of, a few of, little of, a number of,* etc.
He gave several reasons. *Only a few of **them*** were valid. (b) He gave several reasons, *only a few of **which*** were valid.	The expression of quantity precedes the pronoun. Only ***whom**, **which***, and ***whose*** are used in this pattern.
The teachers discussed Jim. *One of **his** problems* was poor study habits. (c) The teachers discussed Jim, *one of **whose** problems* was poor study habits.	Adjective clauses that begin with an expression of quantity are more common in writing than speaking. Commas are used.

☐ **EXERCISE 23:** Combine the two sentences. Use (b) as an adjective clause.

1. (a) The city has sixteen schools. (b) Two of them are junior colleges.
   → *The city has sixteen schools, two of which are junior colleges.*
2. (a) Last night the orchestra played three symphonies. (b) One of them was Beethoven's Seventh.
3. (a) I tried on six pairs of shoes. (b) I liked none of them.
4. (a) The village has around 200 people. (b) The majority of them are farmers.
5. (a) That company currently has five employees. (b) All of them are computer experts.
6. (a) After the riot, over one hundred people were taken to the hospital. (b) Many of them had been innocent bystanders.

☐ **EXERCISE 24:** Complete the following sentences.

1. Al introduced me to his roommates, both of *whom are from California.*
2. The Paulsons own four automobiles, one of _____
3. I have three brothers, all of _____
4. I am taking four courses, one of _____
5. I have two roommates, neither of _____
6. This semester I had to buy fifteen books, most of _____
7. The company hired ten new employees, some of _____
8. In my apartment building, there are twenty apartments, several of _____

6-10 USING *NOUN + OF WHICH*

We have an antique table. *The top of it* has jade inlay. (a) We have an antique table, **the top of which** has jade inlay.	An adjective clause may include *a noun + of which* (e.g., *the top of which*). This pattern carries the meaning of *whose* (e.g., We have *an antique table whose top has jade inlay.*). This pattern is used in an adjective clause that modifies a "thing" and occurs primarily in formal written English. Commas are used.

☐ **EXERCISE 25:** Combine the sentences. Use (b) as an adjective clause.

1. (a) We toured a 300-year-old house. (b) The exterior of the house consisted of logs cemented with clay.
   → *We toured a 300-year-old house, the exterior of which consisted of logs cemented with clay.*

2. (a) They own an original Picasso painting. (b) The value of the painting is over a million dollars.

3. (a) I bought a magazine. (b) The title of the magazine is *Contemporary Architectural Styles*.

4. (a) My country is dependent upon its income from coffee. (b) The price of coffee varies according to fluctuations in the world market.

5. (a) The genetic engineers are engaged in significant experiments. (b) The results of the experiments will be published in the *Journal of Science*.

6. (a) The professor has assigned the students a research paper. (b) The purpose of the research paper is to acquaint them with methods of scholarly inquiry.

6-11 USING *WHICH* TO MODIFY A WHOLE SENTENCE

(a) Tom was late. (b) **That** surprised me. (c) Tom was late, **which** surprised me.	The pronouns **that** and **this** can refer to the idea of a whole sentence which comes before. In (b): The word **that** refers to the whole sentence "Tom was late."
(d) The elevator is out of order. (e) **This** is too bad. (f) The elevator is out of order, **which** is too bad.	Similarly, an adjective clause with **which** may modify the idea of a whole sentence. In (c): The word **which** refers to the whole sentence "Tom was late."*

*Using **which** to modify a whole sentence is informal and occurs most frequently in spoken English. This structure is generally not appropriate in formal writing. Whenever it is written, however, it is preceded by a comma to reflect a pause in speech.

□ **EXERCISE 26:** Use the second sentence as an adjective clause.

1. Max isn't home yet. That worries me.
   → *Max isn't home yet, which worries me.*
2. Jack was fired from his job. That surprised all of his co-workers.
3. My roommate never picks up after herself. This irritates me.
4. Mrs. Anderson responded to my letter right away. I appreciated that very much.
5. There was an accident on Highway 5. That means I'll be late to work this morning.
6. I shut the car door on my necktie. That was really stupid of me.

□ **EXERCISE 27:** Make up a sentence to precede the given sentence. Then combine the two sentences, using the second sentence as an adjective clause.

1. <u>The student next to me kept cracking his knuckles.</u> That bothered me a lot. →

   The student next to me kept cracking his knuckles, which bothered me a lot.

2. _____ That disappointed me.
3. _____ That made me nervous.
4. _____ That shocked all of us.
5. _____ That means he's probably in trouble.
6. _____ That was a pleasant surprise.
7. _____ That made her very unhappy.
8. _____ I appreciated that very much.
9. _____ That made it difficult for me to concentrate.
10. _____ That bothered me so much that I couldn't get to sleep.

6-12 REDUCTION OF ADJECTIVE CLAUSES TO ADJECTIVE PHRASES: INTRODUCTION

Terms: **clause:** *A clause* is a group of related words that contains a subject and a verb.	
phrase: *A phrase* is a group of related words that does not contain a subject and a verb.	
(a) ADJECTIVE CLAUSE: The girl ***who is sitting next to me*** is Mary. (b) ADJECTIVE PHRASE: The girl ***sitting next to me*** is Mary.	An adjective phrase is a reduction of an adjective clause. It modifies a noun. It does not contain a subject and a verb. The adjective clause in (a) can be reduced to the adjective phrase in (b). (a) and (b) have the same meaning.
(c) CLAUSE: The boy ***who is playing the piano*** is Ben. (d) PHRASE: The boy ***playing the piano*** is Ben. (e) CLAUSE: The boy ***(whom) I saw*** was Tom. (f) PHRASE: *(none)*	Only adjective clauses that have a subject pronoun—***who***, ***which***, or ***that***—are reduced to modifying adjective phrases. The adjective clause in (e) cannot be reduced to an adjective phrase.

6-13 CHANGING AN ADJECTIVE CLAUSE TO AN ADJECTIVE PHRASE

There are two ways in which an adjective clause is changed to an adjective phrase:	

(1) The subject pronoun is omitted AND the ***be*** form of the verb is omitted.
  (a) CLAUSE: The ***man who is talking*** to John is from Korea.
      PHRASE: The ***man*** Ø Ø ***talking*** to John is from Korea.
  (b) CLAUSE: The ***ideas which are presented*** in that book are interesting.
      PHRASE: The ***ideas*** Ø Ø ***presented*** in that book are interesting.
  (c) CLAUSE: Ann is the ***woman who is responsible*** for preparing the budget.
      PHRASE: Ann is the ***woman*** Ø Ø ***responsible*** for preparing the budget.
  (d) CLAUSE: The ***books that are on that shelf*** are mine.
      PHRASE: The ***books*** Ø Ø ***on that shelf*** are mine.	

(2) If there is no ***be*** form of a verb in the adjective clause, it is sometimes possible to omit the subject pronoun and change the verb to its ***-ing*** form.
  (e) CLAUSE: English has an ***alphabet that consists*** of 26 letters.
      PHRASE: English has an ***alphabet*** Ø ***consisting*** of 26 letters.
  (f) CLAUSE: ***Anyone who wants*** to come with us is welcome.
      PHRASE: ***Anyone*** Ø ***wanting*** to come with us is welcome.	

(g) *George Washington⊙ who was the first president of the United States⊙* was a wealthy colonist and a general in the army. (h) *George Washington⊙ the first president of the United States⊙* was a wealthy colonist and a general in the army.	If the adjective clause requires commas, as in (g), the adjective phrase also requires commas, as in (h).

Change the adjective clauses to adjective phrases.

1. Do you know the woman who is coming toward us?
   → *Do you know the woman coming toward us?*
2. The people who are waiting for the bus in the rain are getting wet.
3. I come from a city that is located in the southern part of the country.
4. The children who attend that school receive a good education.
5. The scientists who are researching the causes of cancer are making progress.
6. The fence which surrounds our house is made of wood.
7. They live in a house that was built in 1890.
8. We have an apartment which overlooks the park.

□ EXERCISE 29: Change the adjective clauses to adjective phrases.

1. Dr. Stanton, who is the president of the university, will give a speech at the commencement ceremonies.
2. Did you get the message which concerned the special meeting?
3. Be sure to follow the instructions that are given at the top of the page.
4. The conclusion which is presented in that book states that most of the automobiles which are produced by American industry have some defect.
5. The rules that allow public access to wilderness areas need to be reconsidered.
6. The photographs which were published in the newspaper were extraordinary.
7. There is almost no end to the problems that face a head of state.
8. Nero, who was Emperor of Rome from 54 to 68 A.D., is believed to have murdered both his mother and his wife.
9. The psychologists who study the nature of sleep have made important discoveries.
10. The experiment which was conducted at the University of Chicago was successful.
11. Pictures that showed the brutality of war entered the living rooms of millions of Americans on the nightly news.
12. Kuala Lumpur, which is the capital city of Malaysia, is a major trade center in Southeast Asia.
13. The Indians who lived in Peru before the discovery of the New World by Europeans belonged to the Incan culture.
14. Many of the students who hope to enter the university will be disappointed because only one-tenth of those who apply for admission will be accepted.
15. There must exist in a modern community a sufficient number of persons who possess the technical skill that is required to maintain the numerous devices upon which our physical comforts depend.

☐ **EXERCISE 30**: Change the adjective phrases to adjective clauses.

1. David Keller, a young poet known for his sensitive interpretations of human relationships, has just published another volume of poems.
   → *David Keller, **who is** a young poet **who is** known for his sensitive interpretations of human relationships, has just published another volume of poems.*

2. Corn was one of the agricultural products introduced to the European settlers by the Indians. Some of the other products introduced by the Indians were potatoes, peanuts, and tobacco.

3. He read *The Old Man and the Sea*, a novel written by Ernest Hemingway.

4. The sunlight coming through the window wakes me up early every morning.

5. Mercury, the nearest planet to the sun, is also the smallest of the nine planets orbiting the sun.

6. The pyramids, the monumental tombs of ancient Egyptian pharaohs, were constructed from 3000 to 1800 B.C.

7. The sloth, a slow-moving animal found in the tropical forests of Central and South America, feeds entirely on leaves and fruit.

8. Two-thirds of those arrested for car theft are under twenty years of age.

9. St. Louis, Missouri, known as "The Gateway to the West," traces its history to 1793, when Pierre Laclede, a French fur trader, selected this site on the Mississippi River as a fur-trading post.

10. Any student not wanting to go on the trip should inform the office.

☐ **EXERCISE 31**: Combine the sentences. Use the second sentence as an adjective phrase.

1. Louisville was founded in 1778. It is the largest city in Kentucky.
   Louisville, the largest city in Kentucky, was founded in 1778.

2. John Quincy Adams was born on July 11, 1767. He was the sixth president of the United States.

   _____

   _____

3. Two languages, Finnish and Swedish, are used in Helsinki. It is the capital of Finland.

   _____

   _____

4. The Washington National Monument is a famous landmark in the nation's capital. It is a towering obelisk made of white marble.

   _____

   _____

5. Honolulu has consistently pleasant weather. It is best known to the traveler for Waikiki Beach.

_____

_____

6. Libya is a leading producer of oil. It is a country in North Africa.

_____

_____

☐ **EXERCISE 32—ERROR ANALYSIS:** All of the following sentences adapted from student compositions contain errors. Test your skill by seeing how many of the errors you can find and correct.

1. It is important to be polite to people who lives in the same building.

2. She lives in a hotel is restricted to senior citizens.

3. My sister has two childrens, who their names are Ali and Talal.

4. He comes from Venezuela that is a Spanish-speaking country.

5. There are ten universities in Thailand, seven of them locate in Bangkok is the capital city.

6. I would like to write about several problems which I have faced them since I come to United State.

7. There is a small wooden screen separates the bed from the rest of the room.

8. At the airport, I was waiting for some relatives which I had never met them before.

9. It is almost impossible to find two person who their opinions are the same.

10. On the wall, there is a colorful poster which it consists of a group of young people who dancing.

☐ **EXERCISE 33—PREPOSITIONS:** Supply appropriate prepositions.

1. Max is known _____ his honesty.

2. Mr. and Mrs. Jones have always been faithful _____ each other.

3. Do you promise to come? I'm counting _____ you to be there.

4. Trucks are prohibited _____ using residential streets.

5. The little girl is afraid _____ an imaginary bear that lives in her closet.

6. Do you take good care _____ your health?

7. I'm worried _____ this problem.

8. I don't agree _____ you.

9. We decided _____ eight o'clock as the time we should meet.

10. Who did you vote _____ in the last election?

11. How many students were absent _____ class yesterday?

12. It is important to be polite _____ other people.

13. The farmers are hoping _____ rain.

14. Jason was late because he wasn't aware _____ the time.

15. We will fight _____ our rights.

☐ **EXERCISE 34—PHRASAL VERBS:** Supply appropriate prepositions for the following two-word or three-word verbs.

1. A: Are you ready to leave?

   B: Almost. I'll be ready to go just as soon as I get _____ putting the clean dishes away.

2. A: I'm going crazy! I've been trying to solve this math problem for the last hour and I still can't get it.

   B: Why don't you give _____ for a while? Take a break and then go back to it.

3. A: I hear you had a frightening experience yesterday. What happened?

   B: Ed suddenly got dizzy and then passed _____. I tried to revive him, but he was out cold. Luckily there was a doctor in the building.

4. A: What happened when the pilot of the plane passed out during the flight?

   B: The co-pilot took _____.

5. A: Cindy is only three. She likes to play with the older kids, but when they're running and playing, she can't keep _____ with them.

   B: Does she mind?

   A: She doesn't seem to.

6. A: I made a mistake in my composition. What should I do?

   B: Since it's an in-class composition, just cross it _____.

7. A: I need my dictionary, but I lent it to Jose.

   B: Why don't you get it _____ from him?

8. A: I wish the teacher wouldn't call _____ me in class.

   B: Why not?

   A: I get nervous.

   B: Why?

   A: I don't know.

9. I took a plane from Atlanta to Miami. I got _____ the plane in Atlanta. I got _____ the plane in Miami.

10. It was a snowy winter day, but I still had to drive to work. First I got _____ the car to start the engine. Then I got _____ of the car to scrape the snow and ice from the windows.

11. Last year I took a train trip. I got _____ the train in Chicago. I got _____ the train in Des Moines.

12. Phyllis takes the bus to work. She gets _____ the bus at Lindbergh Boulevard and gets _____ the bus about two blocks from her office on Tower Street.

CHAPTER *7*

Noun Clauses

7-1 NOUN CLAUSES: INTRODUCTION

A noun is used as a subject or an object.	
A noun clause is used as a subject or an object. In other words, a noun clause is used in the same ways as a noun.	
(a) **His story** was interesting. (b) **What he said** was interesting.	In (a): **story** is a noun. It is used as the subject of the sentence. In (b): **what he said** is a noun clause. It is used as the subject of the sentence. The noun clause has its own subject (*he*) and verb (*said*).
(c) I heard **his story**. (d) I heard **what he said**.	In (c): **story** is a noun. It is used as the object of the verb **heard**. In (d): **what he said** is a noun clause. It is used as the object of the verb **heard**.

WORDS USED TO INTRODUCE NOUN CLAUSES		

(1) *question words:**
    when   *who*
    where   *whom*
    why   *what*
    how   *which*
             whose
	(2) *whether*
	    if
		(3) *that*

*See Appendix 1, Unit B, for more information about question words and question forms.

7-2 NOUN CLAUSES WHICH BEGIN WITH A QUESTION WORD

QUESTION	NOUN CLAUSE	
Where does she live? What did he say? When do they arrive?	(a) I don't know **where she lives**. (b) I couldn't hear **what he said**. (c) Do you know **when they arrive?**	In (a): **where she lives** is the object of the verb *know*. Do not use question word order in a noun clause. In a noun clause, the subject precedes the verb. Notice: **does, did,** and **do** are used in questions but not in noun clauses.
S V Who lives there? What happened? Who is at the door?	S V (d) I don't know **who lives there**. (e) Please tell me **what happened**. (f) I wonder **who is at the door**.	In (d): The word order is the same in both the question and the noun clause because **who** is the subject in both.
V S Who is she? Who are those men? Whose house is that?	S V (g) I don't know **who she is**. (h) I don't know **who those men are**. (i) I wonder **whose house that is**.	In (g): **she** is the subject of the question, so it is placed in front of the verb **be** in the noun clause.*
What did she say? What should they do?	(j) **What she said** surprised me. (k) **What they should do** is obvious.	In (j): **what she said** is the subject of the sentence. Notice in (k): A noun clause subject takes a singular verb (e.g., **is**).

*COMPARE: *Who is at the door?* = **who** is the subject of the question.
                   Who are those men? = **those men** is the subject of the question, so **be** is plural.

□ **EXERCISE 1:** Change the question in parentheses to a noun clause.

1. (*How old is he?*) I don't know ___how old he is___.

2. (*What was he talking about?*) ___What he was talking about___
   was interesting.

3. (*Where do you live?*) Please tell me _____.

4. (*What did she say?*) _____ wasn't true.

5. (*When are they coming?*) Do you know _____?

6. (*How much does it cost?*) I can't remember _____.

7. (*Which one does he want?*) Let's ask him _____.

8. (*Who is coming to the party?*) I don't know _____.

9. (*Who are those people?*) I don't know _____.

10. (*Whose pen is this?*) Do you know _____?

11. (*Why did they leave the country?*) _____ is a secret.

12. (*What are we doing in class?*) _____ is easy.

13. (*Where did she go?*) _____ is none of your business.

14. (*How many letters are there in the English alphabet?*) I don't remember

_____.

15. (*Who is the mayor of New York City?*) I don't know _____.

16. (*How old does a person have to be to get a driver's license?*) I need to find

out _____.

☐ **EXERCISE 2—ORAL (BOOKS CLOSED):** Begin your response with "I don't know . . . ."

Example: What time is it?
Response: I don't know what time it is.

1. Where does (. . .) live?
2. What country is (. . .) from?
3. How long has (. . .) been living here?
4. What is (. . .)'s telephone number?
5. Where is the post office?
6. How far is it to (*Kansas City*)?
7. Why is (. . .) absent?
8. Where is my book?
9. What kind of watch does (. . .) have?
10. Why was (. . .) absent yesterday?
11. Where did (. . .) go yesterday?
12. What is (. . .)'s favorite color?
13. How long has (. . .) been married?
14. How did (. . .) meet his wife/her husband?
15. What is the capital of (*Texas*)?
16. What is the population of (*Texas*)?

17. Why was (. . .) late to class?
18. Why are we doing this exercise?
19. What kind of government does (*Italy*) have?
20. Where is (. . .) going to eat lunch/dinner?
21. When does (the semester) end?
22. When does (*Thanksgiving*) vacation start?
23. Where did (. . .) go after class yesterday?
24. Why is (. . .) smiling?
25. How many questions have I asked in this exercise?
26. How often does (. . .) go to the library?
27. Whose book is that?
28. How much did that book cost?

☐ **EXERCISE 3:** Make a question from the given sentence. The words in parentheses should be the answer to the question you make. Use a question word (***who, what, how,*** *etc.*). Then change the question to a noun clause.

1. That man is (*Mr. Robertson*).

   QUESTION: ___Who is that man?___

   NOUN CLAUSE: I want to know___who that man is.___

2. George lives (*in Los Angeles*).

   QUESTION: _____

   NOUN CLAUSE: I want to know_____

3. Ann bought (*a new dictionary*).

   QUESTION: _____

   NOUN CLAUSE: Do you know_____

4. It is (*350 miles*) to Denver from here.

   QUESTION: _____

   NOUN CLAUSE: I need to know_____

5. Jack was late to class (*because he missed the bus.*)

   QUESTION: _____

   NOUN CLAUSE: The teacher wants to know_____

6. That is (*Ann's*) pen.

   QUESTION: _____

   NOUN CLAUSE: Tom wants to know_____

7. Alex saw (*Ms. Frost*) at the meeting.

   QUESTION: _____

   NOUN CLAUSE: I don't know_____

8. (*Jack*) saw Ms. Frost at the meeting.

   QUESTION: _____

   NOUN CLAUSE: I don't know_____

9. Alice likes (*this*) book best, (*not that one*).

   QUESTION: _____

   NOUN CLAUSE: I want to know_____

10. The plane is supposed to land (*at 7:14 P.M.*).

    QUESTION: _____

    NOUN CLAUSE: Could you tell me_____

☐ **EXERCISE 4—ORAL:** Make questions and noun clauses.

> *Student A:* Make a question from the given sentence. The words in parentheses should be the answer to your question.
>
> *Student B:* Keep your book closed. Change Student A's question into a noun clause. Begin your sentence with ''(Name of Student A) wants to know . . . .''

1. Fred* lives (*in an apartment*).
   Student A: Where does Fred live?
   Student B: (Yoko) wants to know where Fred lives.
2. It's (*ten o'clock*).
   Student A: What time is it?
   Student B: (Roberto) wants to know what time it is.
3. Tom wants (*a watch*) for his birthday.
4. Jane gets to school (*by bus*).
5. Vacation starts (*on June 3rd*).
6. Sue left class early (*because she didn't feel well*).
7. The movie is going to last (*two hours and ten minutes*).
8. Mary called (*Jim*).
9. (*Mary*) called Jim.
10. Alice talked to the teacher about (*the test*).
11. Alice talked to (*the teacher*) about the test.
12. (*Alice*) talked to the teacher about the test.
13. Sue's plane will arrive (*at 8:05*).
14. (*Two*) students will be absent from class tomorrow.
15. There are (*over 10,000*) lakes in Minnesota.
16. It's (*twenty-five miles*) to Springfield from here.
17. Jane (*studied*) last night.
18. We're supposed to buy (*this*) book, (*not that book*).
19. Ann likes (*chocolate*) ice cream the best.
20. A robin's egg is (*turquoise blue*).
21. That woman is (*Mrs. Anderson*).
22. (*Mr. Anderson*) is talking on the telephone.
23. That's (*Sam's*) notebook.
24. (*Jessica's*) car was stolen.

---

*To Student A: Use the name of a class member instead of the name in the exercise if you wish. For example: *Where does Ali live?* (instead of *Where does Fred live?*).

7-3 NOUN CLAUSES WHICH BEGIN WITH *WHETHER* OR *IF*

YES/NO QUESTION	NOUN CLAUSE	
Will she come?	(a) I don't know *whether she will come*. I don't know *if she will come*.	When a yes/no question is changed to a noun clause, *whether* or *if* is used to introduce the clause.
Does he need help?	(b) I wonder *whether he needs help*. I wonder *if he needs help*.	(Note: *whether* is more acceptable in formal English, but *if* is quite commonly used, especially in speaking.)
	(c) I wonder *whether or not* she will come. (d) I wonder *whether* she will come *or not*. (e) I wonder *if* she will come *or not*.	In (c), (d), and (e): Notice the patterns when *or not* is used.
	(f) *Whether she comes or not* is unimportant to me.	In (f): Notice that the noun clause is in the subject position.

☐ **EXERCISE 5—ORAL (BOOKS CLOSED):** Begin your response with "I wonder . . . ."

Example: Does (. . .) need any help?
Response: I wonder whether/if (. . .) needs any help.

Example: Where is (. . .)?
Response: I wonder where (. . .) is.

1. Where is your friend?
2. Should we wait for him?
3. Should you call him?
4. Where is your dictionary?
5. Who took your dictionary?
6. Did (. . .) borrow your dictionary?
7. Did you leave your dictionary at the library?
8. Who is that woman?
9. Does she need any help?
10. Who is that man?
11. What is he doing?
12. Is he having trouble?
13. Should you offer to help him?
14. How far is it to (Florida)?
15. Do we have enough time to go to (Florida) over vacation?
16. Whose book is this?
17. Does it belong to (. . .)?
18. Why is the sky blue?
19. How long does a butterfly live?
20. What causes earthquakes?
21. When was the first book written?
22. Why did dinosaurs become extinct?
23. Is there life on other planets?
24. How did life begin?
25. Will people live on the moon someday?

☐ **EXERCISE 6—ORAL (BOOKS CLOSED):** Begin your response with ''Could you please tell me . . . .''

> *Example:* What is this?
> *Response:* Could you please tell me what this is?

1. Where is the library? The nearest phone? The rest room?
2. How much does this book cost?
3. When is Flight 62 expected to arrive?
4. Does this bus go downtown?
5. Is this word spelled correctly?
6. What time is it?
7. Is this information correct?
8. How much does it cost to fly from (*Chicago*) to (*New York*)?
9. Where is the bus station?
10. Whose pen is this?

7-4 QUESTION WORDS FOLLOWED BY INFINITIVES

(a) I don't know *what I should do.* (b) I don't know **what to do.** (c) Pam can't decide *whether she should go or stay home.* (d) Pam can't decide **whether to go or (to) stay home.** (e) Please tell me *how I can get to the bus station.* (f) Please tell me **how to get to the bus station.** (g) Jim told us *where we could find it.* (h) Jim told us **where to find it.**	Question words (**when, where, how, who, whom, whose, what, which**) and **whether** may be followed by an infinitive. Each pair of sentences in the examples has the same meaning. Notice that the meaning expressed by the infinitive is either **should** or **can/could.**

☐ **EXERCISE 7:** Give sentences with the same meaning by using infinitives.

1. He told me when I should come. → *He told me when to come.*
2. The plumber told me how I could fix the leak in the sink.
3. Please tell me where I should meet you.
4. Don had an elaborate excuse for being late for their date, but Sandy didn't know whether she should believe him or not.
5. Jim found two shirts he liked, but he had trouble deciding which one he should buy.
6. I've done everything I can think of to help Andy get his life straightened out. I don't know what else I can do.

Complete the following; use infinitives in your completions.

7. I was tongue-tied. I didn't know what _____.

8. A: I can't decide _____ to the reception.

   B: How about your green suit?

9. A: Where are you going to live when you go to the university?

   B: I'm not sure. I can't decide whether _____.

10. A: Do you know how _____?

    B: No, but I'd like to learn.

11. A: I don't know what _____ for her birthday. Got any

    suggestions?

    B: How about a book?

12. My cousin has a dilemma. He can't decide whether _____

    or _____. What do you think he should do?

13. Before you leave on your trip, read this tour book. It tells you where

    _____ and how _____.

7-5 NOUN CLAUSES WHICH BEGIN WITH *THAT*

STATEMENT *(Expression of an idea or fact)*	NOUN CLAUSE	
He is a good actor.	(a) I think *that he is a good actor.* (b) I think *he is a good actor.*	In (a): *that he is a good actor* is a noun clause. It is used as the object of the verb *think*.
The world is round.	(c) We know *(that) the world is round.*	The word *that*, when it introduces a noun clause, has no meaning in itself. It simply marks the beginning of the clause. Frequently it is omitted, as in (b), especially in speaking. (If used in speaking, it is unstressed.)
She doesn't understand spoken English.	(d) *That she doesn't understand spoken English* is obvious. (e) *It* is obvious *(that)* she doesn't understand spoken English.	In (d): The noun clause (*That she doesn't understand spoken English*) is used as the subject of the sentence. The word *that* is not omitted when it introduces a noun clause used as the subject of a sentence, as in (d) and (f).
The world is round.	(f) *That the world is round* is a fact. (g) *It* is a fact *that the world is round.*	More commonly, the word *it* functions as the subject, and the noun clause is placed at the end of the sentence, as in (e) and (g).

☐ EXERCISE 8—ORAL:

Student A: Change the given sentence into a noun clause. Use *it* + any appropriate expression from the list.

Student B: Give the equivalent sentence by using a "*that* clause" as the subject.

a fact	*surprising*	*obvious*	*too bad*	*a shame*
a well-known fact	*strange*	*apparent*	*unfortunate*	*a pity*
true	*unfair*			

1. The world is round.
   Student A: It is a fact that the world is round.
   Student B: That the world is round is a fact.
2. Drug abuse can ruin one's health.
3. Tim hasn't been able to make any friends.
4. Some women do not earn equal pay for equal work.
5. The earth revolves around the sun.
6. Irene failed her entrance examination.
7. Smoking can cause cancer.
8. English is the principal language of the business community throughout much of the world.

☐ EXERCISE 9—ORAL:

Student A: Make an original sentence by using *it* and the given expression.

Student B: Give the equivalent sentence by using a "*that* clause" as the· subject.

1. true
   Student A: It is true that plants need water in order to grow.
   Student B: That plants need water in order to grow is true.
2. a fact
3. surprising
4. obvious
5. too bad
6. a well-known fact
7. unfortunate
8. true
9. strange
10. unlikely

☐ EXERCISE 10—ORAL/WRITTEN: Complete the following.

1. It is my belief that . . . *the war between those two countries will end soon.*
2. It seems to me that . . . .
3. It is my impression that . . . .
4. It is my belief that . . . .
5. It is my theory that . . . .
6. It is widely believed that . . . .
7. It is thought that . . . .
8. It has been said that . . . .
9. It is a miracle that . . . .

□ **EXERCISE 11—ORAL:** "*That* clauses" may follow *be* + *certain adjectives* that express feelings or attitudes. Complete the following.

1. I'm sorry (that) . . . *I was late for class.*
2. I'm glad (that) . . . .
3. I'm disappointed (that) . . . .
4. I'm pleased (that) . . . .
5. I'm surprised (that) . . . .
6. I'm sure (that) . . . .
7. I'm amazed (that) . . . .
8. I'm happy (that) . . . .
9. Yesterday I was annoyed (that) . . . .
10. I'm afraid (that)* . . . .

□ **EXERCISE 12:** A "*that* clause" may follow *be* directly. Complete the sentences with your own ideas by using "*that* clauses."

1. He says he is twenty-one, but the truth is . . . *that he is only eighteen.*
2. There are two reasons why I do not want to go out tonight.
   The first reason is . . . *that I have to study.*
   The second reason is . . . *that I do not have enough money.***
3. There are several reasons why I am studying English.
   One reason is . . . .
   Another reason is . . . .
   A third reason is . . . .
4. I have had three problems since I came here.
   One problem is that . . . .
   Another problem is that . . . .
   The third problem I have had is that . . . .
5. One advantage of owning your own car is . . . .
   Another advantage is . . . .
   One disadvantage, however, of owning your own car is . . . .

□ **EXERCISE 13:** A "*that* clause" is frequently used with *the fact*. Combine the sentences using "the fact that" to introduce a noun clause.

1. Ann was late. *That* didn't surprise me.
   → *The fact that Ann was late didn't surprise me.*
2. Mary didn't come. *That* made me angry.
3. I'm a little tired. I feel fine except for *that.*

To be afraid has two possible meanings:
    (1) It can express fear: *I'm afraid of dogs. I'm afraid that his dog will bite me.*
    (2) In informal English, it often expresses a meaning similar to "to be sorry": *I'm afraid that I can't accept your invitation. I'm afraid you have the wrong number.*

Notice: *That* is used, not *because*, to introduce the clause. (*Because* might occur only in very informal spoken English: *The first reason is because I have to study.*)

4. She didn't pass the entrance examination. She was not admitted to the university due to *that*.

5. Many people in the world live in intolerable poverty. *That* must concern all of us.

6. He is frequently absent from class. *That* indicates his lack of interest in school.

7. I was supposed to bring my passport to the examination for identification. I was not aware of *that*. As a result, I was not allowed to take the test.

8. The people of the town were given no warning of the approaching tornado. Due to *that*, there were many casualties.

7-6 QUOTED SPEECH*

Quoted speech refers to reproducing words exactly as they were originally spoken. Quotation marks (". . .") are used.**	
QUOTING ONE SENTENCE (a) She said, "My brother is a student."	In (a): Use a comma after **she said**. Capitalize the first word of the quoted sentence. Put the final quotation marks outside of the period at the end of the sentence.
(b) "My brother is a student," she said.	In (b): Use a comma, not a period, at the end of the quoted sentence when it precedes **she said**.
(c) "My brother," she said, "is a student."	In (c): If the quoted sentence is divided by **she said**, use a comma after the first part of the quote. Do not capitalize the first word of the second half of the quoted sentence.
QUOTING MORE THAN ONE SENTENCE (d) "My brother is a student. He is attending a university," she said.	In (d): Quotation marks are placed at the beginning and end of the complete quote. Notice: There are no quotation marks after **student**.
QUOTING A QUESTION OR AN EXCLAMATION (e) She asked, "When will you be here?"	In (e): The question mark is inside the quotation marks.
(f) "When will you be here?" she asked.	In (f): If a question mark is used, no comma is used before **she asked**.
(g) She said, "Watch out!"	In (g): The exclamation point is inside the quotation marks.

Quoted speech is also called *direct speech*. *Reported speech* (discussed in Chart 7-7) is also called *indirect speech*.
**In British English, quotation marks are called *inverted commas*.

□ **EXERCISE 14:** Add the necessary punctuation and capitalization to the following.

1. Henry said   there is a phone call for you
2. There is a phone call for you   he said
3. There is   said Henry   a phone call for you   *
4. There is a phone call for you   it's your sister   said Henry
5. There is a phone call for you   he said   it's your sister
6. I asked him   where is the phone
7. Where is the phone   she asked
8.   When the police officer came over to my car, he said   let me see your driver's license, please

   What's wrong, Officer   I asked   was I speeding

   No, you weren't speeding   he replied   you went through a red light at the corner of Fifth Avenue and Main Street   you almost caused an accident

   Did I really do that   I said   I didn't see the red light   **

□ **EXERCISE 15:** Choose two of your classmates to have a brief conversation in front of the class, and decide upon a topic for them (what they did last night, what they are doing right now, sports, music, books, etc.). Give them a few minutes to practice their conversation. Then, while they are speaking, take notes so that you can write their conversation. Use quoted speech in your written report. Be sure to start a new paragraph each time the speaker changes.

---

*Notice in sentences 3 and 4: The noun subject (Henry) follows **said**. A noun subject often follows the verb when the subject and verb come in the middle or at the end of a sentence. A pronoun subject almost always precedes the verb.

**Notice: A new paragraph begins each time the speaker changes.

7-7 REPORTED SPEECH AND THE FORMAL SEQUENCE OF TENSES IN NOUN CLAUSES

Reported speech refers to using a noun clause to report what someone has said. No quotation marks are used. Notice the changes in the verb forms from quoted speech to reported speech in the following examples.

QUOTED SPEECH		REPORTED SPEECH
(a) She said, "I *watch* TV every day."	→	She said (that) she *watched* TV every day.
(b) She said, "I *am watching* TV."	→	She said she *was watching* TV.
(c) She said, "I *have watched* TV."	→	She said she *had watched* TV.
(d) She said, "I *watched* TV."	→	She said she *had watched* TV.
(e) She said, "I *will watch* TV."	→	She said she *would watch* TV.
(f) She said, "I *am going to watch* TV."	→	She said she *was going to watch* TV.
(g) She said, "I *can watch* TV."	→	She said she *could watch* TV.
(h) She said, "I *may watch* TV."	→	She said she *might watch* TV.
(i) She said, "I *might watch* TV."	→	She said she *might watch* TV.
(j) She said, "I *must watch* TV."	→	She said she *had to watch* TV.
(k) She said, "I *have to watch* TV."	→	She said she *had to watch* TV.
(l) She said, "I *should watch* TV."	→	She said she *should watch* TV.
(m) She said, "I *ought to watch* TV."	→	She said she *ought to watch* TV.
(n) She said, "*Watch* TV."	→	She *told me to watch* TV.*
(o) She said, "*Do* you *watch* TV?"	→	She *asked (me) if* I *watched* TV.

GENERAL GUIDELINES ON TENSE USAGE IN A NOUN CLAUSE

(1) If the reporting verb (the main verb of the sentence, e.g., *said*) is in the past, the verb in the noun clause will usually also be in a past form.

(2) This formal sequence of tenses in noun clauses is used in both speaking and writing. However, sometimes in spoken English, no change is made in the noun clause verb, especially if the speaker is reporting something immediately or soon after it was said.

Immediate reporting: *A: What did the teacher just say? I didn't hear him.*
*B: He said he **wants** us to read Chapter Six.*

Later reporting: *A: I didn't go to class yesterday. Did Mr. Jones make any assignments?*
*B: Yes. He said he **wanted** us to read Chapter Six.*

(3) Also, sometimes the present tense is retained even in formal English when the reported sentence deals with a general truth: *She said that the world **is** round.*

(4) When the reporting verb is simple present, present perfect, or future, the noun clause verb is not changed.

She *says*, "I *watch* TV every day." → She *says* she *watches* TV every day.
She *has said*, "I *watch* TV every day." → She *has said* that she *watches* TV every day.
She *will say*, "I *watch* TV every day." → She *will say* that she *watches* TV every day.

*In reported speech, an imperative sentence is changed to an infinitive. ***Tell*** is used instead of ***say*** as the reporting verb. (See Chart 4-5 for other verbs followed by an infinitive that are used to report speech.) Also note that ***tell*** is immediately followed by a (pro)noun object, but ***say*** is not:

*He told **me** he would be late. He said he would be late.* Also possible: *He said **to me** he would be late.*

☐ **EXERCISE 16:** Complete the sentences by reporting the speaker's words in a noun clause. Use formal sequence of tenses where appropriate.

1. Bob said, "I will help you."

   Bob said ___(that) he would help me.___

2. "Do you need a pen?" Annie asked.

   Annie asked me ___if I needed a pen.___

3. Jennifer asked, "What do you want?"

   Jennifer asked me ___what I wanted.___

4. Sid asked, "Are you hungry?"

   Sid wanted to know _____

5. "I want a sandwich," Jennifer said.

   Jennifer said _____

6. "I'm going to move to Ohio," said Bruce.

   Bruce informed me _____

7. "Did you enjoy your trip?" asked Connie.

   Connie asked me _____

8. Dick asked, "What are you talking about?"

   Dick asked me _____

9. Nancy asked, "Have you seen my grammar book?"

   Nancy wanted to know _____

10. Susan said, "I don't want to go."

    Susan said _____

11. Sam asked, "Where is Amanda?"

    Sam wanted to know _____

12. "Can you come to my party?" asked David.

    David asked me _____

13. "I may be late," said Mike.

    Mike told me _____

14. Felix said, "You should study harder."

    Felix told me _____

15. Barbara said, "I have to go downtown."

    Barbara said _____

16. "Why is the sky blue?" my young daughter often asks.

My young daughter often asks me _____

17. My mother asked, "Why are you tired?"

My mother wondered _____

18. "I will come to the meeting," said Juan.

Juan told me _____

19. Ms. Adams just asked, "Will you be in class tomorrow?"

Ms. Adams wants to know _____

20. "The sun rises in the east," said Mr. Clark.

Mr. Clark, an elementary school teacher, explained to his students _____

_____

☐ **EXERCISE 17:** Complete the sentences by changing the quoted speech to reported speech. Use formal sequence of tenses.

1. "Have you ever met Ms. Powell?"

Mr. Peterson asked me *if I had ever met Ms. Powell.*

2. "I'm going to postpone the examination."

Professor Williams announced _____

3. "Someday we'll be in contact with beings from outer space."

The scientist predicted _____

4. "I think I'll go to the library to study."

Joe said _____

5. "Is there anything I can do to help?"

Sally wanted to know _____

6. "Does Jim know what he's doing?"

I wondered _____

7. "Is what I've heard true?"

I wondered _____

8. "Is what I wrote correct?"

Maria wanted to know _____

9. "I need to go to the market before it closes."

Janet suddenly remembered _____

10. "Sentences with noun clauses are a little complicated."

Elsa thinks _____

☐ **EXERCISE 18:** Change the quoted speech to reported speech. Study the example carefully and use the same pattern: *said that . . . and that* OR *said that . . . but that.*

1. "My father is a businessman. My mother is an engineer."
   He said that _his father was a businessman and that his mother was an engineer._

2. "I'm excited about my new job. I've found a nice apartment."
   I got a letter from my sister yesterday. She said _____

3. "Your Uncle Harry is in the hospital. Your Aunt Sally is very worried about him."
   The last time my mother wrote to me, she said _____

4. "I expect you to be in class every day. Unexcused absences may affect your grades."
   Our sociology professor said _____

5. "Highway 66 will be closed for two months. Commuters should seek alternate routes."
   The newspaper said _____

6. "I'm getting good grades, but I have difficulty understanding lectures."
   My brother is a junior at the state university. In his last letter, he wrote _____

7. "I'll come to the meeting, but I can't stay for more than an hour."
   Julia told me _____

8. "Every obstacle is a steppingstone to success. You should view problems in your life as opportunities to prove yourself."
   My father often told me _____

□ **EXERCISE 19—WRITTEN:** Think of a letter written in English that you have received recently. In a short paragraph, summarize some of the news or information in this letter. (If you have not received a letter written in English recently, invent one.) Include at least one or two sentences that use the pattern you practiced in the preceding exercise: ***said that . . . and that/said that . . . but that***.

□ **EXERCISE 20—ORAL (BOOKS CLOSED):** Begin your response with "He (She) asked me . . . ."

(To the teacher: Suggest to the students that they practice using the formal sequence of tenses.)

Example: Where is your friend?
Response: He (She) asked me where my friend was.

1. What time is it?
2. What is your name?
3. Can you speak Arabic?
4. Have you met my brother?
5. Where are you living?
6. Will you be here tomorrow?
7. What kind of camera do you have?
8. How tall are you?
9. What courses are you taking?
10. Do you feel okay?
11. Have you read any good books lately?
12. How do you like living here?
13. Did you finish your assignment?
14. What are you doing?
15. Whose briefcase is that?
16. May I borrow your dictionary?
17. Where will you be tomorrow around three o'clock?
18. Did you go to class yesterday?
19. What are you going to do during vacation?
20. What is the capital city of your country?
21. Did you go to a party last night?
22. How many people have you met in the last couple of months?
23. Can I use your pen?
24. Where should I meet you after class?
25. Do you understand what I am saying?
26. What country are you from?
27. Is what you said really true?
28. How do you know that it is true?
29. Who do you think will win the game?
30. Is what you want to talk to me about important?

□ **EXERCISE 21:** Using the information in the conversation, complete the sentences in the reported conversation.

CONVERSATION:

"Where are you from?" asked the passenger sitting next to me on the plane.

"Chicago," I said.

"That's nice. I'm from Mapleton. It's a small town in northern Michigan."

"Oh yes. I've heard of it," I said. "Michigan is a beautiful state. I've been there on vacation many times."

"Were you in Michigan on vacation this year?"

"No. I went far away from home this year. I went to India," I replied.

"Oh, that's nice. Is it a long drive from Chicago to India?" she asked me. My mouth fell open. I didn't know how to respond. Some people certainly need to study geography.

REPORTED CONVERSATION:

(1) The passenger sitting next to me on the plane _____*asked*_____ me

(2) where I _____*was*_____ from. I _____ her I _____

(3) from Chicago. She _____ that she _____ from

(4) Mapleton, a small town in northern Michigan. She wondered if I _____

(5) _____ of it, and I told her that I _____. I went on to

(6) say that I thought Michigan _____ a beautiful state and

(7) explained that I _____ there on vacations many times. She

(8) _____ me if I _____ in Michigan on vacation

(9) this year. I replied that I _____ and _____ her

(10) that I _____ far away, to India. Then she asked me if it

(11) _____ a long drive from Chicago to India! My mouth fell open. I didn't know how to respond. Some people certainly need to study geography.

☐ **EXERCISE 22—WRITTEN:** Complete the following. Use formal sequence of tenses if appropriate.

1. I cannot understand why . . . .
2. One of the students remarked that . . . .
3. I was not sure whose . . . .
4. What . . . surprised.
5. That she . . . surprised me.
6. One of the students stated that . . . .
7. I could not . . . due to the fact that . . . .
8. What he said was that . . . .
9. No one knows who . . . .
10. The instructor announced that . . . .
11. What I want to know is why . . . .
12. What . . . is not important.
13. We discussed the fact that . . . .
14. I wonder whether . . . .

Student A: Ask a question on the given topic—whatever comes into your mind. Use a question word (**when, how, where, what, why,** *etc.*).

Student B: Answer the question in a complete sentence.

Student C: Report what Student A and Student B said.

Example: tonight   ROSA: What are you going to do tonight?

ALI: I'm going to study.

YUNG: Rosa asked Ali what he was going to do tonight, and Ali replied that he was going to study.

1. tonight
2. music
3. courses
4. tomorrow
5. book
6. this city
7. population
8. last year
9. television
10. dinner
11. next year
12. vacation

□ **EXERCISE 24—ORAL/WRITTEN:** Give a one-minute impromptu speech. Your classmates will take notes, and then in a short paragraph, or orally, they will report what you said. Choose any topic that comes to mind (pollution, insects, soccer, dogs, etc.), or have your classmates help select a topic.

□ **EXERCISE 25—ERROR ANALYSIS:** All of the following sentences contain errors. These sentences are from student compositions. Test your skill by seeing how many of the errors you can find and correct.

1. Tell the taxi driver where do you want to go.

2. My roommate came into the room and asked me why aren't you in class? I said I am waiting for a telephone call from my family.

3. It was my first day at the university, and I am on my way to my first class. I wondered who else will be in the class. What the teacher would be like?

4. He asked me that what did I intend to do after I graduate?

5. Many of the people in the United States doesn't know much about geography. For example, people will ask you where is Japan located.

6. What does a patient tell a doctor it is confidential.

7. The reason I decided to come here, because this university has a good meteorology department.

8. We looked back to see where are we and how far are we from camp. We don't know, so we decided to turn back. We are afraid that we wander too far.

9. After the accident, I opened my eyes slowly and realize that I am still alive.

10. My country is prospering due to it is a fact that it has become a leading producer of oil.

11. Is true that one must to know english in order to study at an american university.

12. My mother told me what it was the purpose of our visit.

7–8 USING THE SUBJUNCTIVE IN NOUN CLAUSES

(a) The teacher *demands* that we *be* on time. (b) I *insisted* that he *pay* me the money. (c) I *recommended* that she *not go* to the concert. (d) *It is important* that they *be told* the truth.	In (a): *be* is a subjunctive verb. The subjunctive is used in a noun clause that follows certain verbs and expressions. The sentences generally *stress importance*. In these sentences, the subjunctive verb is used only in its simple form. It does not have present, past, or future form; it is neither singular nor plural. Negative: *not* + *simple form*, as in (c). Passive: simple form of *be* + *past participle*, as in (d).
(e) I *suggested* that she *see* a doctor. (f) I *suggested* that she *should see* a doctor.	*Should* is also possible after *suggest* and *recommend*.*

COMMON VERBS AND EXPRESSIONS FOLLOWED BY THE SUBJUNCTIVE IN A NOUN CLAUSE
demand (that)   *suggest (that)*   *it is important (that)* *insist (that)*   *recommend (that)*   *it is necessary (that)* *request (that)*   *advise (that)*   *it is essential (that)* *ask (that)*   *propose (that)*   *it is vital (that)*   *it is imperative (that)*

*The subjunctive is more common in American English than British English. In British English, *should* + *simple form* is more usual than the subjunctive: e.g., *The teacher **insists** that we **should be** on time.*

☐ **EXERCISE 26:** Complete the following. In many of the sentences there is more than one possible completion.

1. Mr. Adams insists that we _____ *be* _____ careful in our writing.

2. They requested that we not _____ after midnight.

3. She demanded that I _____ her the truth.

4. I recommended that Jane _____ to the head of the department.

5. I suggest that everyone _____ a letter to the governor.

6. It is essential that I _____ you tomorrow.

7. It is important that he _____ the director of the English program.

8. It is necessary that everyone _____ here on time.

□ **EXERCISE 27:** Give the correct form of the verb in parentheses. Some of the verbs are passive.

1. Her advisor recommended that she (*take*) _____ five courses.

2. He insisted that the new baby (*name*) _____ after his grandfather.

3. The doctor recommended that she (*stay*) _____ in bed for a few days.

4. The students requested that the test (*postpone*) _____, but the instructor decided against a postponement.

5. I requested that I (*permit*) _____ to change my class.

6. It is essential that pollution (*control*) _____ and eventually (*eliminate*) _____.

7. It was such a beautiful day that one of the students suggested we (*have*) _____ class outside.

8. The movie director insisted that everything about his productions (*be*) _____ authentic.

9. It is vital that no one else (*know*) _____ about the secret government operation.

10. She asked that we (*be*) _____ sure to lock the door behind us.

11. It is essential that no one (*admit*) _____ to the room without proper identification.

12. It is important that you (*be, not*) _____ late.

13. It is imperative that he (*return*) _____ home immediately.

14. The governor proposed that a new highway (*build*) _____.

15. She specifically asked that I (*tell, not*) _____ anyone else about it. She said it was important that no one else (*tell*) _____ _____ about it.

7–9   USING -*EVER* WORDS

The following -*ever* words give the idea of "any." Each pair of sentences in the examples has the same meaning.

whoever	(a)	**Whoever** wants to come is welcome. *Anyone who* wants to come is welcome.
who(m)ever	(b)	He makes friends easily with **who(m)ever** he meets.* He makes friends easily with *anyone who(m)* he meets.
whatever	(c)	He always says **whatever** comes into his mind. He always says *anything that* comes into his mind.
whichever	(d)	There are four good programs on TV at eight o'clock. We can watch **whichever program (whichever one)** you prefer. We can watch *any of the four programs that* you prefer.
whenever	(e)	You may leave **whenever** you wish. You may leave *at any time that* you wish.
wherever	(f)	She can go **wherever** she wants to go. She can go *anyplace that* she wants to go.
however	(g)	The students may dress **however** they please. The students may dress *in any way that* they please.

*In (b): **whomever** is the object of the verb **meets**. In American English, **whomever** is rare and very formal. In British English, **whoever** (not **whomever**) is used as the object form: *He makes friends easily with whoever he meets.*

☐ **EXERCISE 28:** Complete the following by using -*ever* words.

1. He is free to go anyplace he wishes. He can go ___*wherever*___ he wants.

2. He is free to go anytime he wishes. He can go _____ he wants.

3. I don't know what you should do about that problem. Do _____ seems best to you.

4. There are five flights going to Chicago every day. I don't care which one we take. We can take _____ one fits in best with your schedule.

5. I want you to be honest. I hope you feel free to say _____ is on your mind.

6. _____ leads a life full of love and happiness is rich.

7. No one can tell him what to do. He does _____ he wants.

8. If you want to rearrange the furniture, go ahead. You can rearrange it _____ you want. I don't care one way or the other.

9. Those children are wild. I feel sorry for _____ has to be their babysitter.

10. I have a car. I can take you _____ you want to go.

11. He likes to tell people about his problems. He will talk to _____ will listen to him. But he bores _____ he talks to.

12. I know you're failing all of your courses, but there is nothing I can do about it. It is up to you to do _____ is necessary to improve your grades.

13. I have four. Take _____ one pleases you most.

14. Irene does _____ she wants to do, goes _____ she wants to go, gets up _____ she wants to get up, makes friends with _____ she meets, and dresses _____ she pleases.

☐ **EXERCISE 29—PHRASAL VERBS:** Supply appropriate prepositions for the following two-word or three-word verbs.

1. A: Why don't we try to call _____ the O'Briens sometime this weekend? We haven't seen them for a long time.

   B: Sounds like a good idea. I'd like to see them again.

2. A: Did you go _____ your paper carefully before you handed it _____?

   B: Yes. I looked it _____ carefully.

3. A: Do you believe his story about being late because he had a flat tire?

   B: No. I think he made it _____.

4. A: Could you pick _____ a newspaper on your way home from work tonight?

   B: Sure.

5. A: Did you hear the bad news?

   B: About what?

   A: Gary's grandmother passed _____. Gary went home to be with his family and attend the funeral.

6. A: I like your new shoes.

   B: Thanks. I had to try _____ almost a dozen pairs before I decided to get these.

7. A: Have you decided to accept that new job?

   B: Not yet. I'm still thinking it _____.

8. A: I'm tired. I wish I could get _____ of going to the meeting tonight.

   B: Do you have to go?

9. A: Why hasn't Mary been in class for the last two weeks?

   B: She dropped _____ _____ school.

10. A: What time does your plane take _____?

    B: 10:40.

    A: How long does the flight take?

    B: I think we get _____ around 12:30.

11. A: Do you like living in the dorm?

    B: It's okay. I've learned to put _____ with all the noise.

12. A: What brought _____ your decision to quit your job?

    B: I couldn't get _____ _____ my boss.

CHAPTER **8**

Showing Relationships Between Ideas—Part I

8–1 PARALLEL STRUCTURE

One use of a conjunction is to connect words or phrases that have the same grammatical function in a sentence. This use of conjunctions is called *parallel structure*. The conjunctions used in this pattern are: **and**, **but**, **or**, **nor**.*

(a) *Steve **and** his friend* are coming to dinner.	In (a): *noun* + **and** + *noun*
(b) Susan *raised* her hand **and** *snapped* her fingers.	In (b): *verb* + **and** + *verb*
(c) He *is waving* his arms **and** *(is) shouting* at us.	In (c): *verb* + **and** + *verb* (The second auxiliary may be omitted if it is the same as the first auxiliary.)
(d) These shoes are *old* **but** *comfortable*.	In (d): *adjective* + **but** + *adjective*
(e) He wants *to watch* TV **or** *(to) listen* to some music.	In (e): *infinitive* + **or** + *infinitive* (The second **to** may be omitted.)
(f) *Steve, Joe,* **and** *Alice* are coming to dinner.	A parallel structure may contain more than two parts. In a series, commas are used to separate each unit. The final comma that precedes the conjunction is optional but is customarily used. (*No* commas are used if there are only two parts to a parallel structure.)
(g) Susan *raised* her hand, *snapped* her fingers, **and** *asked* a question.	
(h) The colors in that fabric are *red, gold, black,* **and** *green*.	

*More specifically, **and, but, or, nor** are called *coordinating conjunctions*.

☐ **EXERCISE 1:** Underline the parallel structure in each sentence, and give the pattern that is used, as in the examples.

1. The old man is extremely <u>kind</u> and <u>generous</u>. _____*adjective*_____ + and + _____*adjective*_____

2. He received a pocket <u>calculator</u> and a wool <u>sweater</u> for his birthday. _____*noun*_____ + and + _____*noun*_____

3. She spoke angrily and bitterly
   about the war.   _____ + and + _____

4. I looked for my book but   _____ + but + _____
   couldn't find it.

5. I hope to go to that university   _____ + and + _____
   and study under Dr. Liu.

6. In my spare time, I enjoy   _____ + or + _____
   reading novels or watching
   television.

7. He will leave at eight and arrive _____ + and + _____
   at nine.

8. He should have broken his   _____ + and + _____
   engagement to Beth and
   married Sue instead.

☐ **EXERCISE 2:** Parallel structure makes repeating the same words unnecessary.* Combine
the given sentences into one concise sentence that contains parallel structure.
Punctuate carefully.

1. Mary opened the door. Mary greeted her guests.
   → *Mary opened the door and greeted her guests.*
2. Mary is opening the door. Mary is greeting her guests.
3. Mary will open the door. Mary will greet her guests.
4. Alice is kind. Alice is generous. Alice is trustworthy.
5. Please try to speak more loudly. Please try to speak more clearly.
6. He gave her flowers on Sunday. He gave her candy on Monday. He gave
   her a ring on Tuesday.

---

*This form of parallel structure, in which unnecessary words are omitted but are
understood, is termed *ellipsis*.

7. While we were in New York, we attended an opera. While we were in New York, we ate at marvelous restaurants. While we were in New York, we visited some old friends.
8. He decided to quit school. He decided to go to California. He decided to find a job.
9. I am looking forward to going to Italy. I am looking forward to eating wonderful pasta every day.
10. I should have finished my homework. I should have cleaned up my room.
11. The boy was old enough to work. The boy was old enough to earn some money.
12. He preferred to play baseball. Or he preferred to spend his time in the streets with other boys.
13. I like coffee. I do not like tea.
    I like coffee but not tea.*
14. I have met his mother. I have not met his father.
15. Jake would like to live in Puerto Rico. He would not like to live in Iceland.

☐ **EXERCISE 3:** In each group, complete the unfinished sentence. Then combine the sentences into one concise sentence that contains parallel structure. Punctuate carefully.

1. The country lane was narrow.

   The country lane was steep.

   The country lane was _____ *muddy.* _____
   _____ *The country lane was narrow, steep, and muddy.* _____

2. I like to become acquainted with the people of other countries.

   I like to become acquainted with the customs of other countries.

   I like to become acquainted with _____ of other

   countries.

   _____

3. I dislike living in a city because of the air pollution.

   I dislike living in a city because of the crime.

   I dislike living in a city because of _____

   _____

_____
*Sometimes a comma precedes **but not**: *I like coffee, but not tea.*

4. We discussed some of the social problems of the United States.

   We discussed some of the political problems of the United States.

   We discussed some of the _____ problems of the United States.

   _____

5. Hawaii has _____

   Hawaii has many interesting tropical trees.

   Hawaii has many interesting tropical flowers.

   Hawaii has beautiful beaches.

   _____

6. Mary Hart would make a good president because she _____

   Mary Hart would make a good president because she works effectively with others.

   Mary Hart would make a good president because she has a reputation for integrity.

   Mary Hart would make a good president because she has a reputation for independent thinking.

   _____

☐ **EXERCISE 4:** Choose the letter of the phrase from the list that best completes each sentence. Use each phrase in the list only once.

A. affordable health care
B. by leaders who are committed to public service and hard work
C. efficiently
D. excellence in
✔ E. in agriculture
F. integrity

G. provide quality education
H. to reduce health care costs
I. responsible
J. seeking practical solutions
K. tolerant of those who are weak
L. who finds a way to get the important jobs done

1. Mr. Turner has had wide experience. He has worked in business, in the news media, and __*E*__.

2. Judge Holmes served the people of this country with impartiality, ability, and _____.

3. The people want safe homes, good schools, and _____.

4. As a taxpayer, I want my money used wisely and _____.

5. Mr. Adams is respected for researching issues and _____.

6. Ms. Hunter has established a record of effective and _____ leadership in government.

7. The challenges that face us today will not be met by politicians who focus on partisan bickering and political expediency but _____.

8. Resolve to be tender with the young, compassionate with the aged, understanding of those who are wrong, and _____. Sometime in life, you will have been all of these.

9. Carol is a hard-working personnel manager who welcomes challenges and _____.

10. I will continue to fight for adequate funding of and _____ education.

11. She has worked hard to control excess government spending, protect our environment, and _____.

12. I see the need to eliminate unfair taxes, to improve the business climate, and _____.

8-2 USING PAIRED CONJUNCTIONS: *BOTH . . . AND; NOT ONLY . . . BUT ALSO; EITHER . . . OR; NEITHER . . . NOR*★

(a) **Both my mother and my sister** *are* here. (b) **Not only my mother but also my sister** *is* here. (c) **Not only my sister but also my parents** *are* here. (d) **Neither my mother nor my sister** *is* here. (e) **Neither my sister nor my parents** *are* here.	Two subjects connected by **both** . . . **and** take a plural verb. When two subjects are connected by **not only** . . . **but also**, **either** . . . **or**, or **neither** . . . **nor**, the subject that is closer to the verb determines whether the verb is singular or plural.
(f) The research project will take **both** *time* **and** *money*. (g) Yesterday it **not only** *rained* **but (also)** *snowed*. (h) I'll take **either** *chemistry* **or** *physics* next quarter. (i) That book is **neither** *interesting* **nor** *accurate*.	Notice the parallel structure in the examples. The *same* grammatical form should follow each word of the pair. In (f): **both** + *noun* + **and** + *noun* In (g): **not only** + *verb* + **but also** + *verb* In (h): **either** + *noun* + **or** + *noun* In (i): **neither** + *adjective* + **nor** + *adjective*

★Paired conjunctions are also called *correlative conjunctions*.

☐ **EXERCISE 5:** Supply *is* or *are* in the following.

    1. Both the teacher and the student _____ here.

    2. Neither the teacher nor the student _____ here.

    3. Not only the teacher but also the student _____ here.

    4. Not only the teacher but also the students _____ here.

    5. Either the students or the teacher _____ planning to come.

    6. Either the teacher or the students _____ planning to come.

☐ **EXERCISE 6—ERROR ANALYSIS:** What is wrong with the following sentences?

    1. Either John will call Mary or Bob.

    2. Not only Sue saw the mouse but also the cat.

    3. Both my mother talked to the teacher and my father.

☐ **EXERCISE 7—ORAL:** Answer the questions. Use paired conjunctions.

*Use **both . . . and.***

    1. You have met his father. Have you met his mother?
      → *Yes, I have met both his father and his mother.*

    2. The driver was injured in the accident. Was the passenger injured in the accident?

    3. Wheat is grown in Kansas. Is corn grown in Kansas?

    4. He buys used cars. Does he sell used cars?

    5. You had lunch with your friends. Did you have dinner with them?

    6. The city suffers from air pollution. Does it suffer from water pollution?

*Use **not only . . . but also.***

    7. I know you are studying math. Are you studying chemistry too?
      → *Yes, I'm studying not only math but also chemistry.*

    8. I know his cousin is living with him. Is his mother-in-law living with him too?

    9. I know your country has good universities. Does the United States have good universities too?

    10. I know you lost your wallet. Did you lose your keys too?

    11. I know she goes to school. Does she have a full-time job too?

    12. I know he bought a coat. Did he buy a new pair of shoes too?

*Use **either . . . or.***

    13. John has your book, or Mary has your book. Is that right?
      → *Yes, either John or Mary has my book.*

14. You're going to give your friend a book for her birthday, or you're going to give her a pen. Is that right?
15. Your sister will meet you at the airport, or your brother will meet you there. Right?
16. They can go swimming, or they can play tennis. Is that right?
17. You're going to vote for Mr. Smith, or you're going to vote for Mr. Jones. Right?
18. You'll go to New Orleans for your vacation, or you'll go to Miami. Right?

*Use **neither . . . nor.***

19. He doesn't like coffee. Does he like tea?
    → *No, he likes neither coffee nor tea.*
20. Her husband doesn't speak English. Do her children speak English?
21. The students aren't wide awake today. Is the teacher wide awake today?
22. They don't have a refrigerator for their new apartment. Do they have a stove?
23. She doesn't enjoy hunting. Does she enjoy fishing?
24. The result wasn't good. Was the result bad?

□ **EXERCISE 8:** Combine the following into sentences that contain parallel structure. Use appropriate paired conjunctions: ***both . . . and; not only . . . but also; either . . . or; neither . . . nor.***

1. He does not have a pen. He does not have paper.
   → *He has neither a pen nor paper.*
2. Ron enjoys horseback riding. Bob enjoys horseback riding.
3. You can have tea, or you can have coffee.
4. Arthur is not in class today. Ricardo is not in class today.
5. Arthur is absent. Ricardo is absent.
6. We can fix dinner for them here, or we can take them to a restaurant.
7. She wants to buy a Chevrolet, or she wants to buy a Toyota.
8. The leopard faces extinction. The tiger faces extinction.
9. The library does not have the book I need. The bookstore does not have the book I need.
10. We could fly, or we could take the train.
11. The President's assistant will not confirm the story. The President's assistant will not deny the story.
12. Coal is an irreplaceable natural resource. Oil is an irreplaceable natural resource.
13. Small pox is a dangerous disease. Malaria is a dangerous disease.
14. Her roommates don't know where she is. Her brother doesn't know where she is.
15. According to the news report, it will snow tonight, or it will rain tonight.

□ **EXERCISE 9—ERROR ANALYSIS:** Find and correct the errors in parallel structure in the following sentences.

1. By obeying the speed limit, we can save energy, lives, and it costs us less.

2. My home offers me a feeling of security, warm, and love.

3. The pioneers labored to clear away the forest and planting crops.

4. When I refused to help her, she became very angry and shout at me.

5. In my spare time, I enjoy taking care of my aquarium and to work on my stamp collection.

6. Either Mr. Anderson or Ms. Wiggins are going to teach our class today.

7. I enjoy not only reading novels but also magazines.

8. Oxygen is plentiful. Both air contains oxygen and water.

8–3 COMBINING INDEPENDENT CLAUSES WITH CONJUNCTIONS

(a) It was raining hard. There was a strong wind. (b) *INCORRECT PUNCTUATION:* It was raining hard, there was a strong wind.	Example (a) contains two independent clauses (i.e., two complete sentences). Notice the punctuation. A period,* NOT A COMMA, is used to separate two independent clauses. The punctuation in (b) is not correct; the error in (b) is called *a run-on sentence.*
(c) It was raining hard, **and** there was a strong wind. (d) It was raining hard **and** there was a strong wind. (e) It was raining hard. **And** there was a strong wind.	A conjunction may be used to connect two independent clauses. *Punctuation:* In (c): Usually a comma immediately precedes the conjunction. In (d): Sometimes in short sentences the comma is omitted. In (e): Sometimes in informal writing a conjunction may begin a sentence.
(f) He was tired, **so** he went to bed. (g) The child hid behind his mother's skirt, **for** he was afraid of the dog. (h) He did not study, **yet** he passed the exam.	In addition to **and, but, or,** and **nor,** other conjunctions are used to connect two independent clauses: **so** (meaning *therefore, as a result*) **for** (meaning *because*) **yet** (meaning *but, nevertheless*) A comma almost always precedes **so, for,** and **yet** when they are used as conjunctions.**

*In British English, *a period* is called *a full stop*.
So, for, and **yet** have other meanings in other structures: e.g., *He is not **so** tall as his brother.* (**so** = **as**) *We waited **for** the bus.* (**for** = a preposition) *She hasn't arrived **yet**.* (**yet** = an adverb meaning *up to this time*).

☐ **EXERCISE 10:** Punctuate the following sentences by adding commas or periods as necessary. Do not add any words. Capitalize letters where necessary.

1. The boys walked the girls ran. → *The boys walked. The girls ran.*

2. The teacher lectured the students took notes.

3. The teacher lectured and the students took notes.

4. Jessica came to the meeting but Ron stayed home.

5. Jessica came to the meeting her brother stayed home.

6. Her academic record was outstanding yet she was not accepted by the university.

7. I have not finished writing my term paper yet I will not be finished until sometime next week.

8. We had to go to the grocery store for some milk and bread.

9. We had to go to the grocery store for there was nothing in the house to fix for dinner.

10. Frank did not have enough money to buy an airplane ticket so he couldn't fly home for the holiday.

☐ **EXERCISE 11:** Punctuate the following sentences by adding commas or periods as necessary. Do not add any words. Capitalize letters where necessary.

1. A thermometer is used to measure temperature a barometer measures air pressure.

2. Daniel made many promises but he had no intention of keeping them.

3. I always enjoyed studying mathematics in high school so I decided to major in it in college.

4. The ancient Egyptians had good dentists archaeologists have found mummies that had gold fillings in their teeth.

5. Both John and I had many errands to do yesterday John had to go to the post office and the bookstore I had to go to the drugstore the travel agency and the bank.

6. Anna is in serious legal trouble for she had no car insurance at the time of the accident.

7. Last night Martha had to study for a test so she went to the library.

8. I did not like the leading actor yet the movie was quite good on the whole.

9. The team of researchers has not finished compiling the statistics yet their work will not be made public until later.

10. We have nothing to fear for our country is strong and united.

11. He slapped his desk in disgust he had failed another examination and had ruined his chances for a passing grade in the course.

12. I struggled to keep my head above water I tried to yell for help but no sound came from my mouth.

13. The earthquake was devastating tall buildings crumbled and fell to the earth.

14. It was a wonderful picnic the children waded in the stream collected rocks and insects and flew kites the teenagers played an enthusiastic game of baseball the adults busied themselves preparing the food supervising the children and playing a game or two of volleyball.

15. The butterfly is a marvel it begins as an ugly caterpillar and turns into a work of art.

16. Caterpillars eat plants and cause damage to some crops but adult butterflies feed principally on nectar from flowers and do not cause any harm.

17. Some people collect butterflies for a hobby these collectors capture them with a net and put them in a jar that has poison in it the dead butterflies are then mounted on a board.

18. The sight of a butterfly floating from flower to flower on a warm sunny day brightens anyone's heart a butterfly is a charming and gentle creature.

19. When cold weather comes some butterflies travel great distances to reach tropical climates.

20. Butterflies are admired throughout the world because they are beautiful they can be found on every continent except Antarctica.

8–4 ADVERB CLAUSES: INTRODUCTION

(a) ***When we were in New York***, we saw several plays. (b) We saw several plays ***when we were in New York***.	***When we were in New York*** is an adverb clause. It is a dependent clause. It cannot stand alone as a sentence. It must be connected to an independent clause. *Punctuation:* When an adverb clause precedes an independent clause, as in (a), a comma is used to separate the clauses. When the adverb clause follows, as in (b), usually no comma is used.
(c) ***Because he was sleepy***, he went to bed. (d) He went to bed ***because he was sleepy***.	Like ***when***, ***because*** introduces an adverb clause. ***Because he was sleepy*** is an adverb clause.

SUMMARY LIST OF WORDS USED TO INTRODUCE ADVERB CLAUSES*

TIME	CAUSE AND EFFECT	OPPOSITION	CONDITION
after	*because*	*even though*	*if*
before	*since*	*although*	*unless*
when	*now that*	*though*	*only if*
while	*as*		*whether or not*
as	*as/so long as*		*even if*
by the time (that)	*inasmuch as*		*providing (that)*
since		*whereas*	*provided (that)*
until		*while*	*in case (that)*
as soon as	*so (that)*		*in the event (that)*
once	*in order that*		
as/so long as			
whenever			
every time (that)			
the first time (that)			
the last time (that)			
the next time (that)			

*Words that introduce adverb clauses are called *subordinating conjunctions*.

8-5 USING ADVERB CLAUSES TO SHOW TIME RELATIONSHIPS

after	(a) **After** *she graduates*, she will get a job. (b) **After** *she (had) graduated*, she got a job.	A present tense, *not* a future tense, is used in an adverb clause of time. Notice examples (a) and (c). (See Chart 1-21 for tense usage in future time clauses.)
before	(c) I will leave **before** *he comes*. (d) I (had) left **before** *he came*.	
when	(e) **When** *I arrived*, he was talking on the phone. (f) **When** *I got there*, he had already left. (g) **When** *it began to rain*, I stood under a tree. (h) **When** *I was in Chicago*, I visited the museums. (i) **When** *I see him tomorrow*, I will ask him.	***when*** = *at that time* (Notice the different time relationships expressed by the tenses.
while *as*	(j) **While** *I was walking home*, it began to rain. (k) **As** *I was walking home*, it began to rain.	***while, as*** = *during that time*
by the time	(l) **By the time** *he arrived*, we had already left. (m) **By the time** *he comes*, we will already have left.	***by the time*** = *one event is completed before another event* (Notice the use of the past perfect and future perfect in the main clause.)
since	(n) I haven't seen him **since** *he left this morning*.	***since*** = *from that time to the present* (Notice: The present perfect tense is used in the main clause.
until *till*	(o) We stayed there **until** *we finished our work*. (p) We stayed there **till** *we finished our work*.	***until, till*** = *to that time and then no longer* (***Till*** is used primarily in speaking rather than writing.)
as soon as *once*	(q) **As soon as** *it stops raining*, we will leave. (r) **Once** *it stops raining*, we will leave.	***as soon as, once*** = *when one event happens, another event happens soon afterwards*
as long as *so long as*	(s) I will never speak to him again **as long as** *I live*. (t) I will never speak to him again **so long as** *I live*.	***as long as, so long as*** = *during all that time, from beginning to end*
whenever *every time*	(u) **Whenever** *I see her*, I say hello. (v) **Every time** *I see her*, I say hello.	***whenever*** = *every time*
the first time *the last time* *the next time*	(w) **The first time** *I went to New York*, I went to an opera. (x) I saw two plays **the last time** *I went to New York*. (y) **The next time** *I go to New York*, I'm going to see a ballet.	Adverb clauses can be introduced by the following: *the* $\left\{ \begin{array}{l} \textbf{\textit{first}} \\ \textbf{\textit{second}} \\ \textbf{\textit{third}} \\ \textbf{\textit{last}} \\ \textbf{\textit{next}} \end{array} \right\}$ *time*

☐ **EXERCISE 12:** Complete the following. Pay special attention to verb tenses.

1. Last night I went to bed after I _____ my homework.

2. Tonight I will go to bed after I _____ my homework.

3. Ever since I was a child, I _____ afraid of dogs.

4. Jane's contact lens popped out while she _____ basketball.

5. Be sure to reread your composition for errors before you _____ _____ it in to the teacher tomorrow.

6. By the time I left my apartment this morning, the mail carrier _____ _____ the mail.

7. I have known Jim Bates since he _____ ten years old.

8. A black cat ran across the road as I _____ my car to work this morning.

9. By the time I leave this city, I _____ here for four months.

10. Whenever Mark _____ angry, his nose gets red.

11. I _____ to the beach whenever the weather was nice, but now I don't have time to do that because I have to study.

12. We will have a big party when _____.

13. The next time I _____ to Hawaii, I'm going to visit Mauna Loa, the world's largest volcano.

14. I had fried chicken the last time I _____ at that restaurant.

☐ **EXERCISE 13:** Make sentences with **until** from the given situations.

1. I can't pay my bills. I haven't gotten my paycheck yet.

   _____*I can't pay my bills*_____ until ___*my paycheck comes*___.

2. We can't leave yet. We have to wait for Nancy.

   _____ until _____.

3. Tell me the truth, or I am not going to leave this room.

   _____ until _____.

4. Finally, Donald arrived. Before that, it had been a dull party.

   _____ until _____.

5. Dinner won't be ready for a while. I think we should just sit here by the fire.

   Let's _____ until _____.

6. When I go to bed at night, I like to read. After a while, I get sleepy.

   _____ until _____.

☐ **EXERCISE 14:** Combine the ideas by using either **as soon as** or **once**. (**As soon as** and **once** basically have the same meaning, but **as soon as** is more immediate. Often, **just** is used with **as soon as** to emphasize the idea of "immediately": *I'll call him just as soon as I get home*.)

1. The taxi will get here in five minutes or so. Then we can leave for the airport.

   As soon as the taxi gets here, we can leave for the airport.

2. The rice will be done in about ten minutes. Immediately after that, we can eat.

   _____

3. First, I have to graduate. Then I can return home.

   _____

4. Spring will come and the weather will be nice again. Then we can start playing tennis every morning before class.

   _____

5. My roommate walked into the room. Immediately, I knew that something was wrong.

   _____

6. Your English will get better. Then you will begin to feel more comfortable living in the United States.

   _____

7. Immediately after the singer finished her song, the audience burst into applause.

   _____

8. I'm watching a baseball game on TV, but it will be over in a few minutes. Then I'll take out the garbage.

   _____

☐ **EXERCISE 15:** Using the given information, make a sentence in which you use *just after*, *just before*, or *just as*. Notice that *just* adds the idea of "immediately."

1. I got to the airport at 8:15. My plane left ten minutes later.
   I got to the airport just before my plane left.

2. You shouldn't eat a heavy meal and then go to bed immediately afterwards.

   _____

3. I went to bed at 11:00. The phone rang at 11:05.

   _____

4. We were sitting down to eat. At that moment, someone knocked on the door.

   _____

5. I was getting on the bus. At that moment, I remembered that I had left my briefcase at home.

   _____

6. I got up to give my speech. Immediately before that, I got butterflies in my stomach.

   _____

7. The guests will come at 7:00. At 6:55, I'll light the candles.

   _____

8. I was bending over to pick up my pencil. My pants split.

   _____

☐ **EXERCISE 16:** Compare *after* and *afterwards*.

(a) ***After** I ate dinner*, I took a walk. I took a walk ***after** I ate dinner*.	***After*** can be used to introduce an adverb clause.
(b) I ate dinner. ***Afterwards***, *I took a walk*. I ate dinner. *I took a walk* ***afterwards***.	***Afterwards**** is an adverb meaning *"later, after that."*

*****Afterwards*** can also be spelled without *-s*: **afterward**.

> *Combine the sentences by using **after** and **afterwards**, as in the previous examples.*
> *Punctuate carefully.*

1. *First:* I studied.
   Then: I went to bed.
2. *First:* We went to the museum.
   Then: We had some lunch.
3. *First:* He was in an automobile accident.
   Then: He had to walk on crutches for two months.

☐ **EXERCISE 17—WRITTEN:** Complete the following. Punctuate carefully. Pay special attention to verb tense usage.

1. Since I came to . . . .
2. Just as I was falling asleep last night . . . .
3. I'll help you with your homework as soon as I . . . .
4. I was late. By the time I got to the airport . . . .
5. One of my friends gets nervous every time . . . .
6. I will be here until I . . . .
7. . . . as long as I live.
8. I heard . . . while I . . . .
9. Once summer/winter comes . . . .
10. Just before I . . . .
11. I have been in . . . for . . . . By the time I leave, I . . . .
12. The last time I . . . .
13. The next time you . . . .
14. I . . . after I . . . .
15. I . . . . Afterwards I . . . .
16. I had already . . . when . . . .
17. Whenever . . . .
18. Ever since . . . .

8–6 USING ADVERB CLAUSES TO SHOW CAUSE AND EFFECT RELATIONSHIPS

because	(a) ***Because*** *he was sleepy*, he went to bed. (b) He went to bed ***because*** *he was sleepy*.	An adverb clause may precede or follow the independent clause. Notice the punctuation in (a) and (b).
since	(c) ***Since*** *he's not interested in classical music*, he decided not to go to the concert.	In (c): ***since*** means *because*.
now that	(d) ***Now that*** *the semester is finished*, I'm going to rest a few days and then take a trip.	In (d): ***now that*** means *because now*. ***Now that*** is used for present and future situations.
as	(e) ***As*** *she had nothing in particular to do*, she called up a friend and asked her if she wanted to take in a movie.	In (e): ***as*** means *because*.
as/so long as	(f) ***As long as (So long as)*** *you're not busy*, could you help me with this work?	In (f): ***as long as*** means *because*.
inasmuch as	(g) ***Inasmuch as*** *the two government leaders could not reach an agreement*, the possibilities for peace are still remote.	In (g): ***inasmuch as*** means *because*. ***Inasmuch as*** is usually found only in formal writing and speech.

□ **EXERCISE 18:** Using the given information, make sentences using ***now that***.

1. Peggy used to take the bus to school, but last week she bought a car. Now she can drive to school.

   Now that Peggy has a car, she can drive to school.

2. You just had your sixteenth birthday. Now you can get a driver's license.

   Now that you are

3. We have to wear warm clothes. It's winter now.

   _____

4. Bob used to live in the dorm, but a couple of weeks ago he moved into an apartment. Now he can cook his own food.

   _____

5. Whew! I've finally finished painting the house. Now I can go fishing.

   _____

6. I can get a job as a bilingual secretary. I know English now.

   _____

7. My brother got married last month. He's a married man now, so he has more responsibilities.

   _____

8. Do you want to go for a walk? The rain has stopped.

   _____

9. It's been a long, hard week, but final exams are finally over. We can relax.

   _____

10. The civil war has ended. A new government is being formed.

    _____

☐ **EXERCISE 19:** Complete the following.

   1. As long as it's such a nice day, why don't _____

   2. As long as the movie is free, let's _____

   3. As long as it's raining, I think I'll _____

   4. As long as the coffee is already made, I guess I'll _____

   5. As long as you're here, why don't _____

   6. As long as you're up, would you mind _____

☐ **EXERCISE 20:** Combine the given ideas by using *since*. Also, decide which sentences might be found in somewhat formal writing and use *inasmuch as*.

   1. Monday is Bob's birthday. Let's give him a party.

      _____

   2. Monday is a national holiday. All government offices will be closed.

      _____

   3. The guys I live with don't know any Arabic. I have to speak English with them.

      _____

4. Oil is an irreplaceable natural resource. We must do whatever we can in order to conserve it.

_____

5. Mary, maybe you could help me with this calculus problem. You're a math major.

_____

6. Many young people move to the cities in search of employment. There are few jobs available in the rural areas.

_____

□ **EXERCISE 21—WRITTEN:** Complete the following. Punctuate carefully.

1. Now that I . . . .
2. The teacher didn't . . . because . . . .
3. Since heavy fog is predicted for tonight . . . .
4. He was not admitted to the university inasmuch as . . . .
5. Jack can't stay out all night with his friends now that . . . .
6. Since we don't have class tomorrow . . . .
7. Inasmuch as her application arrived after the deadline . . . .

8-7 USING PREPOSITIONS TO SHOW CAUSE AND EFFECT: *BECAUSE OF* AND *DUE TO*

(a) *Because* the weather was cold, we stayed home.	*Because* introduces an adverb clause; it is followed by a subject and verb.
(b) *Because of* the cold weather, we stayed home. (c) *Due to* the cold weather, we stayed home.	*Because of* and *due to* are prepositions; they are followed by a noun object.
(d) *Due to the fact that* the weather was cold, we stayed home.	Sometimes, usually in more formal writing, *due to* is followed by a noun clause introduced by *the fact that*.
(e) We stayed home *because of the cold weather.* We stayed home *due to the cold weather.* We stayed home *due to the fact that the weather was cold.*	Like adverb clauses, these phrases can also follow the main clause, as in (e).

□ **EXERCISE 22:** Using the ideas given in parentheses, complete the sentences.

1. (*My parents are generous.*) Because of ___*my parents' generosity*___,
   all of the children in our family have received the best of everything.

2. (*The traffic was heavy.*) We were late to the meeting due to _____
   _____.

3. (*Bill's wife is ill.*) Bill has to do all of the cooking and cleaning because of
   _____.

4. (*Dr. Robinson has done excellent research on wolves.*) Due to _____
   _____,
   we know much more today about that endangered species than we did
   even five years ago.

5. (*It was noisy in the next apartment.*) I couldn't get to sleep last night
   because of _____.

6. (*Circumstances are beyond my control.*) Due to _____
   _____, I regret to say that I cannot be
   present at your daughter's wedding.

8–8   USING TRANSITIONS TO SHOW CAUSE AND EFFECT: *THEREFORE* AND *CONSEQUENTLY*

(a) Al failed the test because he didn't study. (b) Al didn't study. ***Therefore***, he failed the test. (c) Al didn't study. ***Consequently***, he failed the test.	(a), (b), and (c) have the same meaning. ***Therefore*** and ***consequently*** mean "as a result." In grammar, they are called *transitions* (or *conjunctive adverbs*). Transitions connect the ideas between two sentences.
(d) Al didn't study. ***Therefore***, he failed the test. (e) Al didn't study. He, ***therefore***, failed the test. (f) Al didn't study. He failed the test, ***therefore***. **POSITIONS OF A TRANSITION:** **transition + S + V** (+ rest of sentence) **S + transition + V** (+ rest of sentence) **S + V** (+ rest of sentence) + **transition**	A transition occurs in the second of two related sentences. Notice the patterns and punctuation in the examples. A period (NOT a comma) is used at the end of the first sentence. The transition has several possible positions in the second sentence. The transition is set off from the rest of the sentence by commas.
(g) Al didn't study, *so* he failed the test.	COMPARE: A transition (e.g., ***therefore***) has different possible positions within the second sentence of a pair. A conjunction (e.g., *so*) has only one possible position: between the two sentences. (See Chart 8-3.) *So* cannot move around in the second sentence as ***therefore*** can.

☐ **EXERCISE 23:** Restate the sentences using the given transitions. Use three alternative positions for the transitions, as shown in Chart 8-8. Punctuate carefully.

1. The children stayed home because a storm was approaching. (Use *therefore*.)

   _____

   _____

   _____

2. I didn't have my umbrella, so I got wet. (Use *consequently*.)

   _____

   _____

   _____

☐ **EXERCISE 24:** Punctuate the following sentences. Add capital letters if necessary.

1. *adverb clause:*   Because it was cold she wore a coat.
2. *adverb clause:*   She wore a coat because it was cold.
3. *prepositional phrase:*   Because of the cold weather she wore a coat.
4. *prepositional phrase:*   She wore a coat because of the cold weather.
5. *transition:*   The weather was cold therefore she wore a coat.
6. *transition:*   The weather was cold she therefore wore a coat.
7. *transition:*   The weather was cold she wore a coat therefore.
8. *conjunction:*   The weather was cold so she wore a coat.

☐ **EXERCISE 25:** Punctuate the following sentences. Add capital letters if necessary.

1. Pat always enjoyed studying sciences in high school therefore she decided to major in biology in college.
2. Due to recent improvements in the economy fewer people are unemployed.
3. Last night's storm damaged the power lines consequently the town was without electricity for several hours.
4. Because of the snowstorm only five students came to class the teacher therefore cancelled the class.
5. Anna always makes numerous spelling mistakes in her compositions because she does not use a dictionary when she writes.

8–9 SUMMARY OF PATTERNS AND PUNCTUATION

ADVERB CLAUSE	(a) ***Because*** *it was hot*, we went swimming. (b) We went swimming ***because*** *it was hot*.	An adverb clause may precede or follow an independent clause. *Punctuation:* A comma is used if the adverb clause comes first.
PREPOSITION	(c) ***Because of*** *the hot weather*, we went swimming. (d) We went swimming ***because of*** *the hot weather*.	A preposition is followed by a noun object, not by a subject and verb. *Punctuation:* A comma is usually used if the prepositional phrase precedes the subject and verb of the independent clause.
TRANSITION	(e) It was hot. ***Therefore***, *we went swimming*. (f) It was hot. *We,* ***therefore***, *went swimming*. (g) It was hot. *We went swimming,* ***therefore***.	A transition is used with the second sentence of a pair. It shows the relationship of the second idea to the first idea. A transition is movable within the second sentence. *Punctuation:* A period is used between the two independent clauses.* A comma may NOT be used to separate the clauses. Commas are usually used to set the transition off from the rest of the sentence.
CONJUNCTION	(h) It was hot, ***so*** *we went swimming*.	A conjunction comes between two independent clauses. *Punctuation:* Usually a comma is used immediately in front of a conjunction.

*A semicolon (;) may be used instead of a period between the two independent clauses.

> *It was hot; therefore, we went swimming.*
> *It was hot; we, therefore, went swimming.*
> *It was hot; we went swimming, therefore.*

In general, a semicolon can be used instead of a period between any two sentences that are closely related in meaning. Example: *Peanuts are not nuts; they are beans.* Notice that a small letter, not a capital letter, immediately follows a semicolon.

☐ **EXERCISE 26:** Using the given words, combine the following two ideas.

> **We postponed our trip. The weather was bad.**

> 1. because → *We postponed our trip because the weather was bad.*
>   → *Because the weather was bad, we postponed our trip.*

2. therefore	4. so	6. consequently
3. since	5. because of	7. due to (the fact that)

□ **EXERCISE 27**: Using the given words, combine the following two ideas.

She missed class. She was ill.

1. because of
2. because
3. consequently
4. so
5. due to (the fact that)
6. therefore

8–10 OTHER WAYS OF EXPRESSING CAUSE AND EFFECT: *SUCH . . . THAT* AND *SO . . . THAT*

(a) Because the weather was nice, we went to the zoo. (b) It was **such nice weather that** we went to the zoo. (c) The weather was **so nice that** we went to the zoo.	Examples (a), (b), and (c) have the same meaning.
(d) It was **such good coffee that** I had another cup. (e) It was **such a foggy day that** we couldn't see the road.	**Such . . . that** encloses a modified noun: **such + adjective + noun + that**
(f) The coffee is **so hot that** I can't drink it. (g) I'm **so hungry that** I could eat a horse.	**So . . . that** encloses an adjective or adverb: $so + \begin{Bmatrix} adjective \\ or \\ adverb \end{Bmatrix} + that$
(h) She speaks **so fast that** I can't understand her. (i) He walked **so quickly that** I couldn't keep up with him.	
(j) She made **so many mistakes that** she failed the exam. (k) He has **so few friends that** he is always lonely. (l) She has **so much money that** she can buy whatever she wants. (m) He had **so little trouble** with the test **that** he left twenty minutes early.	**So . . . that** is used with **many**, **few**, **much**, and **little**.
(n) It was **such a good book** *(that)* I couldn't put it down. (o) I was **so hungry** *(that)* I didn't wait for dinner to eat something.	Sometimes, primarily in speaking, **that** is omitted.

□ **EXERCISE 28**: Combine the following sentences by using *so . . . that* or *such . . . that*.

1. This tea is good. I think I'll have another cup.

   → *This tea is so good that I think I'll have another cup.*

2. This is good tea. I think I'll have another cup.

   → *This is such good tea that I think I'll have another cup.*

3. The car was expensive. We couldn't afford to buy it.

4. It was an expensive car. We couldn't afford to buy it.

5. I had to wear my wool coat. It was a cold day.

6. The weather was hot. You could fry an egg on the sidewalk.

7. I don't feel like going to class. We're having beautiful weather.

8. Grandpa held me tightly when he hugged me. I couldn't breathe for a moment.

9. I couldn't understand her. She talked too fast.

10. The audience booed the actors. It was a bad performance.

11. I've met too many people in the last few days. I can't possibly remember all of their names.

12. It took us only ten minutes to get there. There was little traffic.

13. There were few people at the meeting. It was cancelled.

14. The wastepaper basket overflowed. Sally used too much paper when she was writing her report.

☐ **EXERCISE 29:** Combine the sentences by using *so . . . that* or *such . . . that.*

1. The classroom has comfortable chairs. The students find it easy to fall asleep.
2. Ted couldn't get to sleep last night. He was worried about the exam.
3. Jerry got angry. He put his fist through the wall.

4. I have many problems. I can use all the help you can give me.

5. The tornado struck with great force. It lifted automobiles off the ground.

6. During the summer, we had hot and humid weather. It was uncomfortable just sitting in a chair doing nothing.

7. I can't figure out what this sentence says. His handwriting is illegible.

8. David has too many girlfriends. He can't remember all of their names.

9. Too many people came to the meeting. There were not enough seats for everyone.

10. In some countries, few students are accepted by the universities. As a result, admission is virtually a guarantee of a good job upon graduation.

☐ **EXERCISE 30—ORAL (BOOKS CLOSED):** Use *so . . . that* or *such . . . that.*

Example: You are sleepy.
Response: I am so sleepy that . . . (I could fall asleep in five minutes).

Example: "Book" is a common word.
Response: "Book" is such a common word that . . . (everyone knows what it means).

1. The weather is hot/cold/nice today.

2. Mary is a good student.

3. John speaks too softly.

4. You are tired.

5. On your way to class this morning/afternoon/evening, the traffic was heavy.

6. The teacher in one of your classes speaks too fast.

7. Your instructor assigned too much homework.

8. You and your husband/wife have a baby. The baby had a high temperature last night.

9. You took a test last week. It was an easy test.

10. You were home alone last night. You heard a noise. You were frightened.

11. You went to a movie last night. It was a good movie.

12. Your roommate makes too much noise at night.

13. Yesterday, there were too many students absent due to the flu.

14. You waited too long to mail your application to the university.

15. Think of a time you were nervous. How nervous were you?

16. Think of a time you were angry. How angry were you?

17. Think of a time you were happy. How happy were you?

18. Think of a time you were exhausted. How exhausted were you?

19. Think of a time you were surprised. How surprised were you?

20. Think of a time you were unhappy/embarrassed/glad/disappointed/sick.

☐ **EXERCISE 31:** Complete the following.

1. This box is so heavy _that I can't lift it._
2. This box is too heavy _(for me) to lift._
3. That car is too expensive _____
4. That car is so expensive _____
5. The coffee was too hot _____
6. The coffee was so hot _____
7. It is so dark in here _____
8. It is too dark in here _____

8–11 EXPRESSING PURPOSE: USING *SO THAT*

(a) I turned off the TV *in order to enable my roommate to study in peace and quiet.*	*In order to* expresses *purpose*. (See Chart 4-10.) In (a): I turned off the TV for a purpose. The purpose was to make it possible for my roommate to study in peace and quiet.
(b) I turned off the TV *so (that) my roommate could study in peace and quiet.*	*So that* also expresses *purpose.** It expresses the same meaning as *in order to*. The word "that" is often omitted, especially in speaking.
SO THAT + CAN or COULD (c) I'm going to cash a check *so that I can buy my textbooks.*	*So that* is often used instead of *in order to* when the idea of ability is being expressed. *Can* is used in the adverb clause for a present/future meaning. In (c): *so that I can buy = in order to be able to buy.*
(d) I cashed a check *so that I could buy my textbooks.*	*Could* is used after *so that* in past sentences.**
SO THAT + WILL/SIMPLE PRESENT or WOULD (e) I'll take my umbrella *so that I won't get wet.* (f) I'll take my umbrella *so that I don't get wet.* (g) Yesterday I took my umbrella *so that I wouldn't get wet.*	In (e): *so that I won't get wet = in order to make sure that I won't get wet.* In (f): It is sometimes possible to use the simple present after *so that* in place of *will*; the simple present expresses a future meaning. *Would* is used in past sentences.

*NOTE: *In order that* has the same meaning as *so that* but is less commonly used.

  Example: *I turned off the TV (in order) that my roommate could study in peace and quiet.*

Both *so that* and *in order that* introduce adverb clauses. It is unusual, but possible, to put these adverb clauses at the beginning of a sentence: *So that my roommate could study in peace and quiet, I turned off the TV.*

**Also possible but less common: the use of *may* or *might* in place of *can* or *could*: e.g., *I cashed a check so that I might buy my textbooks.*

1. Please turn down the radio. I want to be able to get to sleep.
   → *Please turn down the radio so (that) I can get to sleep.*
2. My wife turned down the radio. I wanted to be able to get to sleep.
   → *My wife turned down the radio so (that) I could get to sleep.*
3. Put the milk in the refrigerator. We want to make sure it won't (OR doesn't) spoil.
   → *Put the milk in the refrigerator so (that) it won't (OR doesn't) spoil.*
4. I put the milk in the refrigerator. I wanted to make sure it didn't spoil.
   → *I put the milk in the refrigerator so (that) it wouldn't spoil.*
5. Please be quiet. I want to be able to hear what Sharon is saying.
6. I asked the children to be quiet. I wanted to be able to hear what Sharon was saying.
7. I'm going to cash a check. I want to make sure that I will have (OR have) enough money to go to the market.
8. I cashed a check yesterday. I wanted to make sure that I had enough money to go to the market.
9. Ann and Larry have a six-year-old child. Tonight they're going to hire a babysitter. They want to be able to go out with some friends.
10. Last week Ann and Larry hired a babysitter. They wanted to be able to go to a dinner party at the home of Larry's boss.
11. Be sure to put the meat in the oven at 5:00. You want to be sure that it will be (OR is) ready to eat by 6:30.
12. Yesterday I put the meat in the oven at 5:00. I wanted it to be ready to eat by 6:30.

☐ **EXERCISE 33**: Combine the ideas by using *so (that)*.

1. I'm going to leave the party early. I want to be able to get a good night's sleep tonight.
2. When it started to rain, Harry opened his umbrella. He wanted to be sure he didn't get wet.
3. It's a good idea for you to learn how to type. You'll be able to type your own papers when you go to the university.
4. Lynn tied a string around her finger. She wanted to make sure that she didn't forget to take her book back to the library.
5. Ed took some change from his pocket. He wanted to buy a newspaper.
6. The little boy pretended to be sick. He wanted to stay home from school.
7. A lot of people were standing in front of me. I stood on my tiptoes. I wanted to see the parade better.
8. I turned on the TV. I wanted to listen to the news while I was making dinner.

9. I unplugged the phone. I didn't want to be interrupted while I was working.

10. Yesterday Linda was driving on the highway when her car started making strange noises. After she pulled over to the side of the road, she raised the hood of her car in order to make sure that other drivers knew that she had car trouble.

□ **EXERCISE 34:** Complete the following.

1. I'm going to take my camera to the zoo so (that) . . . .
2. I stayed home last night so (that) . . . .
3. Tommy, keep your pennies in your pocket so (that) . . . .
4. Please be quiet so (that) . . . .
5. You'd better put the food in the refrigerator so (that) . . . .
6. I'd better call Jane so (that) . . . .
7. I'm going on a diet so (that) . . . .
8. I'll give you my phone number so (that) . . . .
9. She sang a lullaby so (that) the baby . . . .
10. It's winter. Yesterday I put on two pairs of socks under my boots so (that) . . . .

□ **EXERCISE 35—ORAL/WRITTEN:** Using the given words, make sentences about yourself, your friends, your family, your classes, today's weather, current events in the world, etc.

1. now that
2. therefore
3. inasmuch as
4. as (meaning *because*)
5. consequently
6. so (meaning *therefore*)
7. since (meaning *because*)
8. as long as (meaning *because*)
9. in order to
10. so that
11. so . . . that
12. such . . . that
13. because
14. because of
15. due to
16. due to the fact that

8-12 REDUCTION OF ADVERB CLAUSES TO MODIFYING PHRASES: INTRODUCTION

In Chapter 6, we discussed changing adjective clauses to modifying phrases. (See Chart 6-13.) Some adverb clauses may also be changed to modifying phrases, and the ways in which the changes are made are the same:

(1) Omit the subject of the dependent clause and the **be** form of the verb.

    (a) ADVERB CLAUSE: *While **I was walking** to class, I ran into an old friend.*

    (b) MODIFYING PHRASE: *While **walking** to class, I ran into an old friend.*

(2) Or, if there is no **be** form of a verb, omit the subject and change the verb to **-ing**.

    (c) ADVERB CLAUSE: *Before **I left** for work, I ate breakfast.*

    (d) MODIFYING PHRASE: *Before **leaving** for work, I ate breakfast.*

An adverb clause can be changed to a modifying phrase ONLY WHEN THE SUBJECT OF THE ADVERB CLAUSE AND THE SUBJECT OF THE MAIN CLAUSE ARE THE SAME. *A modifying phrase* that is the reduction of an adverb clause *modifies the subject* of the main clause. No change is possible if the subjects of the adverb clause and the main clause are different.

    (e) CHANGE POSSIBLE: While **I** was sitting in class, **I** fell asleep.

                           While sitting in class, **I** fell asleep.

    (f) CHANGE POSSIBLE: While **Ann** was sitting in class, **she** fell asleep.

                           While sitting in class, **Ann** fell asleep.

    (g) NO CHANGE POSSIBLE: While **the teacher** was lecturing to the class, **I** fell asleep.*

    (h) NO CHANGE POSSIBLE: While **we** were walking home, **a frog** hopped across the road in

                                   front of us.

"While lecturing to the class, **I fell asleep." means "While **I** was lecturing to the class, **I** fell asleep."*

8-13 CHANGING TIME CLAUSES TO MODIFYING PHRASES

(a) CLAUSE: ***Since Mary came to this country***, she has made many friends. (b) PHRASE: ***Since coming to this country***, Mary has made many friends.	Adverb clauses beginning with **after**, **before**, **while**, and **since** can be changed to modifying phrases.
(c) CLAUSE: ***After he (had) finished his homework***, he went to bed. (d) PHRASE: ***After finishing his homework***, he went to bed. (e) PHRASE: ***After having finished his homework***, he went to bed.	In (c): There is no difference in meaning between *After he finished* and *After he had finished*. (See Chart 1-17.) In (d) and (e): There is no difference in meaning between *After finishing* and *After having finished*.
(f) PHRASE: He went to bed ***after finishing his homework***.	A modifying phrase may follow the main clause, as in (f).

☐ **EXERCISE 36:** Change the adverb clauses to modifying phrases if possible. Make no change if the subjects of the two clauses in the sentence are different.

1. While Joe was driving to school yesterday, he had an accident.
   → *While driving to school yesterday, Joe had an accident.*
2. While I was watching TV last night, the telephone rang. (*no change*)
3. Before I came to class, I had a cup of coffee.
4. Before the student came to class, the teacher had already given a quiz.
5. Since I came here, I have learned a lot of English.
6. After he (had) finished breakfast, he left the house and went to his office.
7. While I was living in Burma last year, I learned many things about Burmese customs.
8. Jennifer looked in the rearview mirror before she drove onto the main road.
9. Since he entered the Institute of Technology, Michael has begun to feel confident about his future.
10. While I was walking down the street, a car swerved to avoid a dog and almost drove onto the sidewalk.

☐ **EXERCISE 37:** Change the adverb clauses to modifying phrases if possible. Make no change if the subjects of the two clauses in the sentence are different.

1. Before I went to Yellowstone Park last summer, I had never seen a black bear in the wild.
2. After she (had) completed her shopping, she went home.
3. Alex hurt his back while he was chopping wood.
4. You should always read a contract before you sign your name.
5. After the children get home from school, our house buzzes with their many activities.
6. The Wilsons have experienced many changes in their lifestyle since they adopted twins.
7. While I was trying to get to sleep last night, a mosquito kept buzzing in my ear.

8. Before the waiter came to our table, I had already made up my mind to order the fried shrimp.
9. Since I arrived here, I have found an apartment, registered for school, explored the city, and made some new friends.
10. After I heard Mary describe how cold it gets in Minnesota in the winter, I decided not to go there for my vacation in January.
11. While Susan was climbing the mountain, she lost her footing and fell onto a ledge several feet below.
12. Before you ask the librarian for help, you should make every effort to find the materials yourself.

8-14 EXPRESSING THE IDEA OF "DURING THE SAME TIME" IN MODIFYING PHRASES

(a) *While **I was walking*** down the street, ***I*** ran into an old friend. (b) *While **walking*** down the street, ***I*** ran into an old friend. (c) ***Walking*** down the street, ***I*** ran into an old friend. (d) ***Hiking*** through the woods yesterday, ***we*** saw a bear. (e) ***Pointing*** to the sentence on the board, ***the teacher*** explained the meaning of modifying phrases.	Sometimes ***while*** is omitted but the ***-ing*** phrase at the beginning of the sentence gives the same meaning (i.e., "during the same time"). (a), (b), and (c) have the same meaning.

8-15 EXPRESSING CAUSE AND EFFECT RELATIONSHIPS IN MODIFYING PHRASES

(f) ***Because she needed*** some money to buy a book, ***Sue*** cashed a check. (g) ***Needing*** some money to buy a book, ***Sue*** cashed a check. (h) ***Because he lacked*** the necessary qualifications, ***he*** was not considered for the job. (i) ***Lacking*** the necessary qualifications, ***he*** was not considered for the job.	Often an ***-ing*** phrase at the beginning of a sentence gives the meaning of "because." (f) and (g) have the same meaning. ***Because*** is not used in a modifying phrase. It is omitted, but the resulting phrase expresses a cause and effect relationship.
(j) ***Having seen*** that movie before, ***I don't want*** to go again. (k) ***Having seen*** that movie before, ***I didn't want*** to go again.	***Having*** + *past participle* gives the meaning not only of "because" but also of "before."
(l) ***Because she was unable*** to afford a car, ***she*** bought a bicycle. (m) ***Being unable*** to afford a car, ***she*** bought a bicycle. (n) ***Unable*** to afford a car, ***she*** bought a bicycle.	A form of ***be*** in the adverb clause is often changed to ***being***. The use of ***being*** makes the cause and effect relationship clear.

☐ **EXERCISE 38:** Discuss the meaning of the following sentences. Which ones give the meaning of *because*? Which ones give the meaning of *while*? Do some of the sentences give the idea of both *because* and *while*?

1. Sitting on the airplane and watching the clouds pass beneath me, I let my thoughts wander to the new experiences that were in store for me during the next two years of living abroad.

2. Being a self-supporting widow with three children, she has no choice but to work.

3. Lying on her bed in peace and quiet, she soon forgot her troubles.

4. Having already spent all of his last paycheck, he does not have any more money to live on for the rest of the month.

5. Watching the children's energetic play, I felt like an old man even though I am only forty.

6. Having brought up ten children of their own, the Smiths may be considered experts on child behavior.

7. Being totally surprised by his proposal of marriage, Carol could not find the words to reply.

8. Driving to my grandparents' house last night, we saw a young woman who was selling flowers. We stopped so that we could get some flowers for my grandmother.

9. Struggling against fatigue, I forced myself to put one foot in front of the other.

10. Having guessed at the correct answers for a good part of the test, I did not expect to get a high score.

11. Realizing that I had made a dreadful mistake when I introduced him as George Johnson, I went over to him and apologized. I know his name is John George.

12. Tapping his fingers loudly on the desk top, he made his impatience and dissatisfaction known.

☐ **EXERCISE 39:** Change the adverb clauses to modifying phrases.

1. Because he didn't want to hurt her feelings, he didn't tell her the bad news. → *Not wanting to hurt her feelings, he didn't tell her the bad news.*

2. Because the little boy believed that no one loved him, he ran away from home.

3. Because she was not paying attention to where she was going, she stepped into a hole and sprained her ankle.

4. Because I had forgotten to bring a pencil to the examination, I had to borrow one.

5. Because she is a vegetarian, she does not eat meat.

6. Because he has already flunked out of school once, he is determined to succeed this time.

☐ **EXERCISE 40:** Combine the two sentences, making a modifying phrase out of the first sentence, if possible.

1. The children had nothing to do. They were bored.
   → *Having nothing to do, the children were bored.*
2. I heard that Judy was in the hospital. I called her family to find out what was wrong.
3. The little boy was trying his best not to cry. He swallowed hard and began to speak.
4. I did not want to inconvenience my friend by asking her to drive me to the airport. I decided to take a taxi.
5. I was sitting on a large rock at the edge of a mountain stream. I felt at peace with the world.
6. John had run a red traffic light. The police officer arrested him.
7. I am a married man. I have many responsibilities.
8. I was reading the paper last night. I saw an article on solar energy.
9. I had not understood what he said. I asked him to repeat the directions.
10. I was watching the children fly their kites in the park. Suddenly the wind blew my hat off my head.
11. Ann was convinced that she could never learn to play the piano. She stopped taking lessons.

☐ **EXERCISE 41:** Change the adverb clauses to modifying phrases.

1. Before I talked to you, I had never understood that formula.
2. Because he did not want to spend any more money this month, Alfred decided against going to a restaurant for dinner. He made himself a sandwich instead.
3. After I read the chapter four times, I finally understood the author's theory.
4. Because I remembered that everyone makes mistakes, I softened my view of his seemingly inexcusable error.
5. Since he completed his Bachelor's degree, he has had three jobs, each one better than the last.
6. While I was traveling across the United States, I could not help being impressed by the great differences in terrain.
7. Before he gained national fame, the union leader had been an electrician in a small town.
8. Because we were enjoying the cool evening breeze and listening to the sounds of nature, we lost track of time.
9. Because she had never flown in an airplane before, the little girl was surprised and a little frightened when her ears popped.
10. Before he became vice-president of marketing and sales, Peter McKay worked as a sales representative.

8–16 USING *UPON* + *-ING* IN MODIFYING PHRASES

(a) **Upon reaching** the age of 21, I received my inheritance.	Modifying phrases beginning with **upon** + **-ing** usually have the same meaning as adverb clauses introduced by **when**. (a) and (b) have the same meaning.
(b) **When I reached** the age of 21, I received my inheritance.	
(c) **On reaching** the age of 21, I received my inheritance.	**Upon** can be shortened to **on**. (a), (b), and (c) all have the same meaning.

☐ **EXERCISE 42:** Using the given information, make sentences with **upon** + **-ing**.

1. When Tom saw his wife and child get off the airplane, he broke into a big smile.
   → *Upon seeing his wife and child get off the airplane, Tom broke into a big smile.*
2. When Tina crossed the marathon finish line, she fell in exhaustion.
3. When I looked in my wallet, I discovered I didn't have enough money to pay my restaurant bill.
4. I bowed my head when I met the king.
5. When Sam re-read the figures, he found that he had made a mistake.
6. When I got an appraisal of my coin collection, I was surprised how it had increased in value.
7. Mrs. Alexander nearly fainted when she learned that she had won the lottery.
8. When you finish the examination, bring your paper to the front of the room.
9. When the police found the thief, they also found the stolen merchandise.
10. When I was elected a member of the club, I found that the dues were more than I could afford.

☐ **EXERCISE 43:** Complete the following. Add commas where needed.

1. Before going to class _____
2. After coming home from the party _____
3. Having failed the entrance examination _____
4. Since arriving in this city _____
5. Driving home last night _____
6. Being new on the job _____
7. After traveling for four hours _____
8. Receiving no answer when he knocked on the door _____

9. Having been told that there were no more rooms available in the dormitory _____

10. Upon finishing this assignment _____

11. Being the largest city in the United States _____

12. Upon hearing a loud crash and feeling the house shake _____

□ **EXERCISE 44—WRITTEN:** Complete the following. Punctuate carefully.

1. After having finished my . . . .
2. Before going to . . . .
3. Since coming to . . . .
4. Sitting in the park the other day . . . .
5. Having heard a strange noise in the other room . . . .
6. Being only four years old . . . .
7. Being disturbed by the noise from the neighbor's apartment . . . .
8. Upon discovering her car had been stolen . . . .
9. Not having read the directions carefully . . . .
10. Exhausted by the long hours of work . . . .
11. Upon reaching our destination . . . .
12. Before leaving on vacation . . . .

□ **EXERCISE 45—ERROR ANALYSIS:** The errors in the following are adapted from student compositions. Test your skill by finding and correcting as many of the errors as possible.

1. The weather was such cold that I don't like to leave my apartment.

2. I have to study four hour every day because of my courses are difficult.

3. In the evening, I usually go downstairs for watching television.

4. On the third day of our voyage, we sailed across a rough sea before to reach the shore.

5. I can't understand the lectures in my psychology class, therefore my roommate lets me borrow her notes.

6. According to this legend, a man went in search of a hidden village, he finally found it after walk two hundred mile.

7. Because my country is located in a subtropical area, so the weather is hot.

8. I will stay at the united state for two more year. Because I want finish my degree before go home.

9. After graduating from college, my father wants me to join his business firm.

10. We were floating far from the beach, suddenly my mother cried out "shark! a shark is coming," we could see a black fin cutting the water and coming toward us, we are paralyzed with fear.

☐ **EXERCISE 46—WRITTEN:** Read today's newspaper. Find three articles—one on local news, one on national news, and one on international news—that you think are interesting. Read these articles several times, and then, without looking at the newspaper, summarize them. Use one paragraph for each summary. Be prepared to share your summaries orally with the rest of the class.

☐ **EXERCISE 47—PREPOSITIONS:** Supply appropriate prepositions.

1. I am grateful _____ you _____ your assistance.

2. The criminal escaped _____ prison.

3. Elizabeth is not content _____ the progress she is making.

4. Paul's comments were not relevant _____ the topic under discussion.

5. Have you decided _____ a date for your wedding yet?

6. My boots are made _____ leather.

7. I'm depending _____ you to finish this work for me.

8. Patricia applied _____ admission _____ the university.

9. Daniel dreamed _____ some of his childhood friends last night.

10. Mr. Miller dreams _____ owning his own business someday.

11. The accused woman was innocent _____ the crime with which she was charged.

12. Ms. Sanders is friendly _____ everyone.

13. Benjamin was proud _____ himself for winning the prize.

14. The secretary provided me _____ a great deal of information.

15. Ivan compared the wedding customs in his country _____ those in the United States.

□ **EXERCISE 48—PHRASAL VERBS:** Supply an appropriate preposition for each of the following two-word verbs.

1. A: Who do you take _____ the most, your father or your mother?

   B: My mother, I think. I can see many similarities between the two of us.

2. A: Hey, cut it _____, you guys! I'm trying to sleep.

   B: What's the matter? Are we making too much noise?

3. A: Could I help you clean _____?

   B: Sure. Would you mind taking _____ the garbage?

4. A: Miss Ward, what seems to be the problem?

   B: Well, Doctor, for the last two days I haven't been able to keep any food down. Every time I try to eat something, I throw _____ soon afterward.

5. A: Where's my jacket?

   B: I hung it _____ in the closet.

6. A: Why are you going to see Professor Kelly?

   B: He called me _____ to talk about my research project.

7. A: Is that man's story true?

   B: Yes. A newspaper reporter checked _____ his story and found that it was true.

8. A: The city government is planning to redevelop a large section of the inner city.

   B: What's going to happen to the buildings that are there now?

   A: They are going to be torn _____.

9. A: Some people tried to crash our party last night.

   B: What did you do?

   A: We kicked them _____.

10. A: The test is about to begin. Please put _____ all of your books and notebooks.

CHAPTER *9*

Showing Relationships Between Ideas—Part II

9–1 EXPRESSING UNEXPECTED RESULT: USING *EVEN THOUGH*

(a) *Because* the weather was cold, I *didn't go* swimming. (b) *Even though* the weather was cold, I *went* swimming. (c) *Because* I wasn't tired, I *didn't go* to bed. (d) *Even though* I wasn't tired, I *went* to bed.	*Because* is used to express expected results. *Even though* is used to express unexpected results.
	Like *because*, *even though* introduces an adverb clause.

☐ **EXERCISE 1:** Complete the sentences by using either *even though* or *because*.

1. Tim's in good shape physically _____*even though*_____ he doesn't get much exercise.

2. Jerry's in good shape physically _____*because*_____ he gets a lot of exercise.

3. _____ Sue is a good student, she received a scholarship.

4. _____ Ann is a good student, she didn't receive a scholarship.

5. _____ it was raining, we went for a walk.

6. _____ it was raining, we didn't go for a walk.

7. This letter was delivered _____ it didn't have enough postage.

8. That letter was returned to the sender _____ it didn't have enough postage.

9. Susan didn't learn Spanish _____ she lived in Mexico for a year.

10. Joe speaks Spanish well _____ he lived in Mexico for a year.

11. A newborn kangaroo can find its mother's pouch _____ its eyes are not yet open.

12. Some people protest certain commercial fishing operations _____ dolphins, considered to be highly intelligent mammals, are killed unnecessarily.

☐ **EXERCISE 2—ORAL (BOOKS CLOSED):** Use *even though*. Be sure to begin your response with either *yes* or *no*.

Example: It was raining. Did you go to the zoo anyway?
Response: Yes, even though it was raining, I went to the zoo.

Example: You studied hard. Did you pass the test?
Response: No, even though I studied hard, I didn't pass the test.

1. You weren't tired. Did you go to bed anyway?
2. The telephone rang many times, but did John wake up?
3. The food was terrible. Did you eat it anyway?
4. You didn't study. Did you pass the test anyway?
5. The weather is terrible today. Did you stay home?
6. You fell down the stairs. Did you get hurt?
7. You took a nap. Do you still feel tired?
8. You told the truth, but did anyone believe you?
9. You took an aspirin. Do you still have a headache?
10. You turned on the air conditioner. Is it still hot in here?
11. You mailed the letter three days ago. Has it arrived yet?
12. You have a lot of money. Can you afford to buy an airplane?
13. Your grandmother is ninety years old. Is she still young at heart?
14. (. . .) told a joke. You didn't understand it. Did you laugh anyway?
15. Your house burned down. You lost your job. Your wife/husband left you. Are you still cheerful?

9–2 SHOWING OPPOSITION (UNEXPECTED RESULT)

<table>
<tr><td colspan="3">All of the following example sentences have the same meaning.</td></tr>
<tr>
<td>ADVERB
CLAUSES</td>
<td>even though
although
though</td>
<td>(a) Even though it was cold, I went swimming.
(b) Although it was cold, I went swimming.
(c) Though it was cold, I went swimming.</td>
</tr>
<tr>
<td>CONJUNCTIONS</td>
<td>but . . . anyway
but . . . still
yet . . . still</td>
<td>(d) It was cold, but I went swimming anyway.
(e) It was cold, but I still went swimming.
(f) It was cold, yet I still went swimming.</td>
</tr>
<tr>
<td>TRANSITIONS</td>
<td>nevertheless
nonetheless
however</td>
<td>(g) It was cold. Nevertheless, I went swimming.
(h) It was cold. Nonetheless, I went swimming.
(i) It was cold. However, I still went swimming.</td>
</tr>
<tr>
<td>PREPOSITIONS</td>
<td>despite
in spite of</td>
<td>(j) I went swimming despite the cold weather.
(k) I went swimming in spite of the cold weather.</td>
</tr>
</table>

☐ **EXERCISE 3:** Combine the ideas in the two sentences. Use the given words. Discuss correct punctuation. Use the negative if necessary to make a logical statement.

1. *We went to the zoo. It was raining.*
   even though
   but . . . anyway
   nevertheless
   in spite of
   because

2. *His grades were low. He was admitted to the university.*
   although
   yet . . . still
   nonetheless
   despite
   because of

☐ **EXERCISE 4:** Complete the following with your own words. Add commas where appropriate.

1. I had a cold but I _____ anyway.

2. Even though I had a cold I _____

3. Although I didn't study _____

4. I didn't study but _____ anyway.

5. I got an "A" on the test even though _____

6. Even though Howard is a careful driver _____

7. Even though the food they served for dinner tasted terrible _____

8. My shirt still has coffee stains on it even though _____

9. I still trust him even though _____

10. Even though he was drowning no one _____

11. Although I tried to be very careful _____

12. Even though Ruth is one of my best friends _____

13. It's still hot in here even though _____

14. Even though I had a big breakfast _____

☐ **EXERCISE 5:** Change the sentences by using *nevertheless*.

1. He wasn't tired, but he went to bed anyway.★
   → *He wasn't tired. Nevertheless, he went to bed.*
2. She wasn't hungry, but she ate two dishes of ice cream anyway.
3. Even though Jack wasn't feeling good, he went to class.
4. I still trust him even though he lied to me.
5. Sally was very sad, but she smiled and pretended to be having a good time.
6. George did not panic even though he was alone and lost in the woods.
7. Elizabeth is not a citizen of the United States, but she has to pay income taxes anyway.
8. Even though Henry Johnson is an honest politician, I would never vote for him because I do not agree with his positions on foreign policy.
9. The crime rate has continued to rise even though the local police department has implemented several new crime prevention programs.
10. Even though math has always been easy for him, he understands that it is not easy for everyone. As a result, he is a good teacher.

☐ **EXERCISE 6:** Give sentences with the same meaning by using *in spite of* or *despite*.

1. Even though her grades were low, she was admitted to the university.
   → *In spite of her low grades,*
   → *Despite her low grades,*
   → *In spite of the fact that her grades were low,* she was admitted to the
   → *Despite the fact that her grades were low,* university.

★*Nevertheless* and *but . . . anyway* have the same meaning: *but . . . anyway* occurs primarily in speaking, and *nevertheless* occurs primarily in writing.

2. I like living in the dorm even though it is noisy.

3. Even though the work was hard, they enjoyed themselves.

4. They wanted to climb the mountain even though it was dangerous.

5. Although the weather was extremely hot, they went jogging in the park.

6. He is unhappy even though he has a vast fortune.

□ **EXERCISE 7—WRITTEN:** Complete the following. Punctuate carefully. (Correct punctuation is not indicated in the given cues.) Capitalize as necessary.

1. I didn't . . . but . . . anyway.

2. He is very old yet he still . . . .

3. . . . nevertheless we arrived on schedule.

4. Even though she wanted . . . .

5. I wanted . . . however I . . . because . . . .

6. The teacher . . . even though . . . .

7. Although . . . only . . . years old . . . .

8. She never went to school however she . . . despite her lack of education.

9. Despite the fact that my . . . .

10. I have decided to . . . even though . . . .

9–3   SHOWING DIRECT OPPOSITION

ADVERB CLAUSES	*whereas* *while*	(a) Mary is rich, ***whereas** John is poor.* (b) Mary is rich, ***while** John is poor.* (c) John is poor, ***while** Mary is rich.* (d) ***Whereas** Mary is rich,* John is poor.	***Whereas*** and ***while*** are used to show direct opposition: "this" is exactly the opposite of "that." ***Whereas*** and ***while*** may be used with the idea of either clause with no difference in meaning. Note: A comma is usually used even if the adverb clause comes second.
CONJUCTIONS	*but*	(e) Mary is rich, ***but*** John is poor. (f) John is poor, ***but*** Mary is rich.	In (e) through (j): As with ***whereas*** and ***while***, it does not make any difference which idea comes first and which idea comes second. The two ideas are directly opposite.
TRANSITIONS	*however* *on the other hand*	(g) Mary is rich; ***however***, John is poor. (h) John is poor; ***however***, Mary is rich. (i) Mary is rich. John, ***on the other hand***, is poor. (j) John is poor. Mary, ***on the other hand***, is rich.	

☐ **EXERCISE 8:** Complete the following. Discuss other ways of expressing the same idea by moving the position of *whereas* or *while*.

1. Some people are fat, whereas . . . *others are thin. (Whereas some people are fat, others are thin.) (Some people are thin, whereas others are fat.)*
2. Some people are tall, whereas . . . .
3. Some people prefer to live in the country, while . . . .
4. While some people know only their native language, ...
5. A mouse is small, whereas . . . .
6. The climate at sea level at the equator is always hot, whereas the climate at the North and South poles . . . .
7. Some people . . . , while . . . .
8. Some countries . . . , whereas . . . .

☐ **EXERCISE 9:** Give sentences with the same meaning by using *however* or *on the other hand*. Punctuate carefully.

1. Florida has a warm climate, whereas Alaska has a cold climate.
2. While Fred is a good student, his brother is lazy.
3. Sue and Ron are expecting a child. Sue is hoping for a boy, whereas Ron is hoping for a girl.
4. Old people in my country usually live with their children, whereas the old in the United States often live by themselves.
5. In the United States, gambling casinos are not legal in most states, while in my country it is possible to gamble in any city or town.

☐ **EXERCISE 10—ORAL/WRITTEN:** What aspects of your country and the United States are in contrast? Use *while, whereas, however, on the other hand*.

1. Size?
2. Population?
3. Food?
4. Time of meals?
5. Climate?
6. Political system?
7. Economic system?
8. Educational system?
9. Religion?
10. Student life?

11. Coffee-tea?

12. Role of women?

13. Language?

14. Educational costs?

15. Medical care?

16. Family relationships?

17. Public transportation?

18. Length of history?

19. Dating customs?

20. Predictability of the weather?

9–4 EXPRESSING CONDITIONS IN ADVERB CLAUSES: "*IF* CLAUSES"

(a) *If it rains*, the streets get wet.	"*If* clauses" (also called *adverb clauses of condition*) present possible conditions. The main clause expresses results. In (a): POSSIBLE CONDITION = *it rains* RESULT = *the streets get wet*
(b) *If it rains tomorrow*, I will take my umbrella.	A present tense, not a future tense, is used in an "*if* clause" even though the verb in the "*if* clause" may refer to a future event or situation, as in (b).*
WORDS THAT INTRODUCE ADVERB CLAUSES OF CONDITION ("*IF* CLAUSES"):	

if	*in case (that)*	*only if*
whether or not	*in the event (that)*	*providing (that)*
even if	*unless*	*provided (that)*

*See Chapter 10 for uses of other verb forms in sentences with "*if* clauses."

□ **EXERCISE 11:** Make sentences from the given possibilities. Use *if*.

1. It may be cold tomorrow.
   → *If it's cold tomorrow, I'm going to stay home.*
   → *If it's cold tomorrow, let's go skating.*
   → *If it's cold tomorrow, you should wear your wool sweater.*
   → *We can't go on a picnic if it's cold tomorrow.*

2. Maybe it will be hot tomorrow.

3. Robert will probably study for the test.

4. Maybe you will have some free time tomorrow.

5. The teacher may be absent tomorrow.

6. Maybe you won't do your homework tonight.

7. Maybe you will lock yourself out of your apartment.

8. Maybe the sun will be shining when you get up tomorrow morning.

9–5 ADVERB CLAUSES OF CONDITION: USING *WHETHER OR NOT* AND *EVEN IF*

WHETHER OR NOT (a) I'm going to go swimming tomorrow **whether or not it is cold**. (OR: **whether it is cold or not**.)	**Whether or not** expresses the idea that *neither this condition nor that condition matters*; the result will be the same. In (a): If it is cold, I'm going swimming. If it is not cold, I'm going swimming. I don't care about the temperature. It doesn't matter.
EVEN IF (b) I have decided to go swimming tomorrow. **Even if the weather is cold**, I'm going to go swimming.	Sentences with **even if** are close in meaning to those with **whether or not**. **Even if** gives the idea that a particular condition does not matter. The result will not change.
COMPARE: (c) **If** Ann studies hard, she *will pass* the exam. (d) **Even if** Mary studies hard, she *won't pass* the exam.	"**If** clauses" are followed by expected results, as in (c). CONDITION: *Ann studies* EXPECTED RESULT: *she passes the exam* "**Even if** clauses" are followed by unexpected results, as in (d). CONDITION: *Mary studies* UNEXPECTED RESULT: *she doesn't pass the exam*

☐ **EXERCISE 12:** Use the given information to complete the sentences.

1. *Usually people need to graduate from school to get a good job. But it's different for Ed. Maybe Ed will graduate from school, and maybe he won't. It doesn't matter because he has a good job waiting for him in his father's business.*
   a. Ed will get a good job whether or not . . . *he graduates.*
   b. Ed will get a good job even if . . . *he doesn't graduate.*
2. *Sam's uncle tells a lot of jokes. Sometimes they're funny, and sometimes they're not. It doesn't matter.*
   a. Sam laughs at the jokes whether . . . or not.
   b. Sam laughs at the jokes even if . . . .
3. *Maybe you are finished with the exam, and maybe you're not. It doesn't matter. The time is up.*
   a. You have to hand in your examination paper whether . . . or not.
   b. You have to hand in your examination paper even if . . . .
4. *It might snow, or it might not. We don't want to go camping in the snow, but it doesn't matter.*
   a. We're going to go camping in the mountains whether . . . or not.
   b. We're going to go camping in the mountains even if . . . .

5. *Max's family doesn't have enough money to send him to college. He would like to get a scholarship, but it doesn't matter because he's saved some money to go to school and has a part-time job.*
   a. Max can go to school whether or not . . . .
   b. Max can go to school even if . . . .

6. *Sometimes the weather is hot, sometimes the weather is cold. It doesn't matter. My grandfather always wears his gray sweater.*
   a. My grandfather wears his gray sweater whether or not . . . .
   b. My grandfather always wears his gray sweater even if . . . .

7. *Your approval doesn't matter to me.*
   a. I'm going to marry Harry whether . . . or not.
   b. I'm going to marry Harry even if . . . .

Complete the following.

8. I'm really angry! Maybe he'll apologize and maybe he won't. It doesn't matter. Even if . . . , I won't forgive him!

9. I'm exhausted. Please don't wake me up even if . . . .

10. I'm not going to . . . even if . . . .

11. Even if . . . , I'm going to . . . .

12. I'm going to . . . whether or not . . . .

9–6 ADVERB CLAUSES OF CONDITION: USING *IN CASE (THAT)* AND *IN THE EVENT (THAT)*

(a) I'll be at my uncle's house *in case you (should) need to reach me.*	*In case that* and *in the event that* express the idea that something probably won't happen, but it might.*
(b) *In the event that* you (should) need to reach me, I'll be at my uncle's house.	*in case/in the event that* = *if by any chance this should happen* Notes: *In the event that* is more formal than *in case*. The use of *should* in the adverb clause emphasizes the speaker's uncertainty that something will happen.

In case that and *in the event that* introduce adverb clauses. *In case of* and *in the event of* have the same meaning, but they are prepositions followed by a noun object:
   In case of trouble, call the police. = In case (that) there is trouble, call the police.
   In the event of rain, the picnic will be cancelled. = In the event (that) it rains, the picnic will be cancelled.

☐ **EXERCISE 13:** Show the relationship between the ideas in the two sentences by using *in case* and/or *in the event that*.

1. You probably won't need to get in touch with me, but maybe you will. If so, I'll give you my phone number.
   → *I'll give you my phone number in case you (should) need to get in touch with me/in the event that you (should) need to get in touch with me.*

2. You probably won't need to see me, but maybe you will.
   If so, I'll be in my office tomorrow morning around ten.

3. I don't think you need any more information, but maybe you do.
   If so, you can call me.

4. You probably don't have any more questions, but maybe you do.
   If so, ask Dr. Smith.

5. You will probably be satisfied with your purchase, but maybe not.
   If not, you can return it to the store.

6. Jack probably won't call, but maybe he will.
   If so, please tell him that I'm at the library.

Complete the following.

7. I've told you all I know. In the event that you need more information, ...

8. It's a good idea for you to keep a written record of your credit card numbers in case . . . .

9. I think I'd better clean up the apartment in case . . . .

10. I have my umbrella with me just in case . . . .

11. In the event that the two countries agree to a peace treaty, ...

12. I'll try to be there on time, but in case I'm not, ...

13. According to the manufacturer's guarantee, I should return my new camera to the factory in the event that . . . .

9–7 ADVERB CLAUSE OF CONDITION: USING *UNLESS*

(a) I'll go swimming tomorrow ***unless*** *it's cold.* (b) I'll go swimming tomorrow ***if*** *it isn't cold.*	***unless*** = ***if . . . not*** In (a): *unless it's cold* = *if it isn't cold* (a) and (b) have the same meaning.

☐ **EXERCISE 14:** Make sentences with the same meaning by using ***unless***.

1. I will go to the zoo if it isn't cold.
   → *I will go to the zoo unless it's cold.*

2. You can't travel abroad if you don't have a passport.

3. You can't get a driver's license if you're not at least sixteen years old.

4. If I don't get some film, I won't be able to take pictures when Ann and Rob get here.

5. You'll get hungry during class if you don't eat breakfast.

☐ **EXERCISE 15**: Complete the sentences.

1. Your letter won't be delivered unless . . . *it has the correct postage.*
2. I'm sorry, but you can't see the doctor unless . . . .
3. I can't graduate from school unless . . . .
4. . . . unless you put it in the refrigerator.
5. Unless it rains, ...
6. Certain species of animals will soon become extinct unless . . . .
7. . . . unless I get a raise in salary.
8. Tomorrow I'm going to . . . unless . . . .
9. The political situation in . . . will continue to deteriorate unless . . . .
10. Ivan never volunteers in class. He doesn't say anything unless . . . .
11. Unless you . . . .

9-8 ADVERB CLAUSES OF CONDITION: USING *ONLY IF* AND *PROVIDING/PROVIDED THAT*

(a) The picnic will be cancelled *only if it rains.* If it's windy, we'll go on the picnic. If it's cold, we'll go on the picnic. If it's damp and foggy, we'll go on the picnic. If it's unbearably hot, we'll go on the picnic.	*Only if* expresses the idea that there is only one condition that will cause a particular result.
(b) *Only if* it rains **will the picnic be cancelled**.	When *only if* begins a sentence, the subject and verb of the main clause are inverted, as in (b).
(c) *Providing/provided (that)* no one has any *further questions*, the meeting will be adjourned.	*Providing that* and *provided that* = *if* or *only if*.

☐ **EXERCISE 16**: Use the given information to complete the sentences.

1. *John must get a scholarship in order to go to school. That is the only condition under which he can go to school. If he doesn't get one, he can't go to school.*
   He can go to school only if . . . *he gets a scholarship.*
2. *You have to have an invitation in order to go to the party. That is the only condition under which you will be admitted. If you don't have an invitation, you can't go.*
   You can go to the party only if . . . .
3. *You have to have a student visa in order to study here. Unless you have a student visa, you can't go to school here.*
   You can attend this school only if . . . .

4. *Jimmy's mother doesn't want him to chew gum, but sometimes he chews it anyway.*
   Jimmy . . . only if he's sure his mother won't find out.

5. *If you want to go to the movie, we'll go. If you don't want to go, we won't go.*
   We . . . only if you want to.

6. *The temperature has to reach 32°F/0°C before water will freeze.*
   Water will freeze only if . . . .

7. *You must study hard. Then you will pass the exam.*
   Only if you study hard . . . .

8. *You have to have a ticket. Then you can get into the soccer stadium.*
   Only if you have a ticket . . . .

9. *My parents make me finish my homework before I can watch TV in the evening.*
   Only if my homework is finished . . . .

10. *I have to get a job. Then I will have enough money to go to school.*
    Only if I get a job . . . .

Complete the following.

11. Yes, John, I will marry you—but only if _____

12. I _____ only if _____

13. Only if _____

☐ **EXERCISE 17:** Give sentences with the same meaning by using *only if* and **unless**.

1. If you don't study hard, you won't pass the test.
   → *You will pass the test only if you study hard.*
   → *You won't pass the test unless you study hard.*

2. If I don't get a job, I can't pay my bills.

3. Your clothes won't get clean if you don't use soap.

4. I can't take any pictures if I don't buy some film.

5. I don't wake up if the alarm clock doesn't ring.

☐ **EXERCISE 18:** Complete the sentences.

1. I will come to the meeting at City Hall providing that . . . *I can get a ride with someone.*

2. Only students can apply for this low-cost health insurance policy. You are eligible for the insurance provided that . . . .

3. I will take the six-thirty flight to Atlanta providing that . . . .

4. You will be admitted to the university providing that . . . .

5. Provided that no one objects, ...

☐ **EXERCISE 19:** Using the given words, combine the following two ideas.

It may or may not rain. The party will be held inside/outside.

1. if → *If it rains, the party will be held inside.*
   → *If it doesn't rain, the party will be held outside.*

2. whether or not   6. unless
3. even if   7. only if
4. in case   8. providing that
5. in the event that   9. provided that

9–9 EXPRESSING CONDITIONS: USING *OTHERWISE* AND *OR (ELSE)*

(a) I always eat breakfast. ***Otherwise***, I get hungry during class. (b) You'd better hurry. ***Otherwise***, you'll be late.	***Otherwise*** expresses the idea "if the opposite is true, then there will be a certain result." In (a): ***otherwise*** = *if I don't eat breakfast* In (b): ***otherwise*** = *if you don't hurry*
(c) I always eat breakfast, ***or (else)*** I get hungry during class. (d) You'd better hurry, ***or (else)*** you'll be late.	***Or else*** and ***otherwise*** have the same meaning.
	Otherwise is a transition. ***Or (else)*** is a conjunction.

☐ **EXERCISE 20:** Make sentences with the same meaning by using ***otherwise***.

1. If I don't call my mother, she'll start worrying about me.
   → *I am going to/should/had better/have to/must call my mother. Otherwise, she'll start worrying about me.*
2. If I don't wash my clothes tonight, I won't have any clean clothes to wear tomorrow.

3. If you don't leave now, you'll be late for class.

4. If you don't go to bed, your cold will get worse.

5. Unless you have a ticket, you can't get into the theater.

6. You can't enter that country unless you have a passport.

7. If Tom doesn't get a job soon, his family won't have enough money for food.

8. Mary can go to school only if she gets a scholarship.

9. Only if you speak both Japanese and Chinese fluently will you be considered for that job.

□ **EXERCISE 21—WRITTEN:** Complete the following. Punctuate correctly. (Correct punctuation is not indicated in the cues.) Use capital letters where appropriate.

1. I am going to . . . even if . . . .

2. We have no choice we have to . . . whether . . . .

3. I will go to . . . providing that . . . .

4. . . . is very inconsiderate he plays his record player even if . . . .

5. I can't . . . unless . . . .

6. Tomorrow I'd better . . . otherwise . . . .

7. You should . . . in case . . . .

8. I will . . . only if . . . .

9. I will . . . unless . . . .

10. . . . must . . . otherwise . . . .

9–10 SUMMARY OF RELATIONSHIP WORDS: CAUSE AND EFFECT, OPPOSITION, CONDITION

	ADVERB CLAUSE WORDS		TRANSITIONS	CONJUNCTIONS	PREPOSITIONS
CAUSE AND EFFECT	*because* *since* *now that* *as*	*as/so long as* *inasmuch as* *so (that)*	*therefore* *consequently*	*so* *for*	*because of* *due to*
OPPOSITION	*even though* *although* *though*	*whereas* *while*	*nevertheless* *nonetheless* *however* *on the other hand*	*but (. . . anyway)* *yet (. . . still)*	*despite* *in spite of*
CONDITION	*if* *unless* *only if* *even if* *whether or not*	*provided (that)* *providing (that)* *in case (that)* *in the event (that)*	*otherwise*	*or (else)*	*in case of* *in the event of*

□ **EXERCISE 22:** Using the two ideas of *to study* and *to pass or fail the exam*, complete the following. Punctuate correctly. Add capital letters as necessary.

1. Because I did not study _____

2. I failed the exam because _____

3. Although I studied _____

4. I did not study   therefore _____

5. I did not study   however _____

6. I studied   nevertheless _____

7. Even though I did not study _____

8. I did not study   so _____

9. Since I did not study _____

10. If I study for the test _____

11. Unless I study for the test _____

12. I will pass the test providing that _____

13. I must study   otherwise _____

14. Even if I study _____

15. I did not study   consequently _____

16. I did not study   nonetheless _____

17. Inasmuch as I did not study for the test _____

18. I will probably fail the test whether _____

19. I failed the exam   for _____

20. I have to study so that _____

21. Only if I study _____

22. I studied hard   yet _____

23. You'd better study or else _____

□ **EXERCISE 23:** Using the ideas of *to be hungry* (or *not to be hungry*) and *to eat breakfast* (or *not to eat breakfast*), complete the following. Punctuate and capitalize correctly.

1. Because I was not hungry this morning _____

2. Because I ate breakfast this morning _____ now.

3. Because I was hungry this morning _____

4. I did not eat breakfast this morning even though _____

5. Although I was hungry this morning _____

6. I was hungry this morning   therefore _____

7. I was hungry this morning   nevertheless _____

8. I was so hungry this morning _____

9. I was not hungry this morning but _____

10. I ate breakfast this morning even though _____

11. Since I did not eat breakfast this morning _____

12. I ate breakfast this morning   nonetheless _____

13. I was not hungry   so _____

14. Even though I did not eat breakfast this morning _____

15. I never eat breakfast unless _____

16. I always eat breakfast whether or not _____

17. I eat breakfast even if _____

18. Now that I have eaten breakfast _____

19. I eat breakfast only if _____

20. I ate breakfast this morning   yet _____

21. Even if I am hungry _____

22. I was not hungry   however _____

☐ **EXERCISE 24—ORAL:** Using the given words, combine the following two ideas. The time is *now*, so use present and future tenses.

    (a) **to go (or not to go) to the beach**   (b) **hot, cold, nice weather**

    1. because → *Because the weather is cold, we aren't going to go to the beach.*
                → *We're going to go to the beach because the weather is hot.*

2. so . . . that	13. since
3. so	14. but . . . anyway
4. nevertheless	15. unless
5. despite	16. therefore
6. now that	17. only if
7. once	18. nonetheless
8. although	19. in spite of
9. because of	20. even if
10. consequently	21. yet . . . still
11. as soon as	22. whether . . . or not
12. such . . . that	23. as long as . . . let's/why don't

☐ **EXERCISE 25:** Complete the following. Add necessary punctuation and capitalization.

1. While some people are optimists _____

2. Even though he drank a glass of water _____ still _____

3. Even if she invites me to her party _____

4. I have never been to Hawaii my parents however _____

5. I couldn't _____ for my arms were full of packages.

6. I need to borrow some money so that _____

7. The airport was closed due to fog therefore _____

8. _____ therefore the airport was closed.

9. As soon as the violinist played the last note at the concert _____

10. Since neither my roommate nor I know how to cook _____

11. I am not a superstitious person nevertheless _____

12. The crops will fail unless _____

13. Just as I was getting ready to eat my dinner last night _____

14. Now that she is married _____

15. We must work quickly otherwise _____

16. Some children are noisy and wild my brother's children on the other hand _____

☐ **EXERCISE 26—WRITTEN:** Complete the following. Punctuate and capitalize correctly.

1. According to the newspaper, now that . . . .
2. Ever since I can remember . . . .
3. Although my . . . .
4. The United States . . . whereas . . . .
5. I was tired however I . . . because . . . .
6. I . . . my friend on the other hand . . . .
7. You must . . . whether . . . .

8. Even though I . . . .

9. Since my apartment is very small . . . .

10. In spite of the fact that . . . .

11. . . . therefore I have decided to . . . .

12. . . . nevertheless I could not understand what . . . .

□ **EXERCISE 27—ERROR ANALYSIS:** Try to find and correct the errors in the following.

1. Unless I study very hard, I will pass all of my exams.

2. My shoes and pants got muddy. Even though I walked carefully through the wet streets.

3. My neighborhood is quiet and safe however I always lock my doors.

4. Although I usually don't like french food, but I liked the food I had at the french restaurant last night.

5. Although my room in the dormitory is very small, but I like it. Because it is a place where I can be by myself and studying in peace and quiet.

6. Despite I prefer to be a history teacher, I am studying in the Business School in order for I can get a job in industry.

7. A little girl approached the cage however when the tiger shows its teeth and growls she run to her mother. Because she was frightened.

8. Many of the people working to save our environment think that they are fighting a losing battle. Because big business and the government have not joined together to eliminate pollution.

□ **EXERCISE 28:** Complete the following.

1. If what he said _____

2. Because the man who _____

3. Even though she didn't understand what _____

4. Now that all of the students who _____

5. Since the restaurant where we _____

9–11 GIVING EXAMPLES

(a) There are many interesting places to visit in the city. **For example**, the botanical garden has numerous displays of plants from all over the world.	**For example** and **for instance** have the same meaning. They are often used as transitions.
(b) There are many interesting places to visit in the city. The art museum, **for instance**, has an excellent collection of modern paintings.	
(c) There are many interesting places to visit in the city, **e.g.**, the botanical garden and the art museum.	**e.g.** = *for example* (**e.g.** is an abbreviation of the Latin phrase *exempli gratia*.)* (c) and (d) have the same meaning.
(d) There are many interesting places to visit in the city, **for example**, the botanical garden or the art museum.	
(e) I prefer to wear casual clothes, **such as** jeans and a sweatshirt.	**such as** = *for example*
(f) Some countries, **such as** Brazil and Canada, are big.	(f), (g), and (h) have essentially the same meaning even though the pattern varies.**
(g) Countries **such as** Brazil and Canada are big.	
(h) **Such** countries **as** Brazil and Canada are big.	

*Punctuation note: Periods are used with **e.g.** in American English. Periods are generally not used with **eg** in British English.
**Punctuation note:
    (1) When the "**such as** phrase" can be omitted without substantially changing the meaning of the sentence, commas are used.
        Example: Some words, such as *know* and *see*, are verbs. (*Commas are used.*)
    (2) No commas are used when the "**such as** phrase" gives essential information about the noun to which it refers.
        Example: Words such as *know* and *see* are verbs. (*No commas are used.*)

□ **EXERCISE 29:** Complete the following. Use **such as**.

    1. You need a hobby. There are many hobbies you might enjoy, ___such as___ _ceramics or stamp collecting._

    2. There are certain products that almost everyone buys regularly, _____

    _____

    3. You should buy a small, economical car, _____

    4. Medical science has made many advances, yet there are still serious diseases that have not been conquered, _____

    5. Some countries, _____ and _____, are rich in oil.

    6. I enjoy such sports _____

7. Such inventions _____ have contributed greatly to the progress of civilization. However, other inventions, _____ _____, have threatened human existence.

8. There are certain times when I wish to be alone, _____ when _____ or when _____

9. Some subjects have always been easy and enjoyable for me, _____ _____. However, other subjects, _____ _____, _____

10. In certain situations, _____ when _____ or when _____, my English still gives me a little trouble.

11. Numbers _____ are odd numbers, whereas numbers _____ are even numbers.

12. Some languages, _____ and _____, are closely related to English, while others, _____ and _____, are not.

□ **EXERCISE 30—ORAL (BOOKS CLOSED):** Use *such as* in the response.

Example: Give me some examples of sports you enjoy. (*I enjoy . . . .*)
Response: I enjoy sports such as (soccer and boxing).

(*To the teacher: Prompt the response with the words in parentheses only if necessary.*)

1. Give me some examples of places you would like to visit. (*I would like . . . .*)
2. Who enjoys watching television? Give me some examples of programs you enjoy. (*I enjoy . . . .*)
3. Do you like bright colors or dark colors? Can you give me some examples? (*I like . . . .*)
4. What are some examples of gifts that a woman likes to receive? (*A woman . . . .*)
5. And examples of gifts that a man likes to receive? (*A man . . . .*)

6. Give me some examples of problems a foreign student can easily overcome. (*A foreign student can easily overcome problems* . . . .)
7. Are there many sources of protein? Can you give me some examples? (*There are many* . . . .)
8. Give me some examples of emotions we all experience. (*We all* . . . .)
9. Should I buy a big car or a small car? For example? (*You should buy* . . . .)
10. What qualities do you appreciate in a friend? (*I appreciate* . . . .)

9–12 CONTINUING THE SAME IDEA

(a) The city provides many cultural opportunities. It has an excellent art museum. { *Moreover,* *Furthermore,* *In addition,* } it has a fine symphony orchestra.	*Moreover*, *furthermore*, and *in addition* mean *also*. They are transitions.
(b) The city provides many cultural opportunities. { *In addition to* *Besides* } an excellent art museum, it has a fine symphony orchestra.	In (b): *In addition to* and *besides** are used as prepositions. They are followed by an object (*museum*), not a clause.

*COMPARE: *Besides* means *in addition to.*
  Beside means *next to*; e.g., *I sat beside my friend.*

☐ **EXERCISE 31:** Combine the ideas in the following by using *moreover, furthermore, in addition (to), besides,* or *also* where appropriate.

1. I like to read that newspaper. One reason is that the news is always reported accurately. It has interesting special features.
2. There are many ways you can work on improving your English outside of class. For example, you should speak English as much as possible, even when you are speaking with friends who speak your native language. You should read as many magazines in English as you have time for. Watching television can be helpful.
3. Along with the increase in population in the city, there has been an increase in the rate of crime. A housing shortage has developed. There are so many automobiles in the city that the expressways are almost always jammed with cars, regardless of the time of day.
4. Good health is perhaps one's most valuable asset. To maintain good health, it is important to eat a balanced diet. The body needs a regular supply of vitamins, minerals, protein, carbohydrates, and other nutrients. Physical exercise is essential. Sleep and rest should not be neglected.

☐ **EXERCISE 32—WRITTEN:** Write a paragraph of approximately 100 to 150 words in which you give specific examples to support one of the following general ideas. Use connecting words such as *for example, for instance, such as, moreover, furthermore, in addition (to),* and *also.*

1. A newspaper contains a variety of articles to appeal to the different interests of its readers.
2. Some television programs are not suitable for viewing by children.
3. There are several things you should consider before you decide to get married.
4. There are several problems international students face when they first arrive in (the United States).

☐ **EXERCISE 33—PHRASAL VERBS:** Supply an appropriate preposition for each of the following two-word verbs.

1. A: Guess who I ran _____ today as I was walking across campus.

   B: Who?

   A: Ann Keefe.

   B: You're kidding!

2. A: There will be a test on Chapters Eight and Nine next Friday.

   B: (Groan.) Couldn't you put it _____ until Monday?

3. A: You'd better put _____ your coat before you leave. It's chilly out.

   B: What's the temperature?

4. A: I smell something burning in the kitchen. Can I call you _____ in a minute?

   B: Sure. I hope your dinner hasn't burned.

   A: So do I! Bye.

   B: Good-bye.

5. A: I think that if I learn enough vocabulary I won't have any trouble using English.

   B: That's not necessarily so. I'd like to point _____ that language consists of much more than just vocabulary.

6. A: One billion seconds ago, World War II was being fought. One billion minutes ago, Jesus Christ was living. One billion hours ago, the human race had not yet discovered agriculture.

   B: How did you figure that _____?

   A: I didn't. I came _____ that information while I was reading the newspaper.

7. A: Your children certainly love the outdoors.

   B: Yes, they do. We brought them _____ to appreciate nature.

8. A: What forms do I have to fill out to change my tourist visa to a student visa?

   B: I don't know, but I'll look _____ it first thing tomorrow and try to find _____. I'll let you know.

9. A: How long were you in the hospital?

   B: About a week. But I've missed almost two weeks of classes.

   A: It's going to be hard for you to make _____ all the work you've missed, isn't it?

   B: Very.

10. A: Would you mind turning _____ the light?

    B: Not at all.

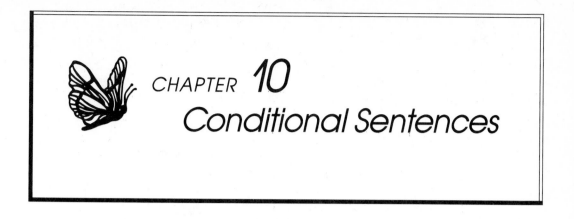

CHAPTER *10*

Conditional Sentences

10–1 SUMMARY OF BASIC VERB FORM USAGE IN CONDITIONAL SENTENCES

MEANING OF THE "*IF* CLAUSE"	VERB FORM IN THE "*IF* CLAUSE"	VERB FORM IN THE "RESULT CLAUSE"	
True in the present/future	*simple present*	*simple present* *simple future*	(a) If I **have** enough time, I **write** to my parents every week. (b) If I **have** enough time tomorrow, I **will write** to my parents.
Untrue in the present/future	*simple past*	***would*** + *simple form*	(c) If I **had** enough time now, I **would write** to my parents. (*In truth, I do not have enough time, so I will not write to them.*)
Untrue in the past	*past perfect*	***would have*** + *past participle*	(d) If I **had had** enough time, I **would have written** to my parents yesterday. (*In truth, I did not have enough time, so I did not write to them.*)

10–2 TRUE IN THE PRESENT OR FUTURE

(e) If I **don't eat** breakfast, I always **get** hungry during class.	In (e): The simple present is used in the result clause to express a habitual activity or situation.
(f) Water **freezes (will freeze)** if the temperature **goes** below 32°F/0°C.	In (f): Either the simple present or the simple future is used in the result clause to express an established, predictable fact.
(g) If I **don't eat** breakfast tomorrow morning, I **will get** hungry during class.	In (g) and (h): The simple future is used in the result clause when the sentence concerns a particular activity or situation in the future.
(h) If the weather **is** nice tomorrow, we **will go** on a picnic.	Note: The simple present, not the simple future, is used in the "*if* clause."

10–3 UNTRUE (CONTRARY TO FACT) IN THE PRESENT/FUTURE

(i) If I *taught* this class, I *wouldn't give* tests.	In (i): In truth, I don't teach this class.
(j) If he *were* here right now, he *would help* us.	In (j): In truth, he is not here right now.
(k) If I *were* you, I *would accept* their invitation.	In (k): In truth, I am not you.
	Note: *Were* is used for both singular and plural subjects. *Was* (with *I, he, she, it*) is sometimes used in very informal speech but is not generally considered grammatically acceptable.

□ **EXERCISE 1:** Complete the sentences with the verbs in parentheses.

1. If I have enough apples, I (bake) _____*will bake*_____ an apple pie this afternoon.

2. If I had enough apples, I (bake) _____ an apple pie this afternoon.

3. I will fix your bicycle if I (have) _____ a screwdriver of the proper size.

4. I would fix your bicycle if I (have) _____ a screwdriver of the proper size.

5. I (make) _____ a tomato salad for the picnic tomorrow if the tomatoes in my garden are ripe.

6. I (make) _____ a tomato salad for the picnic tomorrow if the tomatoes in my garden were ripe.

7. Jack would shave today if he (have) _____ a sharp razor.

8. Jack will shave today if he (have) _____ a sharp razor.

9. Sally always answers the phone if she (be) _____ in her office.

10. Sally would answer the phone if she (be) _____ in her office right now.

11. I (not be) _____ a student in this class if English (be) _____ my native language.

10–4 UNTRUE (CONTRARY TO FACT) IN THE PAST

(l) If you **had told** me about the problem, I **would have helped** you.	In (l): In truth, you did not tell me about it.
(m) If they **had studied**, they **would have passed** the exam.	In (m): In truth, they did not study. They failed the exam.
(n) If I **hadn't slipped** on the ice, **I wouldn't have broken** my arm.	In (n): In truth, I slipped on the ice. I broke my arm.
	Note: The auxiliary verbs are almost always contracted in speech. "If you'd told me, I would've helped you (OR: I'd've helped you)."

☐ **EXERCISE 2:** Complete the sentences with the verbs in parentheses.

1. If I (*have*) _____ enough money, I will go with you.

2. If I (*have*) _____ enough money, I would go with you.

3. If I (*have*) _____ enough money, I would have gone with you.

4. If the weather is nice tomorrow, we (*go*) _____ to the zoo.

5. If the weather were nice today, we (*go*) _____ to the zoo.

6. If the weather had been nice yesterday, we (*go*) _____ to the zoo.

7. If Sally (*be*) _____ at home tomorrow, I am going to visit her.

8. Jim isn't home right now. If he (*be*) _____ at home right now, I (*visit*) _____ him.

9. Linda wasn't at home yesterday. If she (*be*) _____ at home yesterday, I (*visit*) _____ her.

☐ **EXERCISE 3:** Complete the sentences with the verbs in parentheses.

1. It's too bad Helen isn't here. If she (*be*) _____ here, she (*know*) _____ what to do.

2. Fred failed the test because he didn't study. However, if he (*study*) _____ for the test, he (*pass*) _____ it.

3. An aerosol spray can will explode if you (*throw*) _____ it into a fire.

4. You should tell your father exactly what happened. If I (*be*) _____ you, I (*tell*) _____ him the truth as soon as possible.

5. If I (*have*) _____ my camera with me yesterday, I (*take*) _____ a picture of Alex standing on his head.

6. I'm almost ready to plant my garden. I have a lot of seeds. Maybe I have more than I need. If I (*have*) _____ more seeds than I need, I (*give*) _____ some to Nellie.

7. I got wet because I didn't take my umbrella. However, I (*get, not*) _____ wet if I (*remember*) _____ to take my umbrella with me yesterday.

8. I (*change*) _____ the present economic policy if I (*be*) _____ the President of the United States.

9. If the teacher (*be*) _____ absent tomorrow, class will be cancelled.

10. George has only two pairs of socks. If he (*have*) _____ more than two pairs of socks, he (*have to, not*) _____ _____ wash his socks so often.

11. That sounds like a good job offer. If I (*be*) _____ you, I (*accept*) _____ it.

12. The cowboy pulled his gun to shoot at the rattlesnake, but he was too late. If he (*be*) _____ quicker to pull the trigger, the snake (*bite, not*) _____ him on the ankle. It's a good thing he was wearing heavy leather boots.

☐ **EXERCISE 4:** Supply the appropriate auxiliary verb.

1. I don't have a pen, but if I _____*did*_____, I would lend it to you.

2. He is busy right now, but if he _____*weren't*_____, he would help us.

3. I didn't vote in the last election, but if I _____*had*_____, I would have voted for Senator Anderson.

4. I don't have enough money, but if I _____, I would buy that book.

5. The weather is cold today, but if it _____, I would go swimming.

6. She didn't come, but if she _____, she would have met my brother.

7. I'm not a good cook, but if I _____, I would make all of my own meals.

8. I have to go to class this afternoon, but if I _____, I would go downtown with you.

9. He didn't go to a doctor, but if he _____, the cut on his hand wouldn't have gotten infected.

10. I always pay my bills. If I _____, I would get in a lot of trouble.

11. Helium is lighter than air. If it _____, a helium-filled balloon wouldn't float upward.

12. I called my husband to tell him I would be late. If I _____, he would have gotten worried about me.

☐ **EXERCISE 5—ORAL (BOOKS CLOSED):** Answer each question. Begin with "No, but . . . ."

Example: Do you have a dollar?
Response: No, but if I did (No, but if I had a dollar), I would lend it to you.

1. Are you rich?
2. Do you have a car?
3. Are you a bird?
4. Are you in (*student's country/ hometown*)?
5. Do you live in an apartment? Dormitory? Hotel?
6. Are you the teacher of this class?
7. Do you have your own airplane?
8. Are you (*the President of the United States*)?
9. Are you tired?
10. Are you at home right now?
11. Are you married? Single?
12. Do you speak (*another language*)?
13. Is the weather hot/cold today?
14. Are you hungry?
15. Do you live in (*New York City*)?

□ **EXERCISE 6—ORAL (BOOKS CLOSED):** Begin your response with "But if I had known . . . ."

Example: There was a test yesterday. You didn't know that, so you didn't study.
Response: But if I had known (that there was a test yesterday), I would have studied.

1. Your friend was in the hospital. You didn't know that, so you didn't visit her.
2. I've never met your friend. You didn't know that, so you didn't introduce me.
3. There was a party last night. You didn't know that, so you didn't go.
4. Your friend's parents are in town. You didn't know that, so you didn't invite them to dinner.
5. I wanted to go to the soccer game. You didn't know that, so you didn't buy another ticket.
6. I was at home last night. You didn't know that, so you didn't visit me.
7. Your sister wanted a gold necklace for her birthday. You didn't know that, so you didn't buy her one.
8. I had a problem. You didn't know that, so you didn't offer to help.

□ **EXERCISE 7:** Change the following statements into conditional sentences.

1. I didn't buy it because I didn't have enough money. But . . . *I would have bought it if I'd had enough money.*
2. I won't buy it because I don't have enough money. But . . . .
3. You got into so much trouble because you didn't listen to me. But . . . .
4. The woman didn't die because she received immediate medical attention. But . . . .
5. Jack came, so I wasn't disappointed. But . . . .
6. Ann didn't pass the entrance examination, so she wasn't admitted to the university. But . . . .
7. We ran out of gas because we didn't stop at the service station. But . . . .
8. There are so many bugs in the room because there isn't a screen on the window. But . . . .

10–5 USING PROGRESSIVE VERB FORMS

Notice the use of progressive verb forms in the following examples. Even in conditional sentences, progressive verb forms are used in progressive situations. (See Chart 1-2 for a discussion of progressive verbs.)

(a) TRUE:	It *is raining* right now, so I *will not go* for a walk.	
(b) CONDITIONAL:	If it *were not raining* right now, I *would go* for a walk.	
(c) TRUE:	I *am not living* in Chile. I *am not working* at a bank.	
(d) CONDITIONAL:	If I *were living* in Chile, I *would be working* at a bank.	
(e) TRUE:	It *was raining* yesterday afternoon, so I *did not go* for a walk.	
(f) CONDITIONAL:	If it *had not been raining*, I *would have gone* for a walk.	
(g) TRUE:	I *was not living* in Chile last year. I *was not working* at a bank.	
(h) CONDITIONAL:	If I *had been living* in Chile last year, I *would have been working* at a bank.	

☐ **EXERCISE 8:** Change the following statements into conditional sentences.

1. It is snowing, so I won't go with you. But . . . *if it weren't snowing, I would go with you.*
2. The child is crying because his mother isn't here. But . . . .
3. You weren't listening, so you didn't understand the directions. But . . . .
4. Joe got a ticket because he was driving too fast. But . . . .
5. I was listening to the radio, so I heard the news bulletin. But . . . .
6. Grandpa is not wearing his hearing aid because it's broken. But . . . .
7. You were sleeping, so I didn't tell you the news as soon as I heard it. But . . . .
8. I'm enjoying myself, so I won't leave. But . . . .

10–6 USING "MIXED TIME" IN CONDITIONAL SENTENCES

Frequently the time in the "if clause" and the time in the "result clause" are different: One clause may be in the present and the other in the past. Notice that past and present times are mixed in the sentences in the following examples.

(a) TRUE:	I *did not eat* breakfast several hours ago, so I *am* hungry now.	
(b) CONDITIONAL:	If I *had eaten* breakfast several hours ago, I *would not be* hungry now.	
	(past)	*(present)*
(c) TRUE:	He *is not* a good student. He *did not study* for the test yesterday.	
(d) CONDITIONAL:	If he *were* a good student, he *would have studied* for the test.	
	(present)	*(past)*

☐ **EXERCISE 9:** Change the following statements into conditional sentences.

1. I'm hungry now because I didn't eat dinner. But . . . *if I'd eaten dinner, I wouldn't be hungry now.*
2. The room is full of flies because you left the door open. But . . . .
3. You are tired this morning because you didn't go to bed at a reasonable hour last night. But . . . .
4. I didn't finish my report yesterday, so I can't begin a new project today. But . . . .
5. Helen is sick because she didn't follow the doctor's orders. But . . . .
6. I'm not you, so I didn't tell him the truth. But . . . .
7. I don't know anything about plumbing, so I didn't fix the leak in the sink myself. But . . . .
8. I received a good job offer from the oil company, so I won't seriously consider taking the job with the electronics firm. But . . . .

10–7 USING *COULD, MIGHT,* AND *SHOULD*

(a) If I *were* a bird, I **could fly** home. (b) If I **could sing** as well as you, I *would join* the opera. (c) If I'*d had* enough money, I **could have gone** to Florida for vacation.	In (a): **could fly** = *would be able to fly* In (b): **could sing** = *were able to sing* In (c): **could have gone** = *would have been able to go*
(d) If I *don't get* a scholarship, I **might get** a job instead of going to graduate school next fall. (e) If you *were* a better student, you **might get** better grades. (f) If you *had told* me about your problem, I **might have been** able to help you.	In (d): ***I might get*** = *maybe I will get* In (e): ***you might get*** = *maybe you would get* In (f): ***I might have been*** = *maybe I would have been*
(g) If John **should call**, *tell* him I'll be back around five. (h) If there **should be** another world war, the continued existence of the human race *would be* in jeopardy.	In (g): ***If John should call*** indicates a little more uncertainty or doubt than ***If John calls***, but the meaning of the two is basically the same. In (h): ***If there should be*** indicates more uncertainty or doubt than ***If there were***.

☐ **EXERCISE 10:** Complete the following.

1. I could go _____ *to Arizona over vacation if I had enough time.* _____

2. I could buy _____

3. I would buy _____

4. I could have bought _____

5. I would have bought _____

6. If I could speak _____

7. You might have passed the test _____

8. If you should need to get in touch with me later _____

9. If it should rain tomorrow _____

10. I could have finished my work on time _____

10–8 OMITTING *IF*

(a) **Were I** you, I wouldn't do that. (b) **Had I known**, I would have told you. (c) **Should anyone call**, please take a message.	With *were*, *had* (past perfect), and ***should***, sometimes *if* is omitted and the subject and verb are inverted. In (a): ***Were I you*** = *If I were you* In (b): ***Had I known*** = *If I had known* In (c): ***Should anyone call*** = *If anyone should call*

☐ **EXERCISE 11:** Give sentences with the same meaning by omitting *if* from the conditional sentences.

1. The other team committed a foul, but the referee didn't see it. If the referee had seen it, our team would have won the game.
   → *Had the referee seen it, our team would have won the game.*

2. Your boss sounds like a real tyrant. If I were you, I would look for another job.

3. You really should learn how to use a computer. If you had used a computer, you could have finished the work in half the time.

4. I'll be out of my office until 2:00. If you should need to reach me, I'll be in the conference room.

5. The factory was on the verge of bankruptcy. If it had gone out of business, hundreds of people would have lost their livelihood.

6. We would have won the game if Thompson had caught the ball.

7. If Thompson had not dropped the ball, we would have won the game.*

8. The artists and creative thinkers throughout the history of the world have changed all of our lives. If they had not dared to be different, the history of civilization would have to be rewritten.

---

*In the negative, *not* follows the subject. It is not contracted with the auxiliary verb:
   CORRECT: *Had I not seen* it with my own eyes, I wouldn't have believed it.
   INCORRECT: Hadn't I seen it with my own eyes, ...

9. If there should be a global nuclear war, some scientists predict that life on earth as we know it would end forever.

10. If Tom had told the truth about his educational background, he probably wouldn't have gotten the job with the accounting firm. I suspect his boss will figure it out and fire him one of these days.

11. I know you're getting discouraged and are planning to drop out of school. However, if you were to finish your education, many more career opportunities would be open to you.

12. I'm glad I went to the meeting. If I hadn't been there, my proposal probably would not have been accepted.

10-9 IMPLIED CONDITIONS

(a) I **would have gone** with you, but I had to study. (*Implied condition:* . . . **if I hadn't had to study**) (b) I never **would have succeeded** without your help. (*Implied condition:* . . . **if you hadn't helped me**)	Often the "if clause" is implied, not stated. Conditional verbs are still used in the "result clause."
(c) She ran; *otherwise*, she **would have missed** her bus.	Conditional verbs are frequently used following **otherwise**. In (c), the implied "if clause" is: *If she had not run.* . . .

☐ **EXERCISE 12:** Give sentences with the same meaning by using "*if* clauses."

1. I would have visited you, but I didn't know that you were at home.
    → *I would have visited you if I had known you were at home.*

2. It wouldn't have been a good meeting without Rosa.
    → *It wouldn't have been a good meeting if Rosa hadn't been there.*

3. I would have answered the phone, but I didn't hear it ring.

4. I couldn't have finished the work without your help.

5. I like to travel. I would have gone to Nepal last summer, but I didn't have enough money.

6. I stepped on the brakes. Otherwise, I would have hit the child on the bicycle.

7. Cathy turned down the volume on the tape player. Otherwise, the neighbors probably would have called to complain about the noise.

8. Jack would have finished his education, but he had to quit school and find a job in order to support his family.

□ **EXERCISE 13:** Complete the sentences with the verbs in parentheses. Some of the verbs are passive.

1. If I could speak Japanese, I (*spend*) _____ next year studying in Japan.

2. Had I known Mr. Jung was in the hospital, I (*send*) _____ him a note and some flowers.

3. We will move into our new house next month if it (*complete*) _____ _____ by then.

4. How old (*be, you*) _____ now if you (*be*) _____ _____ born in the year 1900?

5. It's too bad that it's snowing. If it (*snow, not*) _____, we could go for a drive.

6. I was very tired. Otherwise, I (*go*) _____ to the party with you last night.

7. I'm broke, but I (*have*) _____ plenty of money now if I (*spend, not*) _____ so much yesterday.

8. That child had a narrow escape. She (*hit*) _____ by a car if her father (*pull, not*) _____ her out of the street.

9. I'm glad I have so many friends and such a wonderful family. Life without any friends or family (*be*) _____ lonely for me.

10. My grandfather is no longer alive, but if he (*be*) _____, I'm sure he (*be*) _____ proud of me.

11. If you (*sleep, not*) _____ last night when we arrived, I would have asked you to go with us, but I didn't want to wake you up.

12. Bill has such a bad memory that he (*forget*) _____ his head if it (*be, not*) _____ attached to his body.

13. According to one report, the average hen lays 247 eggs a year, and the average person eats 255 eggs a year. If hens (*outnumber, not*) _____ people, the average person (*eat, not*) _____ 255 eggs a year.

□ **EXERCISE 14:** Complete the sentences with the verbs in parentheses.

1. A: What would you be doing right now if you (*be, not*) _____
    in class?

    B: I (*sleep*) _____.

2. A: Why were you late for the meeting?

    B: Well, I (*be*) _____ there on time, but I had a flat tire
    on the way.

3. A: How did you get to work this morning?

    B: I drove. I (*take*) _____ the bus, but I
    overslept.

4. A: Did you know that Bob got 100% on the test?

    B: Really? That surprises me. If I didn't know better, I (*think*) _____
    _____ he cheated.

5. A: Boy, is it ever hot today!

    B: You said it! If there (*be*) _____ only a breeze, it (*be,
    not*) _____ quite so unbearable.

6. A: Why isn't Peggy Adams in class today?

    B: I don't know, but I'm sure she (*be, not*) _____ absent
    unless* she (*have*) _____ a good reason.

7. A: When did Mark graduate?

    B: He didn't.

    A: Oh?

    B: He had to quit school because of some trouble at home. Otherwise, he
    (*graduate*) _____ last June.

_____
*__unless__ = __if not__ (see Chart 9-7).

8. A: Hi, sorry I'm late.

   B: That's okay.

   A: I (*be*) _____ here sooner, but I had car trouble.

9. A: Want to ride on the roller coaster?

   B: No way! I (*ride, not*) _____ on the roller coaster even if you paid me a million dollars!

10. A: Hi, Pat. Come on in.

    B: Oh, I didn't know you had company. I (*come, not*) _____ _____ (*know, I*) _____ someone was here.

    A: That's okay. Come on and let me introduce you to my friends.

11. A: How did you do on the test?

    B: Not so well. I (*do*) _____ much better, but I misread the directions for the last section.

12. A: Do you really mean it?

    B: Of course! I (*say, not*) _____ it unless I (*mean*) _____ it.

13. A: Are you coming to the party?

    B: I don't think so, but if I change my mind, I (*tell*) _____ you.

14. A: I hear Dorothy had an accident. Was it serious?

    B: No. Luckily, she wasn't driving fast at the time of the accident. If she

        (*drive*) _____ fast, I'm sure it (*be*) _____

        _____ a more serious accident.

☐ **EXERCISE 15:** Complete the following. Add commas where necessary.

  1. If it hadn't rained _____

  2. If it weren't raining _____

  3. You would have passed the test had _____

  4. It's a good thing we took a map with us. Otherwise _____

    _____

  5. Without electricity modern life _____

  6. If you hadn't reminded me about the meeting tonight _____

  7. Should you need any help _____

  8. If I could choose any profession I wanted _____

  9. If I were at home right now _____

10. Without your help yesterday _____

11. Were I you _____

12. What would you do if _____

13. If I had the chance to live my life over again _____

14. Had I known _____

15. Can you imagine what life would be like if _____

☐ **EXERCISE 16—ORAL (BOOKS CLOSED):** Answer the questions.

    Example: Suppose the student sitting next to you drops his/her pen. What
             would you do?
    Response: I would pick it up for him/her.

  1. Suppose (pretend) there is a fire in this building right now. What would
     you do?
  2. Suppose there is a fire in your room or apartment or house. You have
     time to save only one thing. What would you save?
  3. Suppose you go to the bank to cash a check for twenty dollars. The bank
     teller cashes your check and you leave, but when you count the money,
     you find she gave you thirty dollars instead of twenty. What would you
     do?

4. Same situation, but she gave you only fifteen dollars instead of twenty.

5. John was cheating during an examination. The teacher saw him. Suppose you were the teacher. What would you have done?

6. You go to a party. A man starts talking to you, but he is speaking so fast that you can't catch what he is saying. What would you do?

7. Late at night you're driving your car down a deserted street. You're all alone. In an attempt to avoid a dog in the road, you swerve to one side and hit a parked car. You know that no one saw you. What would you do?

8. Mary goes to a friend's house for dinner. Her friend serves a dish that Mary can't stand, doesn't like at all. What if you were Mary?

9. My friend John borrowed ten dollars from me and told me he would repay it in a couple of days, but it's been three weeks. I think he has forgotten about it. I really need the money, but I don't want to ask him for it. Give me some advice.

10. John was driving over the speed limit. A police car began to chase him, with red lights flashing. John stepped on the accelerator and tried to escape the police car. Put yourself in his position.

11. You are walking down the street and suddenly a large dog jumps in front of you. The dog doesn't look friendly. He is growling and moving toward you. If that happened . . . .

12. Suppose you are walking down the street at night all by yourself. A man suddenly appears in front of you. He has a gun. He says, "Give me your money." Would you try to take his gun away?

13. Suppose you go to (*Chicago*) to visit a friend. You have never been there before. Your friend said he would meet you at the airport, but he's not there. You wait for a long time, but he never shows up. You try to call him, but nobody answers the phone. Now what?

14. You are just falling asleep when you hear a burglar opening your bedroom window and climbing in. What would you do?

15. You ask a very special person to go to dinner with you. You like this person very much and want to make a good impression. You go to a fancy restaurant and have a wonderful meal. But when you reach for your wallet, you discover that it is not there. You have no money with you.

☐ **EXERCISE 17—WRITTEN:** Following are topics for writing.

1. If, beginning tomorrow, you had a two-week holiday and unlimited funds, what would you do? Why?

2. If you had to teach your language to a person who knew nothing about your language at all, how would you begin? What would you do so that this person could learn your language as quickly and easily as possible?

3. If you were Philosopher-King of the world, how would you govern? What would you do? What changes would you make? (A "Philosopher-King" may be defined as a person who has ideal wisdom and unlimited power to shape the world as s/he wishes.)

4. Suppose you had only one year to live. What would you do?

5. Describe your activities if you were in some other place (in this country or in the world) at present. Describe your probable activities today, yesterday, and tomorrow. Include the activities of other people you would be with if you were in this place.

10–10 VERB FORMS FOLLOWING *WISH*

	VERB FORM IN "TRUE" SENTENCE	**VERB FORM FOLLOWING *WISH***	
A wish about the future	(a) She *will not tell* me. (b) He *isn't going to be* here. (c) She *can't come* tomorrow.	I *wish* (that) she *would tell* me. I *wish* he *were going to be* here. I *wish* she *could come* tomorrow.	*Wish* is used when the speaker wants reality to be different, to be exactly the opposite. Verb forms similar to those in conditional sentences are used. Notice the examples.
A wish about the present	(d) I *don't know* French. (e) It *is raining* right now. (f) I *can't speak* Japanese.	I *wish* I *knew* French. I *wish* it *weren't raining* right now. I *wish* I *could speak* Japanese.	
A wish about the past	(g) John *didn't come*. (h) Mary *couldn't come*.	I *wish* John *had come*.* I *wish* Mary *could have come*.	*Wish* is followed by a noun clause. The use of *that* is optional. Usually it is omitted in speaking.

*Sometimes in very informal speaking: *I wish John would have come*.

□ **EXERCISE 18:** Supply appropriate completions in the following.

1. Our classroom doesn't have any windows. I wish our classroom

   _____ windows.

2. The sun isn't shining. I wish the sun _____ right now.

3. I didn't go shopping. I wish I _____ shopping.

4. I don't know how to dance. I wish I _____ how to dance.

5. You didn't tell them about it. I wish you _____ them

   about it.

6. It's cold today. I'm not wearing a coat. I wish I _____ a

   coat.

7. I don't have enough money to buy that book. I wish I _____

   enough money.

8. Martha is tired because she went to bed late last night. She wishes she _____ to bed earlier last night.

9. I can't go with you. I wish I _____ with you tomorrow.

10. My friend won't lend me his car. I wish he _____ me his car for my date tomorrow night.

11. Patricia isn't coming to dinner with us tonight. I wish she _____ _____ to dinner with us.

12. The teacher is going to give an exam tomorrow. I wish he _____ _____ us an exam tomorrow.

13. You can't meet my parents. I wish you _____ them.

14. Jerry didn't come to the meeting. I wish he _____ to the meeting.

15. I am not lying on a beach in Hawaii. I wish I _____ on a beach in Hawaii.

☐ **EXERCISE 19:** Supply an appropriate auxiliary in the following.

1. I'm not at home, but I wish I _____*were*_____.

2. I don't know her, but I wish I _____*did*_____.

3. I can't sing well, but I wish I _____*could*_____.

4. I didn't go, but I wish I _____*had*_____.

5. He won't talk about it, but I wish he _____*would*_____.

6. I didn't read that book, but I wish I _____.

7. I want to go, but I can't. I wish I _____.

8. I don't have a bicycle, but I wish I _____.

9. He didn't buy a ticket to the game, but he wishes he _____.

10. She can't speak English, but she wishes she _____.

11. It probably won't happen, but I wish it _____.

12. He isn't old enough to drive a car, but he wishes he _____.

13. They didn't go to the movie, but they wish they _____.

14. I don't have a driver's license, but I wish I _____.

15. I'm not living in an apartment, but I wish I _____.

10–11 USING *WOULD* TO MAKE WISHES ABOUT THE FUTURE

(a) It is raining. I *wish* it **would stop**. (*I want it to stop raining.*) (b) I'm expecting a call. I *wish* the phone **would ring**. (*I want the phone to ring.*)	**Would** is usually used to indicate that the speaker *wants* something to happen in the future. The wish may or may not come true (be realized).
(c) It's going to be a good party. I *wish* you **would come**. (*I want you to come.*) (d) We're going to be late. I *wish* you **would hurry**. (*I want you to hurry.*)	In (c) and (d): **I wish you would** . . . is often used to make a request.

☐ **EXERCISE 20:** Give the appropriate form of the verbs in parentheses to make wishes about the future.

1. Are you sure you won't be able to come with us? I wish you (*change*)

   _____ your mind.

2. Bob's mother doesn't like his beard. She wishes he (*shave*) _____

   _____ it off.

3. He needs some money. He wishes his parents (*send*) _____

   _____ him some.

4. The newspaper strike has been going on for two weeks. I wish it (*end*)

   _____.

5. My roommate is very messy. I wish she (*pick*) _____ up

   after herself more often.

☐ **EXERCISE 21:** Supply an appropriate form.

1. We need some help. I wish Alfred (*be*) _____ here now. If

   he (*be*) _____, we could finish this work very quickly.

2. We had a good time in Houston over vacation. I wish you (*come*) _____

   _____ with us. If you (*come*) _____ with

   us, you (*have*) _____ a good time.

3. I wish it (*be, not*) _____ so cold today. If it (*be, not*)

   _____ so cold, I (*go*) _____ swimming.

4. I missed part of the lecture because I was daydreaming, and now my

   notes are incomplete. I wish I (*pay*) _____ more attention

   to the lecturer.

5. A: Do you have enough money to buy that antique lamp?

   B: No, but I certainly wish I _____.

6. A: Did you study for the test?

   B: No, but now I wish I _____ because I flunked it.

7. A: Is the noise from the record player in the next apartment bothering you?

   B: Yes. I'm trying to study. I wish he (*turn*) _____ it down.

8. A: What a beautiful day! I wish I (*lie*) _____ in the sun by a swimming pool instead of sitting in a classroom.

   B: I wish I (*be*) _____ anywhere but here!

9. A: I can't go to the game with you this afternoon.

   B: Really? That's too bad. But I wish you (*tell*) _____ me sooner so that I could have found someone else to go with.

10. A: How long have you been sick?

   B: For over a week.

   A: I wish you (*go*) _____ to see a doctor today. You should find out what's wrong with you.

   B: Maybe I'll go tomorrow.

11. A: I wish we (*have, not*) _____ to go to class today.

   B: So do I. I wish it (*be*) _____ a holiday.

12. A: He couldn't have said that! That's impossible. You must have misunderstood him.

   B: I only wish I _____, but I'm sure I heard him correctly.

□ **EXERCISE 22—ORAL (BOOKS CLOSED):** Answer the questions. Use *wish*.

1. Where do you wish you were right now? What do you wish you were doing?
2. Are you pleased with the weather today, or do you wish it were different?
3. Look around this room. What do you wish were different?
4. Is there anything you wish were different about the place you are living?
5. What do you wish were different about this city/town?

6. What do you wish were different about this country?

7. What do you wish were different about a student's life? about a worker's life?

8. Just for fun, what do you wish were or could be different in the world? What about animals being able to speak? People being able to fly? There being only one language in the world? Being able to take vacations on the moon? Speed of transportation?

9. Where do you wish you could go on your next vacation?

10. Your friend gave you his phone number, but you didn't write it down because you thought you would remember it. Now you have forgotten the number. What do you wish?

11. John kept all of his money in his wallet instead of putting it in the bank. Then he lost his wallet. What does he probably wish?

12. You didn't eat breakfast/lunch/dinner before you came to class. Now you are hungry. What do you wish?

13. Mary stayed up very late last night. Today she is tired and sleepy. What does she probably wish?

14. Is there anything in your past life that you would change? What do you wish you had or had not done?

10–12   USING *AS IF/AS THOUGH*

(a) It looks *like* rain.	Notice in (a): *like* is followed by a noun object.
(b) It looks *as if* it is going to rain.	Notice in (b) and (c): *as if* and *as though* are followed by a clause.
(c) It looks *as though* it is going to rain.	
(d) It looks *like* it is going to rain. (*informal*)	Notice in (d): *like* is followed by a clause. This use of *like* is common in informal English but is not generally considered appropriate in formal English. *As if* or *as though* is preferred. (a), (b), (c), and (d) all have the same meaning.

"TRUE" STATEMENT	VERB FORM AFTER *AS IF/AS THOUGH*	
(e) He *is not* a child.	She talked to him *as if* he *were* a child.	Usually the idea following *as if/as though* is "untrue." In this case, verb usage is similar to that in conditional sentences. Notice the examples.
(f) She *did not take* a shower with her clothes on.	When she came in from the rainstorm, she looked *as if* she *had taken* a shower with her clothes on.	
(g) He *has met* her.	He acted *as though* he *had never met* her.	
(h) She *will be* here.	She spoke *as if* she *wouldn't be* here.	

□ **EXERCISE 23:** Using the idea given in parentheses, complete each sentence with *as if/as though*.

1. (*I wasn't run over by a ten-ton truck.*)

   I feel terrible. I feel ___as if (as though) I had been run over by a ten-ton truck.___

2. (*English is not her native tongue.*)

   She speaks English _____

3. (*His animals aren't people.*)

   I know a farmer who talks to his animals _____

4. (*You didn't see a ghost.*)

   What's the matter? You look _____

5. (*His father is not a general in the army.*)

   Sometimes his father gives orders _____

6. (*I didn't climb Mt. Everest.*)

   When I reached the fourth floor, I was winded. I felt _____

   _____ instead of just three flights of

   stairs.

7. (*He does have a brain in his head.*)

   Sometimes he acts _____

8. (*We haven't known each other all of our lives.*)

   We became good friends almost immediately. After talking to each other

   for only a short time, we felt _____

9. (*A giant bulldozer didn't drive down Main Street.*)

   After the tornado, the town looked _____

10. (*I don't have wings and can't fly.*)

I was so happy that I felt _____

11. (*The child won't burst.*)

The child was so excited that he looked _____

12. *Note:* The following sentiments were expressed by Helen Keller, a woman who was both blind and deaf but who learned to speak and to read (Braille).

Use your eyes as if tomorrow you _____ become blind. Hear the music of voices, the song of a bird, as if you _____ become deaf tomorrow. Touch each object as if tomorrow you _____ never be able to feel anything again. Smell the perfume of flowers and taste with true enjoyment each bite of food as if tomorrow you _____ never be able to smell and taste again.

☐ **EXERCISE 24:** General review of verb forms.

1. Some of the students (*speak, never*) _____ English before they came here last fall.

2. I wish I (*come, not*) _____ here last year.

3. It is essential that you (*be*) _____ here tomorrow.

4. Had I known Dan wouldn't be here, I (*come, not*)

_____.

5. My passport (*stamp*) _____ at the airport when I arrived.

6. My seventy-year-old grandfather, who owns his own business, (*continue, probably*) _____ to work as long as he (*live*)

_____.

7. I arrived here in September 1988. By September 1998, I (*be*) _____
_____ here for ten years.

8. Before (*go*) _____ to bed, I have to finish my homework.

9. (*Hear*) _____ that story many times before, I got bored when Jim began to tell it again.

10. Do you know that man (*sit*) _____ in the brown leather chair?

11. Many of the goods that (*produce*) _____ since the beginning of the twentieth century are totally machine-made.

12. The instructor said that she (*give*) _____ an exam next Friday.

13. I (*know*) _____ Beth for six years. When I (*meet*) _____ her, she (*work*) _____ in a law office.

14. If you (*be*) _____ here yesterday, you (*meet*) _____ my father and mother.

15. This evening the surface of the lake is completely still. It looks as if it (*make*) _____ of glass.

16. I don't know why the food service has to be so slow. We (*stand*) _____ here in the cafeteria line for over half an hour and there (*be*) _____ still a lot of people in front of us.

17. Sue says she can't come on the picnic with us. I wish she (*change*) _____ her mind and (*decide*) _____ to come with us.

18. My dog turned her head toward me and looked at me quizzically, almost as if she (*understand*) _____ what I said.

19. (*Be*) _____ an excellent researcher, Dr. Barnes (*respect*) _____ by the entire faculty.

20. Without the sun, life as we know it (*exist, not*) _____.

□ **EXERCISE 25:** General review of the verb forms.

1. Since (*come*) _____ to the United States six months ago, Maria (*learn*) _____ a lot of English.

2. Mrs. McKay (*give, already*) _____ birth to the child by the time her husband arrived at the hospital.

3. I recommended that he (*apply*) ―――――――――― to at least three universities.

4. Thank you for your help. I never (*be*) ―――――――――― able to finish this work without it.

5. Peggy told me she (*be*) ―――――――――― here at six tomorrow.

6. (*Sit*) ―――――――――― on a park bench and (*watch*) ―――――――――― the brightly colored leaves fall gently to the ground, he felt at peace with the world.

7. Why didn't you tell me about this before? I certainly wish I (*inform*) ―――――――――― earlier.

8. The large dormitory (*destroy, completely*) ―――――――――― ―――――――――― by fire last week. Since all of the students (*go*) ―――――――――― home for the holidays, there was no loss of life.

9. James blushed when his friend asked him an (*embarrass*) ―――――――――― ―――――――――― question.

10. Anna is grown up now. You shouldn't speak to her as if she (*be*) ―――――― ―――――――――― a child.

11. I asked all of the people (*invite*) ―――――――――― to the party to RSVP.

12. When the (*puzzle*) ―――――――――― student could not figure out the answer to the (*puzzle*) ―――――――――― problem, she demanded that I (*give*) ―――――――――― her the correct answer, but I insisted that she (*figure*) ―――――――――― it out for herself.

13. Ever since I can remember, mathematics (*be*) ―――――――――― my favorite subject.

14. The people (*work*) ―――――――――― to solve the problems of urban poverty are hopeful that many of these problems (*solve*) ―――――――――― within the next ten years.

15. It's a funny story. I'll tell you the details when I (*call*) ―――――――――― you tomorrow.

□ **EXERCISE 26:** Verb form review. The following is based on compositions written by students who were members of a multicultural class.

Next week, when I _____ _____ my final examinations, I
  (finish) _(take)_

_____ one of the best experiences I _____
(finish, also) _(have, ever)_

_____ in my lifetime. In the last four months, I _____
  (learn)

_____ more about foreign cultures than I _____
  (anticipate)

_____ before _____ to the United
  (come)

States. _____ in a foreign country and _____
  (Live) _(go)_

to school with people from various parts of the world _____
  (give)

_____ me the opportunity _____
  (encounter)

and _____ with people from different cultures. I
  (interact)

_____ to share some of my experiences and thoughts
  (like)

with you.

When I first _____, I _____
  (arrive) _(know)_

no one and I _____ all of my fingers _____
  (need) _(communicate)_

_____ what I was trying to say in English. All of the

international students were in the same situation. When we _____
  (can, find, not)

_____ the right word, we _____
  (use)

strange movements and gestures _____ our meaning.
  (communicate)

_____ some common phrases, such as "How are you?"
  (Know)

"Fine, thank you, and you?" and "What country are you from?", _____
  _(be)_

_____ enough in the beginning for us _____
                                                          (make)
_____ friends with each other. The TV room in the

dormitory _____ our meeting place every evening after
                (become)

dinner. _____ _____ our English,
          (Hope)   (improve)

many of us tried to watch television and _____ what the
                                              (understand)

people _____ on the screen _____
           (appear)   (say)

_____, but for the most part their words were just a

strange mumble to us. After a while, _____ and a little
                                          (bore)

sad, we slowly began to disappear to our rooms. I _____
                                                      (think)

that all of us _____ some homesickness. However,
                  (experience)

despite my loneliness, I had a good feeling within myself because I _____
                                                                        (do)

_____ what I _____ to do for
                            (want)

many years: _____ and _____ in a
                (live)   (study)

foreign country.

After a few days, classes _____ and we _____
                              (begin)   (have)

another meeting place: the classroom. _____ quite what
                                          (Know, not)

_____ the first day of class, I was a bit nervous, but also
    (expect)

_____. After _____ the right
    (excite)   (find)

building and the right room, I walked in and _____ an
                                                  (choose)

empty seat. I _____ myself to the person _____
                  (introduce)   (sit)

_____ next to me, and we sat _____ for a few
                                                   (*talk*)
minutes. Since we _____ from different countries, we _____
                        (*be*)   (*speak*)
_____ in English. At first, I was afraid that the other

student _____ what I _____ ,
           (*understand, not*)   (*say*)
but I _____ when she _____
        (*surprise, pleasantly*)   (*respond*)
_____ to my questions easily. Together we _____
                                                             (*take*)
_____ the first steps toward _____ a friendship.
                                          (*build*)

As the semester _____ , I _____ out
                     (*progress*)   (*find*)
more and more about my fellow students. Students from some countries were

reticent and shy in class. They almost never _____ questions and
                                                   (*ask*)
_____ very softly. Others of different nationalities _____
 (*speak*)   (*be*)
just the opposite: They spoke in booming voices and never _____
                                                                (*hesitate*)
_____ questions—and sometimes they _____
    (*ask*)   (*interrupt, even*)
_____ the teacher. I _____ in a
                                      (*be, never*)
classroom with such a mixture of cultures before. I learned _____
                                                                 (*surprise, not*)
_____ by anything my classmates might say or do.

The time we spent _____ our ideas with each other and
                         (*share*)
_____ about each other's customs and beliefs _____
    (*learn*)   (*be*)
valuable and fun. As we progressed in our English, we slowly learned about

each other, too.

Now, several months after my arrival in the United States, I _____
                                                                (be)

able to understand not only some English but also something about different

cultures. If I _____ here, I _____
              (come, not)   (be, not)

able to attain these insights into other cultures. I wish everyone in the world

_____ the same experience. Perhaps if all the people in
      (have)

the world _____ more about cultures different from their own and
          (know)

_____ the opportunity _____ friends with people
    (have)   (make)

from different countries, peace _____ secure.
                                      (be)

☐ **EXERCISE 27—WRITTEN:** Following are composition topics.

1. Summarize the major events that have occurred in your country and/or in the world in the past three or four months.

2. *For students who have been using this text in a multicultural class:*
   This class has given you the opportunity to meet and interact with students from countries other than your own. Describe your experiences and discuss any insights you might have made into other cultures.

3. *For students who have been using this text in a class where everyone has the same native language:*
   Discuss your experiences in this class, and give advice to people who are going to join this class in the future about how they can improve their English.

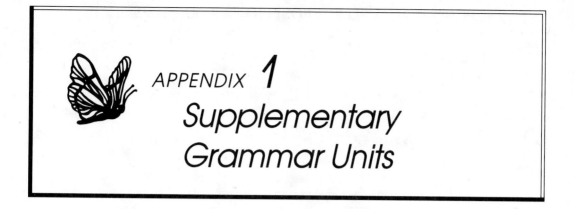

APPENDIX 1
Supplementary Grammar Units

UNIT A: Basic Grammar Terminology

A-1 SUBJECTS, VERBS, AND OBJECTS

S **V** (a) ***Birds*** ***fly.*** (NOUN) (VERB)	Almost all English sentences contain a subject (**S**) and a verb (**V**). The verb may or may not be followed by an object (**O**).
S **V** (b) The ***baby*** ***cried.*** (NOUN) (VERB)	**VERBS:** Verbs that are not followed by an object, as in (a) and (b), are called *intransitive verbs*. Common intransitive verbs: *agree, arrive, come, cry, exist, go, happen, live, occur, rain, rise, sleep, stay, walk.*
S **V** **O** (c) The ***student*** ***needs*** a ***pen.*** (NOUN) (VERB) (NOUN)	Verbs that are followed by an object, as in (c) and (d), are called *transitive verbs*. Common transitive verbs: *build, cut, find, like, make, need, send, use, want.*

S   **V**   **O**
(d) My ***friend*** ***enjoyed*** the ***party.***
     (NOUN)   (VERB)   (NOUN)
	Some verbs can be either intransitive or transitive.
	   intransitive: A student studies.
	   transitive: A student studies books.

	SUBJECTS AND OBJECTS: The subjects and objects of verbs are nouns (or pronouns). Examples of nouns: *person, place, thing, John, Asia, pen, information, appearance, amusement.*

A-2 PREPOSITIONS AND PREPOSITIONAL PHRASES

COMMON PREPOSITIONS				
about	before	despite	of	to
above	behind	down	off	toward(s)
across	below	during	on	under
after	beneath	for	out	until
against	beside	from	over	up
along	besides	in	since	upon
among	between	into	through	with
around	beyond	like	throughout	within
at	by	near	till	without

S   **V**   **PREP**   **O of PREP**
 (a) The student studies *in* *the **library**.*
                       (NOUN)
 	
     S   **V**   **O**   **PREP**   **O of PREP**
 (b) We enjoyed the party *at* *your **house**.*
                           (NOUN)
	An important element of English sentences is the prepositional phrase. It consists of a preposition (**PREP**) and its object (**O**). The object of a preposition is a noun or pronoun. In (a): ***in the library*** is a prepositional phrase.

(c) We went ***to the zoo*** ***in the afternoon***. (place) (time) (d) ***In the afternoon***, we went to the zoo.	In (c): In most English sentences, "place" comes before "time." In (d): Sometimes a prepositional phrase comes at the beginning of a sentence.

☐ **EXERCISE 1:** Find the subjects (**S**), verbs (**V**), objects (**O**), and prepositional phrases (**PP**) in the following sentences.

              S   **V**   **O**   **PP**

1. Jack put the letter in the mailbox.

2. The children walked to school.

3. Beethoven wrote nine symphonies.

4. Mary did her homework at the library.

5. Bells originated in Asia.

6. Chinese printers created the first paper money in the world.

A-3 ADJECTIVES

(a) Mary is an ***intelligent*** *student.*
           (ADJECTIVE) (NOUN)
 (b) The ***hungry*** *children* ate fruit.
       (ADJECTIVE)(NOUN)
	Adjectives describe nouns. In grammar, we say that adjectives modify nouns. The word *modify* means "change a little." Adjectives give a little different meaning to a noun: *intelligent student, lazy student, good student.* Examples of adjectives: *young, old, rich, poor, beautiful, brown, French, modern.*

(c) I saw some ***beautiful*** pictures. *INCORRECT: beautifuls pictures*	An adjective is neither singular nor plural. A final **-s** is never added to an adjective.

A-4 ADVERBS

(a) He walks **quickly**.
(ADVERB)
(b) She opened the door **quietly**.
(ADVERB)
	Adverbs modify verbs. Often they answer the question "*How?*"
	In (a): *How does he walk?* Answer: *Quickly.*
	Adverbs are often formed by adding **-ly** to an adjective.
	    adjective: **quick**
	    adverb: **quickly**

(c) I am **extremely** *happy*. (ADVERB) (ADJECTIVE)	Adverbs are also used to modify adjectives, i.e., to give information about adjectives, as in (c).
(d) Ann will come **tomorrow**. (ADVERB)	Adverbs are also used to express time or frequency. Examples: *tomorrow, today, yesterday, soon, never, usually, always, yet.*
MIDSENTENCE ADVERBS (e) Ann **always** *comes* on time. (f) Ann *is* **always** on time. (g) Ann *has* **always** *come* on time. (h) *Does she* **always** *come* on time?	Some adverbs may occur in the middle of a sentence. Midsentence adverbs have usual positions; they (1) come in front of simple present and simple past verbs (except **be**), as in (e); (2) follow **be** (simple present and simple past), as in (f); (3) come between a helping verb and a main verb, as in (g). In a question, a midsentence adverb comes directly after the subject, as in (h).

COMMON MIDSENTENCE ADVERBS

ever, always, usually, often, frequently, generally, sometimes, occasionally, seldom, rarely, hardly ever, never, not ever, already, finally, just, probably

☐ **EXERCISE 2:** Choose the correct word (*adjective* or *adverb*) in parentheses.

1. George is a (*careless, carelessly*) writer. He writes (*careless, carelessly*).
2. Frank asked me an (*easy, easily*) question. I answered it (*easy, easily*).
3. Sally speaks (*soft, softly*). She has a (*soft, softly*) voice.
4. I entered the classroom (*quiet, quietly*) because I was late.
5. Ali speaks English very (*good, well*). He has very (*good, well*) pronunciation.★

★The word **well** can be either an adverb or an adjective.
  (a) Don *writes* **well**. In (a): **well** = an adverb meaning "in a good manner." It describes how Don writes.
  (b) Mary was sick, but now she *is* **well**. In (b): **well** = an adjective meaning "healthy, not sick." It follows the verb **be** and describes the subject "she"; i.e., Mary is a **well** person, not a sick person.
NOTE: After the linking verb **feel**, either **good** or **well** may be used:
  (c) I *feel* **good**.
  (d) I *feel* **well**.
  (c) and (d) have essentially the same meaning. However, **well** usually refers specifically to health, whereas **good** can refer to one's physical and/or emotional condition.

□ **EXERCISE 3:** Identify the adjectives (**ADJ**) and adverbs (**ADV**) in the following sentences.

ADJ   ADV

1. Jack opened the heavy door slowly.
2. Chinese jewelers carved beautiful ornaments from jade.
3. The old man carves wooden figures skillfully.
4. A busy executive usually has short conversations on the telephone.
5. The young women had a very good time at the picnic yesterday.

□ **EXERCISE 4:** Put the adverb in parentheses in its usual midsentence position.

1. (*never*)   Erica has seen snow. → *Erica has never seen snow.*
2. (*often*)   Ted studies at the library in the evening.
3. (*often*)   Ann is at the library in the evening, too.
4. (*already*)   Fred has finished studying for tomorrow's test.
5. (*seldom*)   Jack is at home.
6. (*always*)   Does he stay there?
7. (*often*)   He goes into town to hang around with his buddies.
8. (*always*)   You should tell the truth.

A-5 THE VERB *BE*

(a) John *is*   **a student**.
     (BE)   (NOUN)
(b) John *is*   **intelligent**.
     (BE)   (ADJECTIVE)
(c) John *was*   **at the library**.
     (BE) (PREP. PHRASE)
	A sentence with *be* as the main verb has three basic patterns:
	
	In (a): *be* + *a noun*
	In (b): *be* + *an adjective*
	In (c): *be* + *a prepositional phrase*

(d) Mary *is writing* a letter. (e) They *were listening* to some music. (f) That letter *was written* by Alice.	*Be* is also used as an auxiliary verb in progressive verb tenses and in the passive. In (d) *is* = *auxiliary*; ***writing*** = *main verb*

TENSE FORMS OF *BE*

	SIMPLE PRESENT	SIMPLE PAST	PRESENT PERFECT
SINGULAR	*I am* *you are* *he, she, it is*	*I was* *you were* *he, she, it was*	*I have been* *you have been* *he, she, it has been*
PLURAL	*we, you, they are*	*we, you, they were*	*we, you, they have been*

A-6 LINKING VERBS

(a) The soup **smells** **good**.
        (LINKING VERB) (ADJECTIVE)
(b) This food **tastes delicious**.
(c) The children **feel happy**.
(d) The weather **became cold**.
	Other verbs like **be** that may be followed immediately by an adjective are called *linking verbs*. An adjective following a linking verb describes the subject of a sentence.*
	Common verbs that may be followed by an adjective:
	    feel, **look**, **smell**, **sound**, **taste**
	    appear, **seem**
	    become (and **get**, **turn**, **grow** when they mean "become")

*COMPARE:
> (1) *The man looks angry.* → An adjective (**angry**) follows **look**. The adjective describes the subject (**the man**). **Look** has the meaning of "appear."
>
> (2) *The man looked at me angrily.* → An adverb (**angrily**) follows **look at**. The adverb describes the action of the verb. **Look at** has the meaning of "regard, watch."

□ **EXERCISE 5:** Choose the correct form (*adjective* or *adverb*) in parentheses.

1. This math problem looks (*easy, easily*). I'm sure I can do it (*easy, easily*).
2. That chair looks (*comfortable, comfortably*).
3. I looked at the problem (*careful, carefully*) and then solved it.
4. I felt (*sad, sadly*) when I heard the news.
5. Susan smiled (*cheerful, cheerfully*). She seemed (*cheerful, cheerfully*).
6. I tasted the soup (*careful, carefully*) because it was hot. The soup tasted (*good, well*).
7. The room got (*quiet, quietly*) when the professor entered. The students sat (*quiet, quietly*) at their desks.
8. The sky grew (*dark, darkly*) as the storm approached.

A-7 PERSONAL PRONOUNS

	SINGULAR	PLURAL	
SUBJECT PRONOUNS	*I* *you* *she, he, it*	*we* *you* *they*	A pronoun is used in place of a noun. It refers to a noun. The noun it refers to is called the *antecedent*. *Examples:* I read the **book**. **It** was good. (The pronoun "it" refers to the antecedent noun "book.")
OBJECT PRONOUNS	*me* *you* *her, him, it*	*us* *you* *them*	Mary said, "**I** drink tea." (The pronoun "I" refers to the speaker, whose name is Mary.)

(continued)

POSSESSIVE PRONOUNS	*mine* *your* *hers, his*	*ours* *yours* *theirs*	Possessive pronouns are not followed immediately by a noun; they stand alone. *Example:* That book is **mine**. Those are **yours** over there.*
POSSESSIVE ADJECTIVES	**my** *name* **your** *name* **her, his, its** *name*	**our** *names* **your** *names* **their** *names*	Possessive adjectives are followed immediately by a noun; they do not stand alone. *Example:* **My** *book* is here. **Your** *books* are over there.

*Possessive nouns require apostrophes; e.g., That book is *Mary's*. (See Chart 5-3.) Possessive pronouns do NOT take apostrophes.
    CORRECT: That book is *hers*, and those books are *theirs*.
    INCORRECT: That book is *her's* and those books are *theirs'*.

□ **EXERCISE 6:** Identify the pronouns and their antecedents in the following sentences.

1. Jack has a part-time job. He works at a fast-food restaurant.

   (**he** = *a pronoun;* **Jack** = *the antecedent*)

2. Many monkeys don't like water, but they can swim well when they have to.
3. The teacher graded the students' papers last night. She returned them during class the next day.
4. The cormorant is a diving bird. It can stay under water for a long time. In some countries, it is used by fishermen to catch fish for them.
5. Tom took an apple with him to school. He ate it at lunch time.

□ **EXERCISE 7:** Choose the correct word in parentheses.

1. This is (*my, mine*) umbrella. (*You, Yours*) umbrella is over there.
2. This umbrella is (*my, mine*). The other one is (*your, yours*).
3. Mary and Bob have (*their, theirs*) books. In other words, Mary has (*her, hers*) and Tom has his.
4. A honeybee has two wings on each side of (*its, it's*) body.*
5. (*Its, It's*) true that a homing pigeon will find (*its, it's*) way home even though it begins (*its, it's*) trip in unfamiliar territory.
6. I have a pet. (*Its, It's*) name is Squeak. (*Its, It's*) a turtle. (*Its, It's*) been my pet for two years.

---

*COMPARE: **its** = a possessive adjective
          it's = a contraction of **it is** or **it has**

A-8 CONTRACTIONS

IN SPEAKING:	In everyday spoken English, certain forms of *be* and auxiliary verbs are usually contracted with pronouns, nouns, and question words.	
IN WRITING:	(1) In written English, contractions with pronouns are common in informal writing, but not generally acceptable in formal writing.	
	(2) Contractions with nouns and question words are, for the most part, rarely used in writing. A few of these contractions may be found in quoted dialogue in stories or in very informal writing, such as a chatty letter to a good friend, but most of them are rarely if ever written.	

In the following, quotation marks indicate that the contraction is frequently spoken but rarely if ever written.

	WITH PRONOUNS	WITH NOUNS	WITH QUESTION WORDS
am	*I'm* reading a book.	Ø	*"What'm"* I supposed to do?
is	*She's* studying. *It's* going to rain.	My *"book's"* on the table. *Mary's* at home.	*Where's* Sally? *Who's* that man?
are	*You're* working hard. *They're* waiting for us.	My *"books're"* on the table. The *"teachers're"* at a meeting.	*"What're"* you doing? *"Where're"* they going?
has	*She's* been here for a year. *It's* been cold lately.	My *"book's"* been stolen! *Sally's* never met him.	*Where's* Sally been living? *What's* been going on?"
have	*I've* finished my work. *They've* never met you.	The *"books've"* been sold. The *"students've"* finished the test.	*"Where've"* they been? *"How've"* you been?
had	*He'd* been waiting for us. *We'd* forgotten about it.	The *"books'd"* been sold. *"Mary'd"* never met him before.	*"Where'd"* you been before that? *"Who'd"* been there before you?
did	Ø	Ø	*"What'd"* you do last night? *"How'd"* you do on the test?
will	*I'll* come later. *She'll* help us.	The *"weather'll"* be nice tomorrow. *"John'll"* be coming soon.	*"Who'll"* be at the meeting? *"Where'll"* you be at ten?
would	*He'd* like to go there. *They'd* come if they could.	My *"friends'd"* come if they could. *"Mary'd"* like to go there, too.	*"Where'd"* you like to go?

☐ **EXERCISE 8—ORAL:** Read the sentences aloud. Practice usual contracted speech.

Example: The streets are wet. → "The streets're wet."

CONTRACTIONS WITH NOUNS:

1. My friend is here.
2. My friends are here.
3. Tom has been here since two.
4. The students have been here since one.
5. Bob had already left.
6. Bob would like to come with us.
7. Don will be here soon.

8. The window is open.
9. The windows are open.
10. Jane has never seen a ghost.
11. The boys have been there before.
12. Sally had forgotten her book.
13. Sally would forget her book if I didn't remind her to take it.

14. Who is that woman?
15. Who are those people?
16. Who has been taking care of your house?
17. What have you been doing?
18. What had you been doing before that?
19. What would you like to do?

20. What did you do yesterday?
21. Why did you stay home?
22. When will I see you again?
23. How long will you be away?
24. Where am I supposed to go?
25. Where did you stay?

UNIT B: Questions

B-1   FORMS OF YES/NO AND INFORMATION QUESTIONS

A yes/no question =	a question that may be answered by *yes* or *no*.
	Yes/no question: Does he live in Chicago?
	Answer: Yes, he does. OR No, he doesn't.

An information question =	a question that asks for information by using a question word.
	Information question: Where does he live?
	Answer: In Chicago.

	QUESTION WORD	AUXILIARY VERB	SUBJECT	MAIN VERB		
(a) *She lives* there.		*Does*	she	live	there?	If the verb is in the simple present, use *does* (with *he, she, it*) or *do* (with *I, you, we, they*) in the question. If the verb is simple past, use *did*.
	Where	*does*	she	live?		
(b) *They live* there.		*Do*	they	live	there?	
	Where	*do*	they	live?		
(c) *He lived* there.		*Did*	he	live	there?	Notice: The main verb in the question is in its simple form; there is no final *-s* or *-ed*.
	Where	*did*	he	live?		
(d) *He is living* there.		*Is*	he	living	there?	If the verb has an auxiliary (a helping verb), the same auxiliary is used in the question. There is no change in the form of the main verb.
	Where	*is*	he	living?		
(e) *They have lived* there.		*Have*	they	lived	there?	
	Where	*have*	they	lived?		
(f) *Mary can live* there.		*Can*	Mary	live	there?	
	Where	*can*	Mary	live?		
(g) *He will be living* there.		*Will*	he	be living	there?	If the verb has more than one auxiliary, only the first auxiliary precedes the subject.
	Where	*will*	he	be living?		

(continued)

	QUESTION WORD	AUXILIARY VERB	SUBJECT	MAIN VERB		
(h) *John lives* there.	*Who*	Ø	Ø	*lives*	there?	If the question word is the subject, do not change the verb. Do not use *does*, *do*, or *did*.
(i) *Mary can come.*	*Who*	*can*	Ø	*come?*		
(j) *They are* there.		*Are*	*they*		there?	*Be* in the simple present (*am, is, are*) and simple past (*was, were*) precedes the subject when *be* is the main verb.
	Where	*are*	*they?*			
(k) *Jim was* there.		*Was*	*Jim*		there?	
	Where	*was*	*Jim?*			

☐ **EXERCISE 9:** For each of the following, first make a yes/no question. Then make an information question using *where*.

> *Example:* They can stay there.
> *Yes/no question:* Can they stay there?
> *Information question:* Where can they stay?

1. She stays there.
2. She is staying there.
3. She will stay there.
4. She is going to stay there.
5. They stayed there.
6. They will be staying there.
7. They should stay there.
8. He has stayed there.
9. He has been staying there.
10. John is there.
11. John will be there.
12. John has been there.
13. Judy will have been there.
14. Ann and Tom were married there.
15. This package should have been taken there.

B-2 QUESTION WORDS

	QUESTION	ANSWER	
WHEN	(a) **When** did they arrive? **When** will you come?	Yesterday. Next Monday.	**When** is used to ask questions about *time*.
WHERE	(b) **Where** is she? **Where** can I find a pen?	At home. In that drawer.	**Where** is used to ask questions about *place*.
WHY	(c) **Why** did he leave early? **Why** aren't you coming with us?	Because he's ill. I'm tired.	**Why** is used to ask questions about *reason*.
HOW	(d) **How** did you come to school? **How** does he drive?	By bus. Carefully.	**How** generally asks about *manner*.
	(e) **How much** money does it cost? **How many** people came?	Ten dollars. Fifteen.	**How** is used with **much** and **many**.
	(f) **How old** are you? **How cold** is it? **How soon** can you get here? **How fast** were you driving?	Twelve. Ten below zero. In ten minutes. 50 miles an hour.	**How** is also used with adjectives and adverbs.
	(g) **How long** has he been here?	Two years.	**How long** asks about *length of time*.
	How often do you write home?	Every week.	**How often** asks about *frequency*.
	How far is it to Miami from here?	500 miles.	**How far** asks about *distance*.
WHO	(h) **Who** can answer that question? **Who** came to visit you?	I can. Jane and Eric.	**Who** is used as the subject of a question. It refers to people.
	(i) **Who is** coming to dinner tonight? **Who wants** to come with me?	Ann, Bob, and Al. We do.	**Who** is usually followed by a singular verb even if the speaker is asking about more than one person.
WHOM	(j) **Who(m)** did you see? **Who(m)** are you visiting? (k) **Who(m)** should I talk **to**? **To whom** should I talk? (*formal*)	I saw George. My relatives. The secretary.	**Whom** is used as the object of a verb or preposition. In spoken English, **whom** is rarely used; **who** is used instead. **Whom** is used only in formal questions. Note: **Whom**, not **who**, is used if preceded by a preposition.

(continued)

	QUESTION	ANSWER	
WHOSE	(1) **Whose book** did you borrow? **Whose key** is this? (**Whose** is this?)	David's. It's mine.	**Whose** asks questions about *possession*.
WHAT	(m) **What** made you angry? **What** went wrong?	His rudeness. Everything.	**What** is used as the subject of a question. It refers to "things."
	(n) **What** do you need? **What** did Alice buy? (o) **What** did he talk **about**? **About what** did he talk? (*formal*)	I need a pencil. A book. His vacation.	**What** is also used as an object.
	(p) **What kind of** soup is that? **What kind of** shoes did he buy?	It's bean soup. Sandals.	**What kind of** asks about the particular variety or type of something.
	(q) **What** *did* you *do* last night? **What** *is* Mary *doing*?	I studied. Reading a book.	**What** + *a form of* **do** is used to ask questions about activities.
	(r) **What countries** did you visit? **What time** did she come? **What color** is his hair?	Italy and Spain. Seven o'clock. Dark brown.	**What** may accompany a noun.
	(s) **What** *is* Ed *like*? (t) **What** *is* the weather *like*?	He's kind and friendly. Hot and humid.	**What** + **be like** asks for a general description of qualities.
	(u) **What** *does* Ed *look like*? (v) **What** *does* her house *look like*?	He's tall and has dark hair. It's a two-story, red brick house.	**What** + **look like** asks for a physical description.
WHICH	(w) I have two pens. **Which pen** do you want? **Which one** do you want? **Which** do you want? (x) **Which book** should I buy?	The blue one. That one.	**Which** is used instead of **what** when a question concerns choosing from a definite, known quantity or group.
	(y) **Which countries** did he visit? **What countries** did he visit? (z) **Which class** are you in? **What class** are you in?	Peru and Chile. This class.	In some cases, there is little difference in meaning between **which** and **what** when they accompany a noun, as in (y) and (z).

☐ **EXERCISE 10:** Make questions from the following sentences. The words in parentheses should be the answer to your question.

1. I need (*five dollars*).
   → *How much money do you need?*
2. Roberto was born (*in Panama*).
3. I go out to eat (*at least once a week*).
4. I'm waiting for (*Maria*).
5. (*My sister*) answered the phone.
6. I called (*Benjamin*).
7. (*Benjamin*) called.
8. The boy has (*a ball*) in his pocket.*

9. "Deceitful" means ("*dishonest*").
10. An abyss is (*a bottomless hole*).
11. He went (*this*) way, (*not that way*).
12. These are (*Jim's*) books and papers.
13. They have (*four*) children.
14. He has been here (*for two hours*).
15. It is (*two hundred miles*) to New Orleans.

☐ **EXERCISE 11:** Make questions from the following sentences. The words in parentheses should be the answer to your question.

1. She bought (*twelve gallons of gas*).
2. The doctor can see you (*at three on Friday*).
3. Her roommate is (*Jane Peters*).
4. Her roommates are (*Jane Peters and Sue Lee*).
5. My parents have been living there (*for three years*).
6. This is (*Alice's*) book.
7. (*The soap bubbles*) made her sneeze.
8. (*Fred and Jack*) are coming over for dinner.
9. Ann's dress is (*blue*).
10. Anne's eyes are (*brown*).
11. I was late (*because the traffic was heavy*).**
12. (*Bob*) can't go on the picnic.
13. Bob can't go (*because he is sick*).
14. I didn't answer the phone (*because I didn't hear it ring*).

---

*A form of **do** is usually used in questions when the main verb is **have** (especially in American English but also commonly in British English); e.g., *Do you have a car?* Using **have** without a form of **do** is also possible but less common; e.g., *Have you a car?*

NOTE: Especially in British English but also in American English, the idiom **have got** is used to indicate possession instead of **have** alone; e.g., *Bob **has got** a car. **Have** you **got** a car?*

In informal spoken English, another way of asking **why is **how come**. Usual question word order is not used with **how come**; instead, the subject comes in front of the verb.
   Example: John isn't here (*because he is sick*). → *Why isn't John here?*
   → *How come John isn't here?*

15. I like (*classical*) music.
16. I don't understand (*the chart on page 50*).
17. Janet is (*studying*) right now.
18. You spell "sitting" (*with two "t's." S-I-T-T-I-N-G*).
19. Tom (*is about medium height and has red hair and freckles*).
20. Tom is (*very serious and hardworking*).
21. Ron (*works as a civil engineer for the railroad company*).
22. Mexico is (*eight hundred miles*) from here.
23. I take my coffee (*black with sugar*).
24. Of Stockholm and Moscow, (*Stockholm*) is farther north.
25. (*Fine.*) I'm getting along (*just fine*).

☐ **EXERCISE 12—ORAL (BOOKS CLOSED):** Make questions. Use question words.

Example: I bought a book.
Response: What did you buy?

1. It is fifty-five miles to (*Springfield*).
2. The fall semester begins on September 10th.
3. I bought the red pen, not the green one.
4. The secretary typed those letters.
5. I took four courses last semester.
6. "Rapid" means "fast."
7. (. . .) went to the library.
8. (. . .) telephoned me.
9. The post office is on Seventh Avenue.
10. It is three blocks to the post office.
11. I slept eight hours last night.
12. (. . .) gave a speech.
13. (. . .) talked about his/her country.
14. (. . .) talked about his/her family.
15. I need twenty-five dollars.
16. (. . .) lives on the fifth floor, not the fourth.
17. I will be in (*the United States*) for four years.
18. This is (. . .)'s pen.
19. I go to the library every day.
20. The next test is on Tuesday.
21. I have been studying English for ten years.
22. I laughed because (. . .) made a funny face.
23. (. . .) dropped his/her pen.
24. You should give that book to (. . .).
25. I didn't come to class yesterday because I wasn't feeling well.

☐ **EXERCISE 13—ORAL (BOOKS CLOSED):** Make questions. Use question words.

1. I had a sandwich for lunch.
2. These are (. . .)'s books.
3. We are supposed to read Chapter Five, not Chapter Six.

4. I talked to (. . .).
5. I talked to (. . .) about the story in this morning's newspaper.
6. I fell asleep in class because I had only two hours of sleep last night.
7. That book belongs to (. . .).
8. "Request" means "ask."
9. It is 325 miles to (*Chicago*).
10. I can speak three languages.
11. (. . .) opened the window.
12. I didn't go to the party because I had to study.
13. I live in this house, not that one.
14. I hung my coat in the closet.
15. The letter is addressed to (. . .).
16. It took me three hours to finish my assignments.
17. Mr. Smith taught English in Japan.
18. You should be here at two o'clock.
19. I found (. . .)'s keys.
20. I visit my aunt and uncle twice a year.

B-3   NEGATIVE QUESTIONS

(a) ***Doesn't she live*** in the dormitory? (b) ***Does she not live*** in the dormitory? (*very formal*)	In a yes/no question in which the verb is negative, usually a contraction (e.g., *does + not = doesn't*) is used, as in (a). Example (b) is very formal and is usually not used in everyday speech. Negative questions are used to indicate the speaker's idea (i.e., what s/he believes is or is not true) or attitude (e.g., surprise, shock, annoyance, anger).

(c)   Bob returns to his dorm room after his nine o'clock class. Dick, his roommate, is there. Bob is surprised.
   Bob says: *"What are you doing here? **Aren't you supposed to be in class now?"***
 	
 (d)   Alice and Mary are at home. Mary is about to leave on a trip and Alice is going to take her to the airport.
   Alice says: *"It's already two o'clock. We'd better leave for the airport. **Doesn't your plane leave at three?"***
	In (c): Bob believes that Dick is supposed to be in class now.
	 Expected answer: **Yes.**
	
	 In (d): Alice believes that Mary's plane leaves at three. She is asking the negative question to make sure that her information is correct.
	 Expected answer: **Yes.**

(e)   The teacher is talking to Jim about a test he failed. The teacher is surprised that Jim failed the test because he usually does very well.
   The teacher says: *"What happened? **Didn't you study?"***
 	
 (f)   Barb and Don are riding in a car. Don is driving. He comes to a corner where there is a stop sign, but he does not stop the car. Barb is shocked.
   Barb says: *"What's the matter with you? **Didn't you see that stop sign?"***
	In (e): The teacher believes that Jim did not study.
	 Expected answer: **No.**
	
	 In (f): Barb believes that Don did not see the stop sign.
	 Expected answer: **No.**

☐ **EXERCISE 14:** Notice the examples in Chart B-3: Sometimes the expected answer to a negative question is *yes* and sometimes *no*. In the following dialogues, make negative questions from the words in parentheses and determine the expected response.

1. A: Why didn't you come to lunch with us? _____*Weren't you hungry?*_____
   (*be hungry*)

   B: _____*No.*_____ I had a late breakfast.

2. A: Did you give Linda my message when you went to class this morning?

   B: No. I didn't see her.

   A: Oh? _____ (*be in class*)

   B: _____ She didn't come today.

3. A: Do you see that woman over there, the one in the blue dress?_____
   _____ (*be Mrs. Robbins*)

   B: _____

   A: I thought so. I wonder what she is doing here.

4. A: It's almost dinner time and you haven't eaten since breakfast.
   _____ (*be hungry*)

   B: _____ I'm starving. Let's go eat.

5. A: You look tired this morning. _____
   (*sleep well last night*)

   B: _____ I tossed and turned all night.

6. A: You look pale. What's the matter? _____ (*feel well*)

   B: _____ I think I might be coming down with something.

7. A: Daddy, Tommy said that the sun rises in the west. _____
   _____ (*rise in the east*)

   B: _____, Annie. You're right. Tommy is a little mixed up.

8. A: See that man over there, the one in the green shirt?

   B: Yes. Who is he?

   A: _____ (*recognize him*)

   B: _____. Am I supposed to?

B-4 TAG QUESTIONS

(a) Jack *can* come, *can't* he? (b) Fred *can't* come, *can* he?	A *tag question* is a question added at the end of a sentence. Speakers use tag questions chiefly to make sure their information is correct or to seek agreement.*

AFFIRMATIVE SENTENCE + NEGATIVE TAG	→ AFFIRMATIVE ANSWER EXPECTED
Mary *is* here, *isn't* she?	Yes, she is.
You *like* tea, *don't* you?	Yes, I do.
They *have left*, *haven't* they?	Yes, they have.

NEGATIVE SENTENCE + AFFIRMATIVE TAG	→ NEGATIVE ANSWER EXPECTED
Mary *isn't* here, *is* she ?	No, she isn't.
You *don't like* tea, *do* you?	No, I don't.
They *haven't left*, *have* they?	No, they haven't.

(c) *This/That* is your book, isn't *it*? *These/Those* are yours, aren't *they*?	The tag pronoun for *this/that* = *it*. The tag pronoun for *these/those* = *they*.
(d) *There is* a meeting tonight, *isn't there*?	In sentences with *there* + *be*, *there* is used in the tag.
(e) *Everything* is okay, isn't *it*? (f) *Everyone* took the test, didn't *they*?	Personal pronouns are used to refer to indefinite pronouns. *They* is usually used in a tag to refer to *everyone*, *everybody*, *someone*, *somebody*, *no one*, *nobody*.
(g) *Nothing is* wrong, *is* it? (h) *Nobody called* on the phone, *did* they? (i) You*'ve never been* there, *have* you?	Sentences with negative words take affirmative tags.
(j) *I am* supposed to be here, *am I not*? (k) *I am* supposed to be here, *aren't I*?	In (j): *am I not?* is formal English. In (k): *aren't I?* is common in spoken English.

*A tag question may be spoken:
   (1) with a rising intonation if the speaker is truly seeking to ascertain that his/her information, idea, belief is correct (e.g., *Ann lives in an apartment, doesn't she?*); OR
   (2) with a falling intonation if the speaker is expressing an idea with which s/he is almost certain the listener will agree (e.g., *It's a nice day today, isn't it?*).

☐ **EXERCISE 15:** Add tag questions to the following.

    1. They want to come, ___*don't they*___?

    2. Elizabeth is a dentist, _____?

    3. They won't be here, _____?

    4. There aren't any problems, _____?

    5. That is your umbrella, _____?

    6. George is a student, _____?

7. He's learned a lot in the last couple of years, _____?

8. He has* a bicycle, _____?

9. Joan can't come with us, _____?

10. She'll help us later, _____?

11. Peggy would like to come with us to the party, _____?

12. Those aren't Fred's books, _____?

13. You've never been to Paris, _____?

14. Something is wrong with Jane today, _____?

15. Everyone can learn how to swim, _____?

16. Nobody cheated on the exam, _____?

17. Nothing went wrong while I was gone, _____?

18. I am invited, _____?

□ **EXERCISE 16—ORAL (BOOKS CLOSED):** Add tag questions.

Example: (*Carlos*) is a student....
Responses: ...isn't he?

1. That's (...)'s pen....
2. (...) is living in an apartment....
3. (...) lives on (*Main Street*)....
4. There isn't a test tomorrow....
5. (...) has his/her book....
6. You had a good time....
7. (...) has been invited to the party....
8. You didn't forget your key....
9. Your parents haven't arrived yet....
10. Turtles lay eggs....
11. (...) can't speak (*Arabic*)....
12. (...) is never late to class....
13. Something will be done about that problem right away....
14. These keys don't belong to you....
15. You used to live in New York....
16. There's a better way to solve that problem....
17. (...) is going to come to class tomorrow....
18. You should leave for the airport by six....
19. (...) doesn't have a car....
20. (...) sat next to (...) yesterday....
21. We have class tomorrow....
22. You've already seen that movie....
23. (...) will help us....
24. Nobody has told you the secret....
25. I am right....
26. Class ends at (*ten*)....

---

*A form of **do** is usually used in the tag when **have** is the main verb: *Tom **has** a car, **doesn't** he?* Also possible, but less common: *Tom **has** a car, **hasn't** he?*

UNIT C: Negatives

C-1 USING *NOT* AND OTHER NEGATIVE WORDS

<table>
<tr>
<td>(a) AFFIRMATIVE: The earth is round.
(b) NEGATIVE: The earth is not flat.</td>
<td>Not expresses a negative idea.</td>
</tr>
<tr>
<td>
AUX + NOT + MAIN VERB
(c) I will   not   go   there.
    I have   not   gone there.
    I am   not   going there.
    I was   not   there.
    I do   not   go   there.
    He does not   go   there.
    I did   not   go   there.
</td>
<td>Not immediately follows an auxiliary verb or be. (Note: If there is more than one auxiliary, not comes immediately after the first auxiliary: I will not be going there.)
Do or does is used with not to make a simple present verb (except be) negative.
Did is used with not to make a simple past verb (except be) negative.</td>
</tr>
<tr>
<td colspan="2">
CONTRACTIONS OF AUXILIARY VERBS WITH NOT

are not = *aren't* *	*do not* = *don't*	*must not* = *mustn't*
cannot = *can't*	*has not* = *hasn't*	*should not* = *shouldn't*
could not = *couldn't*	*have not* = *haven't*	*was not* = *wasn't*
did not = *didn't*	*had not* = *hadn't*	*were not* = *weren't*
does not = *doesn't*	*is not* = *isn't*	*will not* = *won't*
		would not = *wouldn't*

</td>
</tr>
<tr>
<td>(d) I never go there.
    I have hardly ever gone there.

(e) There's no chalk in the drawer.</td>
<td>In addition to not, the following are negative adverbs:
    never, rarely, seldom
    hardly (ever), scarcely (ever), barely (ever)
No also expresses a negative idea.</td>
</tr>
<tr>
<td>COMPARE: NOT vs. NO
(f) I do not have any money.
(g) I have no money.</td>
<td>Not is used to make a verb negative, as in (f).
No is used as an adjective in front of a noun (e.g., money), as in (g). Note: (f) and (g) have the same meaning.</td>
</tr>
</table>

*Sometimes in spoken English you will hear "ain't." It means *am not, isn't,* or *aren't.* "Ain't" is not considered proper English, but many people use "ain't" regularly, and it is also frequently used for humor.

☐ **EXERCISE 17:** Change the following into the negative in two ways: use *not . . . any* in one sentence and *no* in the other.

1. I have some problems. → *I don't have any problems. I have no problems.*
2. There was some food.
3. I received some letters from home.
4. I need some help.
5. We have some time to waste.
6. You should have given the beggar some money.
7. I trust someone. → *I don't trust anyone. I trust no one.* ★
8. I saw someone.
9. There was someone in his room.
10. She can find somebody who knows about it.

★In American English, *no one* is written without a hyphen. In British English, it is written either *no one* (without a hyphen) or *no-one* (with a hyphen).

C-2 AVOIDING "DOUBLE NEGATIVES"

(a) *INCORRECT:* I don't have no money. (b) CORRECT: I **don't** have **any** money. CORRECT: I have **no** money.	(a) is an example of a "double negative," i.e., a confusing and grammatically incorrect sentence that contains two negatives in the same clause.* One clause should contain only one negative.

*NOTE: Negatives in two different clauses in the same sentence cause no problems; for example:
*A person who **doesn't** have love **can't** be truly happy.*
*I **don't** know why he **isn't** here.*

☐ **EXERCISE 18—ERROR ANALYSIS:** Correct the following sentences, all of which contain double negatives.

1. I don't need no help.
2. I didn't see nobody.
3. I can't never understand him.
4. He doesn't like neither coffee nor tea.
5. I didn't do nothing.
6. I can't hardly hear the radio. Would you please turn it up?
7. The beach was deserted. We couldn't see nothing but sand.
8. Methods of horse training haven't barely changed at all in the last eight centuries.

C-3 BEGINNING A SENTENCE WITH A NEGATIVE WORD

(a) **Never will I do** that again. (b) **Rarely have I eaten** better food. (c) **Hardly ever does he come** to class on time.	When a negative word begins a sentence, the subject and verb are inverted (i.e., question word order is used).*

*Beginning a sentence with a negative word is relatively uncommon in everyday usage, but is used when the speaker/writer wishes to emphasize the negative element of the sentence.

☐ **EXERCISE 19:** Change each sentence so that it begins with a negative word.

1. We rarely go to movies. → *Rarely do we go to movies.*
2. I seldom sleep past seven o'clock.
3. I hardly ever agree with her.
4. I will never forget the wonderful people I have met here.
5. I have never known Pat to be dishonest.
6. The mail scarcely ever arrives before noon.

UNIT D: Articles

D-1 BASIC ARTICLE USAGE

<table>
<tr><td colspan="3" align="center">I. USING A or Ø: GENERIC NOUNS</td></tr>
<tr>
<td>SINGULAR COUNT NOUN</td>
<td>(a) A banana is yellow.*</td>
<td rowspan="3">A speaker uses generic nouns to make generalizations. A generic noun represents a whole class of things; it is not a specific, real, concrete thing but rather a symbol of a whole group.

In (a) and (b): The speaker is talking about any banana, all bananas, bananas in general. In (c), the speaker is talking about any and all fruit, fruit in general.

Notice that no article (Ø) is used to make generalizations with plural count nouns and noncount nouns, as in (b) and (c).</td>
</tr>
<tr>
<td>PLURAL COUNT NOUN</td>
<td>(b) Ø Bananas are yellow.</td>
</tr>
<tr>
<td>NONCOUNT NOUN</td>
<td>(c) Ø Fruit is good for you.</td>
</tr>
<tr><td colspan="3" align="center">II. USING A or SOME: INDEFINITE NOUNS</td></tr>
<tr>
<td>SINGULAR COUNT NOUN</td>
<td>(d) I ate a banana.</td>
<td rowspan="3">Indefinite nouns are actual things (not symbols), but they are not specifically identified.
In (d): The speaker is not referring to "this banana" or "that banana" or "the banana you gave me." The speaker is simply saying that s/he ate one banana. The listener does not know nor need to know which specific banana was eaten; it was simply one banana out of that whole group of things in this world called bananas.
In (e) and (f): Some is often used with indefinite plural count nouns and indefinite noncount nouns. In addition to some, a speaker might use two, a few, several, a lot of, etc., with plural count nouns, or a little, a lot of, etc., with noncount nouns. (See Chart 5-8.)</td>
</tr>
<tr>
<td>PLURAL COUNT NOUN</td>
<td>(e) I ate some bananas.</td>
</tr>
<tr>
<td>NONCOUNT NOUN</td>
<td>(f) I ate some fruit.</td>
</tr>
<tr><td colspan="3" align="center">III. USING THE: DEFINITE NOUNS</td></tr>
<tr>
<td>SINGULAR COUNT NOUN</td>
<td>(g) Thank you for the banana.</td>
<td rowspan="3">A noun is definite when both the speaker and the listener are thinking about the same specific thing.
In (g): The speaker uses the because the listener knows which specific banana the speaker is talking about, i.e., that particular banana which the listener gave to the speaker.
Notice that the is used with both singular and plural count nouns and with noncount nouns.</td>
</tr>
<tr>
<td>PLURAL COUNT NOUN</td>
<td>(h) Thank you for the bananas.</td>
</tr>
<tr>
<td>NONCOUNT NOUN</td>
<td>(i) Thank you for the fruit.</td>
</tr>
</table>

*Usually *a/an* is used with a singular generic count noun. Examples:

   A window is made of glass. *A doctor* heals sick people. Parents must give *a child* love. *A box* has six sides. *An apple* can be red, green, or yellow.

The is sometimes used with a singular generic count noun (not a plural generic count noun, not a generic noncount noun). "Generic *the*" is commonly used with, in particular:

   (1) species of animals: *The whale* is the largest mammal on earth.

   The elephant is the largest land mammal.

   (2) inventions: *Who invented the telephone? the wheel? the refrigerator? the airplane?*

   The computer will play an increasingly large role in all of our lives.

   (3) musical instruments: *I'd like to learn to play the piano.*

   Do you play the guitar?

D-2 GENERAL GUIDELINES FOR ARTICLE USAGE

(a) **The sun** is bright today. Please hand this book to **the teacher**. Please open **the door**. Jack is in **the kitchen**.	GUIDELINE: Use **the** when you know or assume that your listener is familiar with and thinking about the same specific thing or person you are talking about.
(b) Yesterday I saw *some dogs*. **The dogs** were chasing *a cat*. **The cat** was chasing *a mouse*. **The mouse** ran into *a hole*. **The hole** was very small.	GUIDELINE: Use **the** for the second mention of an indefinite noun★; in (b): first mention = *some dogs, a cat, a mouse, a hole* second mention = *the dogs, the cat, the mouse, the hole*
(c) INCORRECT: *The apples are my favorite fruit.* CORRECT: **Apples** are my favorite fruit. (d) INCORRECT: *The gold is a metal.* CORRECT: **Gold** is a metal.	GUIDELINE: Do not use **the** with a plural count noun (e.g., *apples*) or a noncount noun (e.g., *gold*) when you are making a generalization.
(e) INCORRECT: *I drove car.* CORRECT: I drove **a car**. I drove **the car**. I drove **that car**. I drove **his car**.	GUIDELINE: Do not use a singular count noun (e.g., *car*) without: (1) an article (**a/an** or **the**); OR (2) **this/that**; OR (3) a possessive pronoun.

★**The** is not used for the second mention of a generic noun. COMPARE:
(1) What color is **a banana** (generic noun)? **A banana** (generic noun) is yellow.
(2) Tom offered me **a banana** (indefinite noun) or an apple. I chose **the banana** (definite noun).

□ **EXERCISE 20:** In the following dialogues, try to decide whether the speakers would probably use *a/an* or *the*.

1. A: I have _____*an*_____ idea. Let's go on _____*a*_____ picnic Saturday.

   B: Okay.

2. A: Did you have fun at _____*the*_____ picnic yesterday?

   B: Sure did. And you?

3. A: You'd better have _____ good reason for being late!

   B: I do.

4. A: Did you think _____ reason Jack gave for being late was believable?

   B: Not really.

5. A: Where's my blue shirt?

   B: It's in _____ washing machine. You'll have to wear _____ different shirt.

6. A: I wish we had _____ washing machine.

   B: So do I. It would make it a lot easier to do our laundry.

7. A: What happened to your bicycle? _____ front wheel is bent.

   B: I ran into _____ parked car when I swerved to avoid _____ big pothole in the street.

   A: Did you damage _____ car?

   B: A little.

   A: What did you do?

   B: I left _____ note for _____ owner of _____ car.

   A: What did you write on _____ note?

   B: My name and address. I also wrote _____ apology.

8. A: Can you repair my car for me?

   B: What's wrong with it?

   A: _____ radiator has _____ leak, and one of _____ windshield wipers doesn't work.

   B: Can you show me where _____ leak is?

9. A: Have you seen my boots?

   B: They're in _____ closet in _____ front hallway.

□ **EXERCISE 21:** Complete the sentences with *a/an*, *the*, or Ø.

1. ___Ø___ beef is a kind of ___Ø___ meat.

2. ___The___ beef we had for dinner last night was excellent.

3. Jack is wearing ___a___ straw hat today.

4. Jack likes to wear _____ hats.

5. _____ hat is _____ article of clothing.

6. _____ hats are _____ articles of clothing.

7. _____ brown hat on that hook over there belongs to Mark.

8. Everyone has _____ problems in _____ life.

9. My grandfather had _____ long life.

10. That book is about _____ life of Helen Keller.

11. Tommy wants to be _____ engineer when he grows up.

12. The Brooklyn Bridge was designed by _____ engineer.

13. John Roebling is _____ name of _____ engineer who designed the Brooklyn Bridge. He died in 1869 from _____ infection. He died before _____ bridge was completed.

14. _____ people wear _____ jewelry to make themselves more attractive.

15. _____ jewelry Diana is wearing today is beautiful.

16. Mary is wearing _____ beautiful ring today. It is made of _____ gold and _____ rubies. _____ gold in her ring was mined in Canada. _____ rubies came from Burma.

17. One of the first things you need to do when you move to _____ new city is to find _____ place to live. Most _____ newspapers carry _____ advertisements (called "want ads") for _____ apartments that are for rent. If you find _____ ad for _____ furnished apartment, _____ apartment will probably contain _____ stove and _____ refrigerator. It will also probably have _____ furniture such as _____ beds, _____ tables, _____ chairs, and maybe _____ sofa.

18. My wife and I have recently moved to this city. Since we're going to be here for only _____ short time, we're renting _____ furnished apartment. We decided that we didn't want to bring our own furniture with us. _____ apartment is in _____ good location, but that's about the only good thing I can say about it. Only one burner on _____ stove works. _____ refrigerator is noisy, and _____ refrigerator door won't stay closed unless we tape it shut. _____ bed sags in the middle and creaks. All of the rest of _____ furniture is old and decrepit too. Nevertheless, we're still enjoying living in this city. We may have to look for _____ another apartment, however.

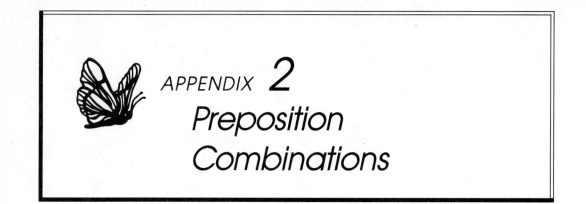

APPENDIX 2
Preposition Combinations

Appendix 2 contains two lists of preposition combinations. The first list consists of preposition combinations with adjectives and verbs. The second list contains phrasal verbs.

Sometimes these lists contain only those preposition combinations used in the exercises in the text and in the accompanying workbooks.

PREPOSITION COMBINATIONS WITH ADJECTIVES AND VERBS

A   *be* absent from
      accuse of
   be accustomed to
   be acquainted with
   be addicted to
   be afraid of
      agree with
   be angry at, with
   be annoyed with
      apologize for
      apply to, for
      approve of
      argue with, about
      arrive in, at
   be associated with
   be aware of

B   believe in
      blame for
   be blessed with
   be bored with

C   *be* capable of
      care about, for
   be cluttered with
   be committed to
      compare to, with
      complain about
   be composed of
   be concerned about
   be connected to
      consist of
   be content with
      contribute to
   be convinced of
   be coordinated with
      count (up)on
      cover with
   be crowded with

D   decide (up)on
   be dedicated to
      depend (up)on

be devoted to
be disappointed in, with
be discriminated against
distinguish from
be divorced from
be done with
dream of, about
be dressed in

E *be* engaged to
be envious of
be equipped with
escape from
excel in
be excited about
excuse for
be exposed to

F *be* faithful to
be familiar with
feel like
fight for
be filled with
be finished with
be fond of
forget about
forgive for
be friendly to, with
be furnished with

G *be* grateful to, for
be guilty of

H hide from
hope for

I *be* innocent of
insist (up)on
be interested in
be involved in

J *be* jealous of

K *be* known for

L *be* limited to
look forward to

M *be* made of, from
be married to

O object to
be opposed to

P participate in
be patient with
be polite to
pray for
be prepared for
prevent from
prohibit from
protect from
be provided with
be proud of
provide with

R recover from
be related to
be relevant to
rely (up)on
be remembered for
rescue from
respond to
be responsible for

S *be* satisfied with
be scared of
stare at
stop from
subscribe to
substitute for
succeed in

T take advantage of
take care of
be terrified of
thank for
be tired of, from

U *be* upset with
be used to

V vote for

W *be* worried about

PHRASAL VERBS (TWO-WORD AND THREE-WORD VERBS)

The term *phrasal verb* refers to a verb and preposition which together have a special meaning. For example, ***put*** + ***off*** means "postpone." Sometimes a phrasal verb consists of three parts. For example, ***put*** + ***up*** + ***with*** means "tolerate." Phrasal verbs are also called *two-word verbs* or *three-word verbs*.

SEPARABLE PHRASAL VERBS (a) I **handed** my paper **in** yesterday. (b) I **handed in** my paper yesterday.	A phrasal verb may be either *separable* or *nonseparable*. With a separable phrasal verb, a noun may come either between the verb and the preposition or after the preposition, as in (a) and (b).
(c) I **handed** it **in** yesterday. (INCORRECT: I handed in it yesterday.)	A pronoun comes between the verb and the preposition if the phrasal verb is separable, as in (c).

NONSEPARABLE PHRASAL VERBS
(d) I **ran into** an old friend yesterday.
(e) I **ran into** her yesterday.
    (INCORRECT: I ran an old friend into.)
    (INCORRECT: I ran her into yesterday.)
	With a nonseparable phrasal verb, a noun or pronoun must follow the preposition, as in (d) and (e).

Phrasal verbs are especially common in informal English. Following is a list of common phrasal verbs and their usual meanings. This list contains only those phrasal verbs used in the exercises in the text. The phrasal verbs marked with an asterisk (*) are nonseparable.

A ask out . . . . *ask someone to go on a date*

B bring about, bring on . . . . *cause*
   bring up . . . . *(1) rear children; (2) mention or introduce a topic*

C call back . . . . *return a telephone call*
   call in . . . . *ask to come to an official place for a specific purpose*
   call off . . . . *cancel*
   *call on . . . . *(1) ask to speak in class; (2) visit*
   call up . . . . *call on the telephone*
   *catch up (with) . . . . *reach the same position or level*
   *check in, check into . . . . . *register at a hotel*
   *check into . . . . *investigate*
   check out . . . . *(1) take a book from the library; (2) investigate*
   *check out (of) . . . . *leave a hotel*
   cheer up . . . . *make (someone) feel happier*
   clean up . . . . *make clean and orderly*
   *come across . . . . *meet by chance*
   cross out . . . . *draw a line through*
   cut out . . . . *stop an annoying activity*

D do over . . . . *do again*
    *drop by, drop in (on) . . . . *visit informally*
    drop off . . . . *leave something/someone at a place*
    *drop out (of) . . . . *stop going to school, to a class, to a club, etc.*

F figure out . . . . *find the answer by reasoning*
    fill out . . . . *write the completions of a questionnaire or official form*
    find out . . . . *discover information*

G *get along (with) . . . . *exist satisfactorily*
    get back (from) . . . . *(1) return from a place; (2) receive again*
    *get in, get into . . . . *(1) enter a car; (2) arrive*
    *get off . . . . *leave an airplane, a bus, a train, a subway, a bicycle*
    *get on . . . . *enter an airplane, a bus, a train, a subway, a bicycle*
    *get out of . . . . *(1) leave a car; (2) avoid work or an unpleasant activity*
    *get over . . . . *recover from an illness*
    *get through . . . . *finish*
    *get up . . . . *arise from bed, a chair*
    give back . . . . *return an item to someone*
    give up . . . . *stop trying*
    *go over . . . . *review or check carefully*
    *grow up (in) . . . . *become an adult*

H hand in . . . . *submit an assignment*
    hang up . . . . *(1) conclude a telephone conversation; (2) put clothes on a hanger or a hook*
    have on . . . . *wear*

K keep out (of) . . . . *not enter*
    *keep up (with) . . . . *stay at the same position or level*
    kick out (of) . . . . *force (someone) to leave*

L *look after . . . . *take care of*
    *look into . . . . *investigate*
    *look out (for) . . . . *be careful*
    look over . . . . *review or check carefully*
    look up . . . . *look for information in a reference book*

M make up . . . . *(1) invent; (2) do past work*

N name after, name for . . . . *give a baby the name of someone else*

P *pass away . . . . *die*
    pass out . . . . *(1) distribute; (2) lose consciousness*
    pick out . . . . *select*
    pick up . . . . *(1) go to get someone (e.g., in a car); (2) take in one's hand*
    point out . . . . *call attention to*

put away . . . . *remove to a proper place*
put back . . . . *return to original place*
put off . . . . *postpone*
put on . . . . *put clothes on one's body*
put out. . . . . *extinguish a cigarette or cigar*
*put up with . . . . *tolerate*

R *run into, *run across . . . . *meet by chance*
   *run out (of) . . . . *finish a supply of something*

S *show up . . . . *appear, come*
   shut off . . . . *stop a machine, light, faucet*

T *take after . . . . *resemble*
   take off . . . . *(1) remove clothing; (2) leave on a trip*
   take out . . . . *(1) take someone on a date; (2) remove*
   take over . . . . *take control*
   take up . . . . *begin a new activity or topic*
   tear down . . . . *demolish; reduce to nothing*
   tear up . . . . *tear into many little pieces*
   think over . . . . *consider carefully*
   throw away, throw out . . . *discard; get rid of*
   throw up . . . . *vomit; regurgitate food*
   try on . . . . *put on clothing to see if it fits*
   turn down . . . . *decrease volume or intensity*
   turn in . . . . *(1) submit an assignment; (2) go to bed*
   turn off . . . . *stop a machine, light, faucet*
   turn on . . . . *begin a machine, light, faucet*
   turn out . . . . *extinguish a light*
   turn up . . . . *increase volume or intensity*

APPENDIX *3*
Guide for Correcting Writing Errors

To the student: Each number represents an area of usage. Your teacher will use these numbers when marking your writing to indicate that you have made an error. Refer to this list to find out what kind of error you have made and then make the necessary correction.

1   **SINGULAR-PLURAL**   He have been here for six month.①
He has been here for six months.

2   **WORD FORM**   I saw a beauty② picture.
I saw a beautiful picture.

3   **WORD CHOICE**   She got on③ the taxi.
She got into the taxi.

4   **VERB TENSE**   He is④ here since June.
He has been here since June.

5+   **ADD A WORD**   I want ∧⑤⁺ go to the zoo.
I want to go to the zoo.

5−   **OMIT A WORD**   She entered to⑤⁻ the university.
She entered the university.

6   **WORD ORDER**   I saw five⑥ times that movie.
I saw that movie five times.

7   **INCOMPLETE SENTENCE**   I went to bed. Because⑦ I was tired.
I went to bed because I was tired.

| 8 | SPELLING | An accident occured.⑧ |
| | | *An accident occurred.* |

| 9 | PUNCTUATION | What did he say.⑨ |
| | | *What did he say?* |

| 10 | CAPITALIZATION | I am studying english.⑩ |
| | | *I am studying English.* |

| 11 | ARTICLE | I had a accident.⑪ |
| | | *I had an accident.* |

| 12? | MEANING NOT CLEAR | He borrowed some smoke.⑫? |
| | | *(? ? ?)* |

| 13 | RUN-ON SENTENCE* | My roommate was sleeping, we didn't want to wake her up.⑬ |
| | | *My roommate was sleeping. We didn't want to wake her up.* |

---

*A run-on sentence occurs when two sentences are incorrectly connected: the end of one sentence and the beginning of the next sentence are not properly marked by a period and a capital letter or by a semicolon. (See Charts 8-3 and 8-9.)

Index—Volume B

Adjective clauses, defined, 238 *(Look on page 238.)*	The numbers following the words listed in the index refer to page numbers in the main text.
Be, A4 *(Look in the back part of this book on the fourth page of the Appendixes.)*	The index numbers preceded by the letter "A" (e.g., A4) refer to pages in the Appendixes, which are found in the last part of the text. The main text ends on page 374, and the Appendixes immediately follow. Page 374 is followed by page A1.
Direct speech, 273*fn.* *(Look at the footnote on page 273.)*	Information given in footnotes to charts or exercises is noted by the page number plus the abbreviation *fn.*